STUDIES IN THE HISTORY OF THE THIRD DYNASTY OF VIJAYANAGARA

STUDIES IN THE HISTORY OF THE THIRD DYNASTY OF VIJAYANAGARA

N. VENKATA RAMANAYYA

GYAN

Studies in the History of the Third Dynasty of Vijayanagara

ISBN : 978-81-212-0066-0

Rs. 990

Reprinted in 2010 in India by
Gyan Publishing House
23, Main Ansari Road, Daryaganj,
New Delhi - 110002
Phone : 23282060, 23261060
Fax : (011) 23285914
e-mail : books@gyanbooks.com
gyanbook@vsnl.com
website : gyanbooks.com

Printed at : G. Print Process, Delhi

PREFACE.

This monograph embodies the result of investigations begun during the last two years of my service in the Madras Christian College. It was in the summer of 1929, while preparing my lectures on the History of Vijayanagara for the Honours students, that I, at first, became interested in the subject. I discovered that the subject needed thorough investigation, notwithstanding the labour of several eminent scholars. As I proceeded with the study, the field of my investigation widened, and the number of problems that had to be tackled increased. Therefore, the work could not be finished as early as I expected.

The present work consists of three parts. The first part narrates the principal events in the history of Vijayanagara between 1529 and 1543. The second describes the system of administration under which the empire of the Rāyas was governed in the sixteenth century; and the third deals with the religious and the social conditions of the same period. The solutions offered to the problems discussed in this volume are often tentative in character, and may have to be modified in the light of future research.

LIMBDI GARDENS,
Royapettah, Madras.
15th July 1935. N. VENKATA RAMANAYYA.

Acknowledgments.

The present work is based on the material gathered by several scholars who had laboured in the field of South Indian History. In the first instance, Surveyor-General Col. Collin Mackenzie collected more than a century ago much valuable historical material which would have otherwise completely perished, and Mr. C. P. Brown saved it from destruction by lapse of time. I am also indebted to many scholars who have made valuable contributions to the history of Vijayanagara, in particular to Messrs. Robert Sewell, A. Rangaswami Saraswati, R. Satyanadhan, R. Narasimhachari, M. S. Purnalingam Pillai, S. Subrahmanya Sastri, Fr. H. Heras, M. Somasekhara Sarma, J. Ramayya Pantulu, and R. Anantakrishna Sarma. My thanks are also due to Professor K. A. Nilakanta Sastri, Mr. C. R. Krishnamacharlu, the Superintendent of Epigraphy, and Mr. M. Somasekhara Sarma for making some valuable suggestions; to Messrs. O. F. E. Zacharias of the Madras Christian College, and P. L. Stephen of St. Xavier's College, Palamcottah for revising the manuscript and reading the proofs; and to Messrs. A. Krishnamurti and M. Venkataramayya for preparing the index. I offer my thanks to the Syndicate of the University of Madras for sanctioning the publication of this work in the University Historical Series.

TABLE OF CONTENTS.

TABLE OF CONTENTS

PART III.

RELIGIOUS AND SOCIAL CONDITIONS.

ABBREVIATIONS.

Abm.	Acyutarāyābhyudayam by Rājanātḥ Ḍiṇḍima.
Ām.	Āmuktamālyada by Kṛṣṇadēvarāya.
ASR.	Reports of the Archaeological Survey of India.
ASPP.	The Āndhra Sāhitya Pariṣat Patrika.
Barbosa.	The Book of Duarte Barbosa, edited by Mansel Longworth Dames.
Bbm.	Bālabhāgavatam by Dōnēri Kōnērinātha.
CC.	Cokkanāthacaritra by Paccakappurapu Tiruvengaḷa Kavi.
Cgc.	Candrāṅgadacaritra by Paiḍimaṟṟi Venkaṭapati.
Cmm.	Cāṭūpadyamaṇimañjari by V. Prabhakara Sastri.
Cpr.	Cāṭūpadyaratnākaram by Dīpāla Pichayya Sastri.
Dvm.	Daivajñavilāsam by Lolla Lakṣmīdhara and Keñcam Yellayārya.
EC.	Epigraphia Carnatica.
ED.	History of India by Sir H. M. Elliot.
EI.	Epigraphia Indica.
FE.	A Forgotten Empire by Robert Sewell.
Glossary	Glossary of Judicial and Administrative Terms by H. H. Wilson.
IA.	Indian Antiquary.
ICD.	Inscriptions of the Ceded Districts (The Mackenzie Collection).

ABBREVIATIONS

JAHRS. Journal of the Āndhra Historical Research Society.

JBBRAS. Journal of the Bombay Branch of the Royal Asiatic Society.

JBHS. Journal of the Bombay Historical Society.

Khm. Kāḷahastimahātmyam by Dhūrjaṭi (Senior).

Kpm. Kaḷāpūrṇōdayam by Pingaḷi Sūranna.

KS. Koṇḍavīṭi Sāmrājyam by M. Gurubrahma Sastri.

LR. The Local Records by C. P. Brown.

LRV. The Lakṣmaṇarāyavyāsāvaḷi (The Vijñāna-candrikāmaṇḍali).

MAR. Mysore Archaeological Reports.

MER. Annual Reports of Epigraphy, Madras.

Mc. Manucaritra by Allasāni Peddana.

M.Mss. The Mackenzie Manuscripts.

NDI. Nellore District Inscriptions by Butterworth and Venugopala Chetti.

NM. The Nāyaks of Madura by R. Satyanadhan.

Npm. Niranku̇śōpākhyānam by Kandukūri Rudra Kavi.

Nss. Nīti Sīsapadya Śatakam by Tāḷḷapākam Peda-Tirumalārya.

Pcp. Pāñcālīpariṇayam by Kākamāni Mūrti.

Phm. Pārijātāpaharaṇam by Nandi Timmana.

Pp. or Ppm. Prabhāvatīpradyumnam by Pingaḷi Sūranna.

Prm. Pāṇḍuraṅgamahātmyam by Tenāli Rāma-kṛṣṇa.

ABBREVIATIONS

Pym. Paramayōgivilāsam by Tāḷḷapākam Tiruvengaḷanātha.

Rbm. Rāmābhyudayam by Ayyalarāju Rāmabhadra.

Rc. Rājaśēkharacaritra by Mallaya, son of Mādana.

Rm. Rādhāmādhavam by Cintalapūḍi Yellayārya-'Rādhāmādhava.'

Sdp. Sudakṣiṇāpariṇayam by Tenāli Annaya.

SII. South Indian Inscriptions.

Snm. or Sns. Sakalanītisammatam by Maḍiki Singanna.

Spm. Sāmbōpākhyānam by Rangappa Rāju.

Sources. The Sources of Vijayanagara History, No. 1 in the Madras University Historical series.

ŚS. Śukasaptati by Pālakāvēri Kadirīpati.

TARC. Tañjāvūru Āndhra Rājula Caritram by V. Prabhakara Sastri.

Tbm. Tārakabrahmarājīyam by Cintalapūḍi Yellayārya-'Rādhāmādhava.'

TDER. Epigraphy Report of the Tirupati, Tirumala Dēvasthānams by S. Subrahmanya Sastri.

Vc. Vasucaritra by Rāmarājabhūṣaṇa.

Vmn. Viṣṇumāyānāṭakam by Cintalapūḍi Yellayārya-'Rādhāmādhava.'

Vpm. Varadāmbikāpariṇayam by Tirumalāmbā.

VR. Topographical List of Inscriptions by V. Rangachari.

VV. Velugōṭivārivamśāvaḷi.

THE SOURCES.

The evidence on which the present monograph is based is drawn from two sources *viz.*, inscriptions and literature.

Inscriptions :—These fall into two classes:—(1) those that have been copied by the Government Epigraphy Department, and (2) those that are included in the *Mackenzie Mss.* Most of the inscriptions copied by the Epigraphy Department still remain unpublished, and therefore nothing more than a bare, and very often an unsatisfactory summary of their contents is available to the non-official investigator of South Indian History. For the purpose of the kind of work that is chalked out in the following pages, a thorough and intimate knowledge of the texts of the inscriptions is indispensable. The value of such publications as the *Epigraphia Carnatica* and the *South Indian Inscriptions* can hardly be overestimated; but these only cover a small area of the field; and therefore the investigation of several important problems is rendered particularly difficult. This difficulty is, however, obviated to some extent by the *Mackenzie Mss.*

Surveyor-General Mackenzie, who took much interest in South Indian History and institutions, conducted a systematic antiquarian survey of the country, about a century ago, at his own expense. At his instance, his assistants visited all the villages, took eye-copies of inscriptions on stone and metal, and collected all the historical traditions current among the villages which they recorded in their reports. After Mackenzie's death, his papers were acquired by the East India Company who deposited all the records written in the South

Indian languages in the Oriental Mss. Library at Madras. Most of Col. Mackenzie's records have been recopied, at the instance of the famous Telugu scholar, C. P. Brown, who, having discovered their value, rescued them from destruction. The copies made under the supervision of Brown are generally known as the *Local Records*.

It is not easy to exaggerate the value of the copies of these inscriptions; but their usefulness is marred to some extent by scribal errors. Nevertheless, they have been of invaluable help in delineating the various aspects of the Vijayanagara polity. Without them, it would have been impossible to do even that little which has been done here. These errors could have been easily corrected by a comparison with the originals; but such a course was rendered impracticable, as it involved much sacrifice of money and time.

Literature:—Much light is thrown upon the political and social history by the literature of the period, which may be divided for the purpose of the present study into three classes: (i) the *prabandhas* and the *kāvyas*; (ii) the travellers' accounts and the chronicles, and (iii) the Local Records.

(i) The *Prabandhas* and the *Kāvyas*:—Most of the *prabandhas* allude to the main events of political and military history. The *Tārakabrahmarājīya* gives an account of Acyuta's military achievements. The *Vasucaritra*, the *Bālabhāgavatam*, the *Sāmbōpākhyānam* as well as the *Narasabhūpālīyam* allude to the struggle between Salakarāju Tirumala and Rāmarāja. In addition to the light which they throw on the events of political and military history, the *prabandhas* yield much interesting and useful information about the social and religious life of the people. The *prabandha* writers wove into the texture of their poems various strands of information pertaining to the society in which they lived. * But the material should be used only after testing it carefully with a view to ascertain its trustworthiness. The records of the Portuguese travellers and merchants who visited Vijayanagara during the reigns of Kṛṣṇarāya and Acyuta serve as useful touchstones to test the value of the material furnished by the *prabandhas*, as they contain accounts of what their authors had seen and heard. A few examples may not be out of place here, as they show the close agreement between the authors of the *prabandhas* and the Portuguese Writers:

The Prabandhas	*The Portuguese Writers.*
1. Almost all the *prabandhas* describe the *jalakrīḍa* or water-sport; sometimes young women alone divert themselves; frequently they are joined by a man, usually the hero of the poem.	1. "The king has in his palace many women of position, daughters of the great lords of the realm, and others as well, some as concubines, and some as handmaids.........They bathe daily in the many tanks of which I spoke about, as kept for that purpose. The King goes to see them bathing, and she who pleases him most is sent for to come to his chamber." *Barbosa* i. p. 208.
2. All the *prabandhas* allude to the extraordinary love	2. "The substances with which they are always anointed

* The credit of having first attempted to tap this source of information belongs to Mr. R. Anantakrishna Sarma of the Mysore University. The originality which he has shown in handling the historical material in the *prabandhas* deserves to be highly commended, as it opens a new and unexplored region to be exploited by the students of South Indian History.

The Prabandhas.	*The Portuguese Writers.*
which the people had for scents. The paste prepared of sandal or aloe wood, musk, saffron, camphor, rose water, civet etc., are said to have been used by them always. Men, it is said, besmeared their bodies with sandal paste, and women anointed their breasts with the paste of sandal or aloe wood, musk saffron etc.	are these : white sanders-wood, aloes, camphor, musk, and saffron all ground fine and kneaded with rose water. With these they anoint themselves after bathing, and so they are always very highly scented." *Barbosa* i. p. 205.
3. All the *prabandhas* refer to the courtesan women ; they praise their beauty, knowledge of arts such as music and dancing, their proficiency in literature and their cultured and witty conversation. They condemn their wiles, and the hollowness of their love, though all men including kings and noblemen are said to seek their company openly.	3. Paes describes the position of the courtesans in a brief paragraph : "These women are of loose character, and live in the best streets that there are in the city ; it is the same in all their cities, their streets have the best rows of houses. They are very much esteemed, and are classed amongst those honoured ones, who are the mistresses of captains ; any respectable man may go to their houses without any blame attaching thereto. These women (are allowed) even to enter the presence of the wives of the kings, and they stay with them and eat betel with them, a thing which no other person may do, no matter what his rank may be." *FE.* p. 242.
4. The *Pāṇḍurangamahātmya* while describing the *jātra* of a village deity alludes to several ceremonies including the hook-swinging. The *Kaḷāpūrṇōdayam* alludes to several daring	4. "The women of this land are so bold in their idolatry and do such marvels for the love of their gods, that it is a terrible thing." (*Barbosa* i. p. 220). To

The Prabandhas.

deeds which people desirous of securing unusual gifts from the goddess *Kāḷi* would perform.

The Portuguese Writers.

illustrate this remark he gives a graphic account of the hook-swinging ceremony.

See *Barbosa* i. pp. 220-3

The account of the *Kaḷāpūrṇōdayam* is borne out by the *Vīrula manṭapam* at Śrīśailam, where people used to cut off their tongues, even heads to win certain objects. (*Paṇḍitārādhya-caritram* v. p. 53).

[The evidence of literature is corroborated by an inscription in the *Vīraśirōmaṇḍapam* at Śrīśailam. It states: "How wonderful it is that here, in this *maṇḍapa,* hosts of Koṅga-Vīras, highly excited under religious fervour, cut off their heads and tongues as (votive) offerings (to god) and attain instantaneously a brilliant body of blessed limbs." *(MER.* C. 20 of 1915, Part II, p. 93).]

5. The *Pāṇḍurangamahātmya* refers to the *veliguḍāra* in which Manmatha temporarily resides before starting for the conquest of the world. (*Prm.* 4: 44). The *Vijayanagarada Sāmrājyavu* alludes to the *veliguḍāra* where Kṛṣṇarāya temporarily halted before he started for his wars against the Muhammadans. (*The Bhārati* v.) The *Rāyavācaka* mentions the *veliguḍāra* in the same context (*ASPP.* iii. p. 130).

5. Before starting on an expedition, 'on an appointed day the king goes forth to an open plain as if he were going for his pleasure......When he arrives at the plain, they bring him a horse whereon he rides holding in his hand a bow and an arrow which arrow he lets fly toward the country with which he i about to wage war. He the gives out in how many days from that time he will start...Thenc he goes forth at once and *fix*

The Prabandhas. — *The Portuguese Writers.*

his camping ground in the open country, where he awaits the time fixed for his advance." (*Barbosa* i. p. 224). This camp outside the city is 'the *veligu-ḍāra*' which means 'a tent fixed outside' (the city).

6. The *Kaḷāpūrṇōdayam* briefly describes the army on the march.

"The merchants who had gone in advance of the army set up small tents called *asimi gollenas,* and offered to the troops all the necessary articles of consumption for sale, where-ever they required them on the road. As all the things which one might desire could be obtained whenever they were considered necessary, and as women could follow the troops in handsomely decorated palanquins, the march of the king's invading army pleased the wealthy, because it offered them the same scope of enjoyment as the city.

Kpm. 8 : 42 : 43.

6. "They (the army) left the city of Bisnaga, and with them a great number of merchants, besides many others who are already in advance with all supplies ; so that wherever you may be, you will at once find all you want. Every captain has his merchants who are compelled to give him all supplies requisite for all his people, and in the same way they carry all other necessaries."

Nuniz : *FE.* p. 329.

The *Kuvalayāśvacaritram,* which describes a military camp vividly, alludes to the formation of streets of shops, where the troops could purchase all the necessary articles. (2 : 85). It also mentions the prostitutes who fell asleep in the tents

Again,—

'All the camp was divided into regular streets. Each captain's division has its market, where you find all kinds of meat.........and this in great abundance ; so much so that it would seem as if you were in the city of Bisnaga. And you

The Prabandhas.	*The Portuguese Writers*
awaiting the arrival of their lovers. (2 : 110)	found many endless kinds of rice, grains, Indian-corn, vetches (*minguo*), and other seeds that they eat. Besides these things, which are necessaries, they had another (market) where you could find in great abundance everything that you wanted ; for in these markets they sell all things that in our parts are sold by professional hucksters.' Nuniz : *FE.* pp. 332-3.
	Again,— '‘I do not here speak of...the public women who accompanied the army ; there were twenty thousand of them with the king during his journey.' *ibid* p. 328.

Sometimes the *prabandhas* serve to clear the obscure statements of the Portuguese writers; for instance, the following passage from the Spanish version of Barbosa's book is really puzzling.

"When this time is fulfilled, he issues a proclamation [ordering that the whole city shall be at once set on fire, saving the palaces, fortresses, and temples, and those of certain lords which are not thatched, and this he does in order] that all men shall attend with their wives and sons and households etc."
Barbosa i. p. 225.

Longworth Dames comments on this passage as follows:—

"The ridiculous statement here quoted from Remusio and the Spanish version does not occur in the Portuguese text, and is evidently an interpolation of an unintelligent copyist. What

Barbosa did say was not that the king set fire to his capital, but that when he was on the march, before starting for the next camping ground, he had this temporary town of grass huts, which had been erected for the accommodation of his army, burnt."

Barbosa i. p. 225.

That this view is correct is proved by a verse in the *Pārijātāpaharaṇam* in which the author compares the blazing sky at the time of sun-rise (which had been the camping ground of the Moon and his army of stars) to the burning camp of an invading king, set fire to by his servants, after his departure. (*Phm.* 2 : 65).

Instances such as these can be multiplied indefinitely; but these are enough to show that the *prabandha* writers, did not altogether draw upon their uncontrolled imagination, but incorporated into their stories the customs and manners of the society with which they were acquainted. The *prabandhas*, therefore can provide us, if properly handled, much excellent material that is greatly needed for the reconstruction of the social history of the period.

The *Varadāmbikāpariṇayam*, and the *Acyutarāyābhyudayam* give much accurate information about the events connected with the reign of Acyuta. Of these, the *Acyutarāyābhyudayam* is more important than the other. The contents of this work may be divided into four parts. The first three cantos briefly narrate the history of the Tuluva kings from the time of Narasā Nāyaka to the coronation of Acyuta. The next three cantos deal with the rebellion of Sāḷuva Narasingarāya Nāyaka *alias* Cellappa. As the genuineness of the events mentioned in these six cantos has been proved by a comparison with the inscriptions, it is needless to go into the matter at present. Cantos VIII and IX may be left out of consideration, as they only describe the pleasures of the Rāya. The last three cantos, which give an account of Acyuta's visit to Śrīrangapaṭṭaṇam and his invasion of Bijāpūr territory, deserve special attention, as they have not been dealt with by any writer. Did this invasion take place? If it did, when? It is not an easy matter to answer these questions. The Muhammadan historians of Golkonda and Ahmadnagar have nothing to say about this invasion, probably because it had no bearing upon the history of these two kingdoms; but the Bijāpūr historian, Ferishta, who should have mentioned it, is also silent. Are we, therefore, to conclude that Acyuta's invasion of the Bijāpūr kingdom is a pure invention of the poet who manufactured imaginary victories to tickle the vanity of his patron? Some such conclusion we would have arrived at, had we no access to material of a more trustworthy character, which corroborates the narrative of the *Acyutarāyābhyudayam* in almost every important particular. According to an epigraph 1534-35, Acyuta lay encamped in that year on the banks of the Kṛṣṇā. Rādhāmādhava, a contemporary of Ḍiṇḍima, the author of the *Acyutarāyābhyudayam*, refers also to Acyuta's victory over the Ādil Shāh. The Portuguese writers allude also to the main events of this invasion. The following table may be helpful in grasping all the evidence pertaining to the subject.

The table offers a satisfactory account of all the particulars connected with the campaign. What is of immediate interest, however, is the agreement between the accounts of De Barros and Ḍiṇḍima. Ignoring the details, for the present, the following three points may be considered as firmly established. (1) In 1535, the Vijayanagara army invaded Bijāpūr territory and laid siege to the fortress of Rāicūr. (2) The Ādil Shāh came to meet the Rāya, and (3) he was forced to sue for peace. The establishment of these three points is enough to rise the *Acyutarāyābhyudayam* to the level of a first rate contemporary historical document which illumines one of the darkest recesses of Vijayanagara history.

How are we to account for the silence of the Muhammadan historians, especially of Ferishta? An examination of the Muhammadan histories of the Deccan reveals the fact that the Muhammadan writers, while scrupulously recording all the victories of the faithful over the Hindus, generally ignore the Hindu victories over their co-religionists. It is no wonder that they suppressed all the information about this campaign to terminate which the Sultān had to supplicate the Hindu monarch. Ferishta was a hero-worshipper. For instance, Asad Khān, one of the greatest of his heroes, would not have looked, if the facts of this war were related, so innocent and honest, as he is made to appear in the pages of Ferishta. Therefore, he kept judicious silence over this inconvenient affair; and the students of our mediaeval history, who are taught to regard Ferishta's work as a true and accurate record of past events, are frequently led astray.

(ii) *The Travellers' accounts and the Chronicles*:—
(a) The Travellers' accounts:—Two works of this class

deserve notice. One of them is an account of the travels of Duarte Barbosa, one of the servants of the Portuguese Government in India; he visited Vijayanagara about 1510 A.D. Barbosa was a keen observer, and his book is said to be a faithful record of what he had seen during his visit. The same remark applies to the work of Paes who was at Vijayanagara about 1520 A.D. As the accounts of these two writers are admitted by all to be thoroughly accurate and trustworthy, an examination of their value as source books cannot but be superfluous.

(b) The Chronicles :—These are of three kinds, the Hindu, the Portuguese, and the Mussalman. (1) The *Rāmarājīya* is the only Hindu chronicle that partially describes the political events of this period. It was written in the first half of the 17th century during the very last days of the empire. Though a work of comparatively late origin, its evidence is reliable, as it is corroborated by the testimony of contemporary writers such as Rāmarājabhūṣaṇa (1525-1570), and Kōnēri-nātha (1549). The *Rāyavācaka* offers much information which is both useful and interesting. There is considerable uncertainty regarding the date of its composition. It professes to be a work written by a certain Bhaktaparādhīna, the *sthānāpati* of Viśwanātha Nāyaka, the founder of the Nāyak kingdom of Madura. As the kingdom of Madura did not come into existence before the battle of Rakṣasi-Tangiḍi, the work could not have been written earlier. That the author was certainly not a contemporary of Kṛṣṇadēvarāya whose history he chronicles is proved by the statement that he "had recorded in clear language the story of Kṛṣṇarāya as he had heard it from others." As the author of this work frequently mentions Bhāgānagara, a city which was founded subsequent to 1580 A.D., he must have written it only after the foundation of that city. It must

have been composed earlier than the middle of the 17th century, when Kumāra-Dhūrjaṭi versified its contents in his *Kṛṣṇarāyavijaya*. It is probable that it was written in the 16th century itself. Whatever be the date of its composition, it stands the test of facts remarkably well. The genuineness of the various items of information which it supplies can be proved by a comparison with the inscriptions, and the contemporary *prabandhas* and the Portuguese records.

(2) The most valuable of the Portuguese chronicles is, no doubt, the work compiled by Nuniz. He must have visited Vijayanagara more than once between 1520 and 1540, when he appears to have sojourned in the city for sometime. He seems to have drawn his information from two sources: the earlier part of his work, that is the part which closes with the Sāḷuva usurpation, appears to have been based upon some Hindu chronicle. For the rest, he either depended upon the evidence of people who were eye-witnesses, or on his own experience. It is only with the second part of Nuniz's work that the present monograph has anything to do. His work appears to be a fairly accurate version of facts, and so far as it is based upon his personal knowledge it is thoroughly trustworthy. It is fashionable with a certain class of writers to belittle the value of his evidence. This seems to be the result of a desire to state something definite, where definiteness is not possible in the present state of our knowledge. On a deep and thorough investigation of the problems, Nuniz is found to be invariably accurate.

Of the Portuguese historians properly so called De Barros claims our attention first. The first three of the four *Decadas* of which he was the author were published during his life-time between 1552 and 1563.

THE SOURCES

Though De Barros himself was never in India, he is believed to have collected his material from men who either visited the country or were residents therein. Paes and Nuniz are said to have compiled their accounts at his instance. His history, so far as it relates to Vijayanagara, is of immense importance, as it lifts the curtain of mist that has been hanging over the events of this period. Correa, the author of the *Lendas da India*, was in India from 1512 and 1528. It is also stated that his *Lendas* are based on the *Conquista da India* of Castanheda, who lived in India from 1528 to 1538. The work of Castanheda is said to be valuable and trustworthy. *

The Mussalman Historians:—There are four Mussalman historians whose works are made accessible to the public in English translations. (1) The anonymous author of the history of the Qutb Shāhi kings of Golkonda. (2) Syed Ali bin Azīz-ul-la Tabātaba, the author of *Burhān-ī-ma'asir*, (3) Raffi-ud-Dīn Shīrāzi, the author of *Tuzaful-ul-Muluk*, and (4) Ferishta, the famous historian of Muhammadan India.

The first two writers deal with the history of Vijayanagara in an incidental manner. Most of what they say is in agreement with known facts. Shīrāzi, who knew Vijayanagara before its destruction by the Mussalmans, appears to be, judging him from a brief summary of his work available in English, the most impartial of all the Muhammadan historians. The information which he gives is not found in other sources. The most important, and, at the same time, the least trustworthy of the Muhammadan writers, is Ferishta. He gives what looks like a concise account of the history of Vijayanagara from A.D. 1485 to 1543. He says:

* *FE.* p. 142.

"The government of Beejanuggur, had remained in one family in uninterrupted succession for seven hundred years, when Shew Ray dying, he was succeeded by his son a minor, who did not long survive him, and left the throne to a younger brother. Not long after, he died also, leaving an infant only three months old. Timraj, one of the principal ministers of the family, celebrated for his wisdom and experience, became sole regent, and was cheerfully obeyed by the nobility and the vassals of the kingdom for forty years. On the occasion of the young King's attaining the age of manhood, Timraj poisoned him, and put an infant of the family on the throne, in order to have a pretence for retaining the regency in his hands. Timraj at length dying, was succeeded in his office by his son Ramraj, who having married a daughter of Shew Ray, added by that alliance greatly to his influence and power." (Brigg's *Ferishta* iii. pp. 80-81).

(1) According to Ferishta, the first dynasty held sway over Vijayanagara for seven hundred years without interruption. In another context, he attributes the construction of the city of Vijayanagara to Ballāḷa III, who reigned from 1290 to 1343. Between 1344 when the city is said to have been built and 1495 when Timrāj became regent, there were only 150 years, and not seven hundred as Ferishta would have us believe. Moreover, it is discovered from a study of the inscriptions that the kingdom of Vijayanagara was founded in or about 1336 A.D., and that the first or the Sangama Dynasty came to an end in 1486 A.D. Therefore, the Sangama line of kings reigned for (1486—1336) 150 years. The account of Nuniz is roughly in agreement with this. As the evidence of the inscriptions is admitted to be most trustworthy, the statement of Ferishta must be regarded as absolutely unreliable.

(2) Shew Rāy is said to have died a few years before Timrāj's assumption of power as regent. Ferishta seems to regard him as the last important member of the first or the Sangama Dynasty; but neither the inscriptions nor Nuniz mention a king of this name as

having ruled at Vijayanagara. Even if it be said that Sadāśiva might be the original of Shew Rāy, he could not have died during the last decade of the fifteenth century. There is ample evidence to show that Sadāśiva ascended the throne in 1543 and died sometime after 1570. Therefore, Shew Rāy must be considered as a mythical person, who is not met with in any trustworthy historical document.

(3) Even if Shew Rāy is identified with Sāḷuva Narasimha, the four youngsters, who are said to have succeeded him, must be accounted for. The two minor sons of Shew Rāy may be identified with the two minor sons of Sāḷuva Narasimha viz., Immaḍi Narasimha and his elder brother; but the other two princes, whom Timrāj is said to have placed upon the throne, have no room for accommodation. Ferishta appears to have multiplied the two successors of Sāḷuva Narasimha, if he were really identical with Shew Rāy, into four, for reasons best known only to himself.

(4) The regent's name, according to Ferishta, is Timrāj; but according to Nuniz and the inscriptions, his name is Narasā Nāyaka. Timrāj is said to have wielded his authority as regent for forty years; but Narasā Nāyaka held the office only for nine years from 1493 to 1502.

(5) It is said that Timrāj died sometime before 1535, and that he was succeeded by his son Rāmrāj.* Ferishta does not leave any room for doubt regarding

* The text of Ferishta available in the market does not mention the relationship of Timrāj and Rāmrāj: *b'ad az ānki Timrāj dar guzasht ba masnadash Rāmrāj qā'yam gashta, dukhtar-i-pisar-i-Sīvrāj bah 'aqad-i-khīsh dar āvard.* After that Timrāj died; Rāmrāj becoming established upon his throne, married a daughter of the son of Sīvrāj. *Tārikh-i-Ferishta.*

his identity. He is the same prince who ultimately perished on the battle-field of Rakṣasi-Tangiḍi. The inscriptions and literature clearly state that Rāmrāj was one of the sons of Śrīrangarāja, a grandson of Āravīṭi Bukka. Śrīranga was but an obscure nobleman, and he never rose even to the position of a minister. If Timrāj is identified with Narasā Nāyaka, Rāmrāj cannot be regarded as his son. Ferishta does not even remotely allude to Narasā Nāyaka's famous sons, Vīra-Narasimha, Kṛṣṇadēva, and Acyuta.

(6) Rāmrāj is said to have married a daughter of Shew Rāy.* The names of the fathers of all the wives of Rāmarāja are mentioned in the *Rāmarājīya*. None of them bore the name of Shew Rāy; but the father of one of his wives is said to be Kṛṣṇadēvarāya.

It is obvious from what has been said above, that Ferishta was almost totally ignorant of the history of Vijayanagara during the first three decades of the sixteenth century. His account of the next decade stands the test of facts a little better. Although it deals with some of the main events of the period, it is so garbled as to make it impossible for us to discover the true course of affairs. According to him, Ibrahim Ādil Shāh led his army to Vijayanagara at the request of Bhōj Tirumal who desired to put down, with his assistance, his rival Rāmrāj. When the Ādil Shāh reached the Hindu capital, he was given a rousing reception by Bhōj Tirumal. His rival was apparently crushed; and he pretended submission. Bhōj Tirumal who was completely taken in, persuaded his ally to go back to his capital after paying him large sums of money. No sooner did the Ādil Shāh turn his back upon the Hindu capital than Rāmrāj marched upon it

* In the foot-note on p. xxix, Rāmrāj is said to have married a daughter of the son of Sivrāj.

with all his troops, and, putting Bhōj Tirumal to death, seized the supreme power. All these events are said to have taken place in A.H. 942 which corresponds, according to Sewell's calculations, to 1535-36 A.D. *

Bhōj Tirumal, at whose request the Ādil Shāh marched to Vijayanagara, is identified with Salakarāju Tirumala (junior), who usurped the throne after murdering his nephew, Venkaṭa I, in A.D. 1543, and who was slain by Rāmrāja during the course of the same year. If the retirement of the Ādil Shāh preceded the death of Salakarāju Tirumala only by a few days, it must have occurred also in the same year. It seems as if the Ādil Shāh who led his troops to Vijayanagara in 1535-36 remained there until 1543, leaving the affairs of his own kingdom to be managed by his ministers. Such a prolonged stay in the midst of an enemy's country is extremely unlikely. As Syed Ali, the author of *Burhān-i-ma'asir*, gives a different account of the affairs of Vijayanagara, at this time, a comparative study of the narratives of the two historians may offer some solution to the problem.

FERISHTA.	SYED ALI.
1. Ismail Ādil Shāh died in September 1534.	1. Ismail Ādil Shāh died in A.D. 1534-5.
2. Malloo Ādil Shāh ruled for six months (*i.e.*, until March 1535).	2. Mallu Adil Shāh ascended the throne in 1534-35, and was deposed in 1535.
3. Ibrahim Ādil Shāh ascended the throne in 1535.	3. Ibrahim Ādil Shāh ascended the throne in 1535.

* *FE.* p. 171.

FERISHTA.	SYED ALI.
4. He led his army to Vijayanagara at the request of Bhōj Tirumal after March 1536.	4. Rāmrāj rebelled against the Rāya in 1537-38. Ibrahim Ādil Shāh invaded the Vijayanagara territory and laid siege to the city, where he stayed for a long time until (?) 1539. Asad Khān's intrigues; and Burhān Nizām Shāh's invasion of the Bijāpūr kingdom in 1540-41.
5. War between the Ādil Shāh and the Nizām Shāh in 1542.	5. The Ādil Shāh's retirement from Vijayanagara territory, and his war with the Nizām Shāh (?) 1540-41.
6. Peace was concluded between the two Sultāns in 1542.	6. Peace was concluded between the two Sultāns in 1542.

Both the Muhammadan historians agree in stating that a war broke out between the Ādil Shāh and the Nizām Shāh about 1541, and that it was preceded by the Ādil Shāh's invasion of the Vijayanagara empire. If the death of Salakarāju Tirumala took place, as the inscriptions and the Portuguese writers declare, in 1543, it could not have occurred at the close of the Ādil Shāh's invasion which terminated before 1540-1541. No doubts need be entertained, regarding the truth of the Ādil Shāh's invasion, as Ferishta's account is not only borne out by Syed Ali but also by Nuniz, though it is probable that it took place in 1539 rather than in 1536. Since Salakarāju Tirumala was alive until 1543, it appears as if his death had no connection whatever with the Ādil Shāh's invasion. However, Correa associates his death with the Ādil Shāh's invasion even as Ferishta does, but he places both the events after 1542. Therefore, the only reasonable conclusion is that the Ādil Shāh invaded the Vijayanagara territory twice. The first invasion took place in 1539, and it terminated before 1540-41. The second invasion must be assigned to 1542-43.

It is evident that Ferishta causes great confusion by mixing up the events connected with two different invasions. On the whole, the testimony of Ferishta is very untrustworthy, so far as the history of this period is concerned. He must be treated as a treacherous guide whose help has to be accepted with great caution, if it cannot be avoided altogether.

(iii) *The Local Records*:—The Local Records, as has already been noticed, contain much historical information of a traditional character. In the preparation of this work, information of a purely traditional kind has been systematically avoided; but wherever tradition is supported by the inscriptions and contemporary literature, it has been fully utilised. A few instances may serve as illustrations of the manner of its treatment.

(1) It is said in an inscription of Kavutāḷam dated A.D. 1533 that Salakarāju Cina Tirumala, who was then a minister of Acyuta, paid a visit to Kavutāḷam and, having summoned all the ryots of the *sīma*, offered them lands for cultivation at low rates. Another fragmentary record in the same place appears to mention the details regarding the rate of assessment.

The Local Records narrate the circumstances under which Cina Tirumala granted the lands. Owing to the oppressive tyranny of the local officials, the ryots abandoned their farms, and repaired to the neighbouring Māneveya *sīma*, which belonged to the Ādil Shāh.

The agriculture of the Kavutāḷa *sīma* was ruined, and the imperial exchequer suffered heavy loss. In order to restore the prosperity of the district, and to replenish the state treasury, Cina Tirumala visited the locality and effected a reconciliation between the Rāya and his ryots.

There is no reason why the evidence of tradition should not be accepted here; for several inscriptions of this period record similar migrations and compromises in many districts of the empire.

(2) According to the *Karnāṭakarājula Vṛttāntamu*, (*LR.* 10) which is probably a translation of the *Kongudēśarājākkaḷ*, Dēvarāja, the chief of Ummattūr, though defeated and subjugated by Narasā Nāyaka, rose up in rebellion against his son, Vīra Narasimha, and defeated him in battle when he invaded the Ummattūr territory. Therefore, it became incumbent upon Kṛṣṇarāya to reduce the rebel soon after his accession to the throne. Before he could take up the task, however, Dēvarāja died, and he was succeeded by his son Nañjarāja, who strengthened his position not only by repairing the fort of Ummattūr but by building a new one on the island of Śivansamudram. In the meanwhile, Kṛṣṇarāya having detached Mallarāja *alias* Cikkarāja from Nañjarāja, invaded the Ummattūr principality. He defeated Nañjarāja and destroyed his stronghold. While attempting to flee from the fort of Śivansamudram, Nañjarāja was accidentally drowned in the waters of the Kāvērī and perished.

This account is in complete agreement with the facts known from the inscriptions and the contemporary literature. The *Varadāmbikāpariṇayam*, the *Acyutarāyābhyudayam*, and the *Pārijātāpaharaṇam* allude to Narasā Nāyaka's march from Madura to Śrīranga-paṭṭaṇam. His route must necessarily have passed along the banks of the Kāvērī through the principality of Ummattūr. His presence in the neighbourhood in 1486 is also mentioned in a few inscriptions. It is not unlikely that he must have subdued the Ummattūr chieftain on his way, if he had assumed an attitude of defiance. The fact that Kṛṣṇarāya had to subdue the Ummattūr chief as soon as he ascended the throne shows that the rebellion of the said chief must have had its origin during the reign of Vīra-Narasimha. Kṛṣṇa-rāya's conquest of Ummattūr is mentioned by several contemporary writers including the Portuguese. Therefore, it is not unreasonable to accept the *Karṇāṭakarājula Vṛttāntamu* as a genuine record of historical events.

(3) The events connected with the war between Salakarāju Tirumala and Rāmarāja are recorded in the traditional histories of three or four places. What Ferishta has to say on the subject is very meagre and faulty. The events recorded in local histories are also mentioned by contemporary writers like Rāmarāja-bhūṣaṇa, whose testimony is corroborated by Venkayya, the author of *Rāmarājīyam*, who lived about a century later. There is no reason, under the circumstances, why the evidence of the Local Records should not be accepted in this context.

(4) A few words must be said, in passing, about the *Aṭṭhavaṇa Tantram*, one of the most interesting documents preserved in the Mackenzie Collection. It is a late document drawn up in the 18th century by an anonymous author at the request of one of the earliest officers of the East India Company, who desired to know the manner of government that was obtaining in the Vijayanagara empire. As that empire

finally fell to pieces in the middle of the 17th century, the author's information could not have been collected from his own personal knowledge. Nor could he have based his account upon some earlier work on the subject, for no such work existed. However, the administrative system of the old empire remained almost intact in certain parts of the country where the subordinates of the last emperors asserted their independence. Citradurga was one of the principalities which came into existence in this fashion. As the administrative system under which this principality was governed was the same as the one obtaining during the age of the Rāyas, the author of the *Aṭṭhavaṇa Tantram* took that as a basis for reconstructing the old Vijayanagara polity. Nevertheless, the *Aṭṭhavaṇa Tantram* cannot be regarded as a primary source. The Vijayanagara administrative system that is described in the present work is not based upon the *Aṭṭhavaṇa Tantram*; but the information supplied by this document is fully taken advantage of, wherever such a course appeared reasonable. The meaning of several taxes which prominently figure in the inscriptions of the sixteenth century is hardly intelligible; but a proper knowledge of their nature is of inestimable value to a student of the fiscal system of the Rāyas. The *Aṭṭhavaṇa Tantram* is of immense importance in this connection, as it explains the nature of some of the most important taxes. As the Vijayanagara system of taxation remained almost unaltered until the days of the East India Company, the adoption of the explanations offered by the *Aṭṭhavaṇa Tantram* is not unjustified. The *āyagārs* are frequently mentioned in the inscriptions of the period. Some of them, the *Reḍḍi* (*gauḍ*), the *karṇam* (*Sānbhōg*), and the *talāri* are referred to by their official designations. The *Aṭṭhavaṇa Tantram* is the only work which fully describes the *āyagār* system.

THE SOURCES

Of all the parts of the old Hindu polity, the village administration is generally admitted to be least affected by the passage of time and the changes in government. Therefore, it stands to reason to take the *āyagār* system to have been the same in the 16th century as it was in 18th.

PART I

THE HISTORY OF VIJAYANAGARA FROM A. D. 1530–1542

Chapter I.

ACCESSION OF ACYUTADĒVARĀYA.

Section 1 :— The Portuguese historian Nuniz states:

"Before the death of Crisnarao from his disease .... being sick and already despairing of his life, he made a will, saying that of his three brothers whom he had sent to be confined in the fortress of Chamdegary, with his nephew, son of King Busbalrao, they should make king, his brother Achetarao. After his (Crisnarao's) death, Salvany became minister of the kingdom, and governed it till the arrival of King Achetarao from the fortress of Chamdegary, where he was detained." *

This account of Nuniz seems to be corroborated by the evidence of Rājanātha Diṇḍima. According to him Acyuta's first coronation took place at Tirupati in the presence of the god Venkaṭēśvara. † It is said in an inscription at Kāḷahasti that Acyuta's coronation took place in that town on *Kārtika ba* 5 of *Virōdhi*, corresponding to the Śaka year 1452 (Oct. 21 Thursday 1529). ‡ As Kṛṣṇarāya died about the middle of that year (May-Oct. 1529), Acyuta was not at Vijayanagara at the time of his brother's death, but somewhere in the neighbourhood of Tirupati and Kāḷahasti, probably at Candragiri which was the most important fortress in that locality.

Acyutarāya whom Kṛṣṇadēva nominated as his successor seems to have gone to Vijayanagara to ascend the throne from his prison at Candragiri, 'where he was detained.' However, a study of the inscriptions seems to indicate that Acyuta was enjoying freedom for three or four years before the death of

* *FE.* 366-67. † *The Sources* 161. ‡ *MER.* 157 of 1924.

his brother. Thus, an inscription from Kammarapūḍi in the Nellore district dated Śaka 1448 *Pārthiva* (A. D. 1526) states that he was ruling the kingdom of the world, seated on his diamond throne at Vijayanagara. * Another from Hosepēṭe in the Sidlaghaṭṭa tālūka of the Mysore State, dated Śaka 1450 *Sarvadhāri* (1528) mentions him with imperial titles, and states that he was ruling from Vijayanagara. † It appears from these records that Acyuta was ruling as the emperor of Vijayanagara from A. D. 1526 onwards, although his coronation was celebrated in A. D. 1530.

This conclusion is in agreement with the date assigned in some of the Local Records to Kṛṣṇadēva's death. He is said to have breathed his last on *Jyēṣṭha śu* 6 Sunday of the cyclic year *Tāraṇa*, corresponding to Śaka 1447. ‡ According to an inscription of Tirumaladēva, son of Kṛṣṇarāya dated Śaka 1446 (expired) *Tāraṇa*, *Mārg. śu* 2, Saturday (1525 A. D), a certain Kōnappa Nāyaka is said to have administered *gangōdaka* to Kṛṣṇarāya. § It is customary among the Hindus of the South to offer a spoonful of pure water to a dying man, and this water is usually called *gangōdaka* (water of the Ganges). The death of Kṛṣṇarāya about this date is inferred from this record. Again, a *kaul* (lease deed) which Aḷiya Rāmarāja granted to Namalanēni Kumāra Peda Bucci Nāyaningāru dated Śaka 1448 *Vyaya*, *Vaiśākha*, *śu* 15 (1526-27) describes Rāmarāja with all the imperial titles. ¶ He is said to have been ruling the kingdom of the earth seated on his throne at the city of Vijayanagara. It is inferred from these that the reign of Kṛṣṇadēvarāya came to an end sometime before

* *NDI.* N. 34-A. p. 892. † *EC.* Sg. 15. ‡ *LRV.* p. 48.

§ *EC.* ix, Mi. 82. ¶ *LR.* 18. p. 407.

A. D. 1526, and that the succession to the throne was disputed by Acyuta, Rāmarāja, and Tirumala who were fighting with one another until 1530, when the civil war ended, and Acyuta the most successful candidate ascended the throne. Further, it is pointed out that during the interregnum each of the three claimants to the throne made grants, and issued *kauls*, as if he were the real king himself. All the feudatories, and private donors, it is assumed, dated their inscriptions in the reign of Kṛṣṇarāya which they supposed to be continuing, until the accession of one of the rival candidates to the throne. *

The epigraphical evidence against this view is overwhelming. We have to deal with several inscriptions belonging to this period not only of the feudatories but of Kṛṣṇarāya himself. † It is impossible to ignore these inscriptions, and accept the statement that Kṛṣṇarāya died in A. D. 1526. What then is the explanation of the inscriptions of Acyuta and Tirumala referred to above, even if the *kaul* of Rāmarāja may be left out of consideration? Only one explanation seems possible. Kṛṣṇarāya seems to have fallen ill about 1525 A. D., and his condition became so critical that his life was despaired of. Even the last rite of offering '*gangōdaka*' was performed; but he evidently recovered from his illness, and assumed the control of affairs. Tirumalarāya in whose favour the emperor abdicated in A. D. 1524 seems to have fallen ill sometime later and died. ‡ Kṛṣṇarāya was, therefore, obliged to make fresh arrangements for the succession to the throne. Among the possible candidates, there were, according to Nuniz, his three brothers, his nephew, the son of Busbalrao, and a son

* *LRV.* p 52. † *MER.* 1891 ii, p. 5. ‡ *FE.* p. 359.

who was only eighteen months old. * Setting aside the claim of the other candidates including that of his infant son, he nominated his brother Acyuta as his successor, because he was the most competent person among the members of the royal family to sit upon the throne. † However, while deciding the question of succession, he had also to consider the case of his son-in-law, Rāmarāja who seems to have played an active part in the administration of the empire during the last years of his reign. Although Nuniz does not at all mention Rāmarāja, several contemporary and later records bear ample testimony to his activity during Kṛṣṇarāya's reign. An early but damaged epigraph of the Āravīḍu chiefs refers to Rāmarāja as 'the son-in-law of Kṛṣṇadēvarāya, the conqueror of the Gajapati.' He appears to have distinguished himself in some of Kṛṣṇadēva's wars against the Mussalmans. ‡ Ayyalarāju Rāmabhadra, a contemporary writer alludes to the marriage of Rāmarāja with a daughter of Kṛṣṇadēvarāya. § The ananymous historian of Gōlkoṇḍa declares that Rāmarāja after his disgrace at Gōlkoṇḍa 'took the route to Beejanuggur, and entered the service of Kṛṣnarāja, who, shortly afterwards forming a high opinion of him, gave him his daughter in marriage.' ¶ 'Couto states also that Rāmarāya was a great general in the army of Kṛṣṇadēvarāya, and was actually in the province of the Baḍagas and Teligas.' ‖ According to Father Queyros, Kṛṣṇadēvarāya, in the last days of his reign, 'entrusted the government of the *kingdom*' to his son-in-law Rāmarāja, and 'the command of the troops'

* *FE.* p. 367. † *ibid.*

‡ *MER.* 164 of 1905; *ASR.* 1908. p. 194. n. 8.

§ *Rm.* 1: 55. ¶ Brigg's *Ferishta* iii. p. 381.

‖ Heras: *The Āravīḍu Dynasty* p. 25.

to Tirumala, his brother. * The Kaifiyat of Penugoṇḍa declares that Kṛṣṇadēvarāya who had no sons to succeed him, gave his daughter in marriage to Rāmarāja, and appointed him at the same time as *yuvarāja.* †

These extracts from contemporary and later records show that Rāmarāja, who married Kṛṣṇadēvarāya's daughter, was a person of considerable importance at the time of the death of that monarch. It is extremely unlikely that the dying emperor would have altogether ignored him in his last will and testament. That this was not the case is shown by the statements of several historians. Ferishta says that Rāmrāja became 'one of the principal ministers' of the state after the death of his father Timrāj. ‡ As Ferishta's Timrāj is a mythical person, what he says about the son should be regarded as something whose value is at best doubtful. But in view of what the ananymous historian of Gōlkoṇḍa says, the evidence of Ferishta need not totally be rejected. Here is what he says:

> "At length his father-in-law (Kṛṣṇarāja) died. *The heir to the throne was a child in arms*; and being, therefore, unfit to manage his affairs, Rāmrāj first assumed the office of the protector." §

Rāmarāja was known to the author of the *Burhān-i-ma'asir* as "*Vakīl* (chief Minister) of the King of Vijayanagara." ¶ These allusions to the early career of Rāmarāja show that after the death of Kṛṣṇarāya, he became one of the principal ministers of the kingdom. The Kaifiyat of Penugoṇḍa seems to throw some light on the problem. ‖ According to this document

* Queyros: *The Conquest of Ceylon* ii. p. 383.

† *M. Mss.* 15-6-8.

‡ Brigg's *Ferishta* iii. p. 81.

§ *ibid.* iii. p. 381.

¶ *IA.* xlix. p. 201.

‖ *M. Mss.* 15-6-8.

Kṛṣṇadēvarāya commanded Rāmarāja at the time of his death, to continue in the office of *yuvarāja*, and assist Acyuta, whom he nominated to succeed him, in the administration of the empire. This is corroborated by Father Queyros who declares that before his death Kṛṣṇarāya ordered his son-in-law Rāmarāja 'to restore the power' to his brother Acyuta, and 'administer justice jointly with him.' Rāmarāja acted according to his father-in-law's wishes. Acyuta who was 'pleased with this courtesy' allowed him to administer the kingdom with him. Consequently, Rāmarāja became "better recognised as king than the natural one, a penalty which all pay to favouritism." * Although the writers whose evidence we have cited agree with one another regarding Rāmarāja's position in the state, they differ about the person who was actually seated on the throne of Vijayanagara at the time. According to some, it was Acyuta that ascended the throne after the demise of Kṛṣṇadēva; but others mention an infant son of the latter as having succeeded him.

Section 2 :—Who was the person that succeeded Kṛṣṇarāya, Acyuta or Kṛṣṇarāya's own infant son? That is the problem which we have to solve first. The problem is a very difficult one. The inscriptions seem to speak unequivocally that Acyuta ascended the throne after Kṛṣṇarāya. They are supported by several Hindu and Portuguese writers, both contemporary and later. But all the Muhammadan historians not only ignore the name of Acyuta altogether but refer to Rāmarāja as the ruler of Vijayanagara after the death of Kṛṣṇadēvarāya. Thus the evidence in the light of which this problem is to be solved is very conflicting and even contradictory. And any

* Queyros: *Conquest of Ceylon*. ii. p. 383.

conclusion that may be arrived at needs necessarily be tentative.

That Kṛṣṇarāya had an infant son at the time of his death is vouched for by the following passage from the chronicle of Nuniz:

"King Crisnarao . . . being sick and already despairing of his life, ... made a will, saying that . . . they should make king his brother Achetarao . . . ; for the latter seemed to him to be better fitted for that than any of the others, *for the reason that he had no son of fit age for the throne, but only one of the age of eighteen months.*" *

It is evident that, while settling the question of succession, Kṛṣṇarāya not only considered the case of his infant son, but rejected him on the ground that he was not 'of fit age for the throne.' But Rafī-ud-Dīn Shirāzi, a contemporary of Rāmarāja declares:

"Rāmarāja became king of Vijayanagara in H. 942. He used to hold his court *in the name of Kṛṣṇarāya's son*, the real emperor, and people used to make their obeisance to the boy. Rāmarāja conducted the administration for two years nominally for the son of Kṛṣṇarāya." †

This is corroborated by the testimony of the anonymous historian, of Golkonda who says:

"The heir to the throne (after Kṛṣṇarāya's death) was *a child in arms*: § and being, therefore, unfit to manage his affairs, Rāmrāj first assumed the office of the protector.' ‡

* *FE.* pp. 366-67. † *JBBRAS.* xxii. p. 28.

‡ Brigg's *Ferishta* iii p. 381.

§ Father Heras identifies this "child in arms" with Sadāśiva. 'Indeed,' says he, 'a contemporary anonymous chronicler of Golkonda' says that the heir to the throne was a 'child in arms,' although according to Couto, at the time of his installation, Sadāśiva 'was a little more than thirteen years of age,' and according to Correa 'about sixteen.' Fr. Heras forgets the context in which 'the child in arms' is mentioned by the contemporary anonymous chronicler. It is this: Rāmarāja 'took the route to Beejanuggur and entered the service of Krishnaraj, who, shortly afterwards, forming a high opinion of him, gave him his daughter in marriage.

According to these Muhammadan historians, the person who succeeded Kṛṣṇarāya was his infant son; and the government of the empire was actually carried on by Rāmarāja who married a sister of the infant monarch. This is supported by the account of the Portuguese historian, Correa who was in India from A. D. 1512 to 1528.

"Correa states that in 1542 Achyuta, king of Vijayanagar, died leaving a young son in the power of his uncle, brother of the dead king who had been king *contrary to the right*. The nobles wished to keep the boy at liberty nominating two ministers to carry on the government; but the uncle disagreed, since in this way he would lose all power, and he contrived to get some partisans to his side. The queen, the mother of the boy, begged the Ādil Shāh to come to her aid and secure the kingdom for her son, promising him, in return for this favour, immense riches. The Sultān set out for the purpose, but on the road he was met by emissaries from the minister, and bought off with lavish gifts. *The king by real right* who had been detained in a fortress was then liberated, and he also sought the aid of the Sultān of Bijāpūr. The Sultān took advantage of the opportunity to set out afresh nominally to aid the *true king* but really to acquire the kingdom for himself. The Hindus, in fear for their safety, placed on the throne the brother of the dead king, and succeeded in defeating the Ādil Shāh close to Vijayanagar. The new king in order to strengthen his position for the future, caused the boy, his rival, to be assassinated. . . . Then, in dread of the power of the principal nobles, he summoned them to court, and put out the eyes of those who arrived first; so that the rest returned in great anger and began to intrigue with the Sultān." "The Ādil Shāh therefore

At length his father-in-law died. The heir to the throne was a 'child in arms.' It is clear that the heir referred to in this passage is the heir of Kṛṣṇarāya, not of Acyuta, nor of Venkaṭa I, as the Rev. Father tries to make out. He also forgets that Kṛṣṇadēvarāya had a son of the age of eighteen months at the time of his death. 'The child in arms' of the anonymous chronicler describes the infant son of Kṛṣṇarāya more accurately than Sadāśiva, who, at the time of his installation, was at least more than 13 years old. Sadāśiva for whose merit grants had been made in 1518, 1523 and 1524 could not have been 'the heir to the throne,' who was a 'child in arms', at the time of Kṛṣṇarāya's death. The 'child in arms' mentioned by the anonymous chronicler can be none other than the infant son of Kṛṣṇarāya himself.

advanced, entered the kingdom of Vijayanagar." "Meanwhile *a new king* had seized the throne of Vijayanagar, a great lord from Paleacate, *married to a sister of the king that preceded the dead king*, and in the end he secured the kingdom." *

This passage sums up correctly but briefly, the leading events of the history of Vijayanagara between 1530 and 1543 A. D. At present, however, what interests us most is the identity of the personalities that are mentioned therein.

The uncle in whose power Acyuta left his son Venkaṭa I should be identified with Salakarāju Cinna Tirumaladēva. Tirumala, was, of course, a brother-in-law of the dead king. It is not unusual with the European writers to refer to the brother-in-law as the brother. 'The queen, the mother of the boy' was, no doubt, Varadādēvi, the queen of Acyutadēvarāya. Tirumaladēva murdered Venkaṭa I, as admitted by all the historians, soon after his coronation. 'The king by real right who had been detained in a fortress' was Sadāśiva, who was kept in prison at Gutti. † The new king from Paleacate was, as pointed out by Sewell, Rāmarāja. And the king who 'preceded the dead king' Acyuta, and whose sister Rāmarāja had married was that infant son of Kṛṣṇadēvarāya of whom Rāmarāja is said to have become the protector.

Therefore, according to Correa, the person that preceded Acyuta on the throne of Vijayanagara was not Rāmarāja's father-in-law, but his brother-in-law. And so far, he is in perfect agreement with the Muhammadan writers whose evidence we have already cited. It is not reasonable to set aside the evidence of these writers as untrue. There seems to be a great deal of truth in what they say.

* Sewell: *FE.* pp. 182-183. † *The Sources* p. 191.

The question of succession appears to have been finally settled in 1526. Although Acyuta was recognised as the heir-apparent, he preferred to stay in the fortress of Candragiri itself. However, Kṛṣṇarāya's act of settlement failed to give satisfaction to several people the most important of whom was Rāmarāja himself; but until the death of the old monarch no one had the courage to express openly his feeling of discontent.

As soon, however, as Kṛṣṇarāya breathed his last, Rāmarāja seems to have made an attempt to place his young brother-in-law upon the throne. Rafī-ud-Dīn Shirāzi, and the anonymous historian of Golkonda state this explicitly, as we have already noticed. Although Kṛṣṇarāya set aside the claim of his young son, in the interests of the state, Rāmarāja who was disappointed by the final arrangements made by him seems to have promptly proclaimed his young brother-in-law emperor, and made an attempt to seize the throne. He must have been strongly backed up by the queens of Kṛṣṇadēva, as well as those officers who were loyal to the family of the late monarch. Besides, the numerous progeny of the patriarch, Āravīṭi Bukka who held several important forts such as Kandanavōlu, Awuku, Ādavani, Nandyāla etc., and several other chiefs should have been ready to join his standard against Acyuta. To counteract the activities of this party, the supporters of Acyuta had to bestir themselves. The strongest supporters of his claim were no doubt his two brothers-in-law, Salakarāju (Pedda and Cinna) Tirumaladēvas. If we can trust the Kaifiyat of Bukkasamudram one of them was already holding an important post in the state, as the superintendent of the royal treasury. * In his capacity as the treasurer, he had access to all the

* *The Sources* p. 179.

stored up wealth of the empire. He was in a position to command the services of all those who cared more for money than for the interests of the family of the dead monarch. Besides, Salvany, Sāḷuva Nāyaka or Sāḷuva Narasingarāya Daṇṇāyaka, the most powerful nobleman in the empire, had declared himself to be a partisan of Acyuta. He was the governor of the Cōḷa country, and was 'the lord of Charamãodel, Negapatão, Tamgor, Bomgarin, Dapatao, Trueguel, and Caullim' His territories were very large, and they bordered upon Ceylon. He maintained an army consisting of 'thirty thousand foot, and three thousand horse, and thirty elephants.' * He seems to have seized the throne on behalf of Acyuta, and held it until the arrival of the latter from Candragiri. "Salvany became the minister of the kingdom," says Nuniz, "and governed it till the coming of Achetarao from the fortress of Chamdegary where he was detained." † The combination of Salakarāju brothers with Sāḷuva Nāyaka frustrated the first attempt of Rāmarāja to secure the supreme power for himself.

It was probably the opposition of Rāmarāja that induced Acyuta to take an unusual step. As soon as he heard the news of his brother's death, instead of hastening to the capital, he leisurely proceeded to Tirupati where he had his coronation celebrated. ‡ Thence he went to Kāḷahasti where the coronation ceremony was repeated. § It must be noted that Acyuta was the first ruler of Vijayanagara, who had his coronation celebrated in a place outside the capital. He was also the first king to crown himself on more than one occasion. It looks as if, fearing the opposition of his rival in the capital, Acyuta had his

* *FE.* pp. 384-85.

† *ibid* p. 367.

‡ *The Sources* p. 161.

§ *MER.* 157 of 1924.

coronation purposely celebrated in the two holy cities of the empire, to strengthen his claim to the throne. This view is supported by an inscription of Ankavalli, Sorab tālūka dated A. D. 1529, the donor of which made a grant in order that Acyutarāya might be firmly established in the empire. * Having then come to know that his friends destroyed the power of Rāmarāja, he proceeded to the capital which he seems to have reached early in 1530 A. D.

Although Rāmarāja failed to grasp the supreme power, his influence in the capital as well as in the provinces should have been considerable. Acyuta appears to have realised that to antagonise Rāmarāja would not help him very much in holding his power successfully. Having the infant son of Kṛṣṇarāya under his protection, Rāmarāja could put forward the claim of his protégé which was legally sounder than his own. Therefore, Acyuta appears to have opened negotiations with Rāmarāja, as soon as he reached the capital, and seems to have succeeded in persuading him to enter into a sort of partnership with him, on behalf of his ward, in governing the empire. The coronation of Acyuta was then celebrated for the third time at Vijayanagara ; and his authority was recognised by all.

Rāmarāja thus became the joint ruler of the empire with Acyuta, and began to exercise as of old great authority in governing the state. This arrangement appears to have worked satisfactorily until the commencement of A. D. 1535 ; for, according to an inscription dated February 7, 1535, Rāmappaya †

* *EC.* viii Sb. 39

† Rāmappaya has been wrongly identified by the epigraphist with the famous Rāmābhaṭlayya, one of the Brāhmaṇa officers of Acyutarāya. It must be noted that he is always mentioned in the inscriptions as Rāmābhaṭlayya

(Rāmarāja) was 'bearing the burden of the kingdom with the king;' *i. e.*, 'partner of the king in the administration of the country.' * Rāmappaya was not "evidently the chief minister of Achyuta," as the epigraphist believes, † but was really his co-regent. This state of friendliness, however, was not destined to last long; for Rāmarāja seems to have set up the standard of rebellion even during the course of that year.

and never as Rāmappaya, whereas Rāmarāja is frequently referred to in the inscriptions as well as literature as Rāmappaya (cf. 121. of 1894; 464 of 1914; 65 of 1915; 14 of 1904; 595 of 1925; 352 of 1926.) Instances can easily be multiplied. Literature also confirms the evidence of inscriptions.

మహిం నెవ్వా రెన సల్కు-రాజు చినతిమ్మక్ష్మాప కంఠారుణాం
బుహావిశ్చర్వణ తర్పితాసి శిఖికిం బుష్పాయుధస్నిగ్ధవి
గ్రహ సౌభాగ్య పరంపరా పరిధికిం గర్ణాటకైశ్వర్యని
ర్వహణావార్య భుజద్వయాయుధ పరీవారుండు రామప్పకుక్ష—

Spm: I: 34

Rāmarāja is also very constantly referred to as Rāmappaya in the Local Records. Moreover, in 1535 Rāmābhaṭlayya was the governor of Udayagiri *Rājya*; and there is no evidence to show that he had anything to do with Salem district from which the present inscription comes.

Mr. S. Subrahmanya Sastri identifies him with Bayakāra Rāmappaya the musician in the court of Acyuta. (*TDER*. p. 234.) It is true that he was appointed the governor of Koṇḍavīḍu by Acyuta in recognition of his talents as a great musician. It is, however, extremely unlikely that he could be "the partner of Acyuta in the administration of the country."

* *MER*. 245 of 1953. † *ibid* 1914 p 100.

Chapter II.

THE EARLY WARS.

Section 1:—Acyuta had to face, probably even before his coronation at Vijayanagara, the invasion of some of his northern neighbours, who had been smarting under the blows which Kṛṣṇarāya had inflicted upon them during the past twenty years. The Gajapati king of Orissa who had to be satisfied with only half of his patrimony; the Sultān of Golkonda who had to retire discomfited to the north of the Kṛṣṇa, leaving the much coveted fortress of Koṇḍavīḍu in the possession of the enemy; and the Sultān of Bijāpūr, who had to relinquish his hold upon the much contested Rāicūr doab, heaved a deep sigh of relief, when they heard of the death of their all powerful enemy. They were stimulated by a common desire to recover what they had lost, before Acyuta firmly established himself on the throne of his kingdom. Therefore, they seem to have made a more or less simultaneous attack upon the northern frontiers of the Vijayanagara empire. This attack is alluded to in one of Acyuta's earliest inscriptions dated Ś 1451 (A. D. 1529.) According to this record, he was already 'the conqueror of Oḍḍiya forces' and 'terror to the mind of the Tulukkars.' * It appears from this that as early as A. D. 1529-30, Acyuta came into conflict with the king of Orissa, and one or more of the Muhammadan rulers of the Deccan.

(*a*) The king of Orissa:—That Acyuta overcame the king of Orissa at the commencement of his reign is proved by the evidence of contemporary

* *MER.* 1911 p. 82 ; 256 of 1910.

Telugu literature. The poet Allasāni Peddana who survived his friend and patron, Kṛṣṇarāya, refers to the Orissan invasion in one of his occasional verses; * and Rādhamādhava, the author of *Tārakabrahmarājīya*, † states that Acyuta "had shown mercy (after defeating him) to the king of Utkala." The Orissan invasion should have taken place in 1529-30, as is shown by the Urattūr inscription referred to above. Further, it is also shown by the last two lines of Peddana's verse. The king of Orissa is said to have entered Kannaḍa like a dog that would stealthily enter a house whose doors are left open. The kingdom of Kannaḍa was like a house with closed doors so long as it was protected by the powerful arm of an emperor. However, at the time of the invasion of the Gajapati, there was no king sitting upon the throne of Vijayanagara. Therefore, he was able to encroach upon Vijayanagara territory without serious opposition. Although the Gajapati, Pratāparudra made a final attempt to recover his lost dominion to the south of the Kṛṣṇa, he was defeated and driven away. The rule of the Gajapatis was not destined to be revived again in the southern Telugu country.

(*b*) The Sultān of Golkonda :—The anonymous historian of Golkonda records an expedition of Qūli

* Where were you, Gajapati, at the time when Kṛṣṇarāya's elephants attacked the fort of Āraṭla? Where were you at the time when the Narapati emperor set up the pillar commemorating his victory (over you) at Simhādri? Where were you at the time when he set his elephants to break (open) the bronze doors of your fort (Cuttack)? Where were you on the day on which you gave your daughter in marriage to the Rāya together with the *gaṇḍapeṇḍera*? Did you take leave of your senses? Were you dead? Were you not on this earth? Daring not to approach (him) and losing your head, did you efface yourself? Now that he is dead, how dare you enter Kannaḍa like a dog that (stealthily) enters a house whose doors are by chance kept ajar?

The Sources: p. 154.

† *Tbm.* Canto 1.

Qutb Shāh against the fortress of Koṇḍavīḍu in or about 1530 A. D.

> "From Nulgonda, the king marched to Condbeer to demand tribute which the Raja had hitherto neglected to pay. Condbeer was, as before, vigorously besieged, and was bravely defended for a considerable time ; till at length the Raja bribed some of the Muhammadan officers to recommend to the king to accept the terms ; but he declared that he would not quit the place, till it was taken. It fell in a few days after. The garrison having surrendered at discretion, the king built a tower in the middle of the fort, in commemoration of its reduction, and then returned to his capital." *

There was no subordinate chief of Golkonda ruling at Koṇḍavīḍu in or about 1530 A. D. Ever since its conquest from the Gajapati in 1514 A. D. by Kṛṣṇadēvarāya, it was included within the empire of Vijayanagara. Nādiṇḍla Gōpa, a nephew of the great minister, Sāḷuva Timma, was appointed as its governor. The latest inscription of Gōpa dated Ś. 1447 (A. D. 1525-6) is found in the Paṭṭābhirāma temple at Koṇḍavīdu. † He was succeeded very probably by Rāyasam Timmarusayya who seems to have held the province until 1529-30 A. D. ‡ An inscription of Vēmalūrupāḍu dated A. D. 1530, ' records that Peda Tirumalayadēva Mahārājulu Gāru of the Salaka family built a tank, and planted a garden both of which he presented to the temple of Gōpinātha at Vēlupāḷem in Koṇḍavīḍu. § It is not unreasonable to suppose that Peda Tirumalaya made the gift to Gōpinātha, in his capacity as the governor of the province. Acyuta seems to have placed one of his brothers-in-law in charge of his north-eastern frontier. He was succeeded by Rāyasam

* Brigg's *Ferishta* iii p. 374-75.

† Gurubrahma Sarma : *KS*. pp. 93-94.

‡ *NDI.* i. D. 53.

§ *MER*. 544 of 1909. Vēlupāḷem appears to be a wrong reading for Velipāḷem.

Ayyaparusa in A. D. 1531 who in all probability ruled until 1533 A. D. * Bācarasa, Bāca, or Rāmaya Bhāskara was the next governor, and he governed the province till 1539 A. D., † when he was succeeded by his nephew Rāmaya Mantri, ‡ the Bayakāra Rāmppayya of the inscriptions; and he held the office until at least A. D. 1544. §

Inscriptions thus furnish us with a fairly continuous list of governors of Koṇḍavīḍu from 1514 A. D. to 1544 A. D. It is not possible to understand how there could have been in A. D. 1530 a subordinate Rāja of Koṇḍavīḍu paying tribute to the Sultān of Golkonda. It is a habit of the Muhammadan chroniclers to describe the kings of Vijayanagara as subordinates paying tribute to the Sultāns of Gulburga. Therefore, the statement of the anonymous historian need not be taken seriously. However, there is no reason to doubt the authenticity of Qutb Shāh's invasion of Koṇḍavīḍu. He appears to have made a dash upon the fort, and after severe fighting succeeded in capturing it; but he could not hold it for long. Acyuta seems to have marched with his army to recover it. It was probably on this occasion that Bācarasa and Velugōṭi Timma distinguished themselves. The former is said to have 'conquered all the Muhammadan armies with his valour.' ¶ And the latter won the praise of Acyutarāya by effecting the destruction of the Muhammadan army while attempting to cross the frontier. || The attack of the Sultān of

* *LR.* 42 p. 259.

† *MER.* 422, 445 of 1915.

‡ *MER.* of 1915 para 51.

§ *ibid.*

¶ *MER.* 445 of 1915.

|| *VV.*:—

అచ్యుతదేవరాయలు రాయమన్నీల బోజుగితండని బోటిపాగడ నెగడె
గడిదాటి రాకుండ వడిదాకి మలక కాల్బలము నేలకాల్బలముచేసె.

cf. (*H.P.C.*) *LR.* iv. pp. 273-7.

Golkonda was thus repelled; and the safety of the north-eastern frontier was secured once again.

(*c*) The Sultān of Bijāpūr:—While Acyuta was busy in defending his dominions along the east coast, his northern frontier was exposed to the attacks of the Bijāpūr army. Ismail Ādil Shāh, who vainly attempted, on more than one occasion, to recapture the forts of Rāicūr and Mudkal during the reign of Kṛṣṇadēvarāya, took advantage of the death of that monarch to invade the doab. He was accompanied by Amīr Barīd whom he had recently vanquished. Ferishta describes this invasion briefly:

"The King (Ismail Adil Shah) marched his army to the south, attended by Alla-ood-din Imad Shah, and Ameer Bareed with their forces. The affairs of the kingdom of Beejanuggur had been lately thrown into confusion owing to the death of Hemraj to whom his son Ramraj had succeeded. Against this prince rebellions were excited by several rays, so that the Muhammadans met with no interruption to their progress.

పూర్వం మా మూలపురుషులు . . . పెదతిమ్మనాయణి వారు . . తిరుపతి ఘాటులో సానాగుండ్లు దగ్గర వుండిన బోయపట్నం ఖిలపడి పోయివుండెను. గనుక్క అదిచూచి యిందుకు వుత్తరంగావుండే కొండ, యీకొండకు చతుర్దిక్కులయందు వుండేషువంటి అరణ్యమును నాల్గుదినములు అక్కడ శేవిణీచేసి యావత్తు అరణ్యము సంచారము చేసి లెస్సా నిదానించి చూచి, మహారాజశ్రీ అచ్యుత రాయలు వారి సముఖానకు చంద్రగిరికి పోయి యా వర్తమానం మనివి చేసినంతట వారు శలవు యిచ్చినట్టయితే అరణ్యం యావత్తు కొట్టించి గ్రామం త్రాలేపరిచి చెరువు కుంటలు వగైరాలుతో కూడా మామూలు చేయవచ్చును, అనిన్ని మనస్సుకు తోచి అదే ప్రకారం చంద్రగిరికి రాయలువారి సముఖానకు పోయెను.

* * * *

అటుతర్వాత ఆరునెలలు అయినపిమ్మట మహారాజశ్రీ రాయలువారు గోలకొండకు తర్లేనిమిత్తం వొచ్చి ఆభూమిని మామూలు చేయవలసినందుకు అక్కడ రెండు దినములువుండి మాకు దానపత్రం వ్రాసియిచ్చి యా భూమి అనుభవించుకొని వుండుమని శలవుయిచ్చి గోలకొండకు తర్లిరి.

Rachore and Mudgul both surrendered after a siege of three months, after having remained in the possession of the infidels for seventeen years" *

The account of Ferishta may be taken as true, after making one or two corrections. Hemraj whose death † about 1530 A. D. threw the kingdom of Vijayanagara into confusion was Kṛṣṇarāya himself. Rāmarāja who is said to have succeeded him was not his son but son-in-law. With these modifications, the passage of Ferishta describes accurately, the state of affairs obtaining at Vijayanagara.

The advance of the Ādil Shāhi army was not, however, unopposed. Appalarāja, the valiant son of the famous general Āravīṭi Rāmarāja-Timma, attempted to bar the path of the Muhammadan army probably on the banks of the Kṛṣṇa. According to the *Bāla-bhāgavata* of Konērunātha (A. D. 1549), ‡ Appala 'opposed the combined forces of Sava (Ādil Shāh) and Barīd at Kūrakacerla, and, defeating them, entered the *swarga* by piercing through the orb of the sun.' § This indicates that, in spite of the supposed defeat of Sava and Barīd, the Vijayanagara army was vanquished, and the general killed. The Muhammadans next

* Brigg's *Ferishta* iii. p. 66.

† The name of Rāmarāja's father is Srirangarāja. He was an ordinary *amaranāyaka* who is rarely, if at all, mentioned in the inscriptions of the time. There is absolutely no evidence to show that he ever rose to political prominence, not to speak of his having become a minister of state.

‡ *The Bhārati* vi. pp. 845-867.

§ The date of the battle of Kūrakacerla cannot be fixed at present. One point seems to connect the battle definitely with the siege of Rāicūr by Ismail Ādil Shāh in A. D. 1530. The Vijayanagara general is said to have perished while opposing the advance of the combined forces of Sava and Barīd. Such a combination of the troops of these two Muhammadan chiefs occurred only once before 1549 A.D., and that was, according to Ferishta, in 1530 A.D., when Amīr Barīd was forced to assist his triumphant enemy, Ādil Shāh in recapturing the fort of Rāicūr.

laid siege to the important forts in the doab which they reduced at leisure.

Acyuta would have marched to the rescue of his frontier garrisons, had his attention not been diverted by the outbreak of a serious rebellion in the south. As a consequence of it, he lost what his brother had acquired with considerable trouble some seventeen years ago.

Section 3:—It was, as already noticed, the outbreak of a rebellion in the south which prevented Acyuta from sending reinforcements to his frontier garrisons in the Rāicūr doab. Sāḷuva Nāyaka, or to state his name fully, Sāḷuva Narasingharāya Daṇṇāyakar, alias Cellappa broke his allegiance to the emperor, and set up the standard of rebellion in the Tamil country. The king of Tiruvadi, Tumbicci Nāyaka of Paramakuḍi were in league with him. The chiefs of Ummattūr, Nuggihaḷḷi etc., seems to have been also in open rebellion against the emperor. The rebellion threatened to assume serious proportions, if it was not put down promptly. Acyuta was, therefore, obliged to hasten to the south, leaving the frontier garrisons in the Rāicūr doab to defend themselves as well as they could.

It is suggested that 'Vīra-Narasimha, the viceroy of the Cōḷa country rebelled in the very last years of Kṛṣṇa,' because the latter exercised very close control over the provincial governments. * Vīra-Narasimha mentioned above is the same as Sellappar *alias* Vīra Narasingha Nāyaka-Sāḷuva Daṇṇāyaka of the inscriptions, Cellappa of the *Acyutarāyābhyudayam*, and Salvany or Salvanayaque of Nuniz. He was the son of Taḷuva-kuḷaindan Bhaṭṭar, a Brāhmaṇ

* S. K. Iyengar : *NM.* Intro. pp. 9-10, *The Sources* Intro. pp. 13-14.

of Coñjeevaram. * He seems to have entered the imperial service even before the accession of Kṛṣṇadēvarāya, and was governing the country around Tirupattūr in the Madura district about A. D. 1510. † He was holding sway over the Cōḷa country from A. D. 1515 to 1531.

It is not true that Vīra Narasingha Nāyaka 'rebelled in the very last years of Kṛṣṇa.' A series of inscriptions ranging from A. D. 1510 to 1530 shows that he was a loyal servant of Kṛṣṇadēvarāya. ‡

* *MER.* 487 of 1920 ; 25 of 1916. † *ibid* 91 of 1908.

‡ The following inscriptions are all dated in the reigns of Kṛṣṇadēvarāya and Acyutadēvarāya.

No.	Ref.	Date	Place.	Particulars.
1	*MER.*:— 91/1908	1510	Tirupattūr (Madura).	Gift of land by Singamma Nāyaka for the merit of Vīra Narasimha Nāyaka *alias* the lord and prosperous Sellappa.
2	92/1908	1510	Nārṇamangalam and Karaiyūr (Pāṇḍiamaṇḍalam).	For the merit of Vīra Narasimha Nāyakar *alias* Sellappar. These two villages were clubbed together under the name of Sellappāpuram.
3	361/1908	1515	Māngāḍu (Tanjore).	A gift made to a temple for the merit of Vīra Narasinga Nāyakar called Sellappar.
4	390/1912	1515	Dēvikāpuram ...	Refers to Vīra Narasingarāya.
5	319/1914	1517	Tiruvaranguḷam.	Gift of certain taxes by Kamalālayappaḍi Monnuyappan for the merit of Vīra Narasingarāya Nāyakar.
6	225/1916	1521	Senganmal (Chingleput).	A gift made by Sellappar Vīra Narasinga Nāyakar, son of Taḻuva-kuḻaindan Bhaṭṭar.
7	399/1906	1522	Tirumaiyam (Tanjore)	A gift of Vīra Narasingarāya Nāyakar.
8	233/1901	1528-9	Accarapākkam...	A gift by Vīra Narasingarāya Nāyakar for the merit of the king and on the occasion of lunar eclipse.

Even during the very last year of that emperor he made a grant for the increase of his religious merit. He seems to have been holding the office of the prime minister at the time of Kṛṣṇadēva's death. A grant from Accarapākkam states that in A. D. 1528-29, he was the *Ubhaya-pradhāni* * of the emperor. This is confirmed by the chronicle of Nuniz who declares:

> "Salvany became the minister of the kingdom, and governed till the coming of Achetarao from the fortress of Chamdagery where he was detained." *

He was, as already noticed, the governor of extensive territories containing several rich sea-port towns, the income of which amounted to more than a million gold *pardaos*, and he maintained a powerful military force. It is said in an Urattūr record of A. D. 1529 that Acyuta made 'the gift of the village of Panaittāngal to the temple of Tiruvāgittīsuram Uḍaiya Tambirānār for the merit of Sellappa *alias* Vīra Narasingha Nāyaka Sāḷuva Daṇṇāyakar. † He occupies here, as the epigraphist remarks, 'the position of a superior for whose merit a gift was made by Acyuta-rāya himself.' ‡

No.	Ref.	Date.	Place.	Particulars.
9	*MER.* :— 256/1910	1529	Urattūr ...	Acyutarāya made a grant for the merit of Sellappar *alias* Vīra Narasingarāya Nāyaka-Sāḷuva Daṇṇāyakar.
10	487/1920	Feb. 1531	Singaperumāḷ Koil.	A gift of Tāḷuva-kuḷaindan Bhaṭṭar of Conjeevaram for the merit of Sellappa Sāḷuva Daṇṇāyakar for conducting the festivals of the god Tirumūlasthānam Uḍaiya Nāyanār of Puḷal.

* *MER.* 233 of 1901. † *MER.* 256 of 1910. ‡ *ibid* 1911 p. 83.

The evidence of the inscriptions and Nuniz establishes beyond the shadow of a doubt that 'Vīra Narasimha, the governor of the Cōḷa country' did not rebel against Kṛṣṇadēvarāya. On the contrary, he remained loyal to the great emperor until the latter's death in A. D. 1529-30. He was a friend and firm supporter of Acyuta when the latter ascended the throne, and probably continued to be so until at least A. D. 1530. That he rebelled against Acyuta after this date is proved by the contents of the *Acyutarāyābhyudayam*. Probably, being discontented with the king, he took advantage of the Gajapati and the Qutb Shāhi invasions, and entering into an alliance with the southern governors and chiefs, attempted to overthrow the authority of the emperor.

The causes that led to the outbreak of this rebellion are very obscure. The subject had not been properly discussed so far. It is believed by some that Vīra Narasingha showed a tendency by his acts to set up an independent kingdom, 'if the head-quarters showed weakness.'* No attempt has been made to show what these acts were. Others seem to infer that the rebellion was caused by the interference of the central government in the management of temple properties. Acyutarāya made the gift of a number of villages 'on the occasion of his coronation' to the temples of Śiva and Viṣṇu at Conjeevaram. He 'directed Sāḷuva Nāyaka to assign the villages to the temples of Varadarāja and Ēkāmranātha equally neither more nor less. But, as Sāḷuva Nāyaka gave more to Ēkāmranātha, Acyutarāya hearing this equalised the number of villages by redistribution.' †

* S. K. Iyengar: *MN.* Intro. p. 9; *The Sources*; Intro. pp. 13-14.

† *MER.* 544 of 1919.

Moreover, Vīra Narasingha Nāyaka was charged with 'exacting *jōḍi* from the village of Tiruppanangāḍu, though this tax had been excused in favour of the temple there, under the orders of Sāḷuva Timmayya in the days of Kṛṣṇarāya.' * It appears from this that Vīra Narasingha rebelled against his master, Acyuta, because the latter attempted to interfere with the management of temple properties within his province. This, however, does not seem to be an adequate cause for the outbreak of a serious rebellion. The real cause of the rebellion is to be sought in the changes that came over the central government after Acyuta's coronation at Vijayanagara.

'Salvanayaque,' according to Nuniz, was the prime minister of the kingdom at the commencement of the reign of Acyuta (1529). † A little later (1530-31) he was the leader of an important rebellion. Within the short interval of one year, he lost his office, and assumed the leadership of the rebels. These two events seem to be connected somehow. Speaking of the causes which contributed to the success of Ismail Ādil Shāh at Rāicūr in A.D. 1530, Ferishta declares: "Against this prince (Ramraj who succeeded Hemraj), rebellions were excited by several rays, so that the Muhammadans met with no interruption to their progress." ‡ The rebellions which, according to Ferishta, were excited by several rays against Rāmarāja are the same as those headed by Sāḷuva Nāyaka, Tumbicci Nāyaka, the Tiruvaḍi, and the chiefs of Ummattūr, Nuggihaḷḷi &c. It is not difficult to discover the reason for Sāḷuva Nāyaka's rebellion against Rāmarāja. In accordance with the

* *ASI.* 1908-9 p. 188.

† *FE.* p. 384.

‡ Brigg's *Ferishta* iii. p. 66.

terms of his agreement with Rāmarāja, Acyuta made him his partner in the administration of the country. As Rāmarāja had resumed as of old the direction of the affairs of the state, 'Salvanayaque' lost most of his power, and probably also his ministership. The deprivation of his office by Acyuta seems to have enraged him to such an extent that he retired to his province, and being unable to bear the humiliation, he entered into a conspiracy with Tumbicci Nāyaka of Paramakuḍi and the Tiruvaḍi, and set up the standard of rebellion. It is not improbable that the chiefs of Ummattūr and Nuggihaḷḷi should have joined the rebels.

Why did the Tiruvaḍi join the rebels, the enemies of the emperor of Vijayanagara? It is generally believed that he was the ruler of the independent kingdom of Travancore. In that case his action becomes very inexplicable. Why did he invite trouble upon his head by encouraging the rebellious subjects of his powerful neighbour? He must have had a motive in doing so. What was the motive?

The Tiruvaḍi of the *Acyutarāyābhyudayam* and the inscriptions should not be identified with the king of Travancore, but with his neighbour, the king of Quilon. There was a long standing feud between the kings of Quilon and the emperors of Vijayanagara. It began in the reign of Dēvarāya II who seems to have conquered Quilon and the neighbouring places Abdur Razak, a contemporary of Dēvarāya, refers to his southern conquests in general terms. * The truth of Razak's statements is proved by the evidence of epigraphy. It is, however, Nuniz that furnishes us with the names of places whose kings paid tribute to

* *ED.* iv p. 116.

Dēvarāya II. "The king of Coullao (Quilon), Ceyllao (Ceylon), and Paleacate, Pegū, and Tanacary, and many other countries paid tribute to him." * But soon after his death, the king of Quilon recovered his independence. For nearly forty years, the weakness of the royal family prevented the Vijayanagara emperors from making any efforts to reconquer the place. With the Sāḷuva usurpation, however, the vigour of the imperial government made itself felt upon the neighbouring states. About 1500 A. D. Narasa Nāyaka seems to have made an attempt to capture the important port of Kāyal; but he was defeated and driven back. "The king of Coulao (Quilon) was a very honest man, and very gallant, and in the war which he carried on with the king of Narasinga, who had many soldiers, both horse and foot, he attacked him with sixty thousand archers and overcame him." † Kṛṣṇadēvarāya renewed the attack after 1518 A.D. By that time, however, the Pāṇḍyas of Kāyattār (Catuir of Nuniz) seem to have wrested the port of Kāyal from the king of Quilon. When Kṛṣṇarāya invaded the territory of Kāyattār, the chief of the place took refuge in the fort of Kāyal trusting to the impassability of the arms of the Tāmraparṇī which were swollen with the winter floods. However, Kṛṣṇarāya persisted in his attack upon the place, and it soon capitulated. Kāyattār was annexed to the empire. It was on this occasion that Quilon was also subjugated. ‡

* *FE.* p. 302.

† Albuquerque's *Commentaries* I. p. 11. An epigraph from Śivapūr in the Tirupattūr tāluka of the Madura district (*MER.* 36 of 1928-29) dated 1500 A.D., states that Nāgama Nāyaka held the Pirāṉmalai sīrmai. This may be taken as an indication of the presence of the Vijayanagara army in this region.

‡ *FE.* pp. 320-21. See the appendix, 'Catuir of Nuniz,' at the end of the book.

THE EARLY WARS

The death of Kṛṣṇadēvarāya, and the consequent confusion that prevailed in the capital owing to the quarrels of Acyuta and Rāmarāja regarding succession should have generated fresh hopes in the mind of the king of Quilon of re-establishing his independence. The rebellion of Sāḷuva Narasingha Nāyaka gave him an excellent opportunity of realising his hopes. Therefore, he threw in his lot with the rebel chief without any hesitation.

The Progress of the Rebellion :—Very little is known about the early stages of this rebellion. The *Acyutarāyābhyudayam*, our only authority on the subject, does not offer any details, but states in a summary fashion that " Cellappa (Sāḷuva Narasingha Nāyaka)—had revolted, and after being defeated in battle, escaped from his province, and had taken refuge with the Cēra king in his territory." * Inscriptions do not add anything more to our knowledge. Although the sources are almost silent regarding the events connected with the early phase of the rebellion, there can be no doubt that the imperial army had encountered Cellappa in the Cōḷa country, and inflicted such a crushing defeat upon him that he was obliged to run away from his province, and seek shelter under his ally, the king Tiruvaḍi of Quilon.

It is very difficult in the present state of our knowledge to determine the circumstances under which he was defeated and driven away from his province. The initial success of the imperial army, however, did not put an end to the rebellion; for the rebel Vīra Narasingha instigated the Tiruvaḍi to wage 'war upon the Pāṇḍyan ruler.' † The Pāṇḍya ruler referred here does not appear to be the king of Madura, but a

* *The Sources* p. 162.

† *ibid.*

member of the Tenkāśi branch of the Pāṇḍya family.* He was defeated in battle and driven out of 'his ancestral territories', by Vīra Narasingha and the Tiruvaḍi.

The minister † who obtained information about the activities of the rebels through his spies, placed it before the emperor, and urged him "to protect the Pāṇḍya who was in exile", and "place him once more firmly upon his throne." He also pointed out that the Cēra king and Cellappa (Vīra Narasingha) should be properly punished for their rebellion. Acyuta, whose wrath was roused on hearing the news of the rebellion, sent for the commander of his troops, and ordered him to make preparations for marching against the rebels. ‡

The route followed by the imperial army is described in the *Acyutarāyābhyudayam*. After a few days march, the army reached the fort of Candragiri where

* Madura was the capital of the viceroy of the southernmost province of the Vijayanagara empire. The rebels are nowhere said to have come into clash with that officer. When Salakarāju Tirumala marched with his army to punish the rebels, he met with no opposition until he reached the Tāmraparṇī on the banks of which he pitched his tents. The general is said to have "marched to the south, past the city of Madura, and encamped on the banks of the Tāmraparṇī." The river Tāmraparṇī appears to have been the northern boundary of the zone of the rebel activities. Therefore, the territory of the Pāṇḍya ruler who was driven out by Cellappa and the Cēra king should have extended as far as the southern bank of the river. The Tinnevelly district was at this time governed by the Pāṇḍyas of Tenkāśi and Kāyattār. This dispossessed Pāṇḍya ruler should belong to one of these families, probably to the former.

† The name of the minister is not stated. He is simply mentioned by his official designation, *saciva*. He who had the spies under his command, and who could be inquiring into the conduct of the *amaranāyakas*, could not be an ordinary minister. The minister in question should have been the prime minister. Who could have been the prime minister at that time? It could not have been Salakarāju Tirumala; for he seems to have been the *sēnāpati* or commander-in-chief whom Acyuta commanded to march against the enemy. Therefore, the *saciva*, referred to here should be Rāmarāja himself who was interested in bringing the rebellion to a speedy conclusion.

‡ *The Sources* p. 162.

the emperor halted for a short time, * On this occasion. he visited Tirupati, and presented to the god Venkaṭēśa *kuṇḍalas, padaka,* and a jewelled crown. † Having stayed there for a few days, he next went to Kāḷahasti where he worshipped the god, and offered him gifts. ‡ Acyuta probably went back to Candragiri to rejoin the army which was camping there. Then he proceeded to Kāñcī, where he received 'the tributes and presents' of several forest chiefs. § There Acyuta weighed himself against pearls which he distributed among the poor. Then, he went to Tiruvaṇṇāmalai and offered worship to the god of the place.¶ Thence, he journeyed on to Śrīrangam where he is said to have resided until the end of the campaign.

Acyuta did not proceed personally against Sāḷuva Narasingha and his confederates. He despatched his brother-in-law, Salakarāju Tirumala against the enemy. Tirumala seems to have met with no opposition until he reached the Tāmraparṇī. It is said that he 'marched to the south past the city of Madura, and encamped on the banks of the Tāmraparṇī.'

He commanded one of his subordinate officers to march against the kingdom of the Tiruvaḍi, the firm supporter of the rebel, Sāḷuva Narasingha. The Tiruvaḍi however, did not await the arrival of the enemy's troops in his territory. He placed himself at the head of his army, and marching towards his northern frontier, attempted to bar the path of the enemy, 'near the mountains,' perhaps at the Aruvāmoḷi Pass. Here a battle was fought, in which the Tiruvaḍi

* *The Sources* p. 126. † *ibid.* p. 159.

‡ *ibid.* § *ibid.* ¶ *ibid.*

was completely beaten. He was, therefore, obliged to submit to the victorious Vijayanagara general. The Tiruvaḍi with the remnant of his troops and with the Cōḷa king * (Sāḷuva Narasingha), approached the general, and prostrating before him acknowledged his own defeat. Then he surrendered the fugitive 'Cōḷa king' (Cellappa) and presented also several elephants and horses.

By this time, Salakarāju Tirumala seems to have arrived at the scene of the battle; for, it is said that he accepted these gifts on behalf of his sovereign. Having overcome the rebels, he next reinstated the Pāṇḍyan chief on the throne of his ancestors, and then proceeded to Anantaśayanam to offer worship to the god Padmanābha. Thence he went to Rāmēś-varam, and bathed in the sea near the *Śētu*. Finally, he returned to the imperial camp at Srīrangam, where the emperor was spending 'all his time in the company of poets and scholars.'

When Salakarāju Tirumala reached Śrīrangam, he produced before the emperor, 'the Cēra King and other prisoners, and submitted to him a report of his expedition.' Acyuta commanded his minister to punish the Tiruvaḍi properly for having encroached upon

* It is suggested that the Cōḷa king referred to here was 'probably the ruler of the province of Vijayanagara empire corresponding to the Cōḷa kingdom.' But he should also have been in rebellion against the emperor, for which there is no evidence. The only person that answers this description is Cellappa (Sāḷuva Narasingha Nāyaka) himself. He was 'the ruler of the province of Vijayanagara empire corresponding to the Cōḷa kingdom' until 1530-31, when he rebelled and joined the Tiruvaḍi. Moreover, Acyuta invaded the kingdom of the Tiruvaḍi, because he offended him by giving shelter to the rebel, Cellappa. The expedition would have ended fruitlessly, if Cellappa's capture had not been effected. Lastly, Acyuta declares in his inscriptions of A. D. 1532 that "he went on a war with the Tiruvaḍi and levied tribute from him, brought under subjection Tumbicci Nāyaka, Sāḷuva Nāyaka." For these reasons, I think, the Cōḷa king should be identified with Cellappa (Sāḷuva Narasingha Nāyaka).

the boundaries of his neighbour's estate; and he ordered 'the Pāṇḍya to rule over his ancestral state.' * It was probably on this occasion that Acyuta married a daughter of the Pāṇḍyan king. † How he punished Sāḷuva (Narasinga) Nāyaka and Tumbicci Nāyaka is not known. The Kāḷahasti ‡ and the Tirupati § inscriptions make it clear that both these chiefs were subjugated. They were probably pardoned. Tumbicci Nāyaka seems to have been a subordinate of Acyuta about 1537 A. D. ¶ There is reason to believe that Sāḷuva Nāyaka was holding some office under the crown during the early years of Sadāśiva. ||

Section 4 :— From Śrīrangam, Acyuta marched 'with his army along the banks of the Kāvēri to Śrīrangapaṭṭaṇam.' Why he had taken this route is not explained anywhere. However, it is obvious that he marched along this route to suppress the rebellion of the Ummattūr chief and his allies. The causes which led to the outbreak of this rebellion are different from those of the other. The chief of Ummattūr seems to have acted in accordance with the traditional policy of his family, in setting up the standard of rebellion.

* *The Sources* p. 160. † *TDER.* p. 221.

‡ *MER.* 157 of 1924. § *TDER.* p. 221. ¶ *MER.* 398 of 1907.

|| According to an inscription of Kondagai in the Ramnad district (2/1923) dated A. D. 1545, a Sāḷuva Nāyaka presided over a court of justice. The *Kēladi Nṛpa Vijaya* refers also to a Sāḷuva Nāyaka, whom the Kēladi chief, Sadāśiva Nāyaka captured at Gutti, acting upon the orders of Rāmarāja.

ಬಗಯುದೆ ರಾಯರಟ್ಟಿದ ನಿರೂಪವ ನದ್ಭುತ ಸೈನ್ಯಗೂಡಿ ಸಂ
ಯುಗದೊಳಿದಿರ್ಬಿ ನಿಂದೆಸೆವ ಗುತ್ತಿಯ ಸಾಳುವನಾಯಕೇಂದ್ರನಂ
ಜಗುಳಿಸಿ ಯುದ್ಧದೋಳ್ಪಿಡುದು ರಾಯರಗೊಪ್ಪಿಸಿ ಮನ್ನೆಯರ್ಕಳೊ
ಳ್ಮಿಗಿಲಿನೆ ಸಾಸಮಂ ಮೆರದ ನ್ನೈದೆ ಸದಾಶಿವರಾಯ ನಾಯಕಂ ॥

Very likely, Sāḷuva Nāyaka, mentioned in these two records, is the same as the hero of the rebellion of 1531 A. D. In that case he should have been pardoned by Acyuta.

V—5

The principality of Ummattūr was included within the dominions of the Rāyas of Vijayanagara, from the early days of the empire, although much is not known about the activities of its chiefs during the time of the First Dynasty. But, with the advent of the Sāḷuvas, the chiefs of Ummattūr assumed an attitude of hostility towards the imperial throne, and gave trouble almost continuously to the Sāḷuva and the Tuḷuva emperors. They usually pretended that they were the descendants of the Ganga kings of Talakāḍ, (hence their title, Gangarāja) and laid claims to sovereignty over the districts of Ummattūr, Penugoṇḍa and Śrīrangapaṭṭaṇam. The pretensions of these chiefs are also alluded to by Fr. Luis who was at Vijayanagara in 1510 A.D. "One of his (Kṛṣṇadēvarāya's) vassals had risen up in rebellion and seized the city of Perguṇḍa (Penugoṇḍa) declaring to himself belonged the kingdom itself by right." * Some writers believe that their authority extended as far east as the North Arcot and Chingleput districts; but the available evidence does not lend colour to this belief. The activity of the Ummattūr chiefs was mostly confined to the Canarese country, and on occasions it extended to parts of Anantapūr district. They wanted to make capital out of the title *Penugoṇḍa-Cakrēśvara* which they usually assumed.

The usurpation of Sāḷuva Narasimha was not effected without much trouble. He had to reduce by force of arms several important strongholds both in the Telugu and the Canarese districts. † In effecting the reconquest, so to speak, of several provinces of the empire, he was ably assisted by his generals, Īśvara and Narasa. Little or no information is available

* Albuquerque : *Commentaries* ii. p. 35. † *The Sources* p. 89.

regarding Sāḷuva Narasimha's relations with the chiefs of Ummattūr; but trouble arose during the reign of Narasimha II, owing probably to the feelings of jealousy caused by the position of Narasa Nāyaka at the court as regent, and *de facto* ruler of the empire. Dēpaṇṇa Voḍeyar, the ruler of Ummattūr *, and the Hēuṇa chieftain † who was the governor of Śrīranga-paṭṭaṇam appear to have revolted together, and defied the authority of the government. Narasa had to march against them at the head of his army. He effected the conquest of Ummattūr without much difficulty; ‡ but the fort of Śrīrangapaṭṭaṇam, which stood on an island between the two arms of the Kāvēri, could not be so easily taken. The river was swollen with floods and the Hēuṇa chief had taken refuge under the strong walls of the fort. Narasa, however, rose equal to the occasion. Having constructed a bridge across one of the arms of the Kāvēri, he enabled his troops to reach the walls of the fort, which they stormed soon after. The Hēuṇa chief with all his family and treasures fell into Narasa's hands; but he generously forgave him and allowed him to retain his principality. §

Vīra Narasimha who succeeded Narasa as the regent of the kingdom had to meet with considerable opposition from several nobles and governors. "As soon as his father was dead," says Nuniz, "the whole land revolted under its captains; who in a short time were destroyed by that king and their lands taken and reduced under his rule." ¶ In reducing the rebellious captains, Vīra Narasimha was assisted by

* *I.R.* xi. pp. 614-17. † *The Sources* p. 107.

‡ *I.R.* xi pp. 614-17. § *The Sources* p. 171. ¶ *FE*. p. 314.

the famous general Āravīṭi Rāmarāja-Timma. * However, according to the chronicle *Konkaṇadēśarājula Vṛttāntamu*, Dēpaṇṇa Voḍeyar, the chief of Ummattūr took advantage of the troubles of the regent to make a fresh attempt to assert his independence. He refused to pay the annual tribute which was due to the imperial treasury. Vīra Narasimha thereupon declared war upon Dēpaṇṇa, and leaving his half-brother, Kṛṣṇarāya in charge of the capital, marched against the fortresses of Ummattūr and Talakāḍ, accompanied by Śrī Ranga, Acyuta, and other princes. Vīra Narasimha did not entirely rely upon force; he seems to have employed diplomacy to some extent. Dēpaṇṇa Voḍeyar had two sons, Gangarāja and Mallarāja. He induced the latter to desert his father by conferring upon him his family title, Cikkarāya, thereby recognising him to be the ruler of the principality. † In an inscription of December 15, 1506, Mallarāja is said to be a subordinate of Vīra Narasimha. ‡

Nevertheless, Vīra Narasimha's efforts to reduce the fort of Ummattūr were not crowned with success. Although, according to the chronicle, he besieged the fort for three months, he could not produce the least impression upon it. The besieged, who were strongly supported by the forces of the neighbouring *pāḷaigārs*, rudely repulsed the royal troops, when they made a final attempt to scale the walls of the fort. Giving up all hopes of capturing the fort, Vīra Narasimha retreated along the upper course of the Kāvēri,

* శా॥ శ్రీమద్వీర నృసింహరాయ నృపతి శ్రేయోదయాసాధిత
స్వామిద్రోహరగండనూపుర విరాజద్రామరాట్తిమ్మభూ
పామిత్యర్జిత పుణ్యసత్ఫల సమస్తాశాంతవిశ్రాంత ని
స్సీమోర్వీప్రతిపాదనప్రతియశా శీతాంశు వంశోనిధీ ॥

Bbm. Canto 1. The Bhārati vi, p. 856.

† *LR.* xi. pp. 614-17. ‡ *EC.* iii. I. Ml. 95.

and reached the city of Srīrangapaṭṭaṇam which he closely invested. It was strongly defended by a son of the Hēuṇa chief whom Narasa Nāyaka had defeated. On the approach of the royal army, he seems to have sent for and obtained the help of the chief of Ummattūr. Then he made a sally upon the besiegers, and defeated them with considerable loss. *

This is the account of the operations as given in the *Konkaṇadēśarājula Vṛttāntamu.* So far as we are able to test it with epigraphic and other evidence, it appears to be genuine. Dēpaṇṇa Voḍeyar was a contemporary of Narasa and Vīra Narasimha. † That Vīra Narasimha did not succeed in reducing Ummattūr is proved by the fact that Kṛṣṇadēvarāya was obliged to march against it almost at the very commencement of his reign. Therefore, the account of *Konkaṇadēśarājula Vṛttāntamu* may be taken as true in this connection.

The failure of Vīra Narasimha to reduce the rebellious chiefs of the Canarese country may be attributed to some extent to the diversion caused by Yūsuf Ādil Khān of Bijāpūr who appears to have invaded the Vijayanagara territory with the object of embarassing the Rāya. Placing himself at the head of 70,000 horses, he advanced upon the fort of Kandanavōlu (Karnūl), and after defeating an army that opposed him, he laid siege to it. He had a powerful ally in Kāśappa Voḍeya, the chief of Ādavani who is believed to have been a relation of the recalcitrant ruler of Ummattūr. ‡ Ādil Khān, however, was obliged to raise the siege, owing to the arrival of the reinforcements to the besieged under the command of Āravīṭi

* *LR.* xi. pp. 614-17.

† *EC.* iv. Intro. p. 27.

‡ *MER.* 1921. p. 90.

Bukkarāju Rāmarāju. * He retreated hastily along the upper valley of the Tungabhadrā hotly pursued by the victorious Hindu general, who forced him to halt in the neighbourhood of the fort of Ādavani and give battle. In the engagement that followed, Ādil Khān was defeated and driven away; and Bukkarāju Rāmarāju, then, laid siege to Ādavani which he soon captured. † Rāmarāja's son, Timma appears to have distinguished himself on this occasion, as he is said to have taken the traitor Kāśappa Voḍeya a prisoner. ‡

After Vīra Narasimha's return from the Ummattūr campaign, he busied himself with making preparations for a fresh campaign against the rebels; but before he could complete his preparations, he breathed his last. Therefore, the task of subduing the rebels devolved upon his half-brother, and successor Kṛṣṇadēvarāya.

Kṛṣṇadēvarāya spent the first year of his reign in studying the administrative problems of the empire. During this period, he introduced certain military reforms which were very much needed. By these reforms, he provided himself with 'a million of fighting

* బుక్కరాయ రామ భూభుజు డెల్ల నృపులు
నెక్కువ యిది యని యెన్నంగ జాలి
వీరులు డెబ్బదివేల యాశ్వికులు
జేరి కొల్వంగ వచ్చిన సవానెదిరి
కలనంది పంచ బంగాళంబు జేసి ॥ *Bbm.* Bhārati vi. p. 853.

† *EI.* xvi. p 244.

‡ విక్రమంబున నాచవేని దుర్గంబు
విక్రాంతులెన్న వేవేగ సాధించి
సిరులతో [illegible]నృసింహరాయలకు
బరుషా [illegible]గ్రాధిపతి నొప్పగించె॥ *Bbm.* The Bhārati vi. p. 855.

troops' including 35,000 'cavalry in armour.' * These preparations were probably completed by the end of A.D. 1510, when he marched against certain rebellious chiefs especially against the ruler of Ummattūr.

Meanwhile, Dēpaṇṇa Voḍeyar who successfully defied the authority of Vīra Narasimha, seized a rocky island in the Kēvēri called Śivansamudram, containing a ruined old fort. Recognising the strategic importance of the island, he rebuilt the fort, and provided it with several weapons of defence, including some cannon. Soon after completing the fortifications, Dēpaṇṇa died, and was succeeded by his son, Gangarāja. † It was during the reign of this prince that Kṛṣṇadēva invaded the Canarese country with the object of subduing the rebellious *pāḷaigārs.* He was accompanied by several *amaranāyakas* including Cikkarāja (Mallarāja) of Ummattūr.

The fort of Ummattūr was easily captured; and it was razed to the ground; but the strong island fort of Śivansamudram defied all his attempts for several months. ‡ At last the Rāya's soldiers entered the fort by a secret path, and Gangarāja, while attempting to escape, was drowned in a pool of the Kāvēri. § Kṛṣṇarāya, having taken possession of the fort, posted a garrison there, and advanced upon Śrīrangapaṭṭanam which he easily captured. He then subdivided into three districts the territory which he had conquered and appointed Kamba Gowḍa, Vīrappa Gowḍa, and Cikkarāja as their governors. ¶

* *FE.* p. 279; cf. *Rv.* (*ASPP.* iii p. 33.) † cf. *MAR.* 1917 p. 53.

‡ *LR.* xi. p. 614-617. § *Ibid.*

¶ Cikkarāja is mentioned as a subordinate of Vijayanagara emperors in *EC.* III. i. ML. 95. (1506 A. D.); ML. 90 (1520 A. D.); and Nj. 35 1529 (A. D). His last date is A. D. 1533. Kamba Gowḍa is the same as the famous Kempa Gowḍa I of Bangalore who is said to have fought in Kṛṣṇadēvarāya's army.

The death of Kṛṣṇadēvarāya in A. D. 1529–30 threw the empire into confusion which gave an opportunity to the *pāḷaigārs* in the Ummattūr region to revolt once again. According to the Kāḷahasti inscriptions, Acyuta 'offered protection to certain chiefs like Rāyaṇarāja of Nuggihaḷḷi, Mallarāja of Ummattūr, Venkaṭādri and others,' * It is not at present possible to identify these chiefs definitely. About this time, there lived two princes of Ummattūr bearing the name of Mallarāja. One of them was, as already noticed, a son of Dēpaṇṇa Voḍeyar, and a subordinate of Vīra Narasimha, Kṛṣṇarāya, and probably also of Acyuta. † The other was the son of Vīra Mangaparāya, and he bore the titles of 'the hunter of elephants, *gēṇānka - Cakrēśvara*, *javādi-kōlāhala*, *arasānka-sūnegāra* etc. He was a subordinate, of Acyuta, and only one record of his dated A. D. 1532 is available at present. ‡ Which of these two princes is referred to in the Kāḷahasti inscriptions, it is difficult to say. Whoever he was, it is certain that he was driven out of the Ummattūr principality by the chief or chiefs who rose up in rebellion. Rāyaṇarāja § and Venkaṭādri must have lost their

Vīrappa Gowḍa appears to be the same as Vīrapa or Vīrapp-oḍeyar, a subordinate of Kṛṣṇarāya who figures in *EC.* III My. 5 (1517) ; My. 32 (1517); Sr. 10 (1516). In the first two inscriptions, he is spoken of as the son of Cikkōḍeyar of Śrīrangapaṭṭaṇam. Cikkōḍeyar seems to be different from Cikkarāya (Mallarāja) of Ummattūr. This Vīrapp-oḍeyar is probably identical with Kumāra Vīrya of Śrīrangapaṭṭaṇam mentioned by Nuniz.

* *MER.* 1924. p. 112

† *EC.* iii. I. Nj. 35.

‡ *MAR.* 1920 p. 37.

§ Rao Bahadur Mahamahopadhyaya R. Narasimhacharya refers to this prince in Vol. II. p. 215 of his *Karṇāṭaka Kavicarite*: "It is said in Hasan 117 dated 1573 A. D. that Tirumalarāja...a son-in-law of the Vijayanagara emperor Vīrapratāpa Prauḍhadēvarāya (1419-1446) had a son called Rāyōḍeya. In another inscription (*MER.* for 1900, 28) a Rāyaṇarāja, a subordinate of the Vijayanagara monarch Acyuta is mentioned. The latter appears to be the patron of Linga Kavi who wrote his *Kabbigara Kaipidi* at his instance."

places, because they upheld the cause of the emperor. The latter was probably the same as the Mahānāyakācārya Venkaṭādri Nāyaka who was ruling 'Penugoṇḍa-Marjavadi *sīma*' as a subordinate of Acyuta in A.D. 1540. *

The rebellion of the Ummattūr chiefs was widespread, and appears to have extended over the major part of the present Mysore state. The imperial army marched from Śrīrangam along the valley of the Kāvēri in order to punish the rebels, and to reduce the country into submission. Unfortunately the details of the campaign are not available. The rebels appear to have submitted almost without fighting; for, according to the *Acyutarāyābhyudayam*, the emperor reached Śrīrangapaṭṭaṇam, where 'he was met by the governors of the place who made him large presents of money.' †

The campaign against Ummattūr must have terminated before July 27, 1532; for, in the Kāḷahasti inscriptions, Acyuta's achievements in the south are briefly described. ‡ It is obvious that his expedition against his rebellious subjects proved a brilliant success; and he had the satisfaction of bringing back to allegiance the whole of the south and the west.

Section 5:—The author of the *Acyutarāyābhyudayam* would have us believe that Acyutarāya marched from Śrīrangapaṭṭaṇam directly against the territories of the Sultān of Bijāpūr. § As a matter of fact, however, the invasion did not take place until after the middle of A. D. 1534. About the beginning of July 1532 A.D., he was at Kāñcī; he seems to

* *MER.* 332 of 1922. † *The Sources* p. 160.

‡ *MER.* 157 of 1924. § *The Sources* p. 167.

have performed the *Tulābhāra* ceremony, and made a grant of fourteen villages to the temple of Varadarāja either on 28th July or a few days earlier. * Inscriptions, slightly later in date, add that Acyutarāya, the empress Varadājiamman, and the crown prince Kumāra-Venkaṭādri had themselves weighed against pearls, and made a gift of 'thousand cows' to the Brāhmans. † It was also on this occasion that Acyuta effected the re-distribution of villages between 'the temples of Varadarāja and Ēkāmranātha neither more nor less.' These villages were granted in common to the two temples on the occasion of his coronation, and the task of distribution was originally assigned to Sāḷuva Nāyaka. The re-distribution became necessary, as he did not perform his duty impartially. ‡ Acyuta seems to have visited Kāḷahasti about the end of July 1532 A.D., § and probably he was camping at the fort of Candragiri until the end of the year; for he was at Tirupati at the beginning of 1533 A.D. "On the occasion (31st January 1533) of his visit to Tiruvēnkaṭamuḍaiyan, he was accompanied by his queen Varadājiamman, and his son Kumāra-Venkaṭādri, and he performed the *mahādānas* *kapila-paśu*, *svarṇa-varsham*, and presented to God Venkaṭēśvara a big *kapha* fully decked with pearls, rubies, emeralds, and diamonds, four *pon-valaiyam*, a pair of *uccippu* set with diamonds for the top of the crown; a long string of pearls and other jewels consisting of differently shaped gold beads and nuts." ¶ He seems to have reached Vijayanagara by the end of February of the same year; for, he was residing in the capital when he gave the copper-plate charter to Bālarāja (Ś 1455.

* *M.E.R.* 546 of 1919.

† *ibid* 511 of 1919; 178 of 1924; 543 of 1919.

‡ *ibid* 544 of 1919. § *ibid* 157 of 1924. ¶ *TDER.* p. 221.

Nandana, Puṣya Makara Sankramaṇa, Uttarāṣāḍha), sanctioning the grant of Koliñjavāḍi *agrahāra* to Brāhmans. * What has been said so far, makes it clear that Acyuta did not march against the Bijāpūr Sultānate, but occupied himself with religious activities.

The Bijāpūr invasion commenced either in the latter half of A.D. 1534 or early in 1535. It is stated in an inscription of Sevallimeḍu in the Chingleput district dated 1534-35, that Acyutarāya was on the banks of the Kṛṣṇa at the time. † As he lost the provinces of Rāicūr and Mudkal early in his reign, the Kṛṣṇa could not have been the northern boundary of his dominions. His presence on the banks of the Kṛṣṇa seems to indicate an invasion of Bijāpūr territory.

The time was very well chosen for leading an expedition against the Ādil Shāhi kingdom. After the capture of Rāicūr in 1530 A.D., Ismail Ādil Shāh remained there for one whole month celebrating a splendid festival in commemoration of his victory. At this time 'intelligence was received that Bahādūr Shāh of Gujerat was again preparing to invade the Deccan.' As a consequence, Ismail returned to his capital, where he gave permission to Amīr Barīd to go to his kingdom on the latter's promising to surrender to him the forts of 'Kulliani and Kandahar,' within six months; but, as he neglected to fulfil his promise, Ismail Ādil Shāh resolved to reduce them by force. Amīr Barīd who was aware of his intentions 'applied to Burhān Nizām Shāh for aid'. Burhān sent ambassadors to Bijāpūr to request Ismail to forego his designs against Amīr Barīd; but Ismail did not fall in with the proposal. Therefore, war broke out between the two

* *The Bhārati. IX.* ii. p. 275 f, 422 f.

† *MER*. 47 of 1900.

Sultāns in which victory favoured the Ādil Shāh. A treaty was concluded in A. D. 1532, according to the terms of which the Nizām Shāh 'should be permitted to add Bērār to his possessions without molestation'; whereas the Ādil Shāh "should be at liberty to reduce the country of the Kutb Shāh." In pursuance of this agreement, Ismail Ādil Shāh, accompanied by Amīr Barīd with whom he became reconciled, invaded Telingāṇa about the middle of A. D. 1533., and laid siege to the fort of Kōvilkoṇḍa which held out for one whole year. While the siege was in progress, there was constant fighting between the forces of Bijāpūr and Golkonda. However, before the fort could be reduced, Ismail Ādil Shāh died of fever on the 27th August 1534 A. D. His death in the enemy's country had considerably complicated the situation. Princes Mallū and Ibrahim, each of whom wanted to succeed his father, 'were on the eve of coming to open war, though in an enemy's country and actively conducting the siege of Kōvilkoṇḍa.' The siege was consequently abandoned; and 'the army moved to Kulburga.'

Asad Khān Lāry, whom the late Sultān appointed as the protector of the kingdom, on reaching Kulburga, 'consulted with the principal ladies of the harem of his late sovereign and the nobility on the choice of the king.' As most of them expressed the opinion that prince Mallū should be the king, Asad Khān placed him upon the throne, although he personally did not like the choice. He soon became disgusted with the conduct of the new king, and resigning his office at the court retired to his *jāgīr* at Belgaum. * The real cause of Asad's retirement appears to have been the check which Mallū Ādil Shāh placed upon the power of the

* Brigg's *Ferishta* iii. pp. 66-76.

protector, and the favour which he had shown to the Decanni Muhammadans. The retirement of Asad Khān from the court involved the Sultān in difficulties. A general rebellion headed by foreign noblemen appears to have been in progress in the districts along the west coast. The Portuguese who were anxious to seize the mainland opposite Goa, showed an inclination to fish in the troubled waters. * To multiply the difficulties of Mallū, Acyutarāya, who was carefully gauging the situation, invaded the Rāicūr doab at the head of a large army.

Although the Rāicūr campaign of Acyuta is described at length in the *Acyutarāyābhyudayam*, it is totally ingnored by Ferishta. As Rājanātha Ḍiṇḍima was a contemporary of Acyuta, his account may be taken as more trustworthy than the history of Ferishta. Moreover, Ḍiṇḍima's account of the campaign is corroborated by the Portuguese historian, Barros.

"'Acadachan, like one who is in a safe and lofty place watches some great fire spreading over the plains below, watched from his city of Belgaum the events that were passing'; but did nothing till the Ādil Shāh wrote desiring him to return to Bijāpūr, which he had temporarily left, owing to a disagreement, and to assist him in the government of the kingdom. Asad Khān replied craftily that he had done with the affairs of this life, and proposed to go and die at Mecca. At this, the Ādil Shāh † flew into a passion and vowed revenge against his powerful subject who, to save himself, wrote to Da Cunha, professing his unalloyed friendship for the Portuguese, and inviting them to take possession of certain tracts on the mainland; declaring that his *master, the Sultān, was powerless to defend himself against the armies of Vijayanagar*. . . . Da Cunha sent Christovão de Figueiredo . . . .

**FE*. p. 175.

† Sewell conjectured wrongly that the name of the Sultān was Ismail, but Ismail did not ascend the throne until the latter half of A.D. 1535.

to bear his reply, since the latter was on friendly terms with the lord of Belgaum. A conversation took place, in which Asad Khān said that he was afraid of his master, who was of variable and inconstant character, and that he desired of all things to preserve friendship with the Portuguese. He therefore begged to be allowed to visit Goa, and cement an alliance with the governor-general to whom he faithfully promised that the lands in question should become for ever the property of the king of Portugal. Accordingly the lands were seized by Da Cunha.

Immediately after Asad began to intrigue with the king of Vijayanagar, and being invited to visit that city on the occasion of one of the great *Mahānavami* festivals, left Belgaum with 13,000 men and 200 elephants. Before starting, he wrote to Da Cunha, asking that Figueiredo might be sent to accompany him, and promising to obtain from the Portuguese a definite cession of the lands from the Rāya, since these had formerly been the latter's possession. Accordingly Figueiredo left for Vijayanagar, but learned that the Khān had already arrived there and had joined the king. The Rāya received Asad favourably, and, as a present gave him two towns, 'Tunge and Turugel,' since he hoped for his aid against the Sultān.

When the Sultān heard of Asad Khān's defection, he gave himself up for lost; but assembled an army and advanced to within twelve leagues of the king's camp, where Asad Khān had pitched his tents at some distance from those of the Hindu lords. The Sultān thence wrote to the Rāya demanding the delivery to him of his recalcitrant 'slave,' and the Rāya sent on the letter to Asad Khān who told the king that he would never join the Muhammadans but would remain faithful to Vijayanagar. A short pause ensued during which the Rāya learned that constant messages were passing between the camp of the Sultān and Asad Khān. Both armies then marched towards Rāichūr, the Rāya to retake the place from the Sultān, the Sultān watching for an opportunity to attack the Rāya.

On the third day, Asad Khān started with his forces two hours in advance of the royal troops, crossed the river first, and hastened to join the Sultān. Ādil Shāh received him with great apparent cordiality, and at length freely forgave him on the Khān's protestations that his intrigues with Vijayanagar and the Portuguese were only so many moves in a game undertaken for the advancement of the Sultān's interests . . . . . "The Ādil Shāh secretly fearful of Asad Khān's duplicity, made a treaty of peace with the Rāya, by which the Muhammadans retained Rāicūr but gave up some other territory." *

The trend of events at Bijāpūr, so far as can be inferred from the foregoing extract, seems to be this: Asad Khān left Bijāpūr, and retired to his *jāgīr*, Belgaum, 'owing to temporary disagreement' with the Ādil Shāh. A rebellion broke out at this time along the west coast, which spread like 'some great fire.' Asad Khān watched the progress of this rebellion, without ever trying to check it. The Ādil Shāh, who was alarmed, summoned Asad Khān to Bijāpūr, 'to assist him in the government of the kingdom;' but Asad disobeyed the royal command. Instead, he began to intrigue with the Portuguese. At that time, the emperor of Vijayanagara invaded the Bijāpūr territory, and 'the Sultān was powerless to defend himself against the armies of Vijayanagar.' Asad Khān opened negotiations with the emperor of Vijayanagara, as a consequence of which he was invited to attend the *Mahānavami* festival at the Hindu capital. He accepted the invitation and went to Vijayanagara, where he was treated with great consideration. He accompanied the Rāya to the Bijāpūr frontier, in order to help him to overcome the Ādil Shāh who came thither to defend his territories. Then the armies of both the Sultān and the Rāya "marched towards Rāicūr, the Rāya to retake the place from the Sultān, the Sultān watching for an opportunity to attack the Rāya." At this stage Asad Khān deserted his Hindu ally, and joined the Sultān, who freely forgave him. As he was

* *FE.* pp. 174-76.

unwilling to continue the war, owing to Asad Khān's duplicity, he concluded a treaty with the Rāya who allowed him to retain in his possession Rāicūr fort in return for some other territory.

The account given by Rājanātha Ḍiṇḍima is briefly this:—

Having learnt that the territory of the Ādil Shāh was seething with rebellion, Acyuta marched his army against it, and laid siege to a fort whose name is not mentioned. The fort was vigorously besieged by the Hindus, and as bravely defended by the Mussalmans for sometime. At last it was stormed by the besiegers who put to the sword most of the garrison. The survivors including the commandant fled. Acyuta then proceeded westwards to effect the capture of *Maluka*. The victorious Hindu army laid waste the Bijāpūr territory dismantling forts and burning cities. Acyuta next marched upon the important fortress of Rāicūr. The Sultān who was alarmed at the rapid progress of the enemy, assembled an army with which he marched towards Rāicūr in order to prevent Acyuta from capturing it. Both the armies met somewhere in the neighbourhood of the fort, and a fierce battle was fought in which the Muhammadans were so completely beaten that the Sultān had to run away from the field all alone. Acyuta captured several horses and elephants and looted the Muhammadan camp. Then he marched to the banks of the Kṛṣṇa where he lay encamped for sometime watching closely the movements of the Sultān who was attempting to gather another army on the opposite bank. The Sultān, however, suddenly abandoned the idea of continuing the struggle, owing to the treacherous conduct of *Maluka*. Considering that it was advisable, under the circumstances, to come to terms with the enemy, he crossed the river on horseback, and reached the Vijayanagara camp without any mishap. There he met Acyuta, and saluted him, in the characteristic Muhammadan fashion, signifying submission. Acyuta having accepted the allegiance of the Sultān, returned to his capital. *

* *The Sources* pp. 167-69.

On comparing the accounts of Barros and Ḍiṇḍima, there can be little doubt that they relate to the same invasion, although they seem to differ in certain material particulars. An important point should be considered in this connection. The rebellion of Asad Khān, his intrigues with the Portuguese and the Rāya of Vijayanagara, and the Rāya's invasion of Bijāpūr territory, are placed by the Portuguese writers in A.D. 1534, after the demise of Ismail Ādil Shāh at Kōvilkoṇḍa. Between 1530 and 1543 A.D. the Vijayanagara army invaded Bijāpūr territory only once, and that was in A.D. 1534-5. Rājanātha Ḍiṇḍima describes only one Vijayanagara invasion of Bijāpūr territory during the reign of Acyuta; and that could not have taken place, as already noticed, before A.D. 1534. Both Barros and Ḍiṇḍima describe an invasion which took place in the same year, the contending parties and the scene of activities being the same. It is not unreasonable, therefore, to infer that their accounts relate to the same set of events.

Resemblances :—Both the accounts refer to the outbreak of a rebellion in the Bijāpūr kingdom followed by an invasion of the emperor of Vijayanagara. There is complete agreement between the two writers regarding most of the events of the war. Whereas Barros alludes only to the outstanding events, Ḍiṇḍima, in addition, supplies the details also. According to Barros, Asad Khān, who joined the emperor of Vijayanagara was present in his camp while he was encamped in the neighbourhood of Rāicūr expecting the Ādil Shāh ; but he deserted him subsequently and joined his master once again. Some three days before the desertion the emperor discovered 'that constant messages were passing between the camps of the Sultān and Asad

Khān.' Yet no action seems to have been taken to prevent the progress of this treacherous correspondence. The least that Acyuta could have done was to place Asad under arrest. This is what he exactly attempted to do, according to Ḍiṇḍima.

After the fall of the unnamed fort, Acyuta is said to have proceeded westward '*to bind*' one Maluka (Malik), who, in some mysterious way, seems to have incurred his displeasure. This Maluka appears to be the same as Asad Khān, and Acyuta wanted 'to bind' him for his treacherous conduct.

If this identification be acceptable, it may be said that Ḍiṇḍima and Barros agree about the activities of Asad Khān also. There is perfect agreement between them regarding the events that took place on the arrival of the Ādil Shāh, and the march of the Hindu and Muhammadan armies towards the fort of Rāicūr. Ḍiṇḍima seems to agree with Barros regarding the cause which induced the Ādil Shāh to conclude a treaty of peace with the Rāya. The Sultān, who was apprehensive of the duplicity of Asad Khān, according to Barros, considered it prudent to close the war by concluding a treaty with the Rāya. The Sultān, according to Ḍiṇḍima, having come to know the treacherous conduct of Maluka, considered it advisable to come to terms with Acyuta. It was treachery of Asad according to Barros, and of Maluka according to Ḍiṇḍima, that induced the Sultān to conclude the treaty. Since Asad, in our opinion, is identical with Maluka, there is agreement between the two writers on this point also.

Differences:—Ḍiṇḍima does not mention the activities of Asad Khān before his advent at Vijayanagara.

Even when he alludes to him, he does not mention him by name, but calls him Maluka. Barros, on the contrary, gives him considerable prominence. This may be attributed to the difference in the method of their writing. Barros is an historian, and Ḍiṇḍima is an author of an eulogistic *kāvya*. Whereas Barros gives a comprehensive account of the Portuguese relations with Asad Khān, Bijāpūr, and Vijayanagara, Ḍiṇḍima concentrates his attention upon those events which are calculated to glorify his hero. Therefore, the difference here at any rate seems to be due to the difference in their respective view points.

This explanation does not apply to another important difference between them. Ḍiṇḍima describes at length a battle between the Hindus and the Muhammadans in the neighbourhood of Rāicūr in which the Muhammadans were defeated; but Barros is silent on this point. This is strange; for he asserts that the Ādil Shāh, while marching towards Rāicūr, was 'watching for an opportunity to attack the Rāya.' This shows that the Sultān was very eager to cross swords with the Rāya. Moreover, he became reconciled with Asad Khān who deserted the Rāya and joined him. This should have strengthened his position considerably. There was nothing to prevent the Sultān from attacking the Rāya. It is extremely likely that a battle should have taken place, as told by Ḍiṇḍima, between the Rāya and the Sultān in which the former suffered a defeat. Otherwise, the Sultān would not have submitted to the Rāya, in spite of his fear of Asad Khān's duplicity. Lastly, it is said by Barros that 'the Ādil Shāh made a treaty of peace with the Rāya,' according to the terms of which he managed to retain Rāicūr by surrendering 'some other territory.' Both Barros and

Diṇḍima agree that it was the Ādil Shāh who sued for peace; but Diṇḍima adds, and he is supported by Rādhāmādhava, that the Ādil Shāh went to the Rāya's camp, and throwing himself at the Rāya's feet, begged him to grant him peace. As Diṇḍima does not mention the capture of Rāicūr, his silence may be taken as an instance of his agreement with the Portuguese historian. But it is inconceivable how an emperor of Vijayanagara could give his consent to a proposal ceding Rāicūr to the Ādil Shāh whom he had completely defeated. Nothing could have prevented the Rāya from taking the place. There is reason to believe that he did capture it; for, according to Nuniz, when Ibrahim Ādil Shāh invested the city of Vijayanagara in 1537-38 A. D., 'he demanded that, among other things, the Rāya should yield up to him the city of Rachol (Rāicūr.)' * Accordingly the fort was given up. It is evident that in 1537-38 A. D. Rāicūr belonged to the emperor of Vijayanagara. As it was in the possession of the Ādil Shāh in 1534 A. D., it is reasonable to believe that it should have been wrested from him in the interval, *i. e.*, during Acyutarāya's campaign in the Rāicūr doab.

Reconstruction of the History of the Campaign:—Mallū Ādil Shāh was indeed helpless. He had to face treachery from within, and invasion from without. As he had very grave suspicions regarding the complicity of Asad Khān with the rebels, he summoned him to the court; but Asad did not obey the royal command. Instead, he wrote to Nuno Da Cunha, the Portuguese governor, inviting him to take possession of certain tracts on the mainland. He drew the attention of the Portuguese governor to the fact that 'his

* *FE.* p. 368.

master was powerless to defend himself against the armies of Vijayanagar'. Da Cunha then 'seized upon the country opposed to Goa,' for the protection of which he built a fort at Racōl. At the same time Asad Khān began to intrigue with the emperor of Vijayanagara who invited him to visit his capital during the Mahānavami festival. Asad Khān accepted the invitation and went to Vijayanagara, accompanied by 13,000 men and 200 elephants. He was warmly received by Acyuta, and obtained for his maintenance two towns 'Tunge and Turugel.' He promised Acyuta that 'he would never join the Muhammadans, but would remain faithful to Vijayanagar.' Acyuta 'hoped for his aid against the Sultān.'

The Vijayanagara army, accompanied by Asad Khān, marched northwards, and entering the Bijāpūr dominion, laid siege to a fort whose name is not mentioned. Although it was stoutly defended, the besiegers were able to capture it by scaling its walls. The victorious Hindu army laid waste the Bijāpūr territory burning cities, and dismantling forts. Mallū Ādil Shāh who was no doubt enraged at these outrages, assembled his troops, and, crossing the Kṛṣṇa, began to move towards the Vijayanagara army. He addressed a letter to the Rāya asking him to surrender his "recalcitrant slave,' Asad Khān. The letter was shown to Asad Khān who promised to remain faithful to the Hindus; but in secret, opened negotiations with the Ādil Shāh. Acyuta began to march his troops towards Rāicūr to take the fort, and Mallū Ādil Shāh was also marching in the same direction to prevent his enemy from capturing the place. During this time, Acyuta learnt that 'constant messages were passing between the camps of the Sultān and Asad Khān. He made an unsuccessful attempt to arrest Asad Khān, who, however, managed to escape, and join the Sultān. As both the armies began to move towards Rāicūr, the inevitable clash between them occurred very soon. A fierce battle was fought in which the Muhammadans were completely defeated, and Mallū Ādil Shāh had to run away from the field all alone. Acyuta, having captured several horses and elephants belonging to the enemy, lay encamped on the southern bank of the Kṣṛṇa, and kept a close watch upon the movements of the Ādil Shāh, who was gathering troops afresh on the opposite bank. It was probably during this interval that Vijayanagara troops captured Rāicūr.

The war, however, was brought to an abrupt end. The Ādil Shāh is said to have sued for peace, because he was 'secretly fearful of Asad Khān's duplicity.' The causes of this abrupt submission of the Ādil Shāh are very obscure. Rājanātha Diṇḍima attributes it to the treacherous conduct of Maluka (Asad Khān). Probably he became aware of the intrigues of Asad Khān with Prince Ibrahim and his followers :

> "Subsequent to the death of Ismail Ādil Shāh," says the anonymous historian, "his elder son Mulloo was proclaimed king ; but shortly afterwards, his minister, Asad Khān Lāry conspired against him, and in conjunction with his younger brother, the Prince Ibrahim, dethroned him." *

This is confirmed by the following passage from the *Burhān-ī-Ma'asir* :

> "In this year (A. D 1534-35)—," says Sayyed Ali, "Ismail Ādil Shāh died, and Mallū Khān his eldest son ascended the

* Brigg's *Ferishta* iii p. 375.

throne; but he had scarcely had time to taste the sweets of sovereignty, when Asad Khān, who was the most powerful of the *amīrs* of Bijāpūr, and was ill-content that Mallū should be king with the assistance of the rest of the *amīrs*, and officers of state, deposed Mallū &c." *

On hearing the news of the conspiracy of Asad Khān with Prince Ibrahim, and the *amīrs* and officers of state, Mallū Ādil Shāh might have considered it unwise to wage war against a foreign foe, while his position on the throne was not free from danger. Therefore, he concluded a treaty with Acyuta, according to which the river Kṛṣṇa was probably recognised as the boundary between the two kingdoms.

Acyuta was able to recover within a short period of three or four years, what he had lost during the first year of his reign. Although it cannot be said that he had fought personally like his brother, Kṛṣṇa, in the battle-field, there is no denying the fact that he was always present at the front, probably directing his forces against the enemy. Acyuta, therefore, was a worthy successor of Kṛṣṇadēvarāya, and had shown himself to be a capable ruler.

* *IA.* xlix. 1920, p. 201

Chapter III.

ACYUTA AND RĀMARĀJA

Section 1 :—Acyuta was warmly received by the citizens of his capital when he returned to it after his victory over the Muhammadans.* He did nōt, however, stay there for long. According to the Kaifiyat of Mutyālpāḍu, a certain Timmā Nāyaka who rose up in rebellion, seized the important fort of Gutti, and defied the imperial authority. Acyuta was obliged to go to Gutti in person to subdue the rebel in Ś 1457 (1535-36 A.D.) He was accompanied by most of his officers. The fort of Gutti was besieged, and a breach was effected in one of its walls. The imperial army under the command of Salakarāju Tirumala entered the fort through the breach, and forced the defenders to surrender. † Acyuta appears to have paid a visit to Tirupati on this occasion. He was present in Tirupati on 26th December 1535 A. D., when 'he instituted two new festivals, viz., the *Lakṣmīdēvi mahōtsavam* to be celebrated for Tiruvēnkaṭamuḍaiyan and Alaimelmangai Nāchchiyār for five days, and the *Punarvasu Tirunal* for Raghunāthan (Śrī Rāma), Nāchchiyār (Sītādēvi), and Iḷaiya-Perumāḷ (Lakṣmaṇa) on each of the 13 days of the Punarvasu star occurring in the year." He was accompanied by some of his officers, *e. g.* Rāmābhaṭṭarayyan, Rāyasam Ramacandra Dīkṣita, Malaiyapparayyan, and Sāḷuva Timmarasa. ‡ He seems to have returned to Vijayanagara sometime before Ś. 1458 Durmukhi Kārttika su 12 (1536 A. D.), when he granted the *agrahāra* of

* *The Sources*. p. 169.

† *M. Mss.* 15-3-52.

‡ *TDER.* p. 223.

Pōlēpalli to Cintapalli Annama in the presence of the god Viṭṭhalēśvara on the banks of the Tungabhadrā. *

Section 2:—The year 1536 A. D. marks an important stage in the reign of Acyuta. With this year commences the dark half of Acyuta's reign. The internal trouble and confusion which characterise this period had their origin in his struggle with Rāmarāja whom he had admitted into partnership in the government of the empire in A. D. 1530. Rāmarāja seems to have taken advantage of Acyuta's continued absence from the capital to seize the throne. The causes that led to the usurpation of Rāmarāja are not quite apparent. They are to be sought in the probable attempt of Acyuta to supersede him in his office. The infant son of Kṛṣṇadēvarāya whom Rāmarāja proclaimed emperor in 1530, having died about 1533 A. D., † his position appears to have become considerably weakened, especially in relation to Acyuta. The death of his nephew who had better claims to the throne than himself, should have relieved Acyuta greatly. The need for placating Rāmarāja continuously had at last disappeared; and he was free to adopt an independent course of conduct towards him. Probably Acyuta ceased to consult Rāmarāja, who was obliged consequently to retire into the background, yielding place to the emperor's brothers-in-law, Salakarāju Peda and Cina Tirumaladēvas. Of these, Peda Tirumala was appointed as *pradhāna* in A.D. 1534, as testified by the Madras Museum Plates of Acyuta. ‡ He continued in the office until A.D. 1535, as shown by an epigraph at Hōspēṭ. § Finally he rose to the position of *sarvaśiraḥ pradhāna* in 1538-39. ¶ It is pretty certain that the loss of his position, and the

* *NDI.* i. Cp. 10.

† *JBBRAS.* xxii. 28.

‡ *MER.* 11 A of 1905-6.

§ *ibid* 681 of 1922.

¶ *LR.* 8 p. 113.

elevation of his rival to the highest office in the state must have enraged Rāmarāja. Naturally he took the earliest opportunity of regaining his lost power.

Although Rāmarāja was deprived of his office, he wielded considerable influence in the state. Being a man of great foresight, he strengthened his position, while he was yet in office, by appointing his friends and relations to the most important posts under the government. The Muhammadan historians are unanimous on this point. "By degrees," says Ferishta, "raising his family to the highest rank, and destroying many of the ancient nobility, Rāmrāj aspired to reign in his own name." * According to the anonymous historian, Rāmarāja, while he was the protector of the son of Kṛṣṇarāya, took 'pains to strengthen his power by reduction of many troublesome neighbours, and elevation of his adherents and relatives. †' Raffi-ud-Din Shīrāzi, who visited Vijayanagara before its destruction by the Mussalmans, asserts :

> "Rāmarāja conducted the administration for two years nominally for the son of Kṛṣṇarāya during which period he removed all the old nobles and state servants, and appointed his own relations to high offices." ‡

Pemmasāni Timmā Nāyaka of Gaṇḍikōṭa, Haṇḍe Hanumappa Nāyaka of Anantapūr, Mesā Peddā Nāyaka of Naḍimidoḍḍipāḷaiyam, and Majjhari Toḷasipati Reḍḍi of Allūr were some of his adherents. Yeṟa-Tirumala and Venkaṭādri, his two younger brothers, held the forts of Gutti and Kandanavōlu respectively. One of his uncles, the famous general, Rāmarāja-Timma, was the lord of the fortress of Awuku; another uncle, Rāmarāja-Koṇḍa was in charge of Ādavāni. His

* Brigg's *Ferishta* iii. p. 381.

† *Ibid* p. 79.

‡ *JBBRAS*. xxii. 28.

distant cousins were the hereditary rulers of Nandyāla. All these chiefs were ready to join his standard; and being assured of their support, he had every reason to feel that his position was unassailable. Rāmarāja took steps to strengthen his military power. Ibrahim Ādil Shāh who, deposed and blinded Mallū Ādil Shāh with the aid of Asad Khān, ascended the throne in or about 1535 A.D. One of his first acts was to dismiss almost all the foreign soldiers who were in his service. Several of them, who were thus suddenly deprived of their means of living by the caprice of the new Sultān, entered the service of Rāmarāja.

> "Rāmrāj, the Hindu prince of Beejanuggur entertained 3000 of them; and in order to reconcile them to the act of making obeisance to him, he caused a Qorān to be placed before him when they came to pay their respects; which enabled them to do so without a breach of the ordinances of their religion." *

These three thousand Muslim soldiers were under some six Mussalman nobles. Rāmarāja gave them *jāgīrs* and 'treated them with respect and consideration.' They lived in a part of the city called Turkiwāḍa 'where they built houses and bazaars. They were permitted to build a *masjid*, to repeat the *namāz*, and follow their own customs and practices, including the slaughter of animals.' †

It was probably the recruitment of a large Muhammadan force that stimulated the ambition of Rāmarāja to seize the throne.

No definite information is available regarding the events that had taken place at the capital, since Acyuta's return from Tirupati in 1536 A. D. There was probably some encounter between him and Rāmarāja at Vijayanagara in which he was worsted.

* Brigg's *Ferishta* iii p. 79. † Shīrāzi: *JBBRAS*. xxii p. 28,

Acyuta seems to have been taken a prisoner and kept under custody. 'Rāmarāja, *vakīl* of the king of Vijayanagar,' says Sayyed Ali, 'had rebelled against, and overcame his lord, and, having imprisoned him, usurped the kingdom.' * He attempted to rule in his own name, but was prevented from doing so, on account of opposition. The poet, Rāmarājabhūṣaṇa, who lived at the court of Vijayanagara at least from A.D. 1525 to 1565, and who was intimately acquainted with the events that took place in the royal palace, refers, in his *Vasucaritra*, to Rāmarāja's *paṭṭābhiṣēka* which, however, was not celebrated, on account of the opposition of some people. † Ferishta gives more definite information. He says :

> " Rāmrāj," " aspired to reign in his own name ; many of the nobility, however, opposing this project, he complied with their wishes." ‡

This is corroborated by the evidence of the Local Records. In one of them, it is said :

> 'Cinnādēvi and Tirumaladēvi, the queens of Kṛṣṇarāya, being desirous of placing Rāmarāja upon the throne, made preparations to celebrate his coronation at Vijayanagara, but had to abandon the scheme, owing to the opposition of Salakarāju Tirumala. ' §

There need be no doubt about Rāmarāja's unsuccessful attempt to seize the throne in A. D. 1536.

The failure of Rāmarāja's *coup d'etat* was mainly due to the opposition of the nobles who objected to his accession, as he had no claim to the throne. Although he was the son-in-law of the great Kṛṣṇarāya, he could not persuade the nobles to accept him as their ruler, because he was not a Tuḷuva by birth. He did

* *IA.* (1920.) xlix. p. 201.

† *The Sources* : p. 217.

‡ Brigg's *Ferishta* iii. p. 81.

§ *The Sources* : p. 179.

not, however, relinquish his hold upon the affairs of the state; nor did he set Acyuta at liberty. Instead, he began to look for a desirable candidate to the throne, who might be content with the name of the emperor, leaving the substance of power in his hands. Such a person he discovered in Sadāśiva, a nephew of Acyuta, whom he proclaimed emperor, and began to govern the empire in his name.

Section 3:—Sadāśiva is the subject of one of the most knotty problems in the history of Vijayanagara. It is generally believed that Rāmarāja proclaimed him emperor of Vijayanagara, immediately after Acyuta's death in Ś. 1464 (A. D. 1542). There are several inscriptions of Sadāśiva dated in that year. In fact, some of his inscriptions belong to an earlier period, a fact which induced the epigraphist to declare that Sadāśiva was governing the empire as a co-regent of his uncle, Acyuta.* It must be remembered, however, that Acyuta had a son named Venkaṭādri, whom he had anointed *yuvarāja* as early as A. D. 1529-30.† Under these circumstances, one fails to understand why Acyuta should have accepted Sadāśiva as his co-regent, depriving thereby Venkaṭādri, his own son, of the chance of succeeding him. It is not at all intelligible why Acyuta recognised his nephew as his successor ignoring altogether the claims of his son. The epigraphist, at any rate, does not divulge the reasons for his assertion.

The truth is that Sadāśiva was set up as a rival candidate to the throne by Rāmarāja both against Acyuta and his son. What did he expect to gain by this act? Acyuta, and after him his son should have had a legal claim to the throne, being next of kin to

* *MER.* A 6 of 1906; Part ii. p. 65. † *Vpm. The Sources* p. 176.

Kṛṣṇarāya. Moreover, they were firmly backed up not only by the Salakarāju faction, but by the majority of the nobles of the kingdom. In these circumstances, what justification had Rāmarāja in setting up Sadāśiva as a rival candidate? Rāmarāja who was ambitious to govern the empire, appears to have believed that he could realise his ambition by espousing the cause of Sadāśiva. He hoped to strengthen his position in the state in such a manner as to render the opposition of Salakarāju Tirumala and his adherents ineffective. By upholding the cause of Sadāśiva, Rāmarāja expected to win over to his side some or even all the partisans of his opponents. It must be remembered that the real actors in this political drama were Rāmarāja and Salakarāju Tirumala, and they made use of their respective candidates to gain their own ends. Therefore, Rāmarāja should have had sufficiently strong reasons in putting forward the claims of Sadāśiva. What were they? Nobody has so far attempted to answer this question. Unless it is satisfactorily answered, it is not possible to understand the significance of several events which happened during the second half of Acyuta's reign.

Neither Acyuta, nor his son had any legal claim to the throne. In all the copper-plate grants of Sadāśiva, Narasa's children by Ōbāmbā are described in the following verse:

Raṅga-kṣitīndr-Ācyuta-dēva-rāyau
rakṣā-dhurīṇāviva Rāmakṛṣṇāu
Ōbāmbikāyām Narasa kṣitindrāt
ubhāvabhūtan-urgēndra sārau ||

It is clear from this that Sadāśiva's father, Ranga, was an elder brother of Acyuta. Both the order of the words '*Raṅga-kṣitīndr-Ācyutadēva-rāyau,*' and the comparison, '*iva Rāmakṛṣṇau,*' leave no room for doubt. Therefore, Sadāśiva had a better claim to the throne than Acyuta or his son. Ranga appears to have predeceased Kṛṣṇarāya, who consequently nominated Acyuta as his successor, ignoring the claims of Raṅga's youthful son. Nevertheless, several people in the country should have sympathised with the helpless prince, and regarded Acyuta almost as an usurper. That is why the Portuguese historian Correa refers to Acyuta as one 'who had been king contrary to right,' * and to Sadāśiva as 'the king by real right.' † Rāmarāja considering it worth his while to exploit the situation revived the claims of Sadāśiva.

Sadāśiva is generally believed to have been a prince of tender years, 'a child in arms,' at the time when Rāmarāja took up his cause. This is not true. If the evidence of the inscriptions can be depended on, it must be admitted that he was at least 17 years old in 1535 A. D. ‡

* *FE*. p. 183. † *ibid.*

‡ The following table is bound to be instructive in this context.

No.	Reference.	Cyclic year.	Śaka year.	Christian year.
1	Sewell's Antiquities I. 8...	Pramādi	1440	1518
2	LR. 42	Svabhānu Śrāvaṇa śu 12.	1445	1523
3	EC. X. Mb 240... ...	Tāraṇa, Vaisākha ba 11 ...	1446	1524
4	EC. X. Mb 201... ...	Nandana, Bhādrapada ba 1	1454	1532
5	Rangachari's Index I By 342.	Jaya	1455	1533
6	129/1905 (MER.) ...	Prabhava ?	1457	1535
7	6/1905-06 (MER.) ...	Hēvaḷambi	1459	1537-38
8	167/1904 (MER.) ...	Śōbhakṛit ?	1461	1539
9	Rangachari's Index I. CD. 430.	Raudri ?	1461	1539
10	EC. XII Mi 66 ...	Śārvari Śrāvaṇa śu 1 Bhānu.	1462	1540
11	33/1905 (MER.) ...	... ...	1464	1542

Of the eleven inscriptions listed above, four (6, 8, 9,) may be set aside as untrustworthy, on the ground that the Śaka and Cyclic years do not tally. Of the remaining seven, three (1, 2, 3,) belong to the reign of Kṛṣṇadēvarāya, the earliest being dated in A.D. 1518.

Again, Durate Barbosa who was travelling in the Deccan and South India about 1511 A.D. refers to a nephew of the king of Vijayanagara ruling at Baticala. He says:

"The king of Narasinga," has given this place (Baticala) and others to a nephew of his. who rules and governs them, and rules in great state, and calls himself king, but he is in obedience to the king, his uncle." *

Raṅga, the father of Sadāśiva is mentioned in some of the inscriptions at Bhaṭakal as the ruler of the place. † It is reasonable to suppose that the nephew of the king mentioned by Barbosa is Raṅga's son, Sadāśiva. Raṅga who was governing Bhaṭakal appears to have died sometime before the accession of Kṛṣṇarāya, who allowed Raṅga's son to succeed to his father's estate. If this surmise be correct, Sadāśiva should have been at least an young man of 25 years in 1536 A. D.; and Rāmarāja might have adduced that as an additional reason for placing him upon the throne.

Section 4:—The revolution in the capital must have had its repercussions in the provinces. According to Ferishta, Rāmarāja, 'marched with an army against some of the rays of the country of Malabar, who had withheld tribute', 'leaving the city of Beejanuggur in charge of a slave whom he had raised to a high rank.' ‡ Ferishta's statement seems to be based upon facts. It is said in an inscription of Nañjangūḍ that "Cinnarāja, the father of Cevvappa Nāyaka of Tanjore became the minister of Rāmarāja, the son-in-law of Kṛṣṇarāja. . . . By the orders of Rāmarāja, Cinnarāja subjugated the Dravidian kings, as far as the Sētu, and made Tañjāpuri his capital." § The genuineness

* Barbosa: *East Africa and Malabar* (Stanely's Translation,) p. 80.

† *ASR.* 1908-9 p. 193. *n* 8.

‡ Brigg's *Ferishta* iii. p. 81.

§ *MAR.* 1917 p. 55.

of this record is not above doubt, as the genealogy of the Tanjore Nāyaks given in it, differs in certain material particulars from that given by Raghunātha Nāyaka, Vijayarāghava, and others. Therefore, it is not possible to make any definite assertion on the authority of this grant. Nevertheless, the military expedition referred to by Ferishta appears to have taken place. A copper-plate grant from Tinnevelly dated 1537 A. D. states that Mahāmaṇḍalēśvara Rāmarāja Viṭṭhaladēva was Sadāśiva's governor in that region. * Viṭṭhaladēva mentioned in the inscription was the first cousin and firm supporter of Rāmarāja. There is no reason to doubt that he was ruling in the extreme south about 1537 A.D. as a representative of his cousin Rāmarāja, who could have established his authority in that distant region only by leading an expedition of the kind alluded to by Ferishta.

The cause of Rāmarāja's southern expedition is said to be the refusal of payment of tribute by some of the *rays* of Malabar. The Tiruvaḍi, who was forced to submit to Acyuta's officers during the late war, probably attempted to reassert his independence, taking advantage of the confusion caused by the revolutionary changes in the capital. The presence of Viṭṭhala's army in the south-eastern corner of the

* *MER.* A-6 of 1905-6.

Another grant *MER.* 129 of 1905 dated Ś 1457 (expired) Parābhava found at Kalakkāḍu (Nāṅgunēri, Tinnevelly) also mentions Rāmarāja Viṭṭhala as a subordinate of Sadāśiva. Two points are worthy of attention. The Śaka and cyclic years do not tally. The cyclic year, Parābhava coincides with Ś. 1468 (1546 A.D.). As the grant under consideration refers to Sadāśiva as having conquered the Mussalmans, subdued all, and levied tribute from Ceylon, it is likely that it belongs to a period subsequent to Sadāśiva's coronation, and not before. As we find, Rāmarāja Viṭṭhala's inscriptions in that region dated 1546 A.D. (510/1907) and 1547 A.D. (64/1896), this inscription also may be placed at that time. It was then that Viṭṭhala subdued Travancore. The conquest of Ceylon mentioned in the inscription under consideration might have taken place then.

Tinnevelly district, which was then included in the kingdom of Quilon, lends colour to this view. Periya Rāmappa Nāyaka who appears to have been the governor of Madura at this time might also have opposed Rāmarāja. A poem called *Cokkanātha Caritra* describing the mythological stories connected with the Cokkanātha temple at Madura was dedicated to him. The poet desired that his patron should rule the earth for a long time by the grace of Cokkanātha. * Moreover, Periya Rāmappa made a gift of land to a temple for the merit of Acyuta in Tirupattūr (Rāmnād) in 1538. A.D. † Some of his subordinates made a gift of land four years later in the same place for the merit of Periya Rāmappa. ‡ It is likely that he should have succeeded Viśvanātha in 1535 or 1536 A.D. as the governor of Madura. § As he is called 'the bearer of the burden of Acyutarāya's valour,' and 'Acyutarāya's valorous right arm,' and bore the title of ***swāmidrōharagaṇḍa*** (the slayer of the disloyal or the seditious) ¶, it is not unreasonable to infer that he

* నరనాథ శ్రీచొక్కనాథు సత్కృపను
ధరయేలు మాచంద్రతారార్కముగను.

CC. [Triennial Catalogue of Telugu Mss.]

† ***MER.*** **217 of 1924.**

‡ ***ibid*** **65 of 1916; 121 of 1908; 224 of 1924.**

§ See Appendix.

¶ ఆయతోన్నత శౌర్యు డచ్యుత దేవ
రాయ ప్రతాప కార్య ధురంధరుండ
* *
దీపించు నచ్యుత దేవరాయ ప్ర
తాప దక్షిణ బాహుదండాంకు పేర
* *
ఘనత స్వామిద్రోహగండని పేర.

CC. [Triennial Catalogue of Telugu Mss.]

opposed Rāmarāja. He was probably assisted by another officer of Acyuta called Vākiṭi Cinnabhūvara, * and both of them seem to have won a victory at Upasūru. †

Rāmarāja was obliged to send an army to reduce the rebels to subjection. According to Ferishta, Rāmarāja himself marched against them, leaving Vijayanagara in charge of one of his servants. The details of the warfare between Rāmarāja and the rebels, are not available; but he succeeded in reducing the rebel chiefs whom he deprived of their fortresses. ‡ Leaving his cousin Rāmarāja Viṭṭhala with a contingent to hold the subdued chiefs in check, he marched northwards towards Vijayanagara. But Viṭṭhala did not remain there long. Inscriptions show that after 1537 A.D., the Madura country was under the control of Acyuta's officers. Besides the inscriptions of Periya Rāmappa bearing the dates 1538, 1539 and 1542 which have been already noticed, there is also an epigraph at Aḻagarkoil in Madura tālūka dated 1542 A.D. which records a gift made to the temple of Aḻagar, for the merit of 'the king (Acyuta), queen Varadāji-amman and prince Chikkadēva Mahārāya.' § On

* He seems to be identical with 'Chinnapanaique' who was the chief *alcaid* of Acyuta (*FE*. p. 372). He was also Acyuta's marshal. He was 'the lord of the land of Calaly in the direction of the Cochin in the interior.' Periya Rāmappa was probably his subordinate; for in an inscription (33 of 1928-29), it is stated that he 'gave a *dēvadāna* to the temple of Tāṇḍōnrīśvaram Uḍaiyar, the village of Kaṇṇamangaḷam, for the merit of Cinnappa Nāyaka, the *vāsil-kāriyam* of the king." It is not possible, however, to identify Upasūru.

† అంచిత కోదమ నాయంకర గండ
మించి వర్తించు స్వామిద్రోహగండ
చేకొన్న నుపసూరి సింహధ్వజాంక
వాకిటి చిన్నభూవర సహితుండ.

CC. [Triennial Catalogue of Telugu Mss.]

‡ Brigg's *Ferishta* iii. p. 81.

§ *MER*. 330 of 1929-30.

the contrary, no trace of Sadāśiva or his officers is seen until the year 1544 A.D. It is evident that Sadāśiva's power suffered a sudden eclipse after 1537 ; and consequently Acyuta's authority was re-established, and it remained intact until 1543, when, by slaying Salakarāju Tirumala, Rāmarāja finally installed Sadāśiva upon the throne.

The retirement of Viṭṭhala must be attributed to some great reverse which Rāmarāja's army suffered in the north. On his way to Vijayanagara, he encountered 'a powerful zamindar,' who governed the territory to the south of the capital. It is not easy to identify this zamindar at present, although it may be suggested that he may be identical with 'Chinnapanaique,' whose lands were in the interior, 'in the direction of Cochin.' The encounter with this zamindar, however, proved disastrous to Rāmarāja. He 'was detained for six months without making the smallest impression, though he had been engaged in several actions.' It is not unlikely that he should have summoned Viṭṭhala to his assistance. Nevertheless, he was not able to subdue the rebellious baron. By this time his 'military chest' was exhausted. Consequently, he 'wrote to his deputy to send him a supply of money from Beejanuggur, in order to enable him to continue the war.' But the treacherous 'deputy' instead of obeying his master, rebelled against him. Not only did he set the imprisoned Acyuta at liberty, but induced the emperor's brother-in-law Salakarāju Tirumala to join him. He then became the minister, and 'began to levy troops.' 'Several tributary rays who were offended with Rāmrāj's administration, hastened to Beejanuggur to rally round their lawful king, and in a short time, thirty thousand horse, and vast hosts of foot assembled under his standard at the city.' But the 'deputy' was not destined to enjoy his exalted position for a long time; for his faithless ally Salakarāju Tirumala became considerably alarmed at his rapidly increasing power. 'Apprehending that the slave, now minister, might repent of his rebellion and eventually betray them to Rāmrāj,' he 'put his benefactor to death, and assumed the management of affairs at Beejanuggur.' *

These dramatic developments in the capital had completely changed the situation. Rāmarāja who was, during the past few months, the *de facto* ruler of the empire was reduced to the position of a rebel. Fortune appeared to desert him on every side. He had to abandon the territories which he conquered; his worst enemies whom he imprisoned escaped from prison, and assumed an attitude of open defiance; his troops had to face a series of disasters which seemed to be interminable. But that man of undaunted courage did not despair. Quickly adjusting himself to the changed circumstances, he 'concluded a hasty peace with his enemy,' and hastened towards Vijayanagara. As he advanced upon the capital, he was 'deserted by several of his officers, who left him on the route to join their lawful sovereign.' † Matters became further complicated by the invasion of the Sultān of Bijāpūr. Ibrahim Ādil Shāh, who succeeded Mallū, was, at this time, totally under the influence of the wily Asad Khān. The latter who was eager to regain what Mallū had lost during his late war with Vijayanagara, advised his young sovereign to invade Vijayanagara dominions, taking advantage of the confusion prevailing in the Hindu capital. The advice was accepted, and the Sultān, placing himself at the head of his army, marched towards Vijayanagara. Sayyed Ali says:

* Brigg's *Ferishta* iii. pp. 81-82. † *ibid* p. 82.

"While the success of Rāmrāj was yet doubtful and the whole army of Vijayanagar had not joined his standard, Asad Khān, regarding the state of affairs in Vijayanagar as an opportunity not to be lost, assembled the whole of the army of Bijāpūr, and taking Ibrahim Ādil Shāh with him, invaded Vijayanagar with the intention of conquering the country." *

Rāmarāja felt that the powers which arrayed themselves against him were overwhelming; and under the circumstances, he thought it prudent to retire to his own *jāgīr* and await further developments.

"When Rāmrāj learnt, that Ibrahim Ādil Shāh was invading Vijayanagar, he, having regard to his own uncertain position in the country, was compelled to seek safety, at the expense of his honour and reputation, in flight." †

Ibrahim Ādil Shāh marched upon Vijayanagara unopposed. Nuniz who was present in the city at the time gives a graphic account of what had taken place:

"So he (the Sultān) made his forces ready, and began to invade the king's territory, and arrived within a league of the city of Bisnaga. Chetarao (Acyuta) was in the city with such great forces and power that he could easily have captured him, if

* *I.A.* xlix. p. 202.

† *ibid.*

The invasion of Ibrahim Ādil Shāh took place, according to Ferishta, in A.D. 1535; but this date is not in agreement with the chronological data he supplies. Ismail Ādil Shāh died at Kovilkoṇḍa on Sep. 6, 1534 A.D. Until the 9th of the month, the Bijāpūr army was at Kovilkoṇḍa. The installation of Ismail Ādil Shāh's successor Mallū, took place at Kulburga, after the consultations which Asad Khān had with the nobles and the ladies of the harem. Therefore, the coronation of Mallū might be safely placed in the beginning of Oct. 1534. Mallū ruled only for six months. His reign must have terminated with the end of March 1535. Ibrahim Ādil Shāh, Mallū's successor invaded Vijayanagara one year after his accession. Therefore, the invasion should have taken place in or after April 1536 A.D.

Sayyed Ali, the author of *Burhān-i-Ma'asir*, places the outbreak of Rāmarāja's rebellion in A.D. 1537-38. This is in agreement with epigraphical evidence. Viṭṭhala's inscription from the south of Tinnevelly is dated in Ś 1459 Hēvaḷambi (A.D. 1537-38). As Ferishta is not in agreement with himself, and as Sayyed Ali's date tallies with the date furnished by the inscriptions, Sayyed Ali's date (1537-38) must be taken as the correct date of Rāmarāja's rebellion and Ādil Shāh's invasion.

his heart had allowed him to take action, since the Ydallcao had with him only 12,000 foot and 30,000 horse ; yet with this small force, the Ydallcao entered Nagallapor a league from Bisnaga and razed it to the ground. The king never tried to go out against him, nor had he the strength to fight, and there were only small skirmishes by some captains, good horsemen. These spoke to the king asking that His Highness would give them leave to attack and saying that his presence was unnecessary for so slight an affair ; but the king was terrified and by the advice of his brothers-in-law (of which they gave not a little) decided to send and make peace with Ydallcao." *

The Ādil Shāh's siege of Vijayanagara and the destruction of Nāgalāpūr are also mentioned by Paes:

"On the south side (of Vijayanagara) is the other city called Nagalapor in a plain ; in it the Ydallcao stopped with all his forces when he besieged Bisnaga, and he razed it to the ground. †

Although the Ādil Shāh besieged Vijayanagara with 'a small force,' Acyuta showed no inclination to drive him away. This was not due to any lack of military strength. He had in the city 'such great forces and power that he could have easily captured' the Ādil Shāh. There was no lack of enthusiasm in his officers to oppose the enemy. In fact, his captains who drove the Muhammadans out of the Rāicūr doab only two years before, feeling a deep sense of humiliation, besought Acyuta to grant them permission to attack the Muhammadan forces; but he would not listen to them. What is the explanation of Acyuta's strange behaviour? Nuniz attributes it to his cowardice; but Acyuta was not a coward. He faced the enemy—the Hindu and the Muhammadan—on several battle-fields. Granting for the sake of argument that he was a coward, we have yet to explain the reasons which prompted his brothers-in-law, Salakarāju (Peda and Cina) Tirumalas, in advising him not to fight with the

* *FE*. pp. 367-68.

† *ibid* p. 290.

Ādil Shāh but to make peace with him. The Salakarāju brothers were no cowards, but brave commanders who proved their mettle in many a battle. Why did they advise Acyuta to give up the idea of fighting? Acyuta's disinclination to offer battle to the Ādil Shāh was not due to his cowardice but to a desire to prevent the formation of an alliance between Rāmarāja and the Ādil Shāh. Acyuta and his advisers had probably reasons to suspect that the Sultān, if attacked, might make common cause with Rāmarāja, and deprive them of their liberty and power which they had secured with so much difficulty. Therefore, they remained strictly on the defensive, ready to adopt any course of action which the events might render imperative.

Ibrahim Ādil Shāh who came to conquer the Vijayanagara empire was able to reach the capital city without any opposition, and having laid siege to it, remained there 'for a considerable time.' He became so elated with 'the easy occupation of the enemy's country' that he threatened in an open durbar 'to take vengeance upon Asad Khān and the other *amīrs*'. They became naturally very apprehensive of the Sultān's actions, and took steps to prevent any misfortune befalling them, while it was not yet too late.

"They sent a messenger to Rāmrāj charged with this message.

"What has come to thee that thou hast brought shame on thyself by flying without striking a blow, and hast thus branded thyself as a coward and a craven? Even now, if thou wilt set forth, we shall so arrange matters that Ibrahim Ādil Shāh shall avoid a fight and take the road ; and even if the affair should end in a battle, we will stand aloof so that the day shall be thine. In any case, it behoves thee to shake off despondency and to come to battle." *

* *IA.* xlix. p. 202.

Having despatched this letter to Rāmarāja, Asad Khān addressed another to Burhān Nizām Shāh, the Sultān of Ahamadnagar, whom he urged to take advantage of the absence of the Ādil Shāh from his dominions, and 'seize this opportunity of recapturing his lost districts.' * He pointed out that 'Ibrahim Ādil Shāh had invaded Vijayanagar, and was encamped there, awaiting the army of Rāmrāj.' 'As Ibrahim Ādil Shāh could not leave Vijayanagar, and the Turks who were the flower of his army, were friendly towards the Nizām Shāh,' the latter need not apprehend any resistance to his invasion from the Ādil Shāhi forces. On the recepit of this letter, Burhān Nizām Shāh gathered his army, and invaded the kingdom of Bijāpūr. When the news of this invasion reached the Ādil Shāh at Vijayanagara, 'he was much perturbed.' Having summoned Asad Khān and his other *amīrs* and captains, he consulted them 'as to the best means of meeting the situation. They unanimously advised him that the only wise course was to make peace with Rāmrāj and to return to his own country.' †

Acyuta and his advisers were probably aware of the machinations of the wily Asad Khān and of the approach of Rāmarāja with his army. They felt that it would be more advantageous to them to secure the alliance of the Ādil Shāh, than to allow him to retire, after he came to some sort of understanding with Rāmarāja. In that case, they would not only prevent a combined attack upon the city of the forces of Rāmarāja and the

* The lost districts referred to are thus explained by Sayyed Ali. "While Burhān Nizām Shāh had been engaged in his dispute with the Sultān Bahadūr of Gujerat which had been fomented by Imād-ul-Mulk, Ādil Shāh taking advantage of the opportunity, had annexed some of those districts of the Ahamadnagar kingdom, which lay on his frontier, and had refused to comply with Burhān Nizām Shāh's request for their restoration." *IA.* xlix p. 202.

† *IA* xlix. p. 202.

Adil Shāh, but secure the friendship of the latter who might be expected to act as a check upon the former. Such considerations as these were probably responsible for Acyuta's determination to conclude peace with the Ādil Shāh. The terms of the treaty are described briefly by Nuniz:

"The Ydallcao was very glad, and made peace with him for one hundred years, on condition that the king should give him ten *lakhs* of gold pagodas...and further should yield up to him the city of Rachol which the king Crisnarao had taken from him and which had a revenue with its lands of 150,000 *pardaos* as well as jewels which could be easily valued at a *lakh*. The king accepted these terms." *

By this time, Rāmarāja must have approached Vijayanagara. Probably, he was disappointed at the turn which the events had taken. Nevertheless, he concluded a treaty with the Ādil Shāh, the terms of which are not recorded. It was perhaps at the Ādil Shāh's instance that Rāmarāja came to an understanding with Acyuta. According to the terms of this agreement, Rāmarāja should remain in independent possession of his *jāgīr*, provided that he allowed Acyuta to rule unhampered the rest of the empire. †

Having thus squared up the differences between his new allies, the Ādil Shāh returned to his kingdom. It was perhaps as a token of his gratitude that Acyuta 'sent to him a diamond stone weighing 130 *mangellinis* with fifteen other similar ones worth fully *a lakh*.' ‡

The remaining years of Acyuta's reign were more or less uneventful. He seems to have spent most of

* *FE*. p. 368.

† Brigg's *Ferishta* iii p. 82.

‡ *FE*. p. 368.

his time in the zenana, leaving the government of the realm in the hands of his brothers-in-law * who dominated him completely during this period. The nature of the administration had suffered a change for the worse. Acting upon the advice of his brothers-in-law, he exacted large sums of money from the nobles in order to replenish his treasury.

> "He destroyed the principal people of his kingdom, and killed their sons and taken their goods." "The captains and the troops, both because he made this treaty (with the Ādil Shāh) and because he exacted this sum of money, contrary to the wishes of them all, have lived greatly discontented."

As a consequence, he became the most hated man in the country. Gradually, there grew up a feeling in the minds of the people that if Vijayanagara, 'should ever be brought to destruction,' it should 'take place in the life-time of King Achetarao.' † But, the hand of fate intervened by putting an end to the earthly career of the oppressor about the middle of A. D. 1542.

* Writing some thirty years ago when Vijayanagara studies were still in their infancy, Robert Sewell hazarded a guess about the identity of Acyuta's two brothers-in-law. "These two may be two of the three powerful brothers Rāma, Tirumala and Venkaṭādri of whom the two first married two daughters of Krishṇa Dēva. In such case, however, they would not have been actually brothers-in-law of king Acyuta, but of his brother the late king." (*FE*. p. 367. n 5.) The last sentence of Sewell is utterly incomprehensible. How Rāma and Tirumala who married Kṛṣṇadēva's daughters were his brothers-in-law, and not sons-in-law passes one's understanding. Be that as it may Sewell is wrong in identifying the two brothers-in-law of Acyuta with Rāma and Tirumala He may be excused for committing this fault, as he was a pioneer. Recently, Father Heras has upheld this wrong identification, although he has plenty of material at his disposal to correct the mistake of Sewell. Referring to Sewell's identification, he says, "this seems to be quite probable." Moreover, he attempts to support himself by citing the evidence of some inscriptions which he has not taken the trouble to understand. A glance through the pages of the *Acyutarāyābhyudayam*, would have convinced him that the two brothers-in-law of Acyuta were Salakarāju Peda and Cina Tirumaladēvas, and not Rāmarāja and Tirumala.

†*FE*. p. 369.

Chapter IV.

SALAKARĀJU TIRUMALA AND RĀMARĀJA

Section 1:—The death of Acyuta was the signal for the renewal of the struggle between Rāmarāja and Salakarāju Tirumala for supremacy in the state. Acyuta left his young son, prince Venkaṭādri to succeed him. Venkaṭādri must have been at least some twelve or thirteen years old at the time of his accession; for he is not only mentioned in Acyuta's Coñjeevaram inscriptions dated 1533 A.D. * but also in the *Varadāmbikā Pariṇayam* which 'seems to have been written during the reign of the emperor Kṛṣṇadēvarāya.' † He is referred to by the Portuguese historian Correa as a 'child,' ‡ the reason for which is not quite apparent. However, as he was not of age to assume personally the reigns of government, the nobles, who gathered at the capital probably to attend the funeral of the dead monarch, wanted to make arrangements to carry on the administration of the empire, until Venkaṭa attained his manhood. They were probably apprehensive of the evil influence which Salakarāju Tirumala might exercise upon the mind of their young master, if they did not take steps to remove him from his guardianship. They prepared a scheme of government according to which the young emperor was to be completely free, and two ministers should govern the state in his name. As this arrangement was not acceptable to Salakarāju Tirumala, the maternal uncle of the boy, he, having 'contrived to gain over some partisans to his side,' opposed it. The nobles, who were disgusted with the intrigues of Tirumala and his partisans, returned to

* *MER.* 511 of 1919. † *The Sources* p. 170.

‡ Heras: *The Āraviḍu Dynasty* p. 4. cf. *Lendas da India* iv, p. 247

their estates which they commenced to rule as independent princes. *

The tactics adopted by her brother did not commend themselves to the queen-mother Varadādēvi. She was so alarmed at his attitude that she sent messengers to Bijāpūr begging the Ādil Shāh to help her in securing the empire for her son. She promised him in return for the assistance 'immense riches.' Ibrahim Ādil Shāh who was glad to have an opportunity of interfering with the internal affairs of Vijayanagara started with his army to comply with the request of the queen-mother; but Salakarāju Tirumala, having come to know of her invitation to the Sultān, sent his emissaries, who met him on the road, 'and bought (him) off with lavish gifts.' The efforts of Varadādēvi to free her son from the clutches of her ambitious and designing brother were thus frustrated, and Salakarāju Tirumala became the *de facto* ruler of the empire. †

The position of the Salakarāju Tirumala was not yet securely established. Rāmarāja who had been closely watching the progress of events at the capital since the death of Acyuta, having liberated Sadāśiva from his prison at Gutti, proclaimed him emperor once again, and began to make preparations for seizing the capital. ‡ Sadāśiva's rule as the emperor seems to have commenced immediately after Acyuta's demise, at least in the province of Udayagiri; for, several of his inscriptions dated 1542 A.D. are found all over the province. § Rāmarāja is said to have requested the

* *FE.* p. 182. † *FE.* p. 183.

‡ *The Sources*: p. 191.

§ *LR.* 15. pp. 102-103 Gundlūr: 13, p. 142. (Cintalapattūru) p. 340-4 (Kottakākarla); 14, p. 664 (Yarakallu).

Ādil Shāh to assist him in enthroning Sadāśiva at Vijayanagara. The Sultān once again marched upon Vijayanagara, ostensibly for the purpose of helping Sadāśiva, but really to conquer the empire for himself. However, the people of Vijayanagara, who were frightened at the approach of the enemy, wanted to strengthen their position by making Salakarāju Cina Tirumala their emperor.* By that time, his elder brother Peda Tirumala appears to have died. The latest of his inscriptions is dated in A.D. 1540,† and no inscription of his belonging to a later date has been discovered so far. The coronation of Cina Tirumala appears to have taken place on some day between Puṣya śu 11, and Māgha ba 14 of Śubhakṛt, corresponding to Śaka 1464 (A.D. 1543).‡ The confidence which the people placed in him was very soon justified. Salakarāju Cina Tirumala, now Tirumaladēva Mahārāya, marched against the Ādil Shāh whom 'he succeeded in defeating' very 'close to Vijayanagar.'§ It is probably on account of this victory that Tirumala Rāya claims to have 'conquered his arrogant enemies, acquired the goddess of sovereignty, just as Rāma, having conquered Rāvaṇa, acquired Sīta." ¶

Tirumala Rāya, having put the enemy to flight, returned to the capital victoriously; but he had to face an awkward situation. His nephew, Venkaṭa I, whom the people of Vijayanagara deposed in a moment of panic, was still alive; and, now that the danger of the foreign invasion was over, many in the capital should

* *FE* p. 183. † *MER.* 730 of 1916.

‡ A Mulbāgal inscription dated Ś 1464 Śubhakṛt ba. 11. (*EC.* x. Sg. 52) refers to Venkaṭapati Mahārāya as the reigning monarch. And Salakarāju Cina Tirumala was ruling as *mahārāya* or emperor on Ś 1464 Śubhakṛit Māgha ba 14 Fri. (*MAR.* for 1917. p. 53).

§ *FE.* p. 183. ¶ *MAR.* for 1917 p. 53.

have regarded him as their lawful sovereign. It is true that the people of the city had chosen Tirumala Rāya as their emperor when they had to face sudden danger; but they might also repudiate him now that they were assured of their safety. On account of these considerations, Tirumala made up his mind to murder his nephew, whom subsequently he 'strangled' to death. * At the same time, he is also said to have put to death some other members of the royal family whose rivalry he feared. In spite of the perpetration of these crimes, he could not feel free from danger, because he was 'in dread of the power of the principal nobles.' 'He summoned them to the court, and put out the eyes of those who arrived first.' † The majority of them, however, returned to their estates 'in great anger.' They did not know how to get rid of this 'monster.' Some of them invited Ibrahim Ādil Shāh to help them in deposing the tyrant promising in return to accept him as their overlord.

> "Ādil Shāh therefore advanced, entered the kingdom of Vijayanagar and was received as sovereign by many; but he also assumed such intolea nt haughty airs that he aroused the hatred of all around him, and in the end was obliged, in fear for his own safety, to retire to Bijāpūr." ‡

Tirumala Rāya must have felt considerably relieved when he heard of the retreat of the Sultān.

Section 2:—Rāmarāja, who invited the Ādil Shāh to help Sadāśiva, must have been greatly disappointed at the turn which the events had taken. He was confident that the Sultān would defeat the usurper, Tirumala Rāya; but, contrary to his expectations, Tirumala inflicted a crushing defeat on the Ādil Shāh, and

* Brigg's *Ferishta* iii. p. 83.

† *FE.* p. 183.

‡ *FE.* p. 183.

succeeded in driving him away from his dominions. Rāmarāja met with a rude check, as a consequence of which he had probably to reconsider his plans, and rearrange them. His position was stronger than ever. His old allies still stood by him. The most important of his supporters besides his two brothers, Tirumala and Venkaṭādri was his uncle Rāmarāja Tirumala or Timma, the lord of Awuku. One of the powerful nobles, Pemmasāni Timmā Nāyaka espoused his cause warmly, and helped him to win some of the early battles in the civil war.

Capture of Penugoṇḍa:—Rāmarāja seems to have resolved to fight the enemy single-handed. He was perhaps encouraged to adopt this course of conduct by the invitation of several patriotic nobles, who requested him to return to the capital, and 'assume the administration of affairs.' * Therefore, he left Gutti where he was then staying, and advanced upon the fortress of Penugoṇḍa which was considered second in importance only to Vijayanagara. † It is not known how the fortress fell into his hands. One of Rāmarāja's *birudas*, according to *Rāmarājīya*, was *Penugoṇḍa-durga-sādhaka* 'the capturer of the fortress of Penugoṇḍa.' ‡ This is in agreement with what is said of Rāmarāja in an inscription dated 1544-45 A. D. "He subdued all the enemies at Suragiri (Penugoṇḍa)." § Probably, he wrested it from some one who held it for Tirumala Rāya. Having captured the town and the fortress, he despatched messengers to all his adherents summoning them to meet him in a conference at the place.

* Brigg's *Ferishta* iii. p. 83.

† The movements of Rāmarāja are described by Venkayya thus:
'గుత్తి పెనుగొండ మఱి గండికోట కందనోలిపుర మాదవే నవలీల గెలిచి.'
The Sources p. 185.

‡ *The Sources* p. 182.

§ *EC.* iv. Ng. 58.

The Conference at Penugoṇḍa:—The conference should have been attended by all those that had any reason to be discontented with Tirumala Rāya. Among those that readily responded to the invitation were Pemmasāni Timmā Nāyaka, Haṇḍe Hanumappa Nāyaka, Mesā Peddā Nāyaka, and Majjhari Tuḷasipati Reḍḍi. Rāmarāja described to them vividly the atrocities committed by Tirumala Rāya. Then, he reminded them of the loyal services which they rendered to the royal family in the past. He besought them to assist him in destroying the enemy, and promised that they would be amply rewarded for any help which they might give him. He desired that one of them should send spies to the camp of the enemy in order to discover the exact strength of his troops and their probable movements. The chiefs that attended the conference were favourably impressed with what Rāmarāja had said, and they agreed that they should stand by him. Thereupon, Peddā Nāyaka stood up in his place and declared that he was ready to go into the camp of the enemy to gather the necessary information. And Rāmarāja, who was greatly pleased with the decision of the assembled chiefs, offered the formal *tāmbūla* to Peddā Nāyaka appointing him probably as the captain of the scouts. The conference was then dissolved. *

The Battle of Kōmali (1542-43):—Rāmarāja next moved to the neighbourhood of Gaṇḍikōṭa, where the Pemmasāni chief had considerable influence, in order to collect the troops. The fall of Penugoṇḍa, and the recruitment of troops near Gaṇḍikōṭa were a direct challenge to Tirumala's authority which he could not afford to ignore. If he desired to keep himself in power, he had to take immediate steps to crush his enemy,

* *LR*. 39 p. 16.

while he had not yet become too formidable. Although he was deserted by most of the nobles, he was not left without any following. Among the nobles who adhered to his cause until the very end, the following chiefs deserve to be noticed. The *Bālabhāgavata* mentions a certain chief called Salakaya who was 'a lieutenant of Salakarāju Timmarāja.' * Inscriptions reveal two persons bearing this name. One of them, who is mentioned in an inscription of Kāḷahasti, was the son of a Timmarāja, and he served Salakarāju Tirumala as his *kāryakarta*. † The other Salakaya, who was the son of Minigi Baiyya Nāyaka, was the *pāḷaigār* of Byāḍara Beḍagallu in the Adoni tālūka of the Bellary district. He was the *kāryakarta* of Salakarāju Cikka Tirumaladēva Mahārasu. ‡ It is difficult to determine which of these two Salakayas is the person referred to in the *Bālabhāgavata*. There is some reason, however, for identifying him with the *pāḷaigār* of Byāḍara Beḍagallu. Cintaguṇṭa Raghupati, the *pāḷaigār* of Bētamcarla in the Kurnool district was another adherent of Salakaya Timma. A Raghupatidēva Mahārasu 'a son-in-law of Salakarāju Tirumaladēva Mahārāja,' who is mentioned in a Mysore inscription, § may most probably be the same as the above. In addition to these, a Salakarāju Raghupatidēvayya Mahārāju, and his subordinate, Cintakuṇṭa Siddaya Hanumayadēva Mahārāju make their appearance in an epigraph at

* *The Bhārati* vi. i. p. 865.

"ఏపున ద్రోహిభావము వహించిన సల్కాయ తిమ్మరాజు ద
త్తాపసహాయు సల్కాయ యుతంబుగ శౌర్యముమీర ద్రుంచి వి
ద్యాపురి యందు చాలఘనుఁడయ్యె సదాశివరాయ రాజ్య సం
స్థాపకుఁడై సిరంగ వసుధావర రామనరేంద్రుఁ డున్నతిన్ ॥

† *MER.* 170 of 1924.

‡ *MER.* 524 of 1915.

§ *EC.* v. Bl. 223.

Lēpākṣi. * These also seem to be the partisans of Salakarāju brothers. The fact that Salakarāju Tirumala was able to inflict a defeat upon the Ādil Shāh shows that he still possessed a strong and efficient army on which he could depend for winning him victories.

Tirumala Rāya, therefore, had little hesitation in taking the field against Rāmarāja. He boldly advanced upon Gaṇḍikōṭa and demanded that Pemmasāni Timmā Nāyaka, the lord of the fort, should surrender Rāmarāja to him. But Timmā Nāyaka declined to do so. Moreover, having gathered the forces of the neighbouring *pāḷaigārs*, he marched out of the fortress accompanied by Rāmarāja, and offered battle to the invader. Both the armies met at Kōmali, a village some six miles to the west of Tāḍipatri. In the battle that ensued, the forces of Salakarāju Tirumaladēva broke and fled hotly pursued by the victors. †

The Battles of Bētamcarla and Jūṭūr (1542-43):— The victorious army of Rāmarāja advanced northwards into the province of Kandanavōlu (Kurnool). The reason which prompted them to follow this route is not quite apparent. Probably, the presence of the enemy in the two important strongholds of this region, Bētamcarla and Jūṭūr, may account for it. It is not possible at this distance of time to note the exact sequence of events. There seems to have been considerable fighting in the neighbourhood of Awuku which was the capital of Rāmarāja Tirumala, an uncle of Rāmarāja. As Rāmarāja Tirumala is said to have 'saved the earth which was sinking in the ocean of destruction caused by the monster Salakaya

* *MER.* 680 of 1917. † *LR.* 12 p. 213.

Timma,*' it may be presumed that he had taken the command of his nephew's army. If this assumption is justified, it is only natural that Rāmarāja's army should move to Awuku, which formed an excellent base for conducting military operations against Bētamcarla and other places in its neighbourhood. Akkaya Cina Timmā Nāyaka, a cousin of the captain of Gaṇḍikōṭa, distinguished himself in several engagements throughout this campaign. † Perhaps, he was one of the most active subordinates of Rāmarāja Tirumala.

Meanwhile, the emperor, Salakarāju Tirumala Rāya was not idle. He seems to have been straining every nerve to resist the advance of the enemy. His adherents were actively co-operating with him. Cintaguṇṭa Raghupati, the chief of Bētamcarla, attempted to check the advance of Rāmarāja's army. He was, however, defeated and driven into his fortress, which Cina Timmā Nāyaka besieged and captured. The fort was then razed to the ground. Having cleared the hilly tracts around Awuku of the enemy, Rāmarāja's army moved northwards to Kurnool. Rāmarāja's presence in this region at the time is indicated by two inscriptions at Śrīsailam and Gaḍirēvula respectively bearing

* సలకయ తిమ్మాసుర దు । ర్విలసిత విజయాబ్ధిలగన విహ్వాల వసుధా
వలయాశ్రితకృతి విశ్రుతో । జ్వల తర ధరణీవరాహ వర బిరుదాంకా ॥
Bbm. (The Bhārati vi. i. p. 857.)

† జూటూరి కాడను శూరత్వ మేర్పడ రణభూమిలో సల్కరాజు గెల్చి
కోరి బేతసుచర్ల కోట ధూళిగ జేసి చింతగుంట్రఘుపతి పంతమణచె
బెడకంటి కాడను భీకరాహవముగా వెండియు సల్కని విరుగదోలె
సాహసుండైనట్టి సంజీవఖానుని విదళించి యపు డాదవేని గొనియె
దిమ్మరైనట్టి సలకయ తిమ్మవిభుని । ద్రుంచి రాయల పట్టాన నుంచి తౌర
పృథుల గెల్పుల సురతాని పెమ్మసాని । యక్కభూజాని చినతిమ్మయ
లఘుధమర ॥ *MMss.* 15-3-15.

the date Ś. 1464 (A.D. 1542-43). * At Jūṭūr, however, their path was barred by Salakaya who, assembling his troops at the place, offered battle to the enemy; but he was defeated and driven away. Rāmarāja then entered Kandanavōlu (Kurnool) which was his ancestral seat.

Battle of Beḍagallu (1543) :— Salakaya, although defeated in the battle of Jūṭūr, was not destroyed. He retreated with the remnant of his army to Beḍagallu, his *jāgīr* in the Ādavani *rājya*. † Rāmarāja pursued him, marching his troops along the upper course of the river Tungabhadrā. Salakaya who was obliged to defend his own estate, drew up his forces before Beḍagallu, and awaited the arrival of the enemy. On the approach of Rāmarāja's army fighting commenced. Both the parties fought bravely; but, in the end, Salakaya's troops fled in considerable disorder, and Salakaya himself, unable to resist the might of Rāmarāja any longer, probably retired to Vijayanagara, where he joined his master.

The Fall of Ādavani :—Ādavani was the only fort of any consequence in this region, which still remained in the hands of Salakarāju Tirumala Rāya. He appears to have entrusted the defence of this fort to an enterprising Muhammadan officer called Sanjīva (Sanjār) <u>Kh</u>ān; ‡ however, the fort was besieged, and captured by Cina Timmā Nāyaka who is said to have scattered the <u>Kh</u>ān and his soldiers.

* *LR.* 16. p. 452; *VR.* ii. p. 1181, 178 L; *LR.* 15. p. 345.

† *LR.* 23 p. 24.

‡ సాహసుం డైనట్టి సంజీవ ఖానుని విదళించి యపు డాదవేని గొనియె.

MMss. 15-3-15.

Rāmarāja made the fortress of Ādavani his temporary capital, where he is said to have remained for four months collecting troops from Gadwal, Kurnool and other places. * It was probably on this occasion that he built a palace there, and strengthened the fortifications by erecting several towers at important places. He is also believed to have laid the foundations of Śukravārapupēṭa, one of the suburbs. †

Section 3 :—Rāmarāja, having completed his preparations, finally advanced upon Vijayanagara about the middle of A.D. 1543. He appears to have reached the neighbourhood of the capital in the middle of Bhādrapada of Śōbhakṛt Ś. 1465. An inscription at Niṭṭūr in the Bellary tālūka records a double grant of Sadāśiva. He made a gift of the village of Niṭṭūr in the Tekkalakōṭa *sīma* to the God Viṭṭhaladēva for the merit of Acyutadēvarāya. Moreover, on the order of the Rāya, a *sarvamānya* grant was also made to Madanūr Caṇḍa Vināyaka, so that Rāmarājayya might obtain 'all kinds of merit.' ‡ This inscription shows that Śadāśiva and Rāmarāja were very close to the capital. Salakarāju Tirumala Rāya should have become very apprehensive of his own safety. In despair, he turned to Ibrahim Ādil Shāh, and requested him 'to march to his assistance, in return for which he promised to acknowledge himself tributary, and to pay down a sum of three lakhs of hoons for avery day's march his army might make.' §

* *The Sources* p. 180.

† *LR.* 10. pp. 9-32.

cf. *Ferishta*: "The rays of Beejanuggur," says he, "regarding it (Ādavani) as impregnable, had all contributed to make it a convenient asylum for their families ; and it was fortified with eleven walls, one within another, so that it appeared impossible to reduce it by force." Brigg's *Ferishta* iii p. 134.

‡ *ICD*. p. 399.

§ Brigg's *Ferishta* iii. p. 83.

The offer which the needy emperor made to the Sultān was indeed very tempting. Asad Khān, the most influential of the Sultān's ministers, advised him to accept the offer and proceed to Vijayanagara. Acting upon this advice, Ibrahim Ādil Shāh, 'moved from his capital' and 'arrived at Beejanuggur without opposition.' On his arrival, he was met by Tirumala Rāya who conducted him into the city and seated him on the royal throne. He is also said to have celebrated a festival for several days, in honour of the arrival of the august guest.*

The conduct of Tirumala Rāya on this occasion must have permanently alienated the sympathy of the nobles. They remembered with horror the atrocities committed by the Muhammadans in the past. Having realised that open resistance was useless under the circumstances, they feigned contrition for having revolted against him. In accordance with their professions, they wrote letters to Tirumala Rāya expressing their regret for their rebellious conduct, and promised to be loyal to him for ever, provided that he would persuade his Muhammadan ally to depart to his own kingdom. Rāmarāja gave him a separate undertaking that he would remain for ever loyal to Tirumala Rāya, if he 'would cause the retreat of the king of Bijāpūr to his dominions.'

Tirumala Rāya believed that Rāmarāja and other nobles were sincere in their protestations of loyalty. Feeling that he no longer required the services of his Muhammadan ally, he 'paid down fifty lakhs of hoons, the amount of the settled subsidy,' and making several other valuable presents requested the

* Brigg's *Ferishta* iii. p. 84.

Sultān to return to his capital. The Ādil Shāh then retreated towards his frontier with all his army. *

The departure of the Sultān was the signal for the universal outburst of feelings of indignation against Tirumala Rāya. Rāmarāja and the majority of the nobles who joined him, 'broke their promises,' and began to make brisk preparations to march upon Vijayanagara, and punish the traitor. Several captains, who remained faithful to Tirumala Rāya until then, began to desert him, and his military strength began to show a tendency to dwindle down rapidly. Having resolved to risk a final battle with his enemies before his followers completely deserted him, he placed himself at the head of such troops as he could gather, and marched out in search of the enemy, and lay encamped somewhere on the bank of the Tungabhadrā.

The Battle of the Tungabhadrā (1543):— Meanwhile, Rāmarāja who was at Ādavani or somewhere in the neighbourhood, sent spies to ascertain the movements of Tirumala Rāya's army. He instructed them to penetrate into Tirumala's camp and tamper with the loyalty of his troops. The spies spread a rumour that Tirumala under whom they were serving was only a shepherd by caste, and that it would be a sin to assist him, although he was wealthy. Moreover, they offered his captains bribes on behalf of Rāmarāja, so that they began to entertain ideas of deserting their master, whose star commenced to set. In the meantime, Rāmarāja who was informed of Tirumala's whereabouts marched upon his camp and fell upon it so suddenly that he was taken completely by surprise. The captains of his army deserting him at the same time, he

* Brigg's *Ferishta* iii. p. 84.

considered it prudent to seek safety in flight. As he was fleeing accompanied by a few retainers, he was overtaken by Rāmarāja's officers, who promptly beheaded him and hoisted his head on a flag-staff so that every one might see that the traitor was at last slain.*

* *The Sources* p. 180; *LR.* 12 p. 213; *LR.* 39 p. 16.

There is considerable difference of opinion among historians regarding the manner of Salakarāju Tirumala Rāya's death. Ferishta's account, being most familiar and dramatic, is considered genuine. According to him, 'Ibrahim Ādil Shāh had not yet recrossed the Krishna when Ramraj and the confederates who had bribed many of the troops in the city, broke their promises and hastened towards Beejanuggur, resolving to put the Ray to death, on pretence of revenging the murder of his predecessor. Bhoj Tirumal Ray, finding he was betrayed, shut himself up in the palace, and becoming mad from despair, blinded all the royal elephants and horses, and cut off their tails that they might be of no use to the enemy. All the diamonds, rubies, emeralds, and other precious stones and pearls, which had been collected in the course of many ages, he crushed to powder between heavy millstones and scattered them on the ground. He then fixed a sword blade into a pillar of his apartment, and ran his breast upon it with such force that it pierced through and came out at his back; thus putting an end to his existence, just as the gates of the palace were opened to his enemies." Brigg's *Ferishta* iii. p. 83.

But Ferishta's account is contradicted by several contemporary as well as later writers:

(1) Contemporary: (*a*) The earliest of them is Dōnēru Kōnērinātha, the author of the *Bālabhāgavatam*, a work which the author finished in A.D. 1549, six years after the death of Salakarāju Tirumala. He definitely states that Tirumala was killed by Rāmarāja in battle.

ఏపున ద్రోహిభావము వహించిన సల్కయతిమ్మరాజు ద
త్పాపసహాయు సల్కయ యుతంబుగ శౌర్యముమీర ద్రుంచి
* * * సిరంగవసుధావర రామనరేంద్రుడున్నతిన్ ॥

(*b*) Rāmarājabhūṣaṇa, who was a protégé of Rāmarāja, states that Rāmarāja killed Salakarāju Tirumala in battle:—

ఖలజనస్థానవాసుల బల్విర వధించి మహిమ సలక ఖర స్వాయు మడంచి
హారివీరభట మహోద్ధతి నబ్ధి గంపింప దురమున గదిసి తద్ద్రోహి దునిమి.

(*c*) Similarly, the poet, Mūrti, refers to Salakarāju Tirumala's death on the battle-field:

ఖలు నత్రిదోహి సల్కయతిమ్మని హరించి సకల కర్ణాటదేశంబు నిలిపె

Rāmarāja then ordered his troops to march upon the capital. The news of the battle of the Tungabhadrā seems to have reached it much earlier than the victorious army. It is said that Tirumaladēvī and Cinnadēvī, the queens of Kṛṣṇadēvarāya, were overjoyed to hear the tidings of victory. They commanded the ministers of Tirumala Rāya to surrender the capital.* The ministers hastened to obey the order. Meanwhile, the army approached the capital; and the new sovereign, Sadāśiva Rāya, and his all powerful regent entered it in a triumphant procession, according to one inscription, on Kārttika śu 11 of the cyclic year Śōbhakṛt corresponding to Śaka 1465.† Sadāśiva's coronation was celebrated a few days later with great pomp and festivity.

(*d*) Rangapparāju, the author of the ***Sāmbōpākhyānam***, describes the death of Salakarāju Cina Timmakṣmāpati in battle.

మహిఁ నెవ్వారెన సలకరాజ చినతిమ్మక్ష్మాప కంఠారుణాం
బుహావిశ్చర్వణ తర్పి తాసి శిఖికిన్ ....రామప్పకున్ ॥

(2) Later: Zabīri, the Muhammadan historian, also refers to the death of Salakarāju Tirumala in battle.

In spite of the testimony of so many contemporary and later writers, Father Heras violates one of his own canons of scientific historical composition by clinging to the melodramatic story of Ferishta, who does not deserve one tenth of the adoration which the Rev. Father lavishes upon him, His reason for accepting Ferishta's evidence in preference to that of contemporary writers is that the former gives 'greater details.' A curious position, indeed, for a scientific historian! Does truth depend upon details? For our part we prefer to accept the evidence of contemporary authors, and treat Ferishta's account in the same way in which we are accustomed to treat historical romances.

* *The Sources* p. 180.

† *L.R.* 46 (Udayagiri No. 1); cf. *MER.* 800 of 1917.

PART II

ADMINISTRATIVE INSTITUTIONS

CHAPTER I

THE CENTRAL GOVERNMENT

Section 1: *The Emperor*: --The emperor was the supreme head of the state. Although his power was not checked by any outside body like a council of nobles, or a popular assembly, it cannot be termed undiluted absolutism, as it was subjected to certain restrictions. According to the principles of Hindu political science, the king or the emperor had to regulate the *Dharma* as laid down by the *Dharma Śāstras*; and he could not go against them. The emperors of Vijayanagara during the 16th century were as much subject to the reign of *Dharma* as any monarch during the early ages. According to the *Dharma Śāstras*, a Brahman should not be put to death, whatever crime he might commit. During the time of Kṛṣṇadēvarāya, the greatest monarch whom South India had ever seen, a Brahman was believed to have committed a crime which affected the emperor personally. Kṛṣṇarāya crowned his six year old son, Tirumaladēva, about 1524 A. D; and 'having abdicated his throne and all his power and name', he 'gave it all to his son, and himself became his minister.' He made Sāḷuva Timma, his own minister, the counsellor of the new emperor. Eight months after his coronation, Tirumaladēva 'fell sick of a disease' and died. After his death, Kṛṣṇarāya learnt that his son was poisoned by Timma Daṇṇāik, the son of Sāḷuva Timma. 'In his anger,' Kṛṣṇarāya believed that what he had heard was true. Therefore, he summoned Sāḷuva Timma, his sons, brothers, and relations, and having deprived them of all their estates and titles, imprisoned them all; but Timma Daṇṇāik escaped from prison, and stirred up a rebellion against the emperor in a mountainous province; the rebellion was, however, put down, and Timma Daṇṇāik was taken prisoner to Vijayanagara. He and his relations who committed high treason were not put to death as they deserved; they were merely blinded and sent back to prison. *

Nuniz gives the explanation for the comparative mild punishment inflicted on the prisoners.

"After he (Timma Daṇṇāik) had so come, the king commanded him to be brought before him, with Sallavatinica, his father, and another brother of his who was kept in prison, and he sent them to the place of executions, and there had their eyes put out, *for in this country, they do not put Brahmans to death, but only inflict some punishment, so that they remain alive.*" †

Here is an instance where the emperor had to submit to the injunctions of the *Dharma*, although he might have been inclined to inflict the extreme penalty of the law upon the rebels. In addition to the *Dharma*, the custom of the country must also have served as another check upon the arbitrary exercise of his power.

The emperor could, if he wished, be very oppressive and tyrannical even under these checks. His subjects had no means of legally getting their grievances redressed. They could, of course, in the last extremity rise up in rebellion against the oppressor; but the idea of rebellion did not appeal to them much. There were, no doubt, several rebellions against the Rāyas; but not one of them had any popular support. They

* *FE*. pp. 359-60.

† *ibid* p 361. (cf *Barbosa* i. p. 217.) "Among them all these men (Bramenes) hold the greatest liberties and privileges and *are not liable to death for anything whatsoever which they do.*"

frequently had recourse to less violent but more effective methods of settling their differences with the crown, when oppression became unendurable. The subjects of the emperor, occasionally joined together for opposing the collection of taxes by the tax-collectors. They would even threaten persons who helped the tax-gatherers and Brahman land holders in collecting the taxes with corporal punishment. * More generally, however, they would abandon the emperor's dominions altogether, and migrate to some place beyond his reach. In certain cases, the emigration involved complete desertion of their homes and farms by all the ryots in certain areas, where, as a consequence, agriculture was totally ruined and the imperial exchequer suffered considerable loss of revenue. Several migrations of the kind are recorded in the inscriptions; but the most important one, during the period, is the complete evacuation of the ryots of the Kavutāḷa *sīma* mentioned in an inscription dated 1533 A.D. † Thus, when the tyranny of the government became insufferable, the ryots forced them to redress their grievances by striking at the root of the state's prosperity. The method adopted by the subjects of the Vijayanagara emperor was certainly less demonstrative than an open rebellion, but more effective as it secured them a bloodless victory.

Section 2: *The Council*:—One of the seven members of the state recognized by the ancient Hindu politicians, was the *mantri* or the minister. The importance of the minister in a kingdom is forcibly described by an ancient Telugu writer thus: "A king who governs a kingdom without a minister is like an

* *MER.* 92 of 1918.

† *MMss.* 19-1-4; *LR.* 40 pp. 338-41; *MER.* (B) 492 of 1915.

elephant that goes about without the trunk." * Maḍiki Singana, a contemporary of Dēvarāya II, declares in his *Sakalanītisammata*, that "as a king gets everything done with the aid of his counsellors, he should surround himself with them. He should not consider that he could secure the counsellors, financiers and commanders when he wanted their services; for that would be like an attempt to dig a well to extinguish the fire burning a house." † In another place, the same author observes, "when a king knowing nothing, attempts with much pride to discharge his duties either without consulting his ministers or going against their advice, he falls an easy prey to his enemies who deprive him of his wealth and dominion." ‡ The importance of the counsellors is also indicated by a soliloquy which is attributed to Kṛṣṇadēvarāya in the *Rāyavācaka*:

> "We have been placed upon the throne. That is all. Everything in the world is really done by the counsellors. Who will listen to us? If we follow an independent course of action in the exercise of our authority, nothing will be done owing to divided counsels." §

It is obvious that the emperor of Vijayanagara did not govern the empire without counsellors. They were at times so powerful as to create a feeling of helplessness in the mind of the emperor himself. The *Manucaritra* gives a brief but poetic description of the

* *Sumati*:

మండలపతి సముఖంబున
మెండైన ప్రధాని లేక మెలగుట యెల్లన్ ।
కొండంత మదపుటేనుగు
తొండము లేకుండినట్లు దోచుర సుమతీ ॥

† *Sns.* (The Āndhra Granthamāla) p. 83.

‡ *ibid.* p. 79.

§ *ASPP.* iii. p. 30.

sabhā or the royal assembly as it existed during the time of Kṛṣṇadēvarāya. To this assembly called *Bhuvanavijaya*, flocked the *amaranāyakas* and their representatives, chiefs of subordinate states, princes, *daḷavāys*, merchants, ambassadors from foreign states, pandits, poets, philosophers, theologians, and all those that depended upon the court for eking out a living.* The *Āmuktamālyada* alludes to the *sabhā* which was attended by the ambassadors from foreign kingdoms.† It was here that the emperor gave audience to the representatives of foreign rulers, and heard the disputations of rival theologians and pandits; it was here that Vallabha, Caitanya, ‡ Vyāsatīrtha, and Tātācārya vaxed eloquent over the excellence of their respective creeds; and it was here that Peddana, Timmana, Dhūrjati, Radhāmādhava and a host of others received certificates, and rewards for the beautiful and melodious poems which they had composed. §

This large and unwieldy assembly was not, however, a suitable place for transacting state business. For this purpose, there existed a small, compact body which consisted of the emperor's ministers, and some of his captains whom he held in great esteem. The distinction between the royal assembly and the ministerial council is brought out by Paes in his chronicle:

* *Mc.* 1: 12-13 (Vāviḷḷa edition).

† *Ām.* 1: 18-4: 259 (Kaḷāprapūrṇa's edition).

‡ *EC.* ix. Cp. 1.

§ రాధామాధవ మచ్యుతాంకితముగా బ్రౌఢక్రియం జెప్పి త
న్మాధుర్యంబున గృష్ణరాయవిభుఁ గర్ణాటేశు మెప్పించి నా
నాధాతృప్రతిమాన సత్కవులలోనన్ భూషణశ్రేణితో
రాధామాధవ నామ మందిన జగత్ప్రఖ్యాత చారిత్రుఁడన్ ॥

Tbm. *canto* 1.

"Thence he (the king) goes to a building made in the shape of a porch without walls, which has many pillars hung with cloths right up to the top, and with the walls handsomely painted. . . . In such a building *he despatches his work with those men who bear office in his kingdom, and govern his cities, and his favourites talk with them.* The greatest favourite is an old man called Temersea. . . After the king has talked with these men on subjects pleasing to him, he bids enter the lords and captains who wait at the gate, and these at once enter to make their salaam to him." *

The meeting of the king with his officers and favourites was evidently his council ; and it was transformed into an assembly by the admission of lords and captains. The *Acyutarāyābhyudayam* refers to a gathering held in the *Venkaṭavilāsa manṭapa*, † which was probably the name of Acyuta's council chamber. It was in this *manṭapa* that the prime minister submitted to the emperor a report about the progress of Sāḷuvanāyaka's rebellion. As soon as he heard the report, the emperor summoned the commander-in-chief to his presence. Probably, the commander-in-chief had no place in the council.

According to the *Āmuktamālyada*, the counsellors should preferably be Brahmans of good character, learned in the political science. They should be of fifty or sixty years in age. If, however, a monarch could not secure such counsellors, he should get the work done by others, always keeping the right of decision to himself, and conducting the affairs of state according to the requirements of the *Dharma*. ‡

The small council where the emperor transacted state business was evidently his privy council, where the administrative problems were discussed and foreign policy shaped. Usually the ministers were the only people that attended the meetings of the council ; but

* *FE.* p. 250. † *The Sources* p. 162. ‡ *Ām.* 4 : 211-213.

the emperor could summon to the council any one whom he liked. Moreover, it was not obligatory that he should discuss matters with all the councillors at a meeting. He could consult the prime minister, or some other councillor, ignoring the others altogether.

The meetings of the council were held in secret. Any councillor divulging the secrets of the council chamber was severely dealt with. * The emperor, at any rate Kṛṣṇarāya, used to summon the council frequently. Both the *Rāyavācaka*, and the Portuguese chronicles allude to several meetings of the council. It was not obligatory that the emperor should accept the council's decision; he might ignore it, if he chose to do so. Although on certain occasions he accepted the decision of the council as against his own, he preferred his own judgment to that of his councillors on others. Nuniz reports two meetings of the council, on the eve of Kṛṣṇadēvarāya's declaration of war on the Ādil Shāh. Having decided to wage war on the Ādil Shāh, he summoned his council to discuss the problem with his councillors, and discover a suitable pretext for breaking the peace that then existed between the two states. When the council met, Sāḷuva Timma proposed that the Rāya should demand the surrender of certain refugees who had taken shelter in the Ādil Shāh's dominions.

> "Salvatinia said that since the peace had been made under certain conditions—one of which was that if on either one side or the other any land-owners, captains in revolt, or other evil-doers should be harboured, and their surrender should be demanded, they should forthwith be given up—there was now great reason for breaking the peace, since many land-owners and debtors to His Highness had fled into the kingdom of the Ydallcão. He counselled therefore that the King should send to demand the surrender of these men, and that on refusal to give them up there would be good ground for breaking the peace." †

* *Ām.* 4 : 252.

† *FE.* p. 323.

Evidently, Sāḷuva Timma had in mind the ryots of the Kavutāḷa *sīma* who were then living in the territory belonging to the Sultān of Bijāpūr. Sāḷuva Timma's proposal, however, did not find much support in the council, and several councillors are said to have opposed it.

"Many, however, disagreed with this advice. Now it happened at this time that the King (of Bisnaga) sent Cide Mercar with forty thousand *pardaos* to Goa to buy horses, which Cide Mercar was a Moor in whom the King of Bisnaga confided on account of various affairs with which he had already been entrusted; and this man, when he arrived at a place where the Moors lived which was called Pomdaa, and is two leagues from Goa, fled from that place, Pomdaa, to the Ydallcão, carrying with him all the treasure." *

This matter was brought to the notice of the Rāya; and it was pointed out that the surest way to break the peace was to demand the surrender of the Sayyed. The emperor, having agreed with them, sent a letter to the Sultān demanding the surrender of the faithless horse-dealer. Here is an instance of the emperor's agreement with the views of his councillors.

The Ādil Shāh sent a courteous refusal to surrender the Sayyed. Thereupon Kṛṣṇarāya summoned another meeting of the council. Having read to his counsellors the reply of the Ādil Shāh, he bade them be ready to march upon the port of Dabull in the Ādil Shāh's dominions, where the treacherous Sayyed was then believed to be hiding.

"But the councillors advised the King, saying that for such a small sum of money as this it was not well so to act; that he should think of what would be said and talked of throughout the world." †

* *FE.* p. 323.

† *ibid.* p. 324.

In other words, the council advised the emperor not to declare war upon the Ādil Shāh.

"The councillors, however, saw that the King remained unmoved from his determination to make war, and they then counselled him, saying,—"Sire, do not go to war by that route (Dabull), but go against Rachol." "The King held this advice to be good, and prepared for his departure. . ." *

Although the Rāya accepted the advice of his councillors on a minor point, he rejected it on the major issue. The right of accepting or rejecting the council's advice belonged to the emperor, and therefore the council could not make its decisions binding.

The emperor was expected to work hard in the discharge of his duties. Although Acyuta is said to have neglected to perform his duties, Vīra Narasimha, Kṛṣṇarāya, and Rāmarāya (the *de facto* ruler of the empire during Sadāśiva's reign) appear to have devoted most of their time to the administrative work of the state. The day was divided into a number of equal divisions, each of which was utilised by the emperor for the despatch of the work of a particular kind. The imperial programme of daily work has been preserved in the works of four writers. A comparative study of these four versions seems to show that each emperor had his own programme of work which might or might not agree with those of others. †

* *FE.* p. 325.

†

Vīra Narasimha	Kṛṣṇarāya	Kṛṣṇarāya	Acyuta
Rāyavācaka:	Nuniz	*Āmuktamālyada*:—	Tirumalācārya's *Nītiśīsapadya śataka*
	Before daylight		Before meal.
1. *Brāhmī Muhūrta*: Waking up, and listening to the reading of devotional literature.	1. Drinking of gingelly oil; exercise in the gymnasium, and riding.	1. First *yāma*:— Waking up; audience to the Brahmans, physicians and astrologers who come to inquire after the king's health.	1. Bath, short meditation, and worshipping the deity.

Section 3 : *Ministers* :—The emperor was assisted by his ministers in carrying out the administrative work. The qualifications which Kṛṣṇarāya expected his ministers to possess were indeed very high. The policy of recruiting the ministers mostly from the Brahman community was continued until almost to the middle of the century. The confidence which Kṛṣṇarāya placed in the Brahmans was thoroughly

Vīra Narasimha	Kṛṣṇarāya	Kṛṣṇarāya	Acyuta
2. Looking at his own face in the mirror, touching the black cow, seeing the face of Brahmans, cleaning the teeth, washing the face, and wearing the caste-mark (*vibhūti*).	2. Bath.	2. Second *yāma* :—Audience to the ministers, *sāmantas*, secretaries &c.	2. Paying respects to the Brahmans, and listening to the Purāṇas.
	After sunrise		
3 Acceptance of the *tirtha* and the *prasāda* of the 108 *Tirupatis* ; enquiry into the conditions of temples, *maṭhas* &c.	3. Visit to the Pagoda for worship.	3. The middle of the day ; conversation with wrestlers, hunters, and the cooks of the royal kitchen.	3 Gifts ; concerting measures to put down thieves and enemies.
4. Admission to *daṇṇāiks* in charge of provinces, and enquiry into the condition of provinces, forts &c. Admission to the *talāri* of the city and listening to his report.	4. The audience.	4. Afternoon : Worship of the deity, conversation with wise men, officers of justice, and ascetics ; meal.	4. Concerting measures for the protection of his men, horses and elephants.
5. Admission of the nine secretaries of state.	......	5. Conversation with the court-fool ; listening to the Purāṇas and discussion with the poets.	5. Consultations with friends, ministers and the *purōhit*.
6. Perusal of foreign correspondence.	......	6. Fourth *yāma* :—Audience to the spies, musicians &c.	6. Enquiry about the means of increasing the extent and the wealth of the kingdom ; meal.
			After meal :
7. Admission of ministers and *daḷavāys*.	......	7. Sleep at night in the company of the queen.	7. Music, poetry and amusements.
8. General audience for all.	......	......	8. Audience to the spies, and sleep in secrecy.

justified by the work of his ministers. The prosperity of the kingdom was fostered to a very great extent by the sagacious statesmanship of Sāḷuva Timma. Besides, Rāyasam Timmarasa, Koṇḍamarasa, Ayyaparasa, Rāmābhaṭlayya, and a host of others rendered yeomen service to the empire. *

No information is available at present about the number of ministers serving the crown at any given time. Each minister held office as long as he retained the favour and goodwill of his sovereign. The moment he lost them, even the mightiest minister had to go. This was, of course, true only of the strong monarchs; but the ministers could have more or less their own way under weak rulers. The most important of the ministers was the *sarvaśiraḥpradhāna* or the prime minister, † who was 'the second person' in the kingdom. He commanded the whole imperial household, and all the great lords behaved to him as towards the king. He was the head of the administration in the absence of the king. ‡ Sāḷuva Timma held this high office during the reigns of Vīra Narasimha and Kṛṣṇarāya; and Sāḷuva Nāyaka and Salakarāju Peda Tirumala held it in the time of Acyuta. A minister called *upapradhāna* is occasionally mentioned in the inscriptions, though it is not stated what his duties were. § Another minister of the state was *bhāṇḍāgārika* or the chief treasurer. ¶ The *Rāyavācaka*

* cf. Nuniz (*FE*. p. 390) "They (the Brahmans) are honest men, very acute and of much talent, and very good at accounts, lean men, well-formed but little fit for hard work. By these and by the duties they undertake the kingdom is carried on."

† *LR*. viii. p. 112; *EC*. iii Tn. 120; *LR*. 57 pp. 222-27.

‡ *FE*. p. 250.

§ *MER*. 689 of 1922.

¶ *EC*. ix. Cp. 152, 155.

furnishes the name of *dharmāsanādhikāri* or the minister in charge of law and religious endowments. * There must have been several others; but their designations, and the nature of the duties which they discharged have not been preserved in any of the known sources.

* *ASPP.* iii. p. 12.

CHAPTER II

THE SECRETARIAT

Section 1: The Sampratis:—Occasional references in the inscriptions seem to indicate that the work of the central government was apportioned among a number of departments; but the evidence is not sufficient to enable us to ascertain the number of the departments, and their mutual interrelation.

The *Rāyavācaka* mentions in two places a set of nine officials called *sampratis.* * The word *samprati* is defined as the head *karṇam* or the chief accountant who is at the head of several *karṇams* or accountants. He may be called the chief secretary. The nine *sampratis* of the *Rāyavācaka* should be taken to mean the nine chief secretaries to the government. The nature of the work of these nine *sampratis* is nowhere clearly stated. It is urged that each of the nine *sampratis* was placed in charge of the accounts of a *durga* or *rājya*; † but this view is not tenable; for even during the time of Vīra Narasimha when the extent of the empire was at its lowest, there were twelve provinces besides the territories of the tributary princes. If the accounts of a *durga* or *rājya* were kept by a *samprati*, there ought to have existed more than nine *sampratis*. Apart from this, the *Rāyavācaka* seems to point in a different direction. It is said, in one place, that Vīra Narasimha 'summoned the nine *sampratis* to the palace; and they came and explained to him the accounts of the nineteen ports of the empire.' ‡ It

* *ASPP.* iii. pp. 13, 29.

† M. S. Sarma: *The Sarada* i. p. 274.

‡ *ASPP.* iii. p. 13.

would appear from this that the nine *sampratis* were officials who maintained the accounts of the ports. That this inference is not correct is shown by another passage from the same work :

"One day, Kṛṣṇadēvarāya summoned to his presence in the audience hall the nine *sampratis*, and commanded them to produce accounts on the following items : the number of provinces in the empire, and the amount of money collected therefrom ; the number of mountain fastnesses, forts, forest strongholds, and fortifications surrounded by water ; the number of forts and villages ; the amount of money that stood to the credit of each *durga* or *rājya* in the account books of the treasury ; the amount of cash, and the value of jewellery and precious stones of nine kinds ; the value of the buried treasure ; the money which the *maṇiagars* of (different) *sīmas* had paid ; and the unpaid balance standing against their names ; and the description of the imperial forces (infantry, cavalry, and elephants) that received their salary directly from the treasury." *

According to this passage, the *sampratis* were in charge of accounts of several branches of administration mostly connected with the treasury. Were the nine *sampratis*, the officials of the treasury ? This could

* *ASPP.* iii. p. 29. cf. *Pym.* vi. Tiruvengaḷanātha gives an interesting account of the *sampratis.*

అకట ! యెన్నాళ్లాయె నాకార ! నగరి
కోశకాను చెల్లింప కున్నాఁడ టంచుఁ
గరముల మీస లొక్కట దీటికొనుచు
బెరయంగ గరణాల బిలువు డటన్నఁ
పసమించు తెలివలిపంపు బింజియలు
పొసగ జుట్టినయట్టి బోడకుల్లాలు
చింపి కుప్పసములు చెవి దోరములను
సంపుటంబులతోడ జంపాడు నోడలు
బిగువుగా జెంప దోపిన బలపములును
తగ నలవడ నత్తఱిఁ గరణికులు
చనుదెంచి నిలిచి హస్తములు మోడ్చుటయుం.

not have been the case; for there would have been only one head *karṇam* of the treasury and not nine. In fact, the *Rāyavācaka* distinguishes him from the other *sampratis*. It speaks of Allālanātha, the *samprati*, of *Cinna Bhaṇḍāram* or the Small Treasury. If Allālanātha was the *samprati* of the treasury, the remaining eight *sampratis* must have been in charge of accounts of the eight other departments. What these eight were, it is not possible to assert definitely, but some of them may be surmised.

Section 2: The Rāyābhaṇḍāram or the Imperial Treasury:—The *Rāyavācaka* refers, as noticed already, to Allālanātha, the *samprati* of 'the Small Treasury.' * Although it is not easy to state the exact significance of the term, 'Small Treasury,' it is permissible to infer the existence of another treasury called 'the Big Treasury.' Paes, the Portuguese chronicler, throws some light on the subject.

"And now I wish you to know that the previous kings of this place for many years past have held it a custom to maintain a treasury, which treasury, after the death of each is kept locked and sealed in such a way that it cannot be seen by any one, nor opened, nor do the kings who succeed to the kingdom open them or know what is in them. They are not opened except when the kings have great need, and thus the kingdom has great supplies to meet its needs." †

The existence of this treasury is also alluded to in the *Rāyavācaka*:

"The wealth which Vidyāraṇya buried for the emperor, at the time of the foundation of the capital, amounts to 96 crores and 56 lakhs of *varahas*. The value of jewellery amounts to 4 crores of *varahas*; the precious stones (of nine varieties) are valued at 6 crores of *varahas*. *Besides, the money which the previous*

* *ASPP.* iii. p. 29.

† *FE.* p. 282.

emperors deposited in the treasury, after defraying their expenses amounts to 19 crores and 56 lakhs of *varahas*." *

The Big Treasury whose existence has been inferred must have been identical with the treasuries of the previous monarchs since the time of Harihara I and Bukka I. The Small Treasury of the *Rāyavācaka* should be identified with that belonging to the reigning monarch. Paes says:

"This king, has made his treasury different from those of the previous kings, and he puts in it every year ten million *pardaos* without taking from them one *pardao* more than for the expenses of his house." †

Besides these, inscriptions allude to 'the Golden Treasury' ‡ and 'the Diamond Treasury.' § Nothing more is known about the former. It is not possible to say whether it was the same as the 'Small Treasury.' Probably it was different. Some interesting information is available about the Diamond Treasury. According to Nuniz, all the diamonds exceeding twenty *megellinis* in weight coming from the mines of Vajra-Karūr were given 'to the king for his treasury.' ¶

The accounts of the Small as well as the Big Treasury appear to have been kept by one *samprati*; for the accounts of both the treasuries were explained by Allālanātha of the Small Treasury. The Small Treasury was the only one that had anything to do with the administration of the empire; for the big one remained closed almost always. The work of the Big Treasury could have employed but a few clerks. That seems to have been the reason why Allālanātha was left in charge of it. The mint was attached to the

* *ASPP.* iii. p. 29. † *FE.* p. 282.

‡ *MER.* 280 of 1918. § *ibid* 387 of 1918. ¶ *FE.* p. 389.

treasury. Owing probably to its association with the treasury, the affairs of the latter became mixed up with those of the other departments. The observations of Abdur Razāk are instructive in this connection.

> "The usage of the country is that at a stated period every one throughout the whole empire carries to the mint the revenue which is due from him, and whoever has money due to him from the exchequer receives an order upon the mint. The *sipāhis* receive their pay every four months, and no one has an assignment granted to him on provinces." *

Why Allālanātha of the Small Treasury was commanded to produce accounts pertaining to several matters apparently unconnected with the treasury, has now become intelligible in the light of Abdur Razāk's remarks.

The Golden Treasury had a separate office of its own. Rāyasam Timmarasa, one of Kṛṣṇarāya's officers was its secretary in A. D. 1527. † Similarly, the Diamond Treasury had its own officer. During the early years of Acyutarāya, a certain Lakki Seṭṭi is said to have been its head. ‡ Allālanātha, Timmarasa, and Lakki Seṭṭi were mere secretaries, and it is doubtful whether they had seats in the emperor's council.

All the four treasuries were probably under the control of a single officer of ministerial rank. The inscriptions of Acyuta's early years reveal the name of a certain *Bhaṇḍārada* Timmappa, son of Tipparasa. § It is said in one record that he was the lord of the treasury; ¶ in another he is called Timmappaya of the Rāya's treasury; ** in a third he is described as

* *ED.* iv. p. 109.

† *MER.* 280 of 1918.

‡ *ibid* 387 of 1918.

§ *MER.* 179 of 1913.

¶ *EC.* ix. Cp. 74.

** *ibid* Cp. 155.

Timmappaya, the lord of Acyutarāya's treasury.* It is reasonable to believe that during the 16th century at Vijayanagara, all the treasuries were placed under the control of a single officer of ministerial rank who was probably one of the members of the council.

Section 3: The Religious Endowment Department:—The *Rāyavācaka* introduces a certain Dharmāsanam Dharmayya as one of the principal officers of Vīra Narasimha. The name Dharmayya of the *Dharmāsana* would lead one to the belief that he was connected with the administration of justice. Probably he had something to do with the court of justice in the capital; but according to the *Rāyavācaka*, he was the superintendent of the *brahmādāyas* or the tax-free lands granted to the Brahmans.† An inscription of the Canarese country mentions the *dharmapārupatya* of Aḷiya Rāmarāya. In the capacity of *dharmapārupatyagāra*, he comman[illegible] copy of the *dānaśāsana* which Kṛṣṇarāya granted to the temple of Viṭṭhala to be brought before him so that he might go through the document before passing orders regarding certain landed property of the temple.‡ A very damaged inscription coming from the Bellary district alludes to an office where copies of the *dānaśāsanas* were kept by the government.§ The *Āmuktamālyada* refers to an

* *EC*. ix. Cp. 152.

† *ASPP*. iii. pp. 12-13.

1. "ధర్మాసనం ధర్మయ్యను పిలువనంపగా ఆయనవచ్చి నిలిచి దేవరవారు ఆనతిచ్చినప్రకారం ద్రావిడరాజ్యములోగల అగ్రహారములున్ను ఆంధ్రదేశం, హొయిసనదేశం, మొరసునాడు, ములునాడు, కర్ణాటకం, ఘట్టిశీమ, చేర, చోర, పాండ్య, మగధ, మళయ ఆదిగాగల అగ్రహారములకున్ను అవధి ఆటంకములులేక నిత్యకర్మానుష్ఠానపరులై .... సుఖ వసతిగా వున్నారని విన్నపం శాయగా."

‡ *EC*. xi. Mk. 1.

§ *M Mss*. (Guṇḍiganūr) 19-1-4.

officer in charge of the temple properties and other charitable endowments. * A passage occurring in a charter which a subordinate of Sāḷuva Govindarāja granted to a temple in A.D. 1523 shows that all the temple properties were under the control and supervision of the government.

> "The *pārupatyagāra* (*dharma ?*) has no authority to inquire into the affairs of this god." †

It is reasonable to suppose that all the charitable endowments—the *dēvādāya*, the *brahmādāya*, and the *maṭhapura*—were placed under the control of a single officer who was probably a minister of the crown.

Section 4: The Aṭṭhavaṇa:—The *aṭṭhavaṇa* or the revenue department was the most important of all. The officials of this department were directly responsible to the prime minister. The *aṭṭhavaṇa* is mentioned in a record of about A.D. 1515. ‡ According to the *Aṭṭhavaṇatantra* all the affairs connected with the revenue of the state were under the jurisdiction of the *aṭṭhavaṇa* or the *sīmāmūla*. § At the central office of the department, registers containing the description of the boundaries of villages, *sthalas*, *sīmas*, *nāḍus*, and *rājyas*; their respective areas; the names of land-owners with the extent of their holdings, and the crops raised thereon; and the details of revenue due from each ryot and village were maintained. If the Local Records may be trusted, these registers were consulted by the local officials and the ryots from time to time. ¶

* *Ām.* 4: 218.

† *EC.* iv. Ch. 99.

‡ *EC.* xi. Jl. 7.

§ *MMss.* 15-6-8.

¶ *LR.* 1. (Nandipāḍ) p. 267. In a village dispute about the boundaries which was taken before Dēvarāya II (A. D. 1428), the parties were directed to go back to their villages and settle their dispute in the presence of the *reḍḍis*, *karṇams* and elders of the neighbouring villages, *according to the directions contained in Royal Records.*

Probably, the accounts pertaining to the *dēvādāya*, *brahmādāya*, and *maṭhapura* lands were entered in separate books. A section, perhaps, of the *aṭṭhavaṇa* office looked after the affairs of the *amaranāyakas.* * This section should have maintained registers in which the names of the *amaranāyakas*, the number of troops which each of them had to maintain, the extent of the territories given to them, and the amount of tax due from them to the state, were recorded. Probably the duty of supervising whether each *amaranāyaka* maintained the required number of troops devolved upon the officials of this department. The '*Rāyasaswāmi*' mentioned in an inscription of 1522 A.D. was, perhaps, the chief secretary of the revenue secretariat. †

Section 5: *Excise Department*:—Was there an Excise Department? The expression *sunkamvāru* or *sunkadavaru* which is occasionally met with in the inscriptions is translated as 'people belonging to the Excise Department.' But, as the right of collecting the taxes was sold by auction to the highest bidder, the *sunkadavaru* or *sunkamvāru* must be taken to mean the tax-farmers and their representatives. Under the circumstances, there would have been no need for maintaining a separate department.

* *Rāyavācaka*: *ASPP.* iii. pp. 30-33.

రాయలవారు కరణాలతోను అమరనాయకానకు నగిరికవిలె కావలి ప్రకారానకు యేనుగు గుఱ్ఱంబంటు బయనలకు వివరముగా లెక్కవ్రాసి తెమ్మని ఆనతిచ్చిన తరువాత.

Again —

కులాచారం కరిణీల పిలిపించి వారితోను సింహాసనాన అమరనాయకం యేనుగులెన్ని గుఱ్ఱాలెన్ని కాల్బలంయెంత అని అడిగినందులకు గణికులు పలుకరించిన వివరం.

† *EC.* xii. Pg. 69 (b).

THE SECRETARIAT

According to the *Rāyavācaka*, there were eighteen ports in the empire during the reign of Vīra Narasimha. The accounts of these ports are said to have been kept by a body of the *karṇams.* * It is stated by Abdur Razāk that 300 ports belonged to the empire during the reign of Dēvarāya II. † Although the number of ports might have diminished since Dēvarāya's reign, it could not have reached such a low figure during Vīra Narasimha's time. The eighteen ports mentioned in the *Rāyavācaka* should be regarded only as the principal ports. During the first half of the sixteenth century the number of ports included in the empire must have reached at least the old figure, if it did not actually exceed it. To keep the accounts of so many ports, an establishment consisting of several clerks must have been maintained by the government. The *Āmuktamālyada*, no doubt, refers to the ports; but it does not give the number. It leaves on the mind the impression that the ports were directly under the control of the central government It enjoins that the ruler should so govern the ports as to increase their trade by offering facilities to the traders, and protection to the strangers that might land therein. ‡ The emperor of Vijayanagara must have had several officers to keep him informed of what was taking place in the ports. It was also necessary that he should have accounts of exports and imports, so that he might levy taxes upon them. Whether there was a state department organized separately to look after the affairs of the ports and the harbours is more than one can say

* *ASPP.* iii. p. 13.

రాయలు నగరికి తొమ్మిది సంప్రతుల నంపగా కరణాలు వచ్చి పదునెనిమిది రేవుల లెక్కలున్ను వినుపించిన తర్వాత.

† *ED*. iv. p. 104.

‡ *Ām.* 4 : 25.

in the present state of the knowledge of the subject.

Section 6: The Spy System and the Diplomatic Corps:—During the 16th century, the emperors of Vijayanagara came frequently into contact with the kings of four other countries in their neighbourhood. These were the rulers of Bijāpūr, Ahmadnagar, Golkonda, and Cuttack. Of these the first three were Mussalmans, only the last was a Hindu. It was a recognized principle of international politics in those days for a strong king to undertake the conquest of a neighbour's territory, especially if he were weak. Therefore, the inter-state relations were at no time very cordial, and frequently very hostile. The states which have to be dealt with in this context fall into two groups, the Hindu and the Muslim. Between the Hindu and the Muslim states, there existed normally a feeling of bitter animosity. The relations between the Hindu states themselves were no better. Ever since the downfall of the kingdom of Koṇḍavīḍu, the emperors of Vijayanagara became the neighbours of the Gajapatis of Orissa. The whole of the Reḍḍi kingdom was at first appropriated by Harihara II and his successors. Dēvarāya II led his victorious armies into the very heart of Kaḷinga. * Subsequent to his death, the power of Vijayanagara monarchs rapidly declined, and the Gajapatis embarked upon a very aggressive policy. They not only annexed the dominions of the Koṇḍavīḍu Reḍḍis, but conquered a considerable slice of the Vijayanagara empire which they were able to retain in their possession for nearly four decades. During this period, the Rāyas made strenuous efforts to drive the Uriyas across the Kṛṣṇa; but they were

* *SII.* iv. 1375.

not successful until Kṛṣṇarāya finally expelled them in the second decade of the 16th century.

The Muslim kingdoms were far from being united. "There is little faith," says Nuniz, "among the Moors, and they bite one another like dogs, and like to see one after the other destroyed." * The Sultāns of Bijāpūr, Ahmadnagar, and Golkonda were constantly at war with one another. The bone of contention between the Qutb Shāhis, and the Ādil Shāhis was the fort of Kōvilkoṇḍa in Telingāṇa, whereas the Nizām Shāḥi Sultāns waged war with the Ādil Shāhis for the sake of Parenda. The political atmosphere in the Deccan courts was surcharged with feelings of jealousy and hatred. Under these circumstances, the ruler of each state became naturally suspicious of the intentions and movements of his neighbours. Consequently, it became imperative that he should keep a close watch upon the court, capital, and the kingdom of his neighbours.

Little or no information is available on this subject from the Portuguese writers; but considerable light is thrown upon it by the *Āmuktamālyada* and the *Rāyavācaka*. The information supplied by the former is, however, comparatively meagre.

The *Āmuktamālyada* gives prominence to the spy system by making 'the audience to the spies' one of the daily duties of a monarch. † According to this work, "a spy should be a resident of the capital, and have knowledge of several languages; he should be capable of assuming many disguises; but he should have no knowledge of the other spies employed by his master. The monarch should consider no cost too high for

* *FE.* p. 326. † *Ām* 4: 271.

securing the services of such a spy." * The *Rāyavācaka* gives much interesting information on the subject. The spies seem to have been divided into two classes. As the emperor had to guard himself against the attacks of internal and external foes, he sent some spies into his own dominions to collect information from villages, towns, and forts and to communicate the same to him. They had to make secret inquiries into the affairs of the *amaranāyakas*, and study their disposition towards the emperor. Their work, however, was comparatively easy. The work of the other class of spies whom the emperor despatched into the dominions of his neighbours was far more risky, as they had to penetrate, on occasions, into the very council chambers of the foreign kings. These spies were men of great intelligence. They were capable of speaking several languages, probably with proper accent and idiom, and could assume many disguises. They received very high salaries from the emperor, and on those occasions, when they successfully performed a specially difficult task, they got additional presents from him. †

The spy system appears to have been closely connected with the diplomatic service. It was a common practice in those days for one state to maintain ambassadors at the courts of all the kings with whom it had diplomatic relations. The *Āmuktamālyada* alludes to this practice more than once. ‡ The *Manucaritra* speaks of the foreign ambassadors who were present at the court of Kṛṣṇadēvarāya. § It is, however, the *Rāyavācaka* that offers valuable information for a study of the subject. It frequently

* *Ām* 4: 279.

† *ASPP.* iii. pp. 26-27.

‡ *Ām* 4: 259.

§ *Mc.* 1: 40.

alludes to the presence of foreign ambassadors at the court of Vijayaṇagara. The ambassadors of several states used to meet secretly to discuss the inter-state relations. A meeting of this kind is said to have been held near the Dāḍi Mahal at Bijāpūr, where the ambassadors of Bijāpūr, Golkonda, Ahmadnagar, and Cuttack met to concert measures of defence against the invasion of Kṛṣṇarāya, the common enemy of the states whom they represented. * Another meeting of the ambassadors of the three Muhammadan states is said to have taken place at Vijayanagara. † A list of the ambassadors that were staying at the court of the Gajapati is preserved in the pages of the *Rāyavācaka*. ‡ The ambassadors were known as *sthānāpatis*. Their main duty was to report to their respective masters what they had seen and heard as well as their own opinion on current political problems. The reports submitted by them influenced to a very great extent the policies of the respective courts. Even during the time of war, it does not appear to have been customary to break off diplomatic relations. The belligerent states seem to have had no objection to allow the enemy's representatives at each other's courts. § While the war between the Gajapati and Kṛṣṇarāya was still in progress, a *sthānāpati* of Vijayanagara, Kamalanābhayya by name, was allowed to remain at Cuttack. It was he who secretly informed the Rāya of the decision of the sixteen *Pātras* of Orissa to compass the ruin of the

* *ASPP*. iii. p. 36. † *ibid.* pp. 38-39. ‡ *ibid* p. 63.

§ cf. Fr. Queyros: (The passage refers to India). "When two kings are at war, each has his ambassador, at the other's court and camp, and all hostile plans become known to all, because when the ambassador writes to his king, he orders the letter to be read in the public generally in the presence of the adversary's ambassador, or one of his household, and everything in public, for neither of the kings trusts one single person." *The Conquest of Ceylon* i. p. 95.

Vijayanagara army. * The kings of the time seem to have taken no particular care to guard their state secrets, so that the enemy might not gain any advantage over them.

The *Āmuktamālyada* states that the ruler of a country should treat the ambassadors of foreign countries with much courtesy and consideration in the audience hall. He should intimate to them his intentions towards their masters in such a manner as to give them no offence. He should avoid the use of harsh language in his conversation with them ; for, on occasions, he might require their assistance in concluding a treaty of alliance with their respective masters. † According to an obscure passage from the *Rāyavācaka*, the foreign ambassadors residing at the court of Vijayanagara received not only presents on important occasions from the Rāya, but fixed allowances at regular intervals. ‡

* *ASPP.* iii. p. 177. † *Ām* 4: 259.

‡ *ASPP.* iii. p. 58.

Abdur Razāk who visited the court of Dēvarāya II as an ambassador of Sultān Shāh Rūkh of Persia, gives a brief description of the treatment which he received at the court of Vijayanagara :—

"They then brought a tray, and gave me two packets of betel, a purse containing 500 *fanams*, and about 20 *miskals* of camphor. The daily provision forwarded to me comprised of two sheep, four couples of fowls, five *mans* of rice, one *man* of butter, one *man* of sugar, and two *varahas* in gold. This occurred every day. Twice a week, I was summoned to the presence of the Rāya towards the evening...and each time, I received a packet of betel, a purse of *fanams*, and some *miskals* of camphor" *ED.* iv. p. 113.

The allowance which was given to Razāk should have been given to the ambassadors of other states also. Dēvarāya II must have treated Razāk in the same way in which he was accustomed to treat the ambassadors of other monarchs, according to the customary practice observed at the court of Vijayanagara. The passage from the *Rāyavācaka* shows that the practice remained unaltered even during the Tuḷuva period.

It is not at all clear whether there was a separate foreign department which had jurisdiction both over the spies and the ambassadors. In the *Rāyavācaka*, the minister, Ayyaparasa, is made to speak on behalf of the spies to the Rāya in order to obtain for them an extra reward. * It is just possible that he was their head; but it is not known under whom the Vijayanagara ambassadors stationed at the courts of foreign monarchs were placed. Probably, they were directly under the control of the emperor himself. Problems such as these can only be solved by future investigation.

* *ASPP.* iii. p. 58.

CHAPTER III

MILITARY ORGANISATION, AND THE KANDĀCĀRA DEPARTMENT.

Section 1: *Forts*:—The empire of Vijayanagara was organized, as stated already, on a military basis, in order to make it efficient for defence against the constant attacks of the Mussalmans. The defence of the empire depended, in the first place, upon a series of forts constructed at all strategical places, and secondly, upon the maintenance of a well organised and efficient army.

The people of the age were so much impressed with the importance of these forts that they built them in all conceivable places. Most of them, however, were built of mud, the construction of stone walls being permitted only in the case of places on the frontier. * The most important forts in the interior were also built of stone; and these invariably belonged to the emperor. The Rāyas of Vijayanagara, following the ancient Hindu tradition seem to have divided their forts into several classes. The *Rāyavācaka* mentions four kinds: *giri durga*, *sthala durga*, *jala durga*, *and vana durga*; † but a contemporary writer divides them into eight classes: *giri durga*, *vana durga*, *gaṁhvara durga*, *jala durga*, *kardama durga*, *miśraka durga*, *grāma durga*, *and kōṣṭa durga*. ‡

* *FE*. pp. 237-8.

† *ASPP*. iii. p. 13.

‡ प्रथमं गिरिदुर्गं च वनदुर्गं द्वितीयकं ।
तृतीयं गह्वरंदुर्गं जलदुर्गं चतुर्थकं ।
पञ्चमं कर्दमंदुर्गं षष्ठंस्यान् मिश्रकं तथा ।
सप्तमं ग्रामदुर्गं स्यात्कोष्टदुर्गं तथाष्टकं ॥

Dvm. (*Rājacaritra-khaṇḍam*).

Every conceivable article which was considered necessary to enable the garrisons to live comfortably for a long time was stocked in these forts. These articles were placed under the command of an officer whose loyalty was unquestionable; and a garrison which was sufficient to repel all attacks of an invader was placed under him. * As the defence of the country depended upon the forts, considerable trouble was taken to maintain them in good condition. Important forts like Vijayanagara had no less than seven walls of fortification. † All the *sthala durgas* had deep moats around them which prevented the enemy from coming near the walls. In order to impede the progress of the enemy's cavalry 'pointed stones of great height' were fixed in the ground at the intervals of 'a lance shaft and a half.' ‡ The forts were equipped with up-to-date weapons of offence and defence. On their walls were set up *pāṣāṇa-yantras* or catapults which showered stones, clubs, and battle-axes upon the enemy causing him much harm; § a weapon called *dambhōḷi,* which was worked by gun-powder threw into the midst of the besiegers balls of stone spreading destruction; ¶ *dambhōḷi* was probably the siege gun which is mentioned by contemporary writers; ‖ besides, the *ākāśa bāṇa, arthacandra bāṇa,* and other explosive weapons were

* *Ām* 4: 209. † *ED.* iv. p. 106. cf. *FE.* p. 243. ‡ *FE.* p. 253.

§ *The Sources* p. 167. For a description of the *pāṣāṇa-yantra,* see *the Daivajñavilāsa* (*Rājacaritra-khaṇḍa*) of Yallanārya.

¶ For a description of *dambhōḷi* see *the Daivajñavilāsa* (*Rājacaritra-khaṇḍa*) of Yallanārya.

‖ *Ām.* 2: 9.

అడుగున నుండియుం బదిలమై చదలంటెడు కోట నొప్ప ప్రో
ల్చెడని కడంక దంచనపు చేతుల గంగను కాసె దూరగా
నడుమన యున్కిఁ జేసి యల నాకపురిన్ సరికై పెనంగి లా
వెడలగ బట్టి వ్రేయుటకు నెత్తె నన న్జను మల్లుపోరిలోన్ ॥

used in defending the forts against the invaders. * The defence of the forts was left in the hands of such *amaranāyakas* in whose loyalty and ability the Rāya had great confidence.

Section 2 : Divisions of the army.—The Vijayanagara army was divided from the very beginning into two well-defined sections. One of them consisted entirely of the *amaranāyaka* levies, which received their pay and equipage, not from the emperor, but from the *amaranāyakas*. Each *nāyaka* commanded his own troops, and had to defray their expenses from his own pockets. A brief account of the *amaranāyaka* forces is given by Nuniz :—

> "This King Chitarao (Acyuta) has foot-soldiers paid by his nobles, and they are obliged to maintain six lakhs of soldiers, that is, six hundred thousand men, and twenty-four thousand horse which the same nobles are obliged to have." †

According to Paes, the *amaranāyaka* troops consisted of a million fighting men, in which were included 35,000 cavalry in armour. ‡ They had to maintain elephants also. The *Rāyavācaka* gives more modest

* खेचरं वाणसंधानं वह्निसंयोगि लक्षणं
तद्वह्नि स्पर्शमात्रेण रिपुसैन्यविनाशनं ॥
*   *   *
अर्धेन्दुसदृशं शस्त्रं स्थापयेन्नाळमूलके
अधःस्थितेन रौद्रेण वर्त्तिमंतः प्रवेश्य च
शत्रुसैन्यस्याभिमुखं भूमौ विन्यस्य सज्जितं
प्रज्वाल्य वह्निना वर्त्तिं प्रयोक्तापसरेत्ततः
स गत्वा तूर्णमच्छब्दं शत्रुसैन्ये पतन् क्षणात्
पलायदंत तस्तुते दंभोळिरिव(?).. ....
अर्धचन्द्रकनामासौ बाणो युद्धे जयप्रदः ॥

Daivajña vilāsa-(Rājacaritra-khaṇḍa.)

† *ibid* p. 373.

‡ *FE.* p. 279.

figures: the *amaranāyakas* had to maintain 200,000 infantry and 24,000 cavalry, and 120 *ghats* of elephants. *

The other section of the army was known as *kaijītamvāru* or the troops that received their salary from the hand of the emperor himself.

Paes says:

"The king has his salaried troops to whom he gives pay. He has eight hundred elephants attached to his person, and five hundred horses always attached to his stables, and for the expenses of his horses and elephants, he had devoted the revenues that he receives from this city of Bisnaga." †

Nuniz gives a fuller account.

"This king (Acyutarāya) has continually fifty thousand paid soldiers amongst whom are six thousand horsemen who belong to the palace guard, to which six thousand belong the two hundred who are obliged to ride with him. He has also twenty thousand spearmen and shield-bearers, and three thousand men to look after the elephants in the stables." ‡

The testimony of the Portuguese writers is confirmed by the *Rāyavācaka*, according to which, the *kaijītam* forces consisted of 500 elephants and 12,000 cavalry and 100,000 infantry. §

* కులాచారం కరిణీల పిలిపించి వారితోను సింహాసనాన అమరనాయకం యేనుగలెన్ని గుఱ్ఱాలెన్ని కాల్బలం ఎంత అని అడిగినందులకు గణికులు పలుకరించిన వివరం:—

గుఱ్ఱాలు యిరువై నాలుగువేలు
యేనుగఘట్టాలు నూటయిరువై
కాల్బలము రెండులక్షలు. *ASPP.* iii p. 33.

A *ghat* consisted of ten elephants, so that the elephant corps was made up of 1200 animals.

† *FE.* p. 281. ‡ *ibid* p. 381. § *ASPP.* iii. pp. 33, 34.

Although the strength of the Vijayanagara army is variously estimated by different writers, they are in complete agreement so far as the two-fold division of the army is concerned. It was only with the administration of the *kaijītam* forces that the government had any direct connection. The *kaijītam* forces were reorganized during the time of Kṛṣṇadēvarāya. It is said that he recruited his troopers from the Kabbili, Morasa, and Tulu communities in order to make his cavalry efficient in its encounters with the Mussalmans. *

Section 3: The Recruitment and Training:—The soldiers were recruited to the army with great care.

> "The officials of war in choosing a man for the army strip him naked, and look at him to find out how tall he is, what is his name, in what land he was born, the names of his father and mother, and in this way, he is appointed without leave being given him to go to his country, and if he goes without leave, and afterwards is captured he is very evilly entreated (and among these men at arms are many knights who gather here from various lands to get the pay, and nevertheless do not cease to live according to their own law.") †

The Vijayanagara army, like the other armies in India in those days, consisted of infantry, cavalry and elephants. Although the emperors of Vijayanagara as *Narapatis*, had the largest infantry in India, they did not bestow much attention on training it so as to make it the most powerful instrument of war. The training of the cavalry absorbed all the attention of the emperor and his *nāyakas*.

It is very much to be doubted whether the infantry was at all trained in the modern sense of the term. Speaking of Kṛṣṇarāya, Paes observes:

* *ASPP.* iii. pp. 33, 34.

† *Barbosa* i. p. 212.

"The king is accustomed every day to drink a *quartilho* (three-quarter pint) of oil of *gingelly* before daylight, and anoints himself all over with the said oil; he covers his loins with a small cloth, and takes in his arms great weights made of earthenware, and then taking a sword, he exercises himself till he has sweated out all oil, and then he wrestles with one of his wrestlers." *

It is not unlikely that the nobles and the soldiers were trained to use the sword and other weapons, in special gymnasia constructed for the purpose, where the wrestlers and fencing masters gave them lessons in military exercises. The *Vasucaritra* alludes to the *gariḍis* or the gymnasia of the city. † The *Manucaritra* mentions also *sāmugariḍīlu* or *gariḍis* where fencing and gymnastic exercises were taught. ‡ Owing to the existence of these fencing clubs, the people at Vijayanagara became very fond of sword-play and duels. § Although each soldier was individually skilled in the use of arms, he was not taught to function effectively as a unit in an organised body of men engaged in attack or defence. The soldiers of those days appear to have been strangers to drill, parade, and other exercises which are but ordinary items in modern military education.

The foot-soldiers that were serving in the Vijayanagara army fell into four classes: (1) The spearmen, (2) the archers, (3) the musqueteers, and (4) the Muhammadans. ¶

* *FE.* p. 249. † *Vc.* 4: 72.

‡ *Mc.* 2: 43.

The *Hamsavimśati*, a work of the 18th century, describes the course of physical and military training which the men of the fighting class had to undergo. It consisted 12 kinds of *daṇḍas*, 14 *visarus*, 32 *vinnāṇas*, 12 *paruvaḍis*, 12 *gatis*, 12 *gāyamānas*, 12 *monas*, some kinds of *naṟukus*, 16 *upvītas* and, 32 *pracāras*. (*Hvt.* 1: 206.). These completed the course of physical training in the *gariḍis*, which might have been in existence long before the eighteenth century.

§ cf. *FE.* p. 383. ¶ *ibid* p. 277.

(1) The spearmen and the shield-bearers that were in the emperor's army are said to have numbered twenty thousand. The shields-men carried shields on which several designs in different colours were painted.

> " Shields-men with their shields with many flowers of gold, and silver on them, others with figures of tigers and other great beasts, others all covered with the silver leaf-work beautifully wrought, others with painted colours, and others black and (so polished that) you can see into them as into a mirror." *

They also carried richly ornamented swords.

(2) The archers had bows plated with gold and silver. Some had only bows which were finely polished. "Their arrows (were) very neat and so feathered that they could not be better." Besides, they had 'daggers at their waists and battle-axes with the shafts and ends of gold and silver.' †

(3) The musqueteers were armed with muskets and blunderbusses.

(4) The Muhammadan soldiers carried 'shields, javelins, and Turkish bows with many bombs and spears and fire missiles.' They are said to have been very adept in the use of their arms. ‡

The Dress:—No uniformity was observed regarding the dress which the soldiers and the officers put on. "You will see among them," declares Paes, "dresses of such rich cloths that I do not know where they came from, nor could any one tell how many colours they have." § But, while engaged in fighting, they put on a

* *FE.* p. 277.

† *ibid* p. 277.

‡ *ibid* p. 277.

§ *ibid* p. 277.

kind of armour made of leather, which covered their bodies completely leaving only the face and the feet. * The armour was noticed by the Portuguese writers also. "On the body, head, and arms," says Barros, (they wear *laudees*) "strong enough to protect them against lance-thrusts, or sword cuts." † Paes gives an idea of how the *laudees* were manufactured. "These tunics," says he, "are made of layers of very strong raw leather and furnished with other iron (plates) that make them strong; some have these plates gilded both inside and out, and some are made of silver." ‡ The head-pieces which protected the neck and the face were made of the same material. The shields-men do not appear to have donned any armour. The shields, it is said, were so large that they covered the body completely. § There was, therefore, no need to protect the body.

Section 4: The Cavalry and the Elephants:—As the cavalry was the most important section of the army, a great deal of attention was paid to its training and equipment. The *Manucāritra* describes the equipment of a war-horse in one place.

> "The reins of fine Ormuz workmanship were made of green (twisted) silk. The armour (which covered the body of the animal), the Persian saddle made of silk to which were attached a Paiṭhān bow, a shining quiver, a broad sword with a handle made of gold, a Gujerāti shield; a small dagger of Shirāz make;

* आयान्तीमथ यवनावनीशसेनाम्
निष्णाता युधि रुरुधुः नृपायुधीयाः
चर्मान्तप्रतिकल सङ्कुचच्छरीराः
संदस्याननचरणाः क्षणं तदग्रे ॥ *Abm. Canto* xi.

† *FE.* p. 276 *n.* 2. ‡ *ibid* p. 276. § *ibid* p. 328.

and a case of sharp javelins; these constituted its equipment. The horse was decorated with a richly ornamented plume of *pikili* feathers; and a plate inlaid with imitation precious stones covered its face." *

This description is fully corroborated by Paes: The horses were fully caprisoned.

> They had "on their foreheads plates, some of silver but most of them gilded, with fringes of twisted silk of all colours, and reins of the same; others had trappings of Mecca velvet...; others had them of other silks such as satins and damask, and others of brocade from China and Persia. Some of the men with gilded plates had them set with many large precious stones, and on the borders lace work of small stones. Some of these horses had on their foreheads heads of serpents and of other large animals of various kinds." †

The troopers wore the same kind of armour as the foot-soldiers; their head-pieces appear to have been somewhat different. They were shaped like helmets 'with borders covering the neck' and pieces to protect the face. In addition to this, the horsemen wore gilded or silk gorgets on their necks. They carried at their waists 'swords, (and) small battle-axes' and had in their hands javelins 'with shafts covered with gold and silver.' ‡

Nothing is known about their training. There are some indications to show that some care was bestowed on the training of horses: they were taught to caracole and prance; § they were drawn up in lines, and took part in sham fights on festive occasions. ¶ The *Prabhāvatī-pradyumnam* describes a game in which men seated on horseback drove a ball with a staff which they held

* *Mc.* 4: 28.

† *FE.* pp. 275-6.

‡ *ibid* p. 276.

§ *ibid* p. 272.

¶ *ibid* p. 271.

in one of their hands.* The description reminds one of the game of polo which was a favourite sport of horsemen in Mediaeval India. It is obvious that there existed a system of training the horses, although it is not possible to state whether they were taught to partake in mass movements on the field of battle.

The elephants were protected with an armour of the same kind as the horses which covered all their bodies. Probably the faces of the beasts were protected by steel plates. They were armed with 'much ground and sharpened knives,' fastened to their tusks, with which they caused much harm to the enemy. They were carefully trained to batter the gates of forts in sieges, and charge the ranks of hostile forces. Besides, each elephant carried on its back a *howdah* in which were seated four warriors on each side. †

The Vijayanagara army was weak in artillery. Although the Rāya had a corps of musqueteers in his army, and several cannon which he employed in his wars, the artillery did not play an important part in the battles. The Mussalmans, on the contrary, made use of it fully; and the Turkish gunners whom they usually employed were trained in European wars. The disaster which befell the Hindu empire at Rakṣasa-Tagiḍi may be partly attributable to the neglect of artillery by the emperors.

Section 5: The Army Administration and the Kandācāra Department:— Kṛṣṇadēvarāya who reorganized the army had also made necessary arrangements for its maintenance in an efficient condition. There is no reason for believing that his arrangements had been altered by his successors. He fixed the salaries of his

* *Ppm.* 2 : 33.

† *FE.* p. 333.

12,000 cavalry and 500 *mahouts*. To feed the horses and elephants, and to keep them healthy, he appointed four *pārupatyagāras*, six *karṇams*, sixteen massagers, and six *muḍupu gollas* for each stable. He commanded that the daily expenses of all the stables should be borne by the treasury. Besides, he appointed a board of six *karṇams* to see that the 100,000 foot-soldiers in his service received their salaries regularly. * The details regarding the administration of *kaijītam* forces are described by the Portuguese writers also. Barbosa speaks of 'the great kitchens kept by the king (Kṛṣṇadēvarāya) to feed his elephants and horses.'

> "These are in many large houses where are many great copper cauldrons, and in these are many officials who look after the preparation of food, and others who prepare it," †

Acyuta had three 'thousand men to look after the elephants in the stables', sixteen hundred grooms, three hundred horse trainers, and 'two thousand artificers, namely blacksmiths, masons, and carpenters and washermen'. ‡

In addition to the horses and elephants which the emperors kept in their stables, they would also distribute some animals among the notable warriors and nobles that attended the court.

Barbosa says:

> "To the knights, he gives one horse each, for his own riding, a groom and a slave-girl for his service, and a monthly allowance of four or five *pardaos* as the case may be; and daily supplies as well for the horse and groom, which they fetch from the great kitchens kept up by the King." "The food is rice boiled

* *ASPP.* iii. p. 34.

† *Barbosa* i. pp. 210-11.

‡ *FE.* p. 381.

with chick-peas and other pulse; and each man as I have said comes to draw the ration for his horse or elephant." *

This is corroborated by Nuniz:

"To the six thousand horsemen, the King gives horses free, and gives provision for them every month." †

The army establishment appears to have been very huge, offering employment to thousands of non-military men. Nothing is known about the way in which this huge army was officered, nor about the measures adopted to train the soldiers. Each of the three sections of the army had probably its own chief. Sāhni Cinnappa Nāyaka perhaps commanded the cavalry during the time of Acyuta; ‡ and Madanarque held the office of the master of horse. § It is not unlikely that the elephant and the infantry corps had their respective chiefs.

* *Barbosa* i. pp. 210-11.

The amusing story of the famous jester, Tenāli Rāmakṛṣṇa and the horse alludes to this practice. Rāmakṛṣṇa obtained a horse from Kṛṣṇarāya like the other courtiers for training. Although he received from the treasury all the allowances, he practically starved the animal, by shutting it up in a closed house with only a chink in the wall to admit light and air. Through this chink he used to offer a handful of grass and some water to the poor animal every day. On the day, when the horse was to be produced before the Rāya, he told him that he could not lead the horse, as the animal became very fat and vicious on account of overfeeding. He requested the Rāya to send some one to lead the horse from the stable. The Rāya sent one of his Muhammadan officers, who was known to be a very good horseman, to bring the animal. The *sardar* accompanied Rāmakṛṣṇa according to the royal command. When they approached the stable where the horse was, the *sardar* peeped into the stable through the chink, acting upon the instructions of Rāmakṛṣṇa. As he did so, his long beard first got into the chink; and the poor animal mistaking it to be the daily allowance of grass, began to tug at it. The *sardar* howled with pain. When the Rāya was informed of this matter he came upon the scene, admonished Rāmakṛṣṇa for his wickedness, and released the *sardar*.

† *FE*. p. 381. ‡ *ibid* p. 372. § *ibid* p. 381.

All the military affairs of the empire seem to have been under the control of a department of state known as the *Kandācāra.* * A certain Timmappaya who was the *Kandācāranāyaka* is mentioned in an inscription of A.D. 1545. † The *Kandācāranāyaka* was probably the designation of the head of the *Kandācāra* or military department. Whether he was merely the head of the clerical staff of the war-office, or a minister of the state guiding the military policy of the empire, can, if at all, be decided only by future investigation. ‡

Section 6 :— It may not be out of place, in this connection, to describe the method which the Rāyas of Vijayanagara adopted in waging war with their enemies. They had great regard for tradition which influenced their warlike activities to a great extent. They never invaded an enemy's country without formally declaring war at first. As they had strong faith in omens and astrology they did nothing without consulting diviners and astrologers. The emperor had his own *śākunikas* who accompanied him in his wars to explain to him the will of the gods. It was his invariable custom to consult them before the declaration of war. § One of the

* *EC.* xi Jl. 24.   † *EC.* x. Cb. 19.

‡ It is stated in the *Tārakabrahmarājīya*, that Nañjarasa Timmarasa, one of Acyuta's ministers, was a *rāyasam* in the *Kandācāra* department. The term *rāyasam* means the profession of writing and it is often taken to mean a writer or a clerk in a public office. Nañjarasa Timmarasa who was a minister of the king could not have been an ordinary clerk. Probably he was the *Kandācāranāyaka*, or head of the clerical staff of the war-office.

§ *FE.* p. 329.

cf. క॥ ఆ కోలాగాములు గనుగొని
శాకునికుం డొకఁడు లేచి సంభ్రమ మొదవన్
జ్యాకలితశరాసనుఁడై
వీకను సైనికుల దిట్టి విభుతో ననియెన్. *Mc.* 4: 62.

favourite methods to divine the future was to listen to *upasṛti* or the conversation of two persons, and to foresee the trend of events in the light of an incidental remark or statement made by them. The *Prabhāvatī-pradyumnam* alludes to the habit of listening to the *upasṛti* before the declaration of war. * Tradition also preserves an instance of listening to *upasṛti*, and it may be taken for what it is worth. On the eve of declaring war on Kaḷinga, the emperor Kṛṣṇadēvarāya is said to have sent his minister Appāji into the city in the early hours of a morning to listen to *upasṛti*. As the minister was passing by the side of the house of a washerman, he heard the following couplet sung :

> " Koṇḍavīḍu is ours ; and Koṇḍapalle is ours.
>
> If any one disputes my statement, then the country up to Kaṭakam is also ours. " †

The minister saw in this an indication of future victory ; and he communicated the matter to the Rāya ; the war was immediately declared.

(*a*) *The pitching of the Veli-guḍāra* :—According to Barbosa, the emperor of Vijayanagara seldom went to war himself, but sent his captains and armies. ‡ This is in conformity with the *Āmuktamālyada*, § which enjoins that the monarch should not personally march upon all enemies, but should send his commanders with

* వ॥ ఇవ్విధంబున వటువచనంబు లుపశ్రుతిగం జేకొని తదనుసారంబున వజ్రపురప్రవేశంబును వ్రజనాథవినాశంబును నతి సుకరంబులుగా మనంబున విశ్చయించుకొని. *Ppm* 1: 110.

† కొండవీడు మనదేరా
కొండపల్లె మనదేరా
కాదని యెవ్వరు వాదుకు వచ్చిన
కటకముదాకా మనదేరా. *Cmm*. i. p. 161.

‡ *Barbosa* i. p. 224.

§ *Ām*. 4 : 255.

sufficient forces to overcome them. This policy, however, was not observed by Kṛṣṇadēvarāya who invariably led his troops in person; and his successors more or less followed in his footsteps. They believed evidently in the maxim that 'a battle without a king would not succeed.' * Ever since Kṛṣṇadēvarāya declared war upon the chief of Ummattūr, the emperors generally accompanied their troops to the battle.

As soon as war was declared, it was the custom to pitch a tent called the *veli-guḍāra* in an open space outside the city. The *Rāyavācaka* † as well as the *Vijayanagarada Sāmrājyavu* ‡ refer to the *veli-guḍāra* which was pitched outside the city, when Kṛṣṇarāya declared war upon his neighbours. According to a passage in the *Pāṇḍurangamāhātmya*, the conqueror resided (for a short time) in the *veli-guḍāra*, before starting on his *digvijaya*. § It is said in the *Rāyavācaka* that the Rāya, having shifted to the *veli-guḍāra*, sent orders to his *nāyakas* to join him in an invasion of his enemy's territories. ¶ This practice was noticed at least by one foreign writer :

* Tirumalācārya : *Nsś.* 29. † *ASPP.* iii. p. 130.

‡ *The Bhārati* vi. ii. p. 622.

§ అఖిలదిగ్జయకాంక్ష బుష్పాయుధుండు
వెలిగుడారంబులో వచ్చి విడిదిచేసె *Prm.* 4 : 44.

¶ వ॥ యెదిరితోడట్టు సన్నాహములకోడట్టు బైలుమెరసి వెలిగుడారానకు వచ్చినిలిచి దొరల మన్నీలనున్ను, రవుతుల మావత్తులనున్ను, వినియోగం పైకం వార్లనున్ను, మునుపటివారు, వెనుకవారు, యెడవంకంవార్లనున్ను అందరిని రప్పించి వారివార్లతో మాటపలుకులు ఆడి మీమీ స్తోమములతో ఆయత్తపాటుతో రమ్మని, బలవంకం అమరనాయకం వార్లతోనున్ను, నగరికైజీతం వారితోనున్ను, నగరి సంప్రతుల తోనున్ను, నగరిలెక్క ప్రకారానకు యేనుగ, గుర్రాలు, రౌతు, రాణువ, బంటు, పైదళం వారినిన్ని గణుతి తీసికొని కర్ణాట కానగల స్వతంత్రస్వామ్యం, కావలిగట్లగుంపులవారినిన్ని, పాళెగార్లను తీసు

"When the war has arrived at such a point that he considers it necessary to go in person, and when he has settled in his Council that he will go; on an appointed day the *king goes forth to an open plain* as if he were going out for his pleasure, mounted on an elephant or in a palanquin, each finely adorned with gold and precious stones, accompanied by a great number of horsemen and footmen, and many elephants well-drawn up in line on the right before him, covered with scarlet and silken cloths. When he arrives at the plain, they bring him a horse whereon he rides holding in his hand a bow and an arrow, which he lets fly towards the country with which he is about to wage war. He then gives out in how many days from that time he will start, and this news runs through the whole city and kingdom. Thence he goes forth at once and *fixes his camping ground in the open country where he awaits the time fixed for his advance.* When this time is fulfilled he issues a proclamation...that all men shall attend with their wives, and sons, and households, all are ordered to go thither." *

(*b*) *March*:—The army did not march rapidly towards its destination. It marched but three leagues a day, and then halted for three days. † The reason for this shortness of the march is explained in the *Āmuktamālyada*; it was intended to enable all the captains of the emperor to join him before he finally attacked the enemy. ‡ When all his troops joined him, the pace of the march was quickened and the army rapidly reached the enemy's frontier. The emperor with his *kaijītagars* was in the centre; and the *amaranāyakas* were divided into four groups. One of them was to march in the van; and another in the rear; the remaining two groups had to march on either flank of the royal forces. § The

కాని లెక్క ప్రకారానకు అందరిని రప్పించి పయినంతర్లడా అని కరణీకులతో నున్ను రాయసం, కటికం, అవసరం, వినియోగ పైకంవార్లతోనున్ను ఆనతిచ్చి.

ASPP. iii. p. 130.

* *Barbosa* i. p. 224.

† *ibid* p. 227.

‡ *Ām.* 4 : 27.

§ *ASPP.* iii. p. 130.

Manucaritra mentions *dumudāru dora* or the captain of the rear-guard.* Probably the *āsīra* or the van which carried the royal standard as well as the flanks had their respective commanders. According to a late authority, the armies never marched in ranks, and almost all the soldiers, took their wives and children with them.† All these, as well as the large concourse of the courtesans who always followed the army, were paid by the emperor.‡ All the halting stations on the route were carefully chosen. The camping grounds were selected with great care so that there should be no difficulty for procuring grass, grain, and water.§ The camp resembled a moving city with houses of straw, 'all arranged in streets with many open spaces.'¶ Nuniz describes the camp at some length:

"The tent of the King was surrounded by a great hedge of thorns with only one entrance, and with a gate at which stood his guards. Inside this hedge lodged the Brahman who washes him, and has charge of the idol that he always carries about with him, and also other persons who hold office about the King's person, and the eunuchs who are always found in his chamber. And outside this circle all around are his guards, who watch all night at fixed spots; with this guard are quartered officers of the household; and from thence to the front were all the other captains in their appointed posts, according as each one was entrusted and ordered. Outside of all these people, in a camp by themselves were the scouts of whom I have already spoken, whose duty it was to patrol all night through the camp and watch to see if they can catch any spies. On the other side the washermen (who are those that wash clothes) were in a camp by themselves, and they were near to the place where they could best wash clothes. All the camp was divided into regular streets."‖

* *Mc.* 3: 54.

† Queyros: *The Conquest of Ceylon* i. p. 95.

‡ *Barbosa* i. p. 225.

§ Tirumalācārya: *Nsf.* 30.

¶ *Barbosa* i. p. 227.

‖ *FE.* p. 332.

When the army moved forward, the abandoned camp was burnt down. "When they are to start," declares Barbosa, "a gong is sounded, and at once the town is set on fire and all depart." * The *Pārijātāpaharaṇam* also alludes to this practice. †

Curiously enough, the Vijayanagara government did not maintain a commissariat department to supply the needs of the army in the field; but its absence was not felt owing to the existence of a different arrangement for provisioning the troops. The task of supplying the needs of the army and the numerous camp-followers was left to private enterprise. Large numbers of merchants were always found in all the mediaeval Indian armies. It was their duty to provide the soldiers with everything they wanted. Each *amaranāyaka's* division had its own market, where his soldiers could purchase any article they desired including such luxuries as jewels, and precious stones, as well as grass and straw for the horses and elephants. The *kaijītam* forces had their own market like the *amaranāyaka* troops. ‡ It was not, therefore, necessary for the government to maintain a separate department for the purpose.

As the army reached the enemy's frontier, the forest tribes inhabiting the mountainous tracts of the empire, commenced to plunder the enemy's territory,

* *Barbosa* i. p. 228.

† రాజు వీడెత్తి చనినతారకభటాలి
అంబరాభోగనిజశిబిరాంగణమున
గాలుకొల్పిన పావకజ్వాలలఁగఁ
బ్రాచిగనుపట్టె నవసాంధ్యరాగరుచులు. *Phm.* 2 : 66.

‡ *FE*. p. 333.

acting upon the instructions of the emperor himself. Although Tirumalācārya hoped that the enemy's country would be invaded without abduction, plunder and robbery, * special arrangements were made by the government for the purpose. The forest tribes were treated by the government generously; because they were expected to be useful for plundering purposes during an invasion, if they were kept in good humour. † When Kṛṣṇarāya started on his *digvijaya*, he is said to have invited the Bōya chiefs of the eighteen *Kampaṇas* of Āraga to a feast where he commanded them to march ahead of the army at a distance of thirty miles, and entering the Muslim territory plunder it and carry away men, cattle, sheep, goats and horses. ‡ The burning of villages and towns was a common practice. Kṛṣṇarāya on one occasion is said to have reduced the whole of Bijāpūr kingdom to ashes. § The course of Acyuta's Rāicūr campaign seems to have been marked by the clouds of smoke produced by the burning cities. ¶ Therefore, the invasion must have caused wide-spread misery in the enemy's territory.

* *Nss.* 30. † *Ām* 4: 257.

‡ *The Rāyavācaka*: *ASPP.* iii. p. 130.

§ कृष्णामुत्तीर्य सोऽयं यवनजनपदं वह्निसात्कृत्य सर्वम्

Lakṣmīnārāyaṇa: *SS.*

¶ प्रज्वालो बलनिहितः प्रतीपपुर्याः
प्रासादोपरि परिजृम्भते स्म वह्निः
व्यालीनान् दिशि दिशि वीक्षितुं विपक्षा-
नुद्ग्रीवो मनुजपतेरिव प्रतापः ॥

आलीढाम्बरमपदिश्य धूमजालं
निर्गच्छत्सगरनिवासदुष्कृतानि
भूजानेर्बलनिहितेन बर्हिषापु
र्विद्वेषिक्षितिपपुराण्यहो विशुद्धिम् ॥ *Abm.* Canto xi.

(c) *The Siege*:—As the defence of the country mainly depended upon its forts, much attention was paid to their reduction during the course of an invasion. The forts of the age were equipped with the up-to-date weapons of offence and defence. Usually the forts were captured by effecting breaches in the walls; the elephants were useful in breaking the gates. Very frequently, the forts were captured by escalade. Sometimes, skill in military engineering was exhibited either in the construction of a bridge to span a river, * or in the removal of stones and huge boulders which hampered the movements of troops. † No clear account of the way in which the battles commenced is available. Nuniz briefly indicates what seems to have been the Hindu method of attack. All the divisions of the Hindu army would make a simultaneous attack upon the enemy; and the battle was either won or lost by that single charge. The Muhammadans protected themselves by a furious discharge of their artillery which decimated the Hindu ranks. This was followed by a vigorous charge of the cavalry and the elephants which decided the fate of battles. ‡ Some change seems to have been introduced in the Hindu method of attack by Kṛṣṇadēvarāya on the battle-field of Rāicūr. Instead of making a simultaneous attack with all his troops upon the enemy according to custom, he divided them into seven wings. Out of these seven divisions, only the two forward divisions were commanded to attack the enemy's camp, the remaining five being kept as reserve. When the Muhammadan artillery began its fusilade, these divisions, having sustained considerable loss began to retreat. This was the signal for the Muslim cavalry

* *EC.* iv. Pt. ii. Guṇḍlapet 30.

† *FE.* pp. 316-17. ‡ *ibid* p. 338.

to make a dash upon the retreating Hindu columns, with disastrous consequence to the latter; but the Muhammadan cavalry in its pursuit of the Hindus was thrown into great disorder; and the Rāya commanded his reserve divisions to charge the enemy; and the result was a complete victory to the Rāya. It is not known whether Kṛṣṇarāya's successors followed this method which he seems to have made use of with great effect.

The conquered country was protected by strong garrisons, faithful officers being placed in charge of the important forts. The inhabitants of the land were treated with consideration, and every effort was made to keep them contented. *

Section 7: The Navy:—No definite information is available from our sources regarding the navy of the empire; but the Rāyas had borne from the beginning a title which implies their supremacy over the seas. They describe themselves as the lords of the eastern, southern, western, and northern seas. If the title has any significance, it presupposes the existence of a navy without which it would have been impossible for them to maintain their lordship of the seas. Moreover, inscriptions frequently allude to the conquest of Ceylon by the Vijayanagara kings and their subordinates. Prince Virūpākṣa, one of the sons of Harihara II, is said to have conquered Ceylon; † and the same feat is attributed to *daṇṇāik* Lakkaṇa, one of the commanders of Dēvarāya II. ‡ All the Tuḷuva monarchs, with the exception of Vīra Narasimha, are said to have subjugated the island and exacted tribute from its

* cf. *Nss.* 30, 31.

† *EI.* iii. p. 228.

‡ *MER.* 1904-5 p. 58.

rulers. * It would not have been possible for the Vijayanagara sovereigns to approach the island without a fleet.

A careful examination of the itineraries of foreign travellers lends support to the belief that the Rāyas had a navy strong enough to maintain their authority upon the sea. According to Nuniz, Harihara II 'took Goa and Chaul and Dabul and Ceillão (Ceylon)'. † The same authority states that the kings of 'Coullão (Quilon), Ceyllão (Ceylon), Paleacate (Pulicat), Peguu and Tenaçary (Tenasserim)' 'paid tribute to him.' ‡ Abdur Razāk mentions an expedition of '*Daṇāik*', a minister of Dēvarāya II to Ceylon. § Ludavico Di-Varthema who visited the Vijayanagara kingdom in A. D. 1504 refers to a war that the king of Vijayanagara was then waging against the ruler of Tenasserim.

> "As this country (Vijayanagara) was at fierce war with the king of Tarnassari, we could not remain here (Pulicat) a very long time. But after remaining there a few days, we took our route towards the city of Tarnassari, which is distant a thousand miles from here." ¶

The Portuguese records briefly allude to the activity of the Vijayanagara fleet. Timōja who was the governor of Ōnōr or Honāwar in 1506 'was practically and in effect the commandant of the Vijayanagara fleet,' and he was 'entrusted with the task of waging perpetual war with Goa' which was then in the possession of the Sultān of Bijāpūr. He joined the

* *MER.* 146 of 1903, *Rep.* 1904 p. 23; 40 of 1897, *Rep.* 1900 p. 70; 224 of 1924, *Rep.* 1924 p. 49; 129 of 1905, *Rep.* 1905 p. 34.

† *FE.* p. 301.

‡ *ibid.* p. 302.

§ *ED.* iv. p. 116.

¶ Varthema: *Itinerary* p. 74.

Portuguese fleet in 1510, and assisted Albuquerque in capturing Goa from the Mussalmans. *

It is evident from this that the Rāyas of Vijayanagara maintained a navy with the aid of which they seem to have captured such sea-port towns as Goa, Chaul, Dabul, and Quilon, and subjugated the island of Ceylon and Ṭenasserim across the Bay of Bengal. However, no information is available about the construction of ships, the recruitment of sailors, and the administration of the navy. Our sources leave us entirely in the dark.

* Heras: *Āravīdu Dynasty* p. 57.

CHAPTER IV.

PROVINCIAL AND LOCAL GOVERNMENT.

Section 1: *The Administrative Divisions*:— The empire of Vijayanagara fell into two divisions, according to the manner of its government. The major portion of the empire was sub-divided into provinces which were ruled by the governors and other officers appointed by the emperor. The rest consisted of a number of tributary principalities, which were reduced to submission by the emperors in course of time. These were confined to the west coast and the extreme south. The chief of Gersoppa, the Bhairasa Vōḍeyar of Karakal, the kings of Quilon and Tenkāsi were the most important feudatory princes of the time. They ruled over their respective kingdoms without any interference on the part of the emperor. So long as they paid their tribute regularly, the emperor did not give them any trouble; and they were allowed to remain practically independent.

The territory that was directly under the administration of the imperial government may be divided into two sections according to the way in which it was organized for the purposes of internal administration. In the Tamil districts, the ancient Cōḷa territorial sub-divisions remained intact; and no serious attempts were made to tamper with them by the introduction of the system that had been perfected by the Rāyas in the Telugu and Canarese areas. The ancient Cōḷa and Pāṇḍyan kingdoms were subdued as early as the reign of Bukka I himself. But the conquered territory was not immediately brought under the direct control of the imperial government. The policy of placing the conquered territory under the control of the local chiefs commended itself to the Rāyas; and no departure was made from it until the advent of the Sāḷuvas. It was probably for this reason that the old territorial sub-divisions, *kōṭṭam*, *nāḍu*, *vala-nāḍu* and *maṇḍalam* still functioned as in the days of the Cōḷas. * Only in one locality was any attempt made to impose the northern nomenclature. The Toṇḍamaṇḍalam which was wrested from the Sāmbuvarāyas by Kumāra Kampaṇa in the fourteenth century was organized into two imperial provinces, the Paḍaivīḍu † and the Tiruvaḍi *rājyas*, ‡ and a part of it corresponding to the present Chingleput district was included in the Candragiri *rājya*. § Traces of northern territorial organisation are no doubt, found here and there; but the Cōḷa nomenclature and arrangements still persisted. So far as the administrative divisions in the Tamil provinces are concerned, the emperors of Vijayanagara may be said to have introduced no change.

The administrative system that obtained in the Telugu and Canarese areas was evolved by the Rāyas themselves. ¶ No doubt, some traces of the older systems such as *nāḍus*, and *sthalas* found their

* *MER*. 100 of 1918; 114, 116 of 1918; 370 of 1919; 272 of 1913.

† *ibid* A 7 of 1914-15.

‡ *ibid* 426 of 1909.

§ *ibid* 373 of 1919; 449 of 1919.

¶ The Local Records attribute the introduction of a new system of administrative divisions to Harihara I. It is stated in one *kaifiyat* that "in the region bounded by Siddhavaṭṭam in the east of Gutti (?), Penugoṇḍa in the south, Maddikara in the west, and Drōṇācalam in the north, king Harihara I appointed a *karṇika* over every village comprising four or five hamlets; *sthalakaraṇa* over an area containing twenty to thirty villages, each having a *karaṇa* of its own; he appointed also for the same region *nāḍ-gauḍas* and *nāḍ-talaiyārs* . . . and having made appointments like this, he granted the office holders title deeds which he had caused to be written." *LR*. 37. p. 279.

way into it; but the provincial system which was originally introduced by Harihara I, and perfected by Bukka I remained unaltered to the very last days of the empire.

The sub-division of the empire into provinces was profoundly influenced by military considerations. The history of Vijayanagara may be said to be the history of a fierce struggle between the Hindus of the south and the Muhammadan rulers of the Deccan. The maintenance of an army, under these circumstances, was, therefore, considered a supreme necessity; and no sacrifice was deemed too great in securing the effective defence of the realm against the national enemy. The empire is frequently alluded to in the Local Records as belonging to the *Rāyarāṇuva* or the Rāya's army. The *rājyas* or provinces were so constituted as to centre round the important forts after which they were named. The names of the provinces of Koṇḍavīḍu, Udayagiri, Gutti, Penugoṇḍa, Candragiri, Candra-gutti, Rāyadurga, Niḍugal, Rāicūr, Paḻaivīḍu illustrate the point. The provincial governors were not civil servants of the crown but military commandants of important forts.

The village then, as now, formed the unit of political organisation. A few villages were grouped together to form a *sthala*, corresponding roughly to the present range or firka. The name of *sammat*, later *samutu* which took the place of the *sthala* in the later Āravīḍu period occurs only in two inscriptions dated in 1517 and 1533 A.D. respectively. * A few

* *EC.* iii. Nj. 10; xi. Hr. 36.

In the days of Venkaṭa II, 185 villages of Hireyūr *sime* were organized into eleven *sthalas*. The biggest *sthala* was Hireyūr itself containing fifty-three villages; and the smallest was Araḷihaḷḷi which had only three villages (*EC.*

sthalas were grouped, in the Canarese districts, into a *sīme.* There appears to be a good deal of confusion in the inscriptions regarding the place of the *sīme* in the territorial scheme. In an inscription dated A.D. 1517, Vṛttiye *sīme* in the Balaguḷa *summat* of the Aṣṭagrāma *sīme* is mentioned. * In another, dated A.D. 1540, Sakala *sīme* in Pāṇḍu *dēśa* of Bāgūr *sīme* is mentioned. † The term *sīma* seems to have been used in two different senses. In Aṣṭagrāma *sīme* and Bāgūr *sīme*, it is used in its primitive sense, signifying a tract of land commonly regarded as a unit; but in Vṛttiye *sīme* and Sakala *sīme*, it is used in its technical sense denoting an artificial group of villages created by the government for the purpose of administrative convenience. In the Telugu districts, the division corresponding to the Canarese *sīme*, is *nāḍū.*

South India appears to have been divided into *nāḍus* from very ancient times. In spite of the constant political changes that came upon her, the territorial divisions into *nāḍus* remained unaffected. That they survived until the Vijayanagara times is proved by the evidence of the inscriptions which refer to Hoysala *nāḍ,* ‡ Muliki *nāḍ* § and Rēnaḍ. ¶ During the time of the Rāyas of Vijayanagara, *nāḍu* meant generally an artificial sub-division of territory, comprising several *sīmes* in the Canarese districts; but in the Telugu country it denoted a much smaller sub-division than the Canarese *nāḍu.* The territorial sub-division which corresponded to Canarese *nāḍu* in the Telugu

xi. Hr. 88. dated 1589). According to the *Aṭṭhavaṇavyavahāra Tantra,* ten to forty villages were grouped into a *hōbaḷi,* a name which later supplanted the *sthala* in the Canarese country, and which was just making its appearance in the reign of Srīranga I (*EC.* x. Mr. 57 dated A.D. 1578).

* *EC.* iii. i. Nj. 10. † *ibid* xi. Hk. 71. ‡ *EC.* v. Hn. 19.

§ *LR.* 33 (Sammatūr) pp. 226-7. ¶ *ibid* 14 (Nosam) pp. 376-7.

country was the *sīma* *e.g.* Gaṇḍikōṭa *sīma*, * Cāngalamaṟṟi *sīma*, † Koṇḍavīṭi *sīma*. ‡ At least one of these *sīmas*, *viz.*, Gaṇḍikōṭa was further sub-divided into a number of smaller *sīmas*. According to an inscription at Kāmanūr in the Cuddapah district, dated A.D. 1536, the *sīmas* of Pennabaḍi, Mulkināḍ, Rēnāḍ, Sakili, Awuku, Kovelakunṭla, Peda Nandyāla and Pulivendala were included in it. § Besides these, Ganjikunṭa *sīma*, Siddhavaṭṭa *sīma*, Pottapi *sīma* formed parts of it. ¶

It is generally believed that the next higher sub-division was the *rājya*. This does not seem to be quite accurate; for we find another intermediary sub-division called *vaṇita* or *vaḷita* between the *nāḍu* or *sīma* and the *rājya*. The following table reveals the names of some of these.

No.	Reference	Date A.D.	Name of the *vaḷita*.
1	LR. 36 pp. 452-53; 18 pp. 70-71	1544	Udayagiri
2	MER. A 12/1918-19	1526	Nellore
3	„ A 9/1914-15	1549	Gutti
4	„ 683/1922	1524	Hastināvati
5	„ 720/1922	1542	„
6	„ 402/1922	1554	„
7	„ 212/1913	1556	„

* *LR.* 37 (Lower Brāhmaṇapalli) pp. 156-8.

† *ibid* 18 (Madūr) pp. 70-71.

‡ *MER.* 5 of 1917-18.

§ *LR.* 36 pp. 443-4.

¶ *ibid* (Vanipenṭa) pp. 485-6; *ibid* 44 (Nelandalūr) p. 25.

It appears from the foregoing table that at least three provinces of the empire, Udayagiri, Penugoṇḍa and Hampi were divided at the first instance into *vaṇitas or vaḷitas.* Another territorial division called *venṭheya* or *venṭhe* which is etymologically connected with *vaḷita* may be noticed in this connection. It makes its appearance frequently in the inscriptions of the Canarese country; but its position in relation to the other territorial divisions cannot easily be determined. It was higher than the *sthala*, and lower than the *rājya.* *

* (1) It occurs before the *sthala* in EC. iii. Nj. 35 dated 1529.

(2) It occurs before the *sime* or *sīma* in

i. EC. xii. Ck. 6	1555.
ii. EC. xii. Ck. 10	1525.
iii. MER. 423/1920	1556.
iv. LR. 41 p. 67.	1538.

(3) before *sīma* and *nāḍu,* but after Bānavāse 12000.

i. EC. viii. Sb. 55	1571.
ii. EC. viii. Sb. 265	1527.
iii. EC. viii. Sb. 475	1577.

(4) before *nāḍ* only

i. EC. viii. Nr. 1	1566.
ii. EC. viii. Nr. 66	1506.

(5) after *nāḍ*

i. EC. xi. Dg. 27	1538.
ii. MER. 571/1912	1538.

(6) after *nāḍ* and before *sime*

i. EC. xi. Dg. 31	1531.
ii. EC. xi. Jl. 24	1554.

(7) after *rājya* and before *sime* in EC. xi. Cl. 54.

(8) after *vaḷita* and before *sime* in MER. 212/1913.

(9) after *sima* MER. 11/1920-21.

(10) before *sime* and after *nāḍ* and *vaḷita* ; MER. 402/1920.

(11) after *rājya,* MER. 403/1920.

(12) after *vaḷita,* MER. 720/1922.

These references clearly show that it is impossible to fix definitely the position of *venṭheya* or *venṭhe* in the scheme of the territorial organization of the empire.

PROVINCIAL AND LOCAL GOVERNMENT

The *rājya* represents the highest unit of administration. Sometimes, however, the term is used to denote much smaller areas than the province. It is said in an inscription of Nelandalūr that a certain Parvata Nāyaka was governing '*the rājyas*' of Sirivoḷḷa, Siddhavaṭṭam, Sakili and Pottapi *nāḍu* with Gaṇḍikōṭa as his capital;* moreover, Pottapi *nāḍu rājya* is said to have been granted to him as his *nāyakara*. The term "*rājya*" is used in this inscription in its general sense denoting a tract of land. But in the language of the *Aṭṭhavaṇa* it always meant a province of the empire.

The number of the *rājyas* was not fixed. The *rājyas* included in the empire at the time of Kṛṣṇadēvarāya's accession are enumerated in his famous marriage edict. They are: (1) Ghanagiri (Penugoṇḍa), (2) Gutti, (3) Kandanavōlu (Kurnool), (4) Candragiri, (5) Mulbāgal, and (6) Rāyadurga. In addition to these Gaṇḍikōṭa *sthala*, the *sīmas* of Siddhavaṭṭa, Pottapi and Nāgamangala are mentioned. † The edict seems to describe the territory that was then under the direct control of the imperial government. In the early years of his reign Kṛṣṇarāya subdued the rebellious province of Paḷaivīḍu. Having reduced to submission the upper valley of the Kāvēri, he constituted it into a new province with Śrīrangapaṭṭaṇa as its

* *LR.* xliv. (Nelandalūr) p. 25.

† *MMss.* 15-3-32 pp. 74-75.

घनगिर्यारव्यराज्येच गुत्तिराज्ये च विश्रुते
राज्ये कन्दनवोलारव्ये गण्डिकोटस्थलेऽपि च
सिद्धवट्टारव्यया सिद्ध पोत्तसीमारव्य विश्रुते
चन्द्रगिर्यारव्यराज्यस्यनागमङ्गलसीमनि
मुलपाकाख्ये महाराज्ये रायदुर्गे महत्यपि·

capital. * His wars against the Gajapati resulted in the reconquest of the old province of Udayagiri, and the creation of a new one with Koṇḍavīḍu as its capital. Similarly, the doab between the Kṛṣṇa and the Tungabhadrā, which he wrested from the Ādil Shāh about 1520 A.D. was constituted into the province of Rāicūr. The *rājyas* of Bārakūru, † Śrīsaila, ‡ Nallūr, § and Hampi-Hastināvati ¶ are also mentioned in the inscriptions. Therefore, it may be said that at the commencement of the reign of Acyutadēvarāya the following *rājyas* were included in the empire:—

1. Hampi-Hastināvati. 2. Penugoṇḍa 3. Gutti 4. Kandanavōlu 5. Śrīsailam 6. Rāyadurga 7. Bārakūru 8. Araga ‖ 9. Koṇḍavīḍu 10. Udayagiri 11. Candragiri 12. Mulbāgal 13. Paḻaivīḍu 14. Tiruvaḍi 15. Śrīrangapaṭṭaṇa 16. Rāicūr 17. Niḍugal. **

The province of Rāicūr was lost by Vijayanagara at the very commencement of Acyuta's reign. Although it was reconquered in 1535 A.D. it was lost again in 1538-9 A.D. The *rājyas* of Buruḍakunṭe. †† Kongu, ‡‡ Ādavani, §§ and Cennapaṭṭaṇa ¶¶ are referred to in the inscriptions of the reign of Acyutarāya. It is possible that some of these are called *rājyas* in a very general way, and they may not denote the *rājya* technically so called.

The provinces or *rājyas* seem to have been created from time to time to suit some immediate administrative needs.. Although Gutti *rājya* is mentioned in the inscriptions belonging to the early years of

* *LR.* xi. pp. 617-20.

† *MER.* 368/1927 1525 A.D.

‡ *ibid* 14 of 1915.

§ *EC.* ix. Ht. 28.

¶ *EC.* xi. Jl. 24.

‖ *EC.* vii, i. Sh. 26.

** *EC.* xii. Pg. 75.

†† *MER.* 576 of 1912.

‡‡ *MER.* 13 of 1922-23.

§§ *MMss.* 19-1-4.

¶¶ *EC.* ix. Cp. 53.

Kṛṣṇadēvarāya, * it is spoken of as a sub-division of the Penugoṇḍa *rājya* in A.D. 1529. † In the inscriptions of the reigns of Acyuta and Sadāsiva, it is once again described as a *rājya*. ‡ It is obvious that the province of Gutti was abolished for some reason after 1512 A.D., and reduced to the position of a sub-division of Penugoṇḍa *rājya*; but it was reconstituted once again after the accession of Acyuta. Some of the *rajyās* which are occasionally mentioned in the inscriptions might be temporary creations for administrative purposes.

Section 2: The Provincial Administration: The Durga Daṇṇāik or the Provincial Governor:—The chief executive of the *rājya* or the province was a military officer called the *Durga Daṇṇāik*. It is often said that under the Rāyas of Vijayanagara the provincial governor wielded absolute authority, practically as an independent chief, over all the villages in his province. § This view is untenable as it is not supported by known facts. In the first place, it is extremely doubtful whether a provincial governor had freedom to remain in his province. According to Nuniz, 'the nobles were never suffered to settle in cities or towns, because they could there be beyond the reach of his (emperor's) hand.' They were, however, permitted to go thither sometimes. ¶ Since the provincial governor was also

* *SII.* iv. 802, 803; *EC.* xii. Mi. 64.   † *MER.* 332 of 1926.

‡ *SII.* iv. 801; *MER.* 295 of 1926.

§ Iswar Dutt: *JAHRS.* iv. p. 169.

¶ *FE.* p. 374.

That the provincial governors visited their provinces occasionally is indicated by the following statement of the *Rāyavācaka*: *ASPP.* iii. p. 38.

విన్న వేళకు ఆ ప్రసంగములు తలపక నాలుగార్లదినముల వెనుక సరుమస్థలాలు చూచేనిమిత్యముగా ఆసీమాధిపతి వస్తున్నాడని వదంతి పుట్టించి ఆయా స్థలముల వుండేవారికి కోటకొత్తళములున్ను రస్తుసామగ్రీలున్ను వైచి ...

an *amaranāyaka* or noble, and held his *amaramāgāṇi* in the province over which he had to rule, it is not probable that he usually dwelt in his province. However, an exception seems to have been made in the case of frontier provinces, where the governors and *amaranāyakas* were allowed to remain within their charges to safeguard the frontier: Those who are at the far end of the kingdom," says Paes, "where (an attack) is feared, such as the kingdom of Oria, and the territories of the Ydallcao," were exempted from going to the capital even during the Dasara festival. * Secondly, as one of the *amaranāyakas*, he had to maintain a fixed contingent of troops for the service of the emperor, and pay him every year a stipulated sum of money as tribute. If he failed to maintain the required number of troops, or to pay the tribute, he was severely punished, and his *amaramāgāṇi* lapsed to the state. † Lastly, his authority did not extend over those villages of his province which were granted as *nāyankara* to the other *amaranāyakas*. These villages were given to them by the emperor to whom alone they were responsible. They had direct dealings with the Royal Mint into which they paid their dues every year at the Dasara season. They probably looked after the judicial work connected with their estates. The provincial governor could not have had much to do with the internal affairs of the *dēvādāya*, *brahmādāya* and *maṭhapura* villages. It is not at all known whether they paid their *jōḍi* directly to the exchequer or to the *maṇiagārs*

Probably the governors and the nobles used to visit their estates in the summer.

గ్రామగ్రామంబున నొక । సామంతున కిడిన చలువ చప్పరములు త
న్నై మేదిని గుంపటిలో । దామరలుగ బోలె నట్టి తరి నొప్పారెన్ ॥

Am 2: 69.

* *FE.* pp. 262-63. † *ibid.* p. 374.

of their respective *sīmas.* The *daṇṇāik* or the governor appears to have had control over the *Bhaṇḍāravāḍa* villages alone. It must not be supposed that these formed his estate; a few of them might have been given to him as his *amaramāgāṇi*; but the rest belonged to the emperor.

If the provincial governor was not permitted to reside in his province, how did he carry on its administration? Every person of any importance at Vijayanagara engaged the services of an agent who was usually known as the *kāryakarta*. All the *nāyakas*, governors, and ministers had their own *kāryakartas*; and much of the civil work of the empire was performed through these functionaries. Although the provincial governor was not permitted, except occasionally, to go to his province, he still managed to discharge his duties, by deputing his *kāryakarta* to look after the provincial administration on his behalf. A few examples may be usefully cited in this connection: Kṛṣṇarāya conferred the governorship of the province of Koṇḍavīḍu on his minister Sāḷuva Timma in 1514 A.D.; but he is said to have left one of his brothers to govern the province as his deputy. * It was, in fact, Nādiṇḍla Gōpa, a nephew of the minister, that was appointed as the deputy; and he held this office until 1525. A.D. Rāmābhaṭlayya who was the governor of Udayagiri in 1540 A.D., appointed his nephew Yeṇḍalūri Venkaṭādri Ayya to govern the province on his behalf. † Rāmarāja Viṭṭhala who held the governorship of the Madura country had several *kāryakartas*; a certain Aṇṇan Basavaṇṇa Nāyaka served him in this capacity in 1537 A.D.; ‡ Timmappa Nāyaka

* *FE.* p. 318.

† *LR.* 13 (Mahānandipalle 9) p. 308.

‡ *MER.* A 6 of 1906.

held this office in 1546 A.D.; * and Viśwanātha Nāyaka acted as his agent in 1551 A.D. †

The governors of the provinces, or the *durga-daṇṇāiks*, as they were called, should, according to the *Āmuktamālyada*, be Brahmans, ‡ because they would serve the emperor faithfully and well in the midst of great difficulties lest they should be laughed at by the *kṣatriya* and the *śūdra* officers. § The principles which Kṛṣṇarāya described in this work were carried out in actual practice. Most of the provincial governors of Kṛṣṇadēva and Acyuta were drawn from the Brahman community, and the practice was not altogether abandoned even during the reign of Sadāśiva.

The most important duty of the *durga-daṇṇāik* or the provincial governor was to protect his province from the attacks of the enemy. The real need for such protection existed only in the provinces along the frontiers; and special arrangements were made to guard them well. The governor and the *amaranāyakas* of these provinces were not compelled to attend the imperial court at the capital, and they were permitted to remain in their places, even during the Daśāra season, so that the frontiers might not be exposed to the attacks of the enemy. The governor seems to have collected a tax called *durga-daṇāyi-nivartana*; ¶ probably it was intended to serve as remuneration for giving protection to the people. The governor was also the revenue officer of the province, and probably also its supreme magistrate. According to the *Rāyavācaka*, the *daṇṇāiks* reported to Vīra Narasimha that in all the *rājyas* the defence and police arrangements were

* *MER.* 2 of 1920.   † *ibid* 721 of 1916.

‡ *Ām.* 4: 207.   § *ibid* 4: 217.   ¶ *LR.* 13. (Puṣpagiri) p. 69.

in good condition. * Probably the provincial governor was held responsible, in the first instance, for preserving law and order in his province. In that case, the *kāvalgars* in his province must have been his subordinates.

The term *cāvaḍi* or *sāvaḍi* very frequently occurs in the records of the period. It denotes an office having jurisdiction over a certain area, where the government records were preserved by a staff of officials called generally *karṇams*. The frequent mention of *cāvaḍis* shows that the internal administration of the provinces of the empire was carried on by an organised bureaucracy. Some officials connected with the administration of the provinces are mentioned in a few inscriptions; but it is not possible to define the nature of the work which they were expected to perform.

The Sīma:—The administrative arrangements obtaining in the sub-divisions of the *rājya* cannot at present be described accurately, as the material that has a bearing on the subject is very meagre; but stray allusions in the inscriptions show that the administrative sub-divisions, *sīma*, *nāḍu*, and *sthala* had their respective officials. Several inscriptions of the Kurnool district contain what appears to be an exhaustive list of officials who were connected with the administration of the *sīma*. Venkaṭādri, who was governing the Kandanavōlu *rājya* during the reign of Sadāśiva, exempted, by the command of the king, the *mahājanas* of several *agrahāras* from the payment of certain dues, and issued an order to the *dhoras*, *pārupatyagāras*, *rāyasamvāru*, *avasaramvāru*, and *rācakaraṇālu* connected with the administration of the *sīma*, prohibiting them

* *ASPP.* iii. p. 13.

from collecting the exempted taxes. * The *dhoras* referred to in the inscriptions were the *amaranāyakas* who held some of the villages of the *sīma* under the *nāyakara* tenure. Therefore, they need not be considered in this context. The *pārupatyagāra* or *maṇiagārā*, as he is sometimes called, was the chief executive officer of the *sīma*. † He was appointed by the governor himself or his deputy. Rāyasam Timma, who held sway over Gaṇḍikōṭa about 1525 A.D., appointed one Aṇṇāji Ayya as his *pārupatyagāra*. ‡ Yeṇḍalūru Venkaṭādri Ayya, who ruled Udayagiri in 1540 A.D. as Rāmabhaṭlayya's deputy, appointed a certain Maṇḍali Kāmābhaṭ as the *pārupatyagāra* of Ēruva *sīma*. § Kāmappa Nāyaka held the *pārupatya* of Śrīrangapaṭṭaṇa *sīma* under Rāmabhaṭlayya about the same time. ¶ The *sīma- pārupatyagāras* are mentioned in two inscriptions dated 1526 and 1547 A.D. respectively. ||

The *sīma-pārupatyagāra* appears to have been a revenue officer. Rāmabhaṭlayya's *pārupatyagāra*, Kāmappa Nāyaka, imposed on areca-nut gardens a duty 'which had not existed before,' in the tax-free villages of Śrīrangapaṭṭaṇa *sīma*. His successor, Peddirāja, remitted not only this duty, but the tax upon sugar-cane mills at Hāruvahaḷḷi Vogeyasamudra. ** Aṇṇāji Ayya created a *santa* at Calamardhigaṇḍapaṭṭaṇam. †† Therefore the *pārupatyagāra* could impose taxes and remit them; he could tap fresh sources of revenue; and he

* *MMss.* 15-3-6 (Uppulagūḍem) p. 212. *LR.* 7; (Pārumāncāla) pp. 86-7.

† *EC.* xi. Hk. 112; *LR.* 7. (Pārumāncāla) pp. 86-87; *LR.* 13. (Kattaragaṇḍla) pp. 279-80.

‡ *LR.* 15. (Talamancipaṭṭaṇam) pp. 83-84.

§ *ibid* 13. (Mahānandipalle) pp. 308-309; *ibid* 41. (Mallelaceruvu) p. 353.

¶ *EC.* iii. i. Sr. 6.

|| *LR.* 7. pp. 86-87; 13 pp. 279-80.

** *EC.* iii. i. Sr. 6.

†† *LR.* 15. (Talamancipaṭṭaṇam) pp. 83-84.

had also something to do with the grant of *paṭṭas* to the ryots for the lands which they cultivated *. What other powers he exercised, it is not possible to say. He must have had his own *cāvaḍi*, where a staff of *karṇams* kept the accounts pertaining to his *sīma*.

No information is available at present about the three classes of officials, *rāyasams*, *avasarams*, and *rācakarṇams* mentioned in the inscriptions. The term *rāyasam*, as mentioned already, means the profession of writing; it also denotes people engaged in the profession. The *rāyasams* should be taken to mean clerks or officials connected with the secretariat of the imperial government. It is not easy to define the exact nature of the duties discharged by *avasarams* or *avasarikas*, as they are sometimes called. The term *avasaram* means necessity or urgency; and *avasarika* denotes a person employed to draw the attention of the emperor to urgent business which he had to transact. Though the *avasarikas* are frequently mentioned in the records, their duties are nowhere defined; but Tiruvengaḷanātha gives a hint which enables us to understand the nature of their work to some extent. The *avasarams* seem to denote a class of servants of either sex employed in the imperial household for the purpose of bringing to the notice of the emperor, when he was within the precincts of the zenana, anything that demanded his immediate attention. They informed him when people desiring immediate audience waited for him in the *mōsāla* or the anteroom. They also intimated to him the hour when he had to attend to each of the items of his daily programme. † According to the *Rāyavācaka*, the *rāyasams* and *avasarams* accompanied the king in his campaigns. The *rācakarṇams*

* *EC.* iv. Ch. 38.

† *Pym.* iii. pp. 190, 207.

were probably *karaṇams* of the imperial household. It is evident that these three classes of officials belonged to the imperial household, and that they did not form integral parts of the administrative machinery of the *sīma*. The part played by the *rāyasams*, *avasarams*, and *rācakarṇams* in the administration of the *sīma* cannot, however, be ascertained at present.

Information regarding the officials of the *nāḍu* is almost totally lacking. The *taḷavara* of Kuḍatini *nāḍu* is mentioned in a grant of 1530 A.D. * Probably it had other officials ; but the records of the period do not furnish any information about them.

The *sthala* had a *cāvaḍi* of its own, where the *sthala-karṇams* maintained the accounts of all the villages in the *sthala*. In an inscription of Honganūru in Mysore dated 1549 A.D., besides the village *gauḍa* and *sēnabova*, a *karṇikka* of the *cāvaḍi* is mentioned. † This official was very probably the *karṇam* of the *sthala*. The *sthala-karṇams* are alluded to in several records of the time. In an inscription dated 1568 A.D., the officers of the Duvvūr *sthala* viz., the *reḍḍi*, the *karṇam*, and the *seṭṭi* are referred to. ‡

The officials of the *sthala* were probably in close touch with the village administration. The *karṇikka* of the *cāvaḍi* mentioned above kept in his *cāvaḍi* the *paṭṭas* of all the ryots in the villages. He was expected to prevent any ryot without the *paṭṭa* from cultivating the land. § If the *kaifiyat* of Bukkāyapalle can be trusted, the officers of the *sthala* had to perform some judicial work in discharging their duties. They joined the officers of three other villages to form a

* *MER.* A 10 of 1922-23.

† *EC.* iv. Ch. 38.

‡ *LR.* 36. (Bukkāyapalle) p. 445.

§ *EC.* iv. Ch. 38.

court or *dharmāsana* for deciding a dispute between two claimants of a *reḍḍi mirāsi*. They had probably other duties also, but nothing is known about them.

Section 3 : The Village Administration:—The village administration in South India was carried on from time immemorial by the village assemblies which may be divided for the sake of convenience into two classes. In the villages which belonged to the crown, the village assembly called '*ūr*' transacted all public business on behalf of the villagers. The assembly of this type, which played an important part in the rural administration in the pre-Vijayanagara times, disappeared more or less completely by the end of the fourteenth century. The village assemblies, no doubt, are occasionally mentioned in early Vijayanagara inscriptions; but they were survivals of an era which came to an end with the advent of the Mussalmans. They disappeared gradually owing to the impact of the institutions of a more modern age. Therefore, the assemblies of this class did not play any important part in the local administration of the period under consideration.

In the *brahmādāya* villages, however, the village assemblies, which were known as *sabhās*, continued to function as vigorously as before. Their existence in the *brahmādāya* villages or *agrahāras* was due not so much to the fostering care of the government as to the need inherent in the system of tenure under which lands were held. The king or one of his officers granted a village to one or more Brahmans as a reward for his or their learning and piety. If the donee was a single individual, the village granted was called *ēkabhōga* or the land enjoyed by a single individual. If, on the other hand, the donees were several, the village granted was known as *gaṇabhōga* or the land enjoyed by a *gaṇa* or a group. The distinction between *ēkabhōga* and *gaṇabhōga* was not, however, permanent, as the *ēkabhōga* villages were transformed into *gaṇabhōga* within a generation or two of the original donee.

As the *gaṇabhōga* villages were granted to all the donees collectively, they jointly managed the land which they held together. Since the management of the affairs of the village by all the shareholders, could be carried on only by common consent, they had to meet frequently to discuss the problems affecting the welfare of the whole village. The *sabhā* or the assembly of the *brahmādāya* villages came into existence in this fashion. The shareholders of the villages were known as *vidwan-mahājanas*, or simply *mahājans*, who are frequently mentioned in the inscriptions, as discharging some public duty or other.

No information is available about the manner of the working of this *vidwan-mahājana-sabhā*. The Local Records, no doubt, allude to these bodies frequently; but they do not describe any of the functions of these assemblies excepting the judicial. These *sabhās* took the place of the civil courts of the empire, and tried cases which were referred to them by the king or his subordinates. Besides the judicial duties, the *sabhās* served as a link between the villagers and the government. They collected the *jōḍi* from the ryots, and paid it into the imperial treasury. They brought the grievances of the villagers to the notice of the Rāya, and had them redressed.

The Āyagārs:—The village assemblies in the government villages yielded place to a group of village officers called *āyagārs* who governed the village. They served as a link connecting the village folk with the government and their officials. The origin of the *āyagār* system cannot easily be traced. It was already in full force during the period of the Kākatīya rule. The *āyagārs* were twelve in number:

(1)	*Karṇam or Sēnābova*	(7)	Carpenter
(2)	*Gauḍa or Reḍḍi*	(8)	Goldsmith
(3)	*Talāri*	(9)	*Purōhit*
(4)	Washerman	(10)	Waterman
(5)	Shoemaker	(11)	Potter
(6)	Barber	(12)	Blacksmith

Most of the *āyagārs* were village servants rather than the servants of the government. The first three only had any connection with the government.

The *karṇam* or *sēnābova* maintained the accounts of the village known as *guḍikaṭṭu* or *āyakaṭṭu*. He kept registers in which the extent of the village site, the area of the land belonging to the village, its boundaries, the extent of the rent-free land, groves, gardens, crematoria, tanks, the number of wells and canals, and the exact extent of land belonging to each ryot in the village were entered.* Besides, he had to measure and keep accounts of the cultivable, non-cultivable, and waste lands, gardens, dry fields and pasture lands.

The *karṇam* was closely associated with the *reḍḍi* in the administration of the village. His main duty was the collection of revenue due to the state as stipulated by the *jamābandi* settlement.† The *reḍḍi* and *karṇam* had to work together in the collection

* cf. *Āndhra Patrika*: *Ugādi Sañcika* (1922) p. 157.

† This account of village administration is mainly based upon the *Aṭṭhavaṇa Tantram* (*MMss.* 15-6-8.).

of state dues ; and both of them attended the annual *jamābandi*, when the accounts were balanced, and the next year's dues settled.

Although the *reḍḍi* and the *karṇam* were subject to the authority of the officers of the *Aṭṭhavaṇa*, they were virtually the rulers of the village. The *Aṭṭhavaṇa Tantram* mentions three causes which helped these officers in the acquisition of so much power. (1) The absence of direct contact between the ryots and the government. (2) The fear of the ryots that they might involve them in trouble by submitting false accounts to the *Aṭṭhavaṇam* officials regarding the extent of land cultivated by them. (3) A feeling of loyalty to the officers whose families had been managing the village affairs for several generations. Owing to these considerations, the ryots would not complain to higher authorities against the *reḍḍi* and *karṇam* even when they had specific grievances against them.

Next in importance to these officers was the *talāri* or the village policeman. His duties and the part which he played in the village administration will be described in a different context. As the other *āyagārs* had little or no direct connection with the government, they may be dealt with briefly. The *purōhit* was the village priest. He had to preside over all the ceremonies that might be performed in the ryots' houses ; he had to fix an auspicious day for ploughing the fields and harvesting the crops that might be raised thereon. The carpenter made the ploughs, carts, and other tools necessary for agricultural operations ; the blacksmith made knives, sicles, and other metallic instruments needed by the cultivators ; the barber shaved them, the washerman washed their clothes, and the potter supplied them with pots. The goldsmith measured the grain during the harvest, and the waterman regulated the supply of water to the fields. The shoemaker not only manufactured sandals for the villagers, but provided the ryots with leather ropes and buckets that were needed to bale out water from the wells.

The *āyagārs* were not paid any salary by the government for their services either in coin or in kind; but they were assigned plots of village land, which, like the office which they held, remained hereditary possessions of the family. The plots of land thus assigned to them were known as their *mirāsi* on which they were liable to pay a small quit-rent known as *jōḍi*. In addition to the *mirāsi*, they had another source of income. Each ryot had to measure out to them at the time of the harvest, a fixed quantity of paddy or other produce for every field, *kapila*, or *khaṇḍuga* in accordance with the custom of the village. The share of paddy or other produce which the *āyagārs* obtained from the ryots was known as their '*mēra*.'

CHAPTER V

THE LAND TENURE AND THE NĀYANKARA SYSTEM

Section 1: *The Proprietorship of the Soil*:—The first problem, that should be considered in connection with the land tenure, is that relating to the proprietory right in the soil. Who was the ultimate proprietor of the soil? Was it the emperor or the ryot? Nuniz gives an unequivocal answer to this question. He says:

> "*All the land belongs to the King*, and from him the captains hold it. They make it over to the husbandmen who pay nine-tenths to their lord; and *they have no land of their own* for *the kingdom belongs entirely to the King.*" *

This has been denied by certain writers recently. It is said to be 'exactly the reverse of the Hindu theory.' Inscriptions are said 'to prove to the hilt,' the contrary. † 'That it is a fact,' says one writer, 'is proved by the innumerable epigraphs of the period.' ‡ He supports his contention by adducing two arguments:

> (1) "The provincial governors and their subordinates and the private persons owning landed property grant villages for the benefit of deities and brahmans." §

> (2) "The person who owns the landed property has the right of disposing of the land at his will and pleasure except perhaps in the case of *inām* lands." ¶

It is true that the provincial governors and their subordinates granted villages to the gods and

* *FE*. p. 379.

† K. P. Jayaswal: *Hindu Polity* p. 174.

‡ K. Iswar Dutt: *JAHRS*. v. p. 73.

§ *ibid*.

¶ *ibid*.

Brahmans; but this does not show, 'private property in the soil.' What it may be claimed to show at the most is that the proprietory right in the soil belonged to the governors and their subordinates; but, as a matter of fact, they had no such right. In a large number of instances, the donor of a village or a piece of land (the governor or his subordinate) made the grant with the express permission of the emperor, or one of his ministers acting on his behalf. In several grants, no reference is made to the sanction of the emperor at all. From these it is inferred that the governor or his subordinate could make grants without obtaining the permission of the emperor, and that he was the supreme lord within his own territory. That this was not the case will be shown presently. Even if such grants were taken as having been made without reference to the emperor, they could only indicate the extent of the donor's power, and not his 'property in the soil.' If the emperor, according to this contention, had no 'property in the soil,' how could the governor, who was but his representative, have it? If the governor had it, it was because the emperor had delegated it to him. It is, therefore, reasonable to believe that, even in grants containing no reference to the royal sanction, it was understood to be implicit. Such of the private persons as granted lands to the temples and the Brahmans, were the chief relations, and dependents of the emperor, or his nobles. Their grants are not helpful in determining whose was 'property in the soil.' The fact that the imperial government could resume at will any land granted to a temple or a Brahman is sufficient proof to establish the right of the emperor as the proprietor of the soil.

Taking the sale and purchase of land into consideration, it is necessary to find out what exactly was sold and purchased. Was it 'the property in the soil', or was it only the occupancy right that formed the subject of the transaction? It is very difficult to say which. It may be contended that because the formula *nidhi-nikṣēpa-jala-taru-pāṣāṇa* is found in certain sale-deeds of the time, the seller should be considered to have sold his 'property in the soil,' and the purchaser to have purchased the same. Such an inference need not necessarily follow. Nobody can deny the fact that at present the King Emperor of India is recognised by law to be the owner of every inch of ground in the British territory. Nevertheless, the formula mentioned above is repeated in all the sale-deeds of the *ryotwāri* lands even at the present day. It is needless to point out that the modern seller of such land is only disposing of his rights to occupy and cultivate, and not his proprietory right in the soil. Matters in Vijayanagara times could not have been very different from what they are now.

Two important points must be noticed in this connection: (1) The imperial government exercised the right of surveying lands frequently, and assessing taxes afresh. A similar right is exercised by the present government. They carry on the work of resurvey and resettlement, because they claim 'property in the soil.' This claim is admitted by all. If the imperial government of Vijayanagara exercised the rights of resurvey and resettlement, it was because the Rāya was the owner of all the land in the empire, and others held it of him under some kind of tenure. (2) When taxation became very oppressive the ryots frequently abandoned their homes and farms and migrated to foreign parts. The emperor or on his behalf some of his officers brought them back after granting them concessions. The abandonment of their homes and fields by the ryots indicates that they had no proprietory right in the land. If they had any such right, the emperor could not have legally enhanced the land tax as he liked, and the ryots would never have abandoned their homes and farms in the way in which they did.

Although these and other considerations prove that during the age of the Rāyas, the proprietorship of the soil was vested in the emperor, there is room for conceding the existence of private ownership in certain places. In A.D. 1534, 'by the order of the royal treasurer, Timmapayya,' one of his subordinates, and 'all the Hebbaruva Brahmans of Kūḍalūr and Maṇalūr' made a grant to the temple priest Nārāyaṇayya of some land to the service of the God, 'with the consent of all the farmers and the subjects of those villages.' * The *koḍagi* lands of several Lingāyat *maṭhas* were made *sarvamānya* in A. D. 1545 by Bhaṇḍiya Basavaṇṇa Nāyaka with the approval of two *seṭṭis* and a *gauḍa*. †

In these two cases, the consent of all the farmers, subjects, *seṭṭis* and *gauḍa* was considered necessary to make the grant valid. They must have possessed some sort of proprietory right in the soil; otherwise their consent would not have become necessary. However, grants such as these, come from a particular corner of the Canarese country where the individual ownership of land appears to have been recognised. But this is an exception. The state ownership of land was admitted in all the other parts of the empire.

Section 2: The Classification of Villages:—Before taking up for consideration the kinds of tenure, it is necessary to consider the classes into which the villages

* *EC.* ix. Cp. 155. † *ibid* Nl. 81.

were divided by the *Aṭṭhavaṇam* department. For the convenience of fiscal administration, the villages of the empire were divided into a number of classes. It is said, in an inscription of A.D. 1542, that the villages in the Śrīrangapaṭṭana district were divided into

(1) *Daḷavāyi agrahāras.*
(2) *Mānya grāmas.*
(3) *Kara grāmas.* *

Five classes of villages, are mentioned in several inscriptions of the Udayagiri and Penugoṇḍa *rājyas.* †

(1) *Amara grāmas.*
(2) *Umbaḷa grāmas.*
(3) *Bhaṇḍāravāḍa grāmas.*
(4) *Agrahāras.*
(5) *Agrahāra-dēvasthānas.*

In addition to the *Bhaṇḍāravāḍa-grāmas* and *agrahāras*, *dēvasthāna* villages are referred to in a grant of Gōḍēkallu in the Anantapūr district. ‡ An epigraph from Old Siruvoḷḷa in the Kurnool district alludes to (1) *dēvatāgrāmālu*, (2) *agrahārālu* and (3) *bhaṭavṛttulu.* § The last class seems to refer to service *ināms*. Moreover, three classes of villages, *vara*, *hore*, and *kara grāmas* are frequently mentioned in the inscriptions. ¶ *Kara grāmās* must be villages yielding *kara* or revenue to the government. Therefore, they may be said to belong to the same class as the *Bhaṇḍāravāḍa grāmas* or villages belonging to the imperial treasury. The word *vara* means 'a favour, a gift, a reward, a recompense.' ‖ Therefore, the *vara grāma* may be taken to mean a village which was given as a gift to a temple,

* *EC.* iii. i. Sr. 6.

† *LR.* 13 p. 144.

‡ *MER.* 390 of 1920.

§ *LR.* 40 p. 215.

¶ *LR.* 15 p. 120; *ibid* p. 133.

‖ Kittel: *Canarese-English Dict.* p. 1377.

maṭha, or a Brahman. *Hore* is said to mean 'an allowance of grain to village servants.' * As this allowance was obviously given as a remuneration for some services rendered, *hore grāma* may be taken to mean a village given to a person for some service rendered to government. Probably, it belongs to the same class as the *amaram* villages.

The villages of the empire, therefore, fell into three main groups, viewed from the standpoint of land tenure under which they were held :

I. *The Bhaṇḍāravāḍa grāmas* or crown lands.
II. *The Amara* villages.
III. *The Mānya* villages.

The last two groups are capable of further sub-division.

This classification was neither rigid nor permanent. All the classes ultimately lapsed into the first. The *amara* villages were held by the *nāyakas* at the pleasure of the crown. A *nāyaka* might at any time be deprived of his holding, and his village or villages be transferred to the treasury. † Again, the villages granted to the temples, the Brahmans, and the *maṭhas* might also be absorbed by the treasury, if circumstances necessitated the adoption of such a course. ‡

Of the three classes of villages, the *Bhaṇḍāravāḍa* class is the only one where there was direct contact between the ryot and the imperial government. The *amara* villages were given to the *nāyakas* who formed the intermediaries between the government and the ryot. The holders of *mānya grāmas* were responsible to the treasury for the payment of *jōḍi*, and the

* H. H. Wilson: *Glossary* p. 211.

† *FE.* p. 374.

‡ *MMss.* 19-1-14.

farmer had no chance of coming into contact with the government.

I. The Bhaṇḍāravāḍa Villages:—To this class belonged all the villages of the empire which were not given either to the *amaranāyakas*, or to religious institutions. The *Bhaṇḍāravāḍa* villages were under the control of the provincial governor and his subordinates. The imperial *aṭṭhavaṇa*, under whose jurisdiction they were, sent its officials to supervise the work of the provincial governors. There was a separate treasurer for them, and he was assisted by several 'scribes.' *

II. The Amara Villages:—The most important duty which the Rāya had to discharge was to provide for the defence of the realm. For the purpose of equipping himself with an efficient army, he apportioned the country among his *nāyakas* who in return had to provide him with men and money. Nuniz gives a short but interesting account of the way in which the land was distributed among the nobles during the reign of Acyuta.

> "All the land belongs to the king, and from his hand the captains hold it". "The kingdom of Bisnaga is divided between more than two hundred captains who are all heathen." †

This is confirmed by Paes:

> "These captains whom he has over these troops are the nobles of the kingdom; they are lords, and they hold the city, and the towns and the villages of the kingdom." ‡

The *amaranāyakas* according to the *Rāyavācaka* were holding the territories containing the forts of

* *FE.* p. 384. † *ibid* p. 37˜ ‡ *ibid* p. 280.

Ādavani, Ceyyēṭidurgam, Gutti, Gaṇḍikōṭa, Candragiri, Guṟṟamkoṇḍa, Maddūr, Śōṇagiri, Triśirapura, Kunnattūr, Penugoṇḍa, Nandyāla, Śrīrangapaṭṭaṇam, Ummattūr, Daḷanāyakulakōṭa, Vallamkōṭa, Madura, Pāḷaiyamkōṭa, Diṇḍigal, Satyavīḍu, Koṭṭikallu, Ḍanginīkōṭa, Nārāyaṇavanam and other forest strongholds. * As these forts were scattered all over the empire, it is obvious that nearly three-fourths of it was governed by the nobles or the *amaranāyakas.*

Section 3: *The Nāyankara System*:—The *nāyakas* held land of the emperor under a military tenure called *amaram.* They were consequently known by the name *amaranāyakas.* They claimed to hold the land for *nāyankara*, a word the meaning of which is not quite clear. Sometimes, it is loosely asserted that the country was held by the nobles on feudal tenure. A recent writer says:

> "The country was parcelled out into provinces which were held on feudal tenure. Several of the feudal lords were hereditary princes." †

The *nāyankara* system has no doubt very strong affinities to feudalism but it has also very many differences. Feudalism is said "to contain both a social element based upon land tenure, and a political element expressed by homage and fealty." "The union of the two relationships of lord with man and lord with vassal," is said to be the characteristic feature of feudalism. ‡ It is very much to be doubted whether the political element was present in the *nāyankara system.* No instance of an *amaranāyaka* swearing fealty and rendering homage to his overlord is recorded.

* *ASPP.* iii. p. 29.

† J. Ramayya Pantulu: *JAHRS.* ii. p. 216.

‡ Medley: *English Constitutional History*

Nāyankarism may, therefore, be described as a system of land tenure according to which land was held immediately or mediately of the emperor on condition of military service. People holding land of the emperor on this tenure were known as *amaranāyakas* or more briefly *nāyakas*.

(*a*) Although the tenants of a feudal lord were originally only tenants at will, they soon ceased to be such. "Tenancy at will grew into tenancy for life, which in its turn extended into a heritable holding." * The *amaranāyaka*, on the contrary, always remained a tenant at will, and until the period subsequent to the battle of Tālikōṭa, no *amaranāyaka* could put forward any pretensions of a hereditary character. The emperor could take away the lands of any *nāyaka* when he became displeased with him. The frequent change of *amaranāyakas* is indicated by inscriptions. A few examples are enough to illustrate the point.

(1) The village of Tarnupāḍu with its hamlets was granted by Sadāśiva as *nāyakara* to Nandyāla Avubhaḷayyadēva Mahārāja in 1543 A.D. † The same village with its hamlet Cennāreḍḍipalle was granted by the same monarch to Rāmarāju Peda Tirumalarāju Tirumalayya in A.D. 1552. ‡ Again, Tarnupāḍu with its hamlets was granted to Mādrāju Nāgappa in A.D. 1554. §

(2) The village of Peda Kommerla was granted as *nāyakara* to Nandyāla Timma in A.D. 1544 ; ¶ but in A.D. 1545, it was granted to Nandyāla Avubhaḷarāju

* Medley: *English Constitutional History* p. 28.

† *LR.* 13 (Mārkāpuram) No. 5.

‡ *ibid* No. 7.

§ *ibid* No. 8.

¶ *LR.* 15 p. 107.

Avubhaḷēśvara, * and to Nandyāla Avubhaḷa Avubhaḷēśvara Cina Avubhaḷa in A.D. 1554. †

(3) Śrībhāṣyapuram (Sammaṭūru and Gaḍḍamayapalle) was given to Nandyāla Narasinga-Nārapa for his *nāyakara* in A.D. 1551 ; ‡ and it was granted to Nandyāla Vōbaḷayya Cina Vōbaḷayya in A.D. 1553 ; § and to Nandyāla Avubhaḷēśvara in A.D. 1557. ¶

(4) Pērūr was given to Nandyāla Kṛṣṇamarāju in A.D. 1538 ; to Nandyāla Cina Avubhaḷarāju in 1546 ; and to Nandyāla Avubhaḷarāju in A.D. 1547. ||

(5) Narasā Nāyaka, the regent of Immaḍi Narasimha, granted to Rampā Kannamanāyaka, the villages of Prodduṭūr and Rāmēśvaram in 1498 A.D., ** and to Sāḷuva Govindarāja a little later. ††

(6) The *kavul* of Cintarājupāḷem dated 1526 A.D., refers to the confiscation of the lands given to Namalanēni Kumāra Peda Bucci Nāyuḍu by Kṛṣṇadēvarāya for his supposed complicity in the revolt of Tarigoṇḍa Rāmānāyuḍu. ‡‡

(7) Kṛṣṇarāya granted Awuku in the Duvvūr *sīma* as *nayakara* to his *kāryakarta* Bukkarāju Timmarāju who held it until A.D. 1530. §§ Acyuta who ascended the throne in that year permitted him to continue in the office for two more years *i. e.*, until 1532 A.D. However, in 1533 A.D. Acyuta dismissed

* *LR.* 15 p. 111.

† *ibid* p. 129.

‡ *LR.* 33 p. 227.

§ *ibid* p. 228.

¶ *ibid* p. 228.

|| *MMss.* 15-3-6.

** *MMss.* 15-3-32. Inscription in the *Rangamanṭapam* of Rāmayadēva

†† *ibid.* Inscription in the *manṭapa* opposite to the *gōpura.*

‡‡ *LR.* 18 p. 407.

§§ *LR.* 18 p. 59 ; *LR.* 37 p. 286 (Inscription at Nandipāḍu.)

Timma from his service, and appointed in his place Salakarāju Peda Tirumala.* As Timma was an enemy of Peda Tirumala, the latter poisoned the emperor's mind against Timma, and had his estate of Awuku which was granted to him by Kṛṣṇadēvarāya confiscated. †

These instances are sufficient to prove that the holders of *nāyakara* lands were only tenants at will, and that their tenements were not hereditary possessions. The emperor or his ministers could deprive them of their lands, a practice in which they seem to have indulged frequently.

(*b*) The *nāyakara* system differs from feudalism in another important respect. The practice of sub-infeudation which was such a common feature of feudalism was present in *nāyankarism* to a very mild degree.

> "Just as the crown enfeoffed them (the tenants-in-chief) or granted them feuda or fiefs with right of inheritance for their heirs, so by a similar process known as sub-infeudation or the creation of sub-fiefs, would they carve out portions of their estates, and make them over to tenants to hold on condition of rendering in return services of various kinds." ‡

The process of sub-infeudation might be, and in fact was, carried on indefinitely. Although this practice was not altogether unknown to the *amaranāyakas*, the chain of feudal tenants was not usually lengthened by them beyond the second link. § The sub-tenants like the *amaranāyakas* themselves

* *LR.* 18 p. 61. † *LR.* 33 pp. 368-69.

‡ Medley: *The English Constitutional History* p. 28.

§ *LR.* 15. (Pedamuḍium) p. 139; 16. (Vaḍḍamānu) p. 454; *MMss.* 15-3-9 (Niṭṭūr); *LR.* 14 (Cinapasupula) p. 14.

were only tenants at will, and they never succeeded in establishing themselves as hereditary owners of their holdings. Moreover, they were not obliged to render to their lords any kind of service but military.

(*c*) The tenants of a feudal monarch owed him military service. They were required to be present with their retainers on the battle-field during the time of war. No money payment, except the occasional feudal dues, was demanded of the tenant for his holding. The *amaranāyakas* "besides maintaining these troops," had to make their "annual payments to the king." * These payments were different in nature from the feudal dues which each tenant had to pay from time to time to his feudal superior. The money which the *amaranāyakas* paid to the emperor was called *tribute*, and it was in the nature of a tax which they had to pay on their *amaram* lands.

The Duties of Amaranāyakas :—These have been described by the Portuguese writers fairly well.

(1) Paes:

> "As each one has revenue, so the king fixes for him the number of troops which he must maintain in foot, horse, and elephants. These troops are always ready for duty, whenever they may be called out, and wherever they may have to go." †

This is confirmed by a passage from Nuniz.

> "In this way the kingdom of Bisnaga is divided between more than two hundred captains,—and according to the lands and the revenues that they have, so the king settles for them the forces that they are compelled to keep up.' ‡

* *FE.* p. 281. † *ibid.* ‡ *ibid* p. 389.

(2) Paes:

"Each captain has to make his annual payments to the king." *

This is corroborated by Nuniz. He says:

"The King settles for them . . . how much revenue they have to pay him every month during the first nine days of September when they pay their land rents." †

(3) Nuniz:

"All these captains, who are thus like renters, must always attend the court, and of those whom this King (Acyuta) always has about him and by whom he is accompanied in his court there are more than two hundred. These are obliged always to be present with the King. . . . These nobles are never suffered to settle themselves in cities or towns, because they would there be beyond his hand." ‡

(4) Paes:

"Whenever a son happens to be born to this king or a daughter, all the nobles of the kingdom offer him great presents of money, and jewels of price, and so they do to him every year on the day of his birth." §

In addition to these, 'they give great gifts of money to the king,' on 'new year's day.' 'It is even said that they give on that day to the king in money a million and five hundred thousand gold *pardaos*.' ¶

(5) Nuniz:

"The nobles send it (food) to him (the king) every day to his house, namely, rice and wheat and meat, and fowls with all other necessary things." ‖

* *FE*. p. 281. † *ibid* p. 389. ‡ *ibid* p. 374.

§ *ibid* p. 281. ¶ *ibid* p. 282. ‖ *ibid* p. 371.

The *amaranāyakas* had therefore to maintain a stipulated body of troops. They had to pay not only the tribute on the lands * but offer presents to the sovereign on the occasions of the birth of his children as well as on his birth day and the New Year's Day. They had also to provide the emperor with his daily food. They had to live in the capital, always attending upon the monarch, and were not permitted to reside in any place outside the city. These appear to have been the principal obligations of the *amaranāyakas*, so far as they can be gleaned from the available records.

The failure to fulfil these obligations, specially the first three, was met with severe punishment by the emperor.

"(They) must," says Nuniz, "always maintain the full number of soldiers according to their obligations, for if he finds

* There is reason to believe that the *amaranāyakas* were allowed to deduct from the tribute certain items of revenue. The following passage of Tiruvengaḷanātha is of considerable interest in this connection.

ఏమోయి ! పరకాలుఁ డేలుచునున్న
సీమదా నెంత నేజేసినయట్టి
యుమ్మడియును తాణె యుత్తర సమర
మిమ్మోయి డింప మా కియ్యేటి వఱకుఁ
జెల్లినధన మెంత ? చేసేత నతఁడు
చెల్లింపగావలసిన ధన మెంత ?
* * * *
తలపోయనదియు నుత్తరపు ఘుమ్మళియుఁ
ద్రోయంగ మఱియు నందులకు నిందులకుఁ
బోయెఁ బొమ్మనివారిఁ బలిమిపుచ్చుటయు.

Pym. vi. pp. 460-461.

It is not possible to determine the exact nature of these deductions, as the meaning of some of the terms is not known.

that they have a less number they are severely punished and their estates confiscated." *

Again,

"If they do not pay (tribute) they are well punished, and are ruined and their property taken away." †

Durate Barbosa confirms the statement of Nuniz. He gives a graphic description of the manner in which the Rāya punished the defaulters.

"When he (the king) finds any great Lord or his relation guilty of any crime, he sends for him, and (as among them all go in great state) they come in rich litters borne by their servants, with many led horses and mounted men. On arrival at the palace the king is informed, and orders him to enter, and if he does not give a just excuse for his fault "he chastises him in words as thoroughly as he deserves and besides this, takes from him half of his revenues;" [he immediately orders him to be stripped, and stretched on the ground, and given a severe beating; and if this person happens to be his own near relative, and a great lord, the King himself beats him with his own hand, and after he has been well beaten, he orders that rich vestments should be given him from his wardrobe, and be taken in his palanquin very honourably with music and rejoicing to his own house."] ‡

The drastic corporal punishment which the Rāya is said to have inflicted upon delinquent nobles is not alluded to by other writers. This is, as said by Longworth Dames, 'an improbable story.' § The rest, however, is true. It is also supported by the *Rāyavācaka* which records the default of most of the *amaranāyakas* during the reign of Vīra Narasimha, owing to the weakness of the government. On Kṛṣṇarāya's accession, Sāḷuva Timma supervised their accounts and discovered that most of them owed large sums of money to the imperial exchequer. The

* *FE*. p. 374.

† *ibid* p. 389.

‡ *Barbosa* i. p. 209.

§ *ibid* p. 209. *n*. 1.

amaranāyakas admitted their fault, and begged the Rāya not to deprive them of their lands, but to permit them to hold their tenements as before. They promised that they would surrender to the government their elephants and horses to make up the arrears of rent.* They had, of course, to purchase horses and elephants afresh to make up the full strength of the contingents which they were obliged to maintain. The emperor, having agreed, the proposals were carried out.

Section 4: Kinds of Tenure :—The *amara* lands may be divided into two classes: (1) *amara* or *nāyankara* and (2) *umbali* or *umbalige.*

(1) In most of the inscriptions, the term which is used to describe the holding of an *amaranāyaka* is *nāyankara*; this, however, is only an abbreviated form, the fuller form being *amaranāyankara*, which occurs in a few inscriptions. Another shorter form of the word is '*amaram.*'

What is the meaning of the word *amaranāyankara*? It consists of three members *amara*, *nāyaka*, and *kara*. *Amara* means literally a command of a thousand foot. † It is, however, taken to mean 'a *grant* of a revenue by the prince or a *pāḷaigar* on condition of service generally military or police; such grants were resumable when the grantee failed to perform the stipulated service.' ‡ *Nāyaka* is said to denote 'a military chief under Vijayanagar Rājas.' § *Kara* is really a very difficult word to understand. It very probably means an office. ¶ Therefore, the word

* *ASPP.* iii. p. 33. † H. H. Wilson: *Glossary* p. 21.

‡ *ibid.* § *ibid* p. 372.

¶ "నీవు తలమావి వీడని నిసువువయసు నాడె జేజేలదళవాయి నాయంకరపుఁ బట్టమున నిల్చి......" *Prm.* 1: 145. cf. Brown: *Telugu English Dictionary* p. 645.

amaranāyankara may be understood to mean, a piece of land yielding revenue, granted to a military chief by the Rāyas of Vijayanagara. As the words *amara* and *nāyankara* are but the abbreviated forms of *amaranāyankara*, their meaning need not be separately considered. Most of the land under the Rāyas of Vijayanagara was held by military chiefs on this tenure. The holding of an *amaranāyaka* is sometimes described as his *amara-māgāṇi* * or *amara-mahale.* †

(2) *Umbaḷi or Umbaḷige*:—Kittel defines *umbaḷi* as 'the rent free grant of a plot of ground or of a village'; ‡ but, according to Wilson, it means 'a grant to an individual for his subsistence'; § but he does not mention whether the grant is rent free or not. However, he makes good this omission in defining *umbaḷige* by which he understands 'land granted by the government rent free as a reward for, or in consideration of, public services.' ¶ He makes the sense of the last part of this definition clearer in describing '*umbaḷi-grāma*,' which he takes to mean 'a village granted by the government rent free in reward for, or on condition of, performing public service.' ||

Three points emerge from the above :—

(1) that *umbaḷi* or *umbaḷige* was a grant made by the government of tax-free land.

(2) that it was given to an individual for public services already rendered.

(3) that it was also given on condition of performing public services.

* *E.C.* iii. i. Sr. 6; *ibid* xi. Hr. 35. † *EC.* viii. Sb. 379.

‡ Kittel : *Canarese-English Dictionary* p. 240.

§ *Glossary* p. 532. ¶ *ibid* || *ibid*

It seems that there were two classes of *umbaḷigārs* or holders of *umbaḷi* lands: (*a*) Those that acquired an *umbaḷige* for some public service rendered in the past, and which they were required to do no more. As instances of this class of people, mention may be made of scholars, poets and philosophers, to whom the Rāya made frequent grants of land. An inscription of Kōkaṭam dated 1518 A.D. registers the grant of the village as *umbaḷige* to the poet Allasāni Peddana by Kṛṣṇadēvarāya.* The poet refers to Kōkaṭam as an *agrahāra* which the Rāya granted to him.† It is obvious that between an *umbaḷi-grāma* and an *agrahāra* there was no difference. Such grants as these were probably known as '*mānya-umbaḷiges.*' ‡

Probably, *daṇḍige umbaḷi*, § *pālaki umbaḷi*, ¶ and *hasa umbaḷi* ‖ should be included in this class. The Rāyas honoured the Brahmans and others by conferring upon them the privilege of riding in palanquins, on horses and elephants, and of using umbrellas, and chowries. In addition to this, they were also granted lands from the produce of which they should defray the expenses of maintaining the horses, elephants etc.**

(*b*) Those that obtained *umbaḷiges* on condition of performing public services. The *umbaḷiges* of this class are spoken of as "*amara-umbaḷiges.*" †† Though

* *LR.* 33 (Kōkaṭam) p. 213.

† "కోకట గ్రామ మద్యనేకాగ్రహారంబు లడిగిన సీమలయందు నిచ్చె."
The Sources p. 153.

‡ *LR.* 41 (Yaṟṟaguḍi) pp. 16-17; *EC.* x. Sd. 22.

§ *EC.* xii. Tm. 59.

¶ *ibid.* Gb. 59.

‖ *ibid.* Gb. 49.

** *EC.* iv. Hs. 25.

†† *LR.* 1. (Andirāju Koḍūru) pp. 11-13.

this term is nowhere explained, it is not very difficult to find out its meaning. It is neither a pure *amara*, nor a pure *umbaḷige*, but partakes of the nature of both. The *amara-umbaḷige* appears to be a rent free grant of land, on condition of performing military service to the emperor. The *amaranāyakas*, as already noticed, had not only to maintain a stipulated body of troops, but to pay a fixed sum of money as tribute every year. The *umbaḷigekāra* properly so called had to do neither. The holder of an *amara-umbaḷige* land had probably to perform military service and not pay the tribute. A few grants belonging to the reigns of Sadāśiva and Śrīranga I may be noticed in this context. According to an epigraph of Pedamuḍium dated 1554 A.D., Sadāśiva granted a certain *ṭhāṇya* of Gaṇḍikōta *śīma* as an *umbaḷige* to Nandyāla Timma. * In a grant of Śrīranga I at Cinapasupula dated A.D. 1577, it is said that he granted the Pasupula *māgāṇi* belonging to the Gaṇḍikōṭa *śīma* as an *umbaḷige* to Haṇḍe Kadambarāya. † The subjects of these two grants are not single villages but groups of several villages. It is extremely unlikely that Sadāśiva and Śrīranga I would have granted so many villages to *amaranāyakas* free of all obligations. They must have granted these villages not as pure *umbaḷiges*, but as *amara-umbaḷiges*. This view is confirmed by the fact that the donors of the grants mentioned above gave some of the villages included in their *umbaḷige* on *amara* tenure to their followers. The subject, however, deserves further investigation.

III. The Mānya Grāmas or Tax-free Villages :—The emperors of Vijayanagara were staunch Hindus. They always encouraged the Hindu religion in several ways.

* *LR.* 15 p. 130. † *ibid* 14 p. 366.

Usually, they made grants of lands at very low rent to individuals as well as to institutions. The lands granted in this fashion are divided in the *Rāyavācaka* into four classes: (1) The *brahmādāya* (2) the *dēvādāya* (3) the *maṭhapura* and (4) the *sarvamānya* lands.*

(1) The *brahmādāya* is defined as 'a grant or Perquisite appropriated to Brahmans.' † Such grants usually took the form of land, either small fields or whole villages. The latter were generally known as *agrahāras*, and *śrōtriyas*, which were granted to Brahmans either as a reward for their learning or to enable them to impart religious and secular knowledge to the younger members of the community. (2) The *dēvādāya* grants were made to the temples for the purpose of carrying on daily worship, *brahmōtsava* and *māsōtsava* to deities to whom they were dedicated. (3) The *maṭhapura* lands were granted to the Śaivite, and probably also to the Vaiṣṇavite temples and *maṭhas* in order to enable the religious of the respective sects to study theology and spread their respective tenets among the laity. The holders of these three classes of land had to pay to the government every year a low quit-rent called *jōḍi* or *śrōtriya*. The grants of lands to the *āyagārs* of the village should be taken into consideration in this connection, as they had also to pay the *jōḍi* to the state. (4) The holders of the *sarvamānya* grants were under no obligation of any kind. They seem to have enjoyed the fruit of the land granted to them without paying any tax to the government. Several *agrahāras* and *puras*, were completely tax-free. Another kind of tax-free land known as *koḍagi* may be considered in this connection. The word *koḍagi* or *koḍage*

* *ASPP.* iii. p. 29.

† H. H. Wilson: *Glossary* p. 92.

means a gift or grant, usually of a piece of land free of rent. Inscriptions mention names of two varieties of *koḍagi* grants. *(a) Kaṭṭu-koḍage.** It denotes a *koḍage* granted to a person or persons as a reward for constructing a tank, a temple, or some other public building. This appears to be identical with *daśa-vandha.* † *(b) Nettara* or *rakta-koḍage.* ‡ It means the *koḍage* granted to the relations of deceased warriors who sacrificed their lives in the service of the state.

The Newly-formed Villages:—Another kind of tenure which must be noticed, in this connection, is the one obtaining in the newly-formed villages. According to the *Āmuktamālyada*, § the king, in order to increase the income of the state, should destroy the forests in the interior of the country, and give the reclaimed territory to farmers to bring it under cultivation. The land adjoining new villages built on the sites of old ones belongs to this class. To induce desirable colonists to settle down in these places, the government offered them easy terms. They were exempted from the payment of all taxes during the first year, or more generally, during the first three years. At the end of this initial stage, low taxes were levied which, however, were gradually increased year by year until, at the end of the seventh year, the tax on these lands became adjusted to the rate prevailing in the neighbouring villages. ¶ Although this arrangement was only temporary, it left certain permanent marks upon these settlements which deserve to be noticed. The original colonists seem to have divided the village land into a number of shares, usually sixteen,

* *EC.* xii. Si. 18; ix. Ht. 30. † *MER.* 788 of 1917.

‡ *EC.* x. Mb. 87; *LR.* 18 p. 513. § *Ām.* 4: 256.

¶ *EC.* xi. Hk. 112; *MER.* 307 of 1921; *SII.* iv. No. 810.

which they apportioned among themselves. Villages of this kind were known as the *vīsapaḍi* or 'sixteenth villages.' * The internal arrangements of the *vīsapaḍi* villages regarding cultivation and payment of taxes have been described by Sir Thomas Munro. He says:

> "The land and rents were divided into sixteen shares. When the season of cultivation draws near all the ryots of the *vīsapaḍi* villages, assemble to regulate their several rents for the year......They ascertain the amount of agricultural stock of each individual, and of the whole body, and the quantity of land to which it is adequate, and they divide it accordingly, giving each man a portion which he has the means of cultivating, and fixing his share of rent, and whether his share be one or two sixteenths, he pays this proportion whether the whole rent of the village be higher or lower than that of last year." †

The holdings of the ryots were interchangeable or subject to redistribution.

The Guttige Lands:—The word '*gutta*' means rent, and therefore the *guttige* lands ‡ were lands hired by private individuals from the government. The government used to let the *Bhaṇḍāravāḍa* or crown lands to contractors on which they had to pay the government *gutta* or rent. This practice was also followed by some *amaranāyakas* occasionally. § The *guttadār* was entitled only to collect the rent due to the emperor or *amaranāyaka*, as the case may be; and he had no other rights or privileges.

* Munro: *The Gazetteer of Cuddapah* pp. 146-7.

† *ibid.*

‡ *EC.* ix. Kn. 31.

§ *LR.* 18 (Vanipenṭa) p. 49; *ibid* 20 (Golla-Uppalapāḍu) pp. 147-148.

Chapter VI

IRRIGATION.

Section 1: The State Irrigation Policy:—The Rāyas paid much attention from the very early days of the empire to storing up of water for the purposes of agriculture, the main industry of the country, on which its prosperity depended. The greatest of the Rāyas declared that as the prosperity of the country was a source of profit to the state, the government should create irrigation facilities by the construction of tanks and the excavation of canals; the land should be given on a favourable rate of assessment to poor ryots for cultivation, which would, of course, bring in plenty of money to the treasury. * The government of the Rāyas, however, did not create a special department for storing up water, and regulating its distribution among agricultural population; nevertheless, the ryots did not suffer from water scarcity except during periods of drought and famine. There is reason to believe that, owing to abundant harvests, the country was generally prosperous.

Although the government made no provision for the maintenance of an irrigation department, the country was not without irrigation facilities. The construction of dams across the rivers to divert the water into feeder channels is mentioned in a few inscriptions of the period; † but the information is so scanty that it is not possible to elaborate on the subject. The

* *Ām* 4: 236.

† *The Bhārati* ix. p. 434.

"ಆ ಕೊಂಗು ಧಾರಾಪುರದ ಆಮ್ರಾವತಿಯೆಂಬ ಹೊಳೆಯಲ್ಲಿ ತಂಮ ಉಭಯವಾಗಿ ಹೊಸ ಅಣೆಯನು ಕಟ್ಟಿಸಿ"

excavation of tanks and canals as well as the digging of wells was left to individual enterprise. To provide the country with tanks, wells and canals was believed to bring religious merit to the people. * In an inscription of 1538-39 A.D. the excavation of tanks was included in the *Saptasantānas* or the seven acts productive of religious merit.† In another inscription dated 1540 A.D. recording the excavation of the *Gōpinātha-jaladhi* at Vankāyalapāḍu near Koṇḍavīḍu, it is said that "the gods, men, *pitṛis*, *gandharvas*, *uragas*, *rakṣash*, and the permanent *bhūtas* all depend on a tank. The person in whose tank men, beasts, and birds quench their thirst by drinking its water acquires the merit of performing an *aśvamēdha*. The *pitṛi* of the excavator of a tank rejoices, and his *pitāmaha* dances. Even the *pitṛis* of his cognates join them." ‡ All the

* cf. *EC.* v. Ak. 2.

† *LR.* 14 (Camḷḷapalle, a hamlet of Puṣpagiri) p. 483.

"వనమును గుడియును చెరువును
తనయుఁడు ధర్మప్రతిష్ఠ ధర నిక్షేపం
బును మొదలుగ సంతసమున
ననఘుఁడు భూమసుపుని పాపడవనిపు డిచ్చెన్ ॥

The *Saptasantānas* are described in all the *prabandhas* of the age *e.g.*, *Sṛngāra Śākuntalam* of Pina Vīrabhadra:

నల్లిల్లుం గుడియుం వనంబును నిధానంబుం దటాకంబు రం
జిల్లం గొండొక కాలమేగ నవి విచ్ఛేదంబునుం జొందు నే
పొల్లుం బోనిది కీర్తికిం గృతియపో భూమండలిం దానికిం
చెల్లం బిప్పుడు రామభారత కథా దీన ప్రబంధావళుల్ ॥

‡ *LR.* 48 (in Gōpināthapattaṇa of Koṇḍavīḍu) p. 72.

The following passage from the Mahābhārata is quoted in the inscription:—

देवा मनुष्याः पितरो गन्धर्वोरग राक्षसाः ।
स्थावराणि च भूतानि संश्रयन्ति जलाशयम् ॥
तटाके यस्य गावस्तु पिबन्ति तृषिता जलम् ।
मृगपक्षिमनुष्याश्च सोऽश्वमेधफलंलभेत् ॥
आस्फोटयन्ति पितरः प्रनृत्यन्ति पितामहाः ।
अपिनस्तु कुलेजातो यस्तटाकं करिष्यति ॥

well-to-do people of the age who were desirous of perpetuating their names, performed at least one of the *Saptasantānas*, if they could not do all. The Rāya set the fashion; his ministers, officers, nobles and wealthy subjects followed his example. The empire was, as a consequence, provided with an irrigation system which satisfied all the requirements of the agricultural population. The name of Kṛṣṇadēvarāya is associated with several irrigation works throughout the empire. Paes witnessed the construction of the tank at Nāgalāpūr. He says:

> "In order to make this tank the said king (Kṛṣṇarāya) broke down a hill which enclosed the ground occupied by the said tank. In the tank I saw so many people at work that there must have been fifteen or twenty thousand men, looking like ants, so that you could not see the ground on which they walked, so many there were; this tank the king portioned out amongst his captains, each of whom had the duty of seeing that the people placed under him did their work, and that the tank was finished and brought to completion." *

The Bijāpūr historian Raffi-ud-Din Ibrahim Shīrāzi states that Kṛṣṇadēvarāya began the excavation of a canal at Vijayanagara which he did not, however, complete; and it was only completed by Rāmarāja when he assumed power. † Rāyasam Koṇḍamarasa, Kṛṣṇarāya's minister, was responsible for the construction of Timmasamudra and Koṇḍasamudra in the province of Koṇḍavīḍu. ‡ He had also two or three tanks constructed in the province of Udayagiri. § Although no construction of irrigation works is attributed to Acyuta, several of his ministers and officers excavated tanks, and dug canals in different

* *FE*. pp. 244-245.

† *JBBRAS*. xxii. p. 28.

‡ *MER*. 336 of 1915.

§ *NDI*. i. A 6, 28; *MER*. 336 of 1915.

parts of the empire. Bayakāra Rāmappayya who became the governor of Koṇḍavīḍu built a tank at Māgimāvinahaḷḷi in the Bellary district.* Timmarasa and Bācarasa, two officers of Acyuta had each a tank constructed at Lēbāka in the Cuddapah district.† Vākiṭi Vengaḷarāja, Acyuta's commander of the gate caused the tank of Kukkasamudra to be constructed.‡ Mallappa Nāyaka had a tank built and channels dug at Bilebalu.§ Penugoṇḍa Vīraṇṇa, brother of Virūpaṇṇa, the *talāri* of Vijayanagara, dug up a spring and an irrigation canal called Nūtana-Tungabhadrā at the village of Mōdaya.¶ It is easy to multiply instances. The nobles, merchants, and wealthy persons also contributed their share. Mahānāyakācārya Cāri Narasā Nāyaḍu dug a channel from the river Pennār to feed the tank at Kūcipāpala.‖ The merchants of Gunḍḷahaḷḷi caused a tank to be built in A.D. 1530.** Mādammanagāru caused a tank to be made at Sāmantapūḍi in memory of her son.†† Cinnamāmba, the sister of Rāmaya Bāca, caused a huge tank to be dug at Vankāyalapāḍu.‡‡ Besides, people and institutions holding landed property constructed tanks for the purpose of increasing the productivity of their estates. The Brahmans of Nangali had a tank dug to water the fields of their *agrahāra*.§§ The authorities of the temple of Śiva at Kāḷahasti spent the money, which they received from pious donors on improving the condition of the tanks of the villages belonging to the temple.¶¶

* *MER*. 517 of 1914.

† *LR*. 44 pp. 238-40.

‡ *EC*. vi. Kd. 160.

§ *MER*. 727 of 1919.

¶ *MER*. 68 of 1912.

‖ *LR*. 18 pp. 58-60.

** *EC*. xii. Pg. 12.

†† *NDI*. i. D. 66.

‡‡ *LR*. 48 p. 72.

§§ *EC*. x. Mb. 226.

¶¶ *MER*. 152, 153, 156, 160, 164, 166, 171, 181 and 183 of 1924.

Section 2: *The Construction of Tanks*:—When any person wanted to build a tank or to dig a well or canal, he would never undertake the work himself. He would entrust it to one or more persons in whom he had confidence. The merchants of Guṇḍḷahaḷḷi entrusted the building of the tank to Akalāti, and his sons Allága and Baḷiga. * The Brahmans of Bhūpasamudra employed a certain Basivi Reḍḍi; † Mallappanāyaka engaged the *Bōyās* of Bilebalu. ‡ Sometimes labourers were directly employed by the persons excavating tanks. Timmarasa and Bācarasa who built the tanks at Lēbāka hired the *Vaḍḍes*, and personally supervised the work. § But such instances are rare. The more popular method was to entrust the work to some competent person or persons.

The person or persons to whom the construction of a tank or the digging of a well or canal was entrusted, had to execute the work at his or their own expense. Occasionally they received some money in advance from the person on whose behalf they were executing the work. Gaṇḍikōṭa Cinnamaseṭṭi who was employed by Rāmarāja Tirumala to dig a canal at Prodduṭūr received a sum of 230 *varahas* for executing the work; ¶ but more generally the work was given on *koḍage* or *dasavandha* contract. According to this arrangement, the contractor would agree to construct a tank or dig a well or a canal in return for the permanent assignment of a piece of tax-free land watered by the tank, canal or well. ‖ The extent of the *dasavandha* or the *kaṭṭu-koḍage* land varied

* *EC.* xii. Pg. 12. † *MER.* 782 of 1917.

‡ *ibid* 727 of 1919. § *LR.* 44 p. 238. ¶ *ibid* 41 pp. 52-53.

‖ *MER.* 782 of 1917; *LR.* 15 pp. 434-5; *ibid* 18 pp. 58-60; *ibid.* 33 p. 230 *MER.* 32 of 1917; *ibid* 49 of 1917.

according to the nature of the work to be turned out. A *mānya* of a few acres was the fee for digging a well or canal;* but for the construction of the tank, the extent of land offered as remuneration was much bigger. † The *dasavandha* or *kaṭṭu-koḍage mānya* might consist of wet and dry fields. ‡

The tanks had to be constructed so as to withstand the impact of the winter floods. The embankment had to be made 'with plenty of earth, building it up with stone, fixing a stone sluice, making it secure with brick and mortar.' § Notwithstanding the care with which the embankments were built, they demanded the constant attention of the villagers. Owing to heavy floods in the rainy season, they might breach; the feeder channel might be silted up; the level of the tank bed might rise, rendering the tank useless for the purpose of irrigation. Extraordinary care was taken to keep the tanks in very good condition. In several cases, the people who caused the tanks to be excavated made adequate provision to maintain them in a proper manner:

> "If any damage should come to the tank you build, you will make it good from your four parts of the *mānya*." ¶ "Even if through much rain the tank should be filled up and breach, the tank is for ever yours, to build." ‖ "Enjoying the *dasavandha mānya* of three *puṭṭis*, you must carry on the work of the tank year after year." **

Bāli Reḍḍi who received *dasavandha* land from Kṛṣṇarāya was expected to keep the tank in good

* *LR.* 18 pp. 58-60; *MMss.* 15-3-33 (Vanipenṭa) pp. 34-35; *LR* 36 pp. 296-297.

† *EC.* ix. Cp. 156; *ibid.* x. Mb. 172; *MER.* 49 of 1917.

‡ *EC.* x. Mb. 172. § *ibid.* ¶ *ibid.*

‖ *EC.* x. Kl. 15. ** *LR.* 13 (Reḍḍicerla) pp. 249-51.

repair.* The *Bōyās* of Bilebalu who received *dasavandha* land had to look to the upkeep of the tank. †

Other arrangements for the upkeep of tanks were also known. In several places in the Canarese country a cart was permanently maintained by the builder of the tank, or the state, or the villagers themselves to remove the silt from the tank-bed. ‡ A piece of tax-free land was granted to some person or persons by the emperor or his provincial representative for maintaining a cart exclusively for repairing the tank. In one case, a whole village was granted for the purpose. § The arrangements for preserving the irrigation works in the eastern districts were different. A *ceruvu* or tank *mēra* of one *kunca* per *puṭṭi* on all kinds of grain grown in the village was collected for defraying the expenses of the repair. ¶ The grain so collected was measured out to the *Upparas* for repairing the tank. In the southern districts 'the fish-lease money' was utilised, in certain places for executing repairs. || The upkeep of the tanks belonging to the villages granted to the Brahmans, temples and *maṭhas* devolved on the holders of such grants. ** The money which was received as donations by the temple at Kāḷahasti was invested by the *sthānikas* in improving the condition of tanks in the villages belonging to the temple. †† If, however, these arrangements proved inadequate owing to unusual circumstances, special efforts were, of course, made by

* *ibid* 727 of 1919.

† *MER.* 788 of 1917.

‡ *EC.* ix. Bn. 80 ; *ibid* xii. Ck. 5.

§ *ibid* ix. Cp. .156

¶ *NDI* ii. Gd. 109, 117 ; Kr. 5.

|| *MER.* 194 of 1921 ; 145 of 1924.

** *EC.* x. Mb. 226 ; *MER.* 7 of 1922.

†† *ibid* 152, 153, 156, 160, 164, 166, 171, 180 and 183 of 1924.

the government, the holders of tax-free villages, or the villagers themselves to restore the tank to its former condition ; * but, if the tank was so damaged as to be irreparable, the village was, of course, provided with a new tank. †

During the years when the rainfall was insufficient the ryots would not get as much water from the tanks as their crops required. In order to avoid quarrels among them which might easily lead to crime, the supply of water to the fields was carefully regulated. Such regulations are recorded in an inscription of of 1535 A.D. ‡ The cultivators had to await their turn, to water their fields ; and however urgent their need, they could not get it earlier.

* *EC.* x. Mb. 172. "When that is filled up, if any the least failure occurs, we will levy money and grain from the rice lands." cf. *EC.* xii. Ck. 5 ; xi. Hr. 35.

† *EC.* x. Kl. 15.

‡ *EC.* iv. Gn. 41.

Chapter VII

REVENUE AND TAXATION

Section 1: *The Two Kinds of Income*: —The revenue of the empire was collected from several sources; but it was divided into two classes: (*a*) the *dhānyādāya* and (*b*) the *suvarṇādāya.*

(*a*) *Dhānyādāya* means income in kind. As agriculture was the main industry of the country, the bulk of the state's revenue came from lands. According to a contemporary writer, 'all the lands belonged to the king.' * He let them to the cultivators directly or indirectly. The holders of the land had to measure out to the government a portion of the produce as rent.

Survey and Settlement:—As the land rent or tax was the main source of the state's revenue, it was of the utmost importance to ascertain the exact extent of land which each ryot held. The lands were carefully measured every year, the names of the holders, and the extent of their holdings were entered in registers. The instrument that was made use of in measuring lands was a bamboo pole whose length seems to have varied with the locality. The *kēsari-pāṭighaḍa* of 32 *vitastis* or 42 feet 8 inches was in use in the province of Koṇḍavīḍu; † the measuring pole of 32 *padas* referred to in the Nāgulavaram grant of Kṛṣṇadēvarāya appears to have been shorter in length than the above. ‡ *Dore* or *doraghaḍa* is mentioned

* *FE.* p. 379.

† *MER.* 659 of 1920.

‡ *NDI.* i. Cp. 16.

in several inscriptions of the Ceded districts; * its length, however, is not known. A measuring rod called 'the *mānadaṇḍa*, 18 *padas* in length' was in use in the Canarese districts. † The 'standard rod' which was employed in the Cōḷa country is mentioned in an epigraph of Tāyanūr. ‡ It is said to have measured 34 feet. § There is reason to believe that there was a general survey of lands in the Canarese districts during the reign of Kṛṣṇadēvarāya. Timmarasa's name is associated with the survey of certain Telugu districts. The names of other officers who surveyed the lands and settled the revenue are also preserved in the inscriptions. ¶ As it was customary to measure the land and assess the revenue every year, no special significance need be attached to the survey conducted by the officers mentioned above.

The land belonging to every village was divided into two main classes, the arable fields and the pastures. The former were further sub-divided into *nīrāramba* and *kāḍāramba* fields. ‖ *Nīrāramba* fields are defined as 'wet lands, lands irrigated artificially for rice cultivation.' ** This definition, however, is too narrow, as several crops other than rice must have been dependent upon artificial irrigation. In a *rāyarēkha* of the time of Vīra Narasimha, fields in which sugar-cane, betel, and kitchen vegetables were cultivated, are included in

* *MMss.* 15-3-32: (Rāmēśvaram-Prodduṭūr) pp. 63-64; *LR.* 9 (Pedapasupula) p. 169.

† Rice: *Mysore Gazetteer* i. p. 577.

‡ *MER.* 365 of 1909.

§ M. S. Sarma: *Śārada,* ii. p. 394.

¶ *MER.* A 10 of 1922-23.

‖ *EC.* vii. Ch. 62; *LR.* 16 (Pāṇyam) p. 439.

** H. H. Wilson: *Glossary* p. 378.

the *nīrāramba* land. * Similarly, the *Kaifiyat* of Sirivoḷḷa includes in it fields in which all kinds of kitchen vegetables, fruit bearing trees, sugar-cane, plantain, and betel creeper were cultivated. † The *nīrāramba* lands are, therefore, divided in the *rāyarēkha* mentioned above into rice lands and gardens, the latter being further sub-divided into sugar-cane, betel, vegetable, and plantain gardens. The *kāḍāramba* is said to mean 'dry land or land which depends entirely upon rain for watering; the cultivation of such land.' ‡ All the dry crops such as *rāgi*, *cōḷam*, *javari*, and pulses might be described as *kāḍāramba* crops. This minute classification of the village land was made for the purpose of assessing revenue. The arable fields seem to have been classified further into, 'best, middling, and inferior.' § And very probably taxes were assessed according to the yield of the crops.

It is not, however, possible to assert definitely the exact proportion of the produce which the government claimed as their share. Some writers believe that one sixth of the produce was taken by the state as its due.¶ The belief is based upon theoretical statements contained in the *dharma-śāstrās* ; but it does not seem to correspond with the real state of affairs obtaining in the 16th century. According to some inscriptions, the government claimed *muggōru* and even *sangōru* from certain types of land. ‖ These terms are explained by the author of the *Aṭṭhavaṇa Tantram* :

* *LR.* 6 p. 324.

† *ibid* pp. 338-45.

‡ H. H. Wilson : *Glossary* p. 246.

§ *EC.* x. Kl. 15.

¶ Iswar Dutt : *JAHRS.* iv. p. 171.

‖ cf. *EC.* iv. Yd. 10.

> "By *muggōru* is meant an arrangement according to which the government claim one third of the produce, leaving the remaining two thirds to the ryot. Similarly, by *sangōru* is meant an arrangement by which the government take half of the produce leaving the other half to the ryot." *

Again, in newly formed villages, and in the villages built in the clearings of the jungles and on ruined sites, the state's share of revenue varied with time and place. † It appears from this that no uniformity was observed regarding the proportion of the produce which the government claimed as the share due to them.

The measurement of lands, and several details pertaining to it were entered in palm leaf registers called *kavilas.* Each village had a *kavila* of its own which was maintained by the *karṇam* or the village accountant. In this register were recorded the *guḍi* or the *āyakut* of the village, the extent of the lands given to the Gods and the Brahmans, the names of the donors, the *Śaka* and the cyclic years in which the donations were made, the extent of the land cultivated by each ryot, the tax which he had to pay thereon to the government, the boundaries of the villages ‡ and several other particulars of the kind. The village boundaries were jealously guarded by the villagers against the encroachments of the ryots of the neighbouring villages. Several disputes regarding the boundaries of villages are recorded in the inscriptions.

* *MMss.* 15-6-8.

† *MER.* 10 of 1912-13; *EC.* xi. Hk. 112; *MER.* 380 of 1925; *LR.* 57 p. 181.

‡ It is said that 'the figure of Vāmana was engraved on demarcation stones' marking the boundaries of villages (*JAHRS*. iv. p. 172). This is a mistake. The figure of Vāmana was engraved on the boundary stones only of *agrahāras*. No instance of a non-*agrahāra* boundary stone containing the figure of Vāmana is known to exist.

It is said that the village boundaries were minutely described in the government records. Copies of village *kavilas* were preserved in the *cāvaḍis* or offices of the *sthala*, and *sīma*. Probably copies were also kept in the *Aṭṭhavaṇam* or the imperial revenue secretariat.

It should be noted that taxes on *kāḍāramba* and several *nīrāramba* fields were paid not in coin but in kind ; but taxes on certain types of *nīrāramba* fields *e.g.*, gardens where vegetables, sugar-cane, plantain, and betel were grown, were received not in kind but in coin, probably because their products being soon perishable, could not be stored up for long periods of time.

The Meaning of Dhānyādāya :—Several inscriptions which enumerate the taxes due to the government from the people mention *dhānya* and *davasa.* * The former is described as 'grain in general, especially rice ; but nine principal kinds are enumerated under this title.' † The latter is said to mean 'the produce of fields, grain in general.' ‡ From these definitions, it appears that the words mean more or less the same thing. However, as *dhānya* and *davasa* are used in juxtaposition, the authors of the inscriptions seem to have intended to convey some difference in their meaning. Although the word has become obsolete in Telugu, it is still in use in certain parts of the Canarese country. It is here understood to mean oil seeds, pepper, and coriander, whereas the term *dhānya* is used to denote the nine varieties of grain such as rice, wheat, *rāgi*, *cōḷam*, and pulses. Therefore, the term *dhānyādāya*

* *E.C.* iv. Gu. 67.

† H. H. Wilson: *Glossary* p. 136.

‡ *ibid* p. 130.

should be taken to mean government's income in grain, and *davasa* as their income in oil-seeds, pepper etc.

Section: *2* (*b*) *The Suvarṇādāya* :—The taxes other than *dhānyādāya* were known as *siddhāyas.* * As all the *siddhāya* taxes were paid only in cash, they were frequently referred to as *suvarṇādāya*. This word is usually translated as income in gold. It would be more correct to interpret it as 'income in *suvarṇas*.' The word *suvarṇa*, which is but a Sanskritisation of the Canarese word '*honnu*', was a gold coin, half the value of a *varāha*. There is ample evidence to show that at Vijayanagara money was reckoned in terms of '*honnu*' in the sixteenth century. The state would realise all the money payments due to it in *honnu*. Consequently taxes paid in cash would be *suvarṇādāya*.

Sunka :—Before proceeding to describe the various items of *suvarṇādāya*, it is necessary to define the term *sunka*. It is generally taken to mean toll or duty levied by the government on all articles of merchandise; but this definition does not seem to be adequate; for an inscription of Mysore mentions *nālkusamaya sunka* or dues from four castes. † According to the *Aṭṭhavaṇa Tantram* the government used to appoint over certain castes a *kula-pedda* or caste elder from among their members for the purpose of regulating caste rules and deciding caste disputes. The *kula-pedda* had the right of imposing fines on offenders; and the money collected from them went into his pockets. Moreover, he had the privilege of receiving *nagari-tāmbūla* or the *tāmbūla* due to the state on the occasions of marriages, and festivals. Any person who attempted

* *LR.* 6 p. 324. (*The Rāyarēkha* of the time of Vīra Narasimha)

† *EC.* iv. Hg. 35-36.

to exercise the rights of the *kula-pedda* without the permission of the government was severely dealt with. Therefore, the office of *kula-pedda* brought to the holder of it a good deal of money. He was required to pay a tax to the government, for being permitted to hold the office. * The *nālkusamaya-sunka*, mentioned in the inscription refers to the tax payable to the government by the elders of four castes.

In another inscription dated A.D. 1506, *sunka*, *āleya-sunka*, *heḍage-moṭṭa-sunka* (*sthāvara-sunka*) are mentioned. † Here *sunka* is taken to mean customs dues; *heḍage moṭṭa-sunka* is said to be tax on large baskets of eggs; and *āleya-sunka* is translated as dues on sugar-cane mills. *Sthāvara-sunka* certainly refers to a class of *sunkas* in which *heḍage moṭṭa-sunka* and *āleya-sunka* are at least included. And what is *sthāvara-sunka* ? *Sthāvara* means 'fixed, stationary, immovable, as applied to property.' ‡ *Sunka* means a tax. Therefore, the word *sthāvara-sunka* means a tax upon immovable property. Another inscription dated 1529 A.D. alludes to *maṇḍi-sunka* or the duty upon shops. § "In towns and villages," declares the *Aṭṭhavaṇa Tantram* "those who have a shop should pay tax to the government." ¶ *Kabbina-sunka* or the tax upon sugar-cane is referred to in a grant of A.D. 1528. ‖ An inscription of A.D. 1500 includes the taxes called *jātre*, *sante*, *aḍatere*, and *maggadere* in *sthala-sunkas*.** In another inscription of A.D.1561 it is stated that the *grāma-kaṭna*, and the taxes on oil mongers and *Upparas* are included in the *sunka* payable to the *nāyakara* holder of Cina Veṇuturla. ††

* *MMss.* 15-6-8.

† *EC.* iii. i. Ml. 95.

‡ H. H. Wilson: *Glossary* p. 490.

§ *EC.* xii. Gb. 32.

¶ *MMss.* 15-6-8.

‖ *EC.* xi. Dg. 106.

** *EC.* v. Pt. 1. Ag. 7.

†† *LR.* 15 p. 135.

One of the most important of the *sunkas* was the *maduveya-sunka* or the *peṇḍli-sunka* or the marriage tax.* The most interesting record, however, comes from the village of Cadipirēla dated 1542 A.D. † Three *sunkaris* or *sunkam* officers of the Gaṇḍikōṭa *sīma* made a grant of taxes due to them to the God of the place in the following terms :

"We, three have granted the following items pertaining to our *sunka* in Cadipirēla included within our *sunka-ṭhāṇya* in the Gaṇḍikōṭa *sīma* : (1) *grāma-kaṭnam*, (2) *magga-sthāvaras*, (3) *kōmaṭi siddhāyam*, (4) *pinja siddhāyam*, (5) *golla siddhāyam*, (6) *uppara siddhāyam*, (7) *īḍige siddhāyam*.

From what is said above, it is evident that the word *sunka* cannot be translated as 'tolls'; for it refers to several taxes which can never be brought under customs duties. In the inscriptions of the 16th century the term *sunka* appears to have been employed in two different senses. (1) *Sunka* was used to denote taxes in general (excluding, of course, *dhānyādāya*). (2) It was also employed in a restricted sense to denote tolls and customs. Unless this distinction is kept in mind, a clear understanding of the system of taxation which obtained in the Vijayanagara empire is not possible.

Section 3: *Classification of Taxes*:—The taxes coming under the head *suvarṇādāya* may be roughly divided into ten classes :

(1)	Agricultural	(6)	Professional
(2)	Pasture and Forest	(7)	Social and Communal
(3)	Industrial	(8)	Property
(4)	Commercial	(9)	Religious
(5)	Military and Police	(10)	*Mānya-grāma*

* *EC.* xii. Ck 5 ; *MMss.* 15-3-32 (Rāmēśvaram).

† *LR.* 3 (Cadipirēla) p. 426.

(1) *The Agricultural Taxes.*—The distinction between the *nīrāramba* and the *kāḍāramba* lands has already been noticed. Although the gardens where sugar-cane, plantain, and betel grew were included in the *nīrāramba*, owing to the perishable nature of their produce, taxes upon them were not received in kind but in cash. The rates at which the garden produce was assessed is sometimes given; but it is not possible to understand the principle employed by the government in assessing it. Moreover, only a few instances of this kind have survived, and no inference can reasonably be drawn from them.

(2) *The Pasture and the Forest*:—Though the waste lands and jungles were useless for agricultural purposes, yet they yielded considerable revenue to the state. The staple industry of the country being agriculture, the maintenance of large numbers of cattle became a necessity. Again, the Kurubas and other pastoral communities reared large flocks of goats and sheep on which they depended for their livelihood. The pastures required for grazing cattle were owned by the government who let them to the cattle-breeders on rent. The rent paid by them was known as *pullari* or *hullu-hanni.* * The *āḍatere* † or the goat tax which is so frequently mentioned in the inscriptions of the time must be assigned to this class. Moreover, the wood-cutter who cut wood in the forests for the purpose of selling it in towns and villages had also to pay a tax, which was called *koṇḍa-gutta* or the hill rent. ‡ These taxes were not directly collected by the state; but the right of collecting them was sold in auction to contractors or tax-farmers.

* *LR* 13 (Mārkāpuram) No. 5. † *EC.* iv. Gu. 2, 73.

‡ *MMss.* 15-6-8.

(3) *The Industrial Taxes* :—*Magga*, * *kumbāra-terege*, † *kabbina* or *āleya-sunka*, ‡ *gāṇatere*, § *pinjaṇi-garu*, ¶ *uppinapāḷe*, ‖ and *īḍige-sunka* ** are some of the important industrial taxes that are mentioned in the inscriptions. *Pedda-kolimi* or *hemmala* may be added to this list.

Maggadere or *maggari* was a tax imposed upon the weavers. As weaving was one of the wide-spread industries of the country, *maggadere* or *maggari* must have brought a large sum of money into the imperial exchequer. There was not a single village in the whole empire, which did not possess a few looms. As cloth was not one of the staple exports, most of the cloth manufactured in the empire was sold in the home market itself.

Some information is available regarding the rate of tax imposed upon looms in certain localities. It is said in an inscription dated A.D. 1536-37, that the weavers at Anantapūr should pay ½ *ga* per loom.†† The same rate obtained also at Alavakoṇḍa ‡‡ A Kōṭakoṇḍa grant of 1523 A.D. records a royal command that a tax of ½ *varāha* should be collected from each loom. §§ But the information is not sufficient to formulate a general theory concerning the government policy in taxing the textile industries. The *Aṭṭhavaṇa Tantram*, however, makes a few interesting observations in this connection.

"The tax paid by the weavers to the government every year varies with the caste of the weaver, his *munasību*, the fineness of

* *EC.* ix. Cp. 155.

† *ibid* iv. Gu. 2 ; iii. i. Ml. 95.

‡ *ibid* xi. Dg. 106 ; iii. i. Ml. 95.

§ *ibid* xi. Mk. 1.

¶ *ibid* xi. Mk. 1.

‖ *ibid* v. Cn. 174.

** *LR.* 17 (Pōli) p. 19 ; *ibid* 3 (Andirāju-kōḍūru) p. 426.

†† *ibid* 15 p. 100.

‡‡ *ibid* 6 p. 328.

§ p. 22-23.

the texture and the kind of cloth produced by him. If the cloth be sold in the place of production, the weaver need not pay any excise duty. On the other hand, if it be sold in an outside market, he should not only pay the excise duty but also an annual *paḍitaram* or perquisite to the *sunkam* collectors." *

The tax called *pinjaṇigaru* or *pinja-siddhāyam* † must be considered in this context. *Pinja* or *pinjara* is the bow used in carding or combing cotton. *Pinjaṇigaru* should have been a tax imposed upon the carders and the combers of cotton. No information is available at present about this tax.

Kumbāraterege was a tax paid by the potters. The potters, according to the *Aṭṭhavaṇa Tantram* were required to pay this tax not for the manufacture of pottery, but for selling the manufactured pots in the market place. The tax which the potters paid for making pots was known as *cakra-kānika* or wheel's present. ‡ *Gāṇa*, *gāṇakaḍivaru* § or *gānugari* ¶ was a tax paid by the oil mongers. "The oil mongers" declares the *Aṭṭhavaṇa Tantram* "have to pay to the government every year a tax called *gāniga-gutta* on their mills. The government give them a tree or a stone for making the mill, and a piece of land to erect it on. Moreover, they prohibit all but payers of the tax from pressing oil on pain of severe punishment." ‖ The *āleya-sunka* appears to be a similar tax paid by the manufacturers of jaggery, who had to press sugar-cane in mills similar to those used by the oil mongers. *Uppinapāḷe*, also called *uppara-siddhāya*, ** was a tax imposed upon the manufacturers of salt. One would expect that the salt tax was collected only from coastal regions. But, from

* *MMss.* 15-6-8. † *LR.* 3 (Cadipirēla) p. 426. ‡ *MMss.* 15-6-8.
§ *EC.* xi. Mk. 1. ¶ *LR.* 13 p. 217. ‖ *MMss.* 15-6-8.
** *LR.* 3 p. 426.

the frequent references to the concessions granted by the emperor to the salt manufacturers in the interior, * it appears that the salt tax was also collected from inland districts. It is said in the *Aṭṭhavaṇa Tantram* that the salt tax was collected from those who brought saline earth from public lands, and manufactured salt therefrom. † The tax called *īḍiga* or *īdula-sunkam* is occasionally mentioned in the inscriptions. It appears to have been a tax levied upon toddy drawers. No further information of this tax can be had at present. Lastly, the tax paid by the manufacturers of iron must be noticed. It was known as *pedda kolimi* or *hommal.* ‡ The iron manufacturers had to pay the tax for three reasons: (1) They collected fine black sand out of which the metal was extracted from the beds of streamlets where it lay deposited. (2) They made use of charcoal obtained from the government forests for smelting purposes. (3) They sold the manufactured metal in the markets of the empire. § Iron was also manufactured from stones containing the ore. Probably the manufacturers of this kind of iron were also similarly taxed.

No information is available at present about other industries; but it is obvious that the Vijayanagara government levied taxes upon all the industries of the country.

(4) *Commercial Taxes*:—Inscriptions frequently refer to a tax called *mūlavīsa* paid by the merchants to the government, or some *nāyaka*, or institution to whom the government might alienate a town, market-place, or village. Though the nature of this tax is nowhere described, it is not difficult to comprehend its

* *EC.* xi. Mk. 8, 9.

† *MMss.* 15-6-8.

‡ *EC.* iv. Gu. 67.

§ *MMss.* 15-6-8.

meaning. The term *mūlavīsa* is made up of two words '*mūla*' and '*vīsa*,' which mean 'capital', and 'a sixteenth' respectively. The merchants were probably required to pay a tax equivalent to one sixteenth of their capital to the government. The tax was not collected in a lump sum, but as small duties on the commodities sold in the market. * When the government or the holder of the village or the market-place desired to grant the tax as a gift to some temple or other religious institution, it was considered necessary to secure the consent of the merchants concerned.†

The tax known as *sunka* should be considered next. As noticed already, the word was used in two senses. Here, it must be understood in its restricted sense meaning a toll or an excise duty. *Sunka* may at first be divided into two classes from the standpoint of the sale of the commodities, *herjjunka* ‡ and *kirukula*. "The customs duties or *sunka*," says Rice "are spoken of as the *perjjunka* or *herjjunka*, those on wholesale articles in bulk." '*Kirukula*' is said to be the toll collected on 'miscellaneous petty retail articles.' § In an inscription dated A.D. 1552, 'profit arising from the sale of retail articles' is mentioned. ¶ And this, perhaps, corresponds to the *kirukula* mentioned by Rice.

Next, the taxes known as *sthala-sunka* and *cara-sunka* must be noticed. The *sunkas* or the excise duties are divided in the *Aṭṭhavaṇa Tantram* into three classes: *sthalādāyam*, *carādāyam*, and *māmūlādāyam*.

* *MMss.* 15-3-6. (Śrīśailam) pp. 37-40.

† *MER.* 681 of 1922.

‡ *EC.* v. Pt. i. Cn. 259.

§ Rice: *Mysore and Coorg from the Inscriptions* p. 175.

¶ *NDI.* iii. U. 22.

The first two are the same as the *sthala-sunka* and the *cara-sunka*; but the third, the *māmūlādāyam*, is not met with in the inscriptions. The *Aṭṭhavaṇa Tantram* describes the three kinds of *sunkas* briefly:

(*a*) *Sthalādāyam or Sthala-sunka*: "The *sunka* collected on commodities that are imported from abroad to any given place is known as the *sthalādāyam*." * The rates of dues collected as *sthalādāyam* are described in an inscription of A. D. 1530. † The articles that came to the town of Bukkapaṭṭaṇam had to pay duties as shown hereunder:

No.	Article	Unit taxed	Tax
1.	Pepper	Per *perika*	*Rūka* 2
2.	Jaggery	"	" 2
3.	*Anumulu*	"	" 2
4.	*Cōḷam*	"	" 1
5.	Areca-nuts	"	" 2
6.	*Kāyalu*	"	" 2
7.	Silks	Per bale	" ¼
8.	Vegetables	Per basket	a handful

Pēṭa or *pēṭa-sunkam* ‡ appears to be identical with the *sthalādāyam* or *sthala-sunkam*. *Pēṭi* or *pēṭa* is described as 'a town attached to, but distinct from, a fort,' 'where shops are assembled.' It is 'a trading or manufacturing town.' § As *sunka* means the duty collected upon the articles sold in a place, *pēṭa-sunka* must be interpreted as the duty collected on the

* *MMss.* 15-6-8.

† *LR.* 37 p. 116.

‡ *LR.* 1 (Andirāju-kōḍūru) pp. 9-10.

§ H. H. Wilson: *Glossary* p. 415.

articles sold in the shops of the *pēṭa*. The *pēṭa-mantrāya* alluded to in a grant of Mārkāpūr may be another name for *pēṭa-sunka.** Details regarding the *pēṭa-sunka* are available in some of the inscriptions.† The most interesting record which gives a very good idea of *pēṭa-sunkas* comes from Koṇḍavīḍu. ‡ According to this record, the articles that were sold in the market towns of the province of Koṇḍavīḍu were taxed as shown below.

No.	Article	Unit Taxed	Rate
1	Great millet	Per bag	½ *paikam*
2	Millet	"	"
3	Salt	"	"
4	Mangoes	"	"
5	Myrobalan	"	"
6	Fruits	"	"
7	Brinjals	"	"
8	Clearing nuts	"	"
9	*Māvine* (a fragrant root) ...	"	"
10	Green gram	"	1 *paikam*
11	Black gram	"	"
12	Bengal gram	"	"
13	Horse gram	"	"
14	Red gram	"	"
15	Wheat	"	"

* *LR.* 13 (Mārkāpūr) No. 7

† *LR.* 16 (Gaḍivēmula) pp. 470-71; *LR.* 20 (Sammaṭūr) pp. 292-3; *LR.* 36 (Bollavaram) pp. 430-31; *LR.* 57 (Pedakākandi) p. 197; *LR.* 1. (Andirāju-Kōḍūru) pp. 9-10.

‡ Gurubrahma Sarma: *History of Koṇḍavīḍu* p. 93.

No.	Article	Unit Taxed	Rate
16	Sesamum seeds	Per bag	*1 paikam*
17	Oil seeds	„	„
18	Black pulse	„	„
19	*Anumulu*	„	„
20	Cotton	„	„
21	Tamarind	„	„
22	Gall nuts	„	„
23	Myrobalan seeds	„	„
24	Yarn	„	„
25	*Cāma*	„	„
26	*Kanda*	„	„
27	Onions	„	*1 damma*
28	Turmeric	„	„
29	Dammer	„	„
30	Cumin	„	„
31	Fenugreek	„	„
32	Mustard	„	„
33	New gunny bags ...	Per *śalaga*	„
34	Green ginger	Per bag	„
35	Lime fruits	„	„
36	Cocoanuts	„	„
37	Jaggery	„	*2 dammas*
38	Cleaned cotton	„	„
39	Ghee	„	„
40	Castor oil	„	„
41	*Sangadi* nuts	„	„
42	Dry ginger	„	„

No.	Article	Unit Taxed	Rate
43	Iron	Per bag	*2 dammas*
44	Steel	"	"
45	Chisels	"	"
46	Sugar	"	*4 dammas*
47	Areca-nuts	"	"
48	Cotton thread	"	"
49	Betel leaves	"	"
50	Long pepper	"	*6 dammas*
51	Pepper	"	"
52	Sandal	"	"
53	Cloves	"	"
54	Nutmeg	"	"
55	Mace	"	"
56	Lead	"	"
57	Tin	"	"
58	Copper	"	"
59	Sarees	Double bullock load	*1 tsavela*

Although such elaborate lists of articles are not available for the other parts of the empire, there are distinct indications in the inscriptions which show that all or most of the articles mentioned above were taxed.*

* *EC.* iii. Ml. 95 (A.D. 1506) refers to taxes on horse-gram and Bengal-gram ; *EC.* iii. i. Nj. 118 (A.D. 1491) refers to the duty on cotton; *EC.* v. i. Cn. 174 (A.D. 1500) mentions dues on horse-gram, *rāgi*, oil, ghee, and salt ; *LR.* 13 (Mārkāpūr No. 7) mentions the *mantrāya* on betel; *LR.* 37 p. 116 (A.D. 1560) describes dues on pepper, jaggery, *anumulu*, *cōḷam*, areca-nuts, shawls and vegetables. A record from Śrīśailam dated A.D. 1516 (*MER.* 18 of 1915) describes the tolls collected on the *kāvaḍis*, pack horses, bullocks, asses and head loads. According to Nuniz, everything including 'even men and women' that passed through the gates of Vijayanagara was taxed. (*FE.* p. 364). Evidently what was obtaining in the cities, towns, and *pēṭās* of the empire was only a copy of the tariff system adopted in the metropolis.

Sante :—The duty known as *sante* * may be described as a variety of the *pēṭa-sunka*. *Santa* or *sante* is a place where people gather at regular intervals, usually of a week, for the purpose of selling and purchasing goods. The *santa* must be technically regarded as a temporary *pēṭa*. Therefore, the *sante* which seems to be a tax or duty levied on articles sold in a *santa*, may be considered as a species of *pēṭa-sunka*.

As the *santas* or fairs brought an appreciable sum of money into the treasury, the government encouraged the formation and the continuance of the *santas* all over the empire. In order to attract the stall-keepers to a particular locality, the government would allow the articles to be sold for sometime free of duty. Aṇṇāji Ayya, Timmarasa's *pārupatyagāra* in the Gaṇḍikōṭa *sīma* created a *santa* at Calamardhigaṇḍapaṭṭaṇam in A.D. 1525, and made the following arrangement. "On the articles that are brought for sale at the *santa* held on every Tuesday, no tax will be collected for the first six months; and in the next six months.. ..." † There must have been several *santas* in every province of the empire; and the local officers of the government must have received special instructions from the imperial secretariat to foster their growth.

(ii) *Cara-sunka or Mārgādāya* :—"The *sunka* collected on articles in transit is termed *mārgādāya*." ‡ A few instances of the *mārgādāya* are described in the Local Records. In the *Magava Sādhaka* or *paṭṭa* granted to Peda Cinnama Nāyaḍu of Rōḷḷamaḍugu the following rates of *cara-sunka* are recorded. §

* *EC.* v. Pt. i. Ag. 7.

† *LR.* 15 pp. 82-84.

‡ *MMss.* 15-6-8.

§ *LR.* 44 p. 148.

1	*Rasavargas* ...	Per *perika*	½ *rūka*
2	*Davasa* ...	"	¼ "
3	Bullocks ...	One rope	1 "
4	Cotton ...	Per bale	1 "

A similar list of rates is also recorded in the *nirūpa* which Aḷiya Rāmarāja granted to Namalanēni Kumāra Peda Bucci Nāyaḍu in A. D. 1526-27. * Rāmarāja permitted Bucci Nāyaḍu to collect *rusum* on articles passing on the High Road to Tirupati through the passes of Sūryakumāra, Cerikaṭṭa, and Dongalasāni.

1	Areca-nuts ...	Per *perika*	¼ *rūka*
2	*Rasavargas* ...	"	¼ "
3	Cloth ...	Per bale	⅜ "
4	Tirupati pilgrims: on horseback ...	Per head	4 *nebs*
5	Tirupati pilgrims: on foot	"	1 *neb*

The *ubhayamārga-sunka* † which is often mentioned in inscriptions is identical with *cara-sunka* or *mārgādāya*; for, it is the duty collected (on articles) on both the roads *i.e.*, the duty collected on the articles passing along the road in both the directions.

(iii) *The Māmūlādāya*:—"The duty collected on the articles that are to be exported is called *māmūlādāya.*" ‡ An epigraph dated A.D. 1546 refers to the *sunka* with the *mūla-vīsa* due to the government on several kinds of grain; on *rasavargas* such as ghee, sugar, and jaggery, and on perfumes like sandal, musk,

* *LR.* 18 p. 407.

† *EC.* iii. Nj. 118; *LR.* 18 (Gundūr) pp. 478-9.

‡ *MMss.* 15-6-8.

camphor, and *pilli*-roots which were exported from Udayagiri and other *rājyas**. The *horavaru* † which is sometimes met with in the records of the Canarese districts appears to be identical with the *māmūlādāya*.

A duty called *ubaya-tūga-sunka* is mentioned in an epigraph of Cintakommudinne. ‡ The word when literally interpreted means 'sunka on both the weights.' What these weights were it is not possible to determine at present. Another *sunka* that should be noticed is *maḷige* or *maṇḍi-sunka*. § The shop-keepers in towns and villages had to pay this tax to the government for being permitted to keep their shops in the bazaar.¶

It is evident from what is said above that the economic life of the people was completely surrounded by a bewildering multiplicity of tariff walls. In these circumstances, how trade could have flourished at all is a wonder. The inscriptions do not enable us to ascertain whether a uniform scale of customs duties was enforced in all the markets of the empire. Such at any rate was not the case, if a statement in the *Aṭṭhavaṇa Tantram* is to be taken as true.

"No uniformity is possible in the scale of excise duties. The tax farmers who are eager to obtain whatever profit they can secure from their districts, secretly repair to the merchants, and enter into an agreement with them by offering to levy only an *aḍḍaga*, when they have to pay a *rūka* in a neighbouring district. Consequently, it is not possible to make any general statement about the excise duties. If in one province 10 *ga* (of duty) are collected on every 100 *ga* worth of goods sold, only 2 *ga* are

* *LR.* 42 (Udayagiri) No. 23.
† *EC.* iii. Pt. i. Ml. 95.
‡ *LR.* 14 pp. 393-94.
§ *LR.* 1. pp. 10-13; *EC.* iv. Ch. 37.
¶ *MMss.* 15-6-8.

demanded in a neighbouring district. Therefore, the excise duties are different in different places." *

(5) *Military and Police Taxes*:—*Durga-nivartana* or *Durga-daṇṇāyi-nivartana* is a tax which is prominently mentioned in the inscriptions of the Ceded Districts. † It means a tax paid to the commandant of a fort. That the Vijayanagara empire was organized on a military basis has already been noticed. Each province was so constituted that all the villages within its jurisdiction should be capable of being easily defended from a fort which also served as the provincial capital. The commandant of a fort received *vartana* or fee from the villagers, probably in return for the protection which he was expected to give. The *vartana* was payable to the *daṇṇāyi* every year by the ryots. ‡ The amount of the *vartana* varied from village to village. Whereas Alavakoṇḍa paid 10 *ga* every year, § Ēṭūr Miḍutūr, Sarungapalle, and Gangavaram all of which belonged to a temple at Puṣpagiri paid collectively a sum of 60 *ga*. ¶ Whether the *daṇṇāyi-nivartana* was paid personally to the commandant or to the tax collectors, cannot now be known. It is likely that the *nivartana* represents the salary due to him as the commandant; but of this no information is available.

* *MMss.* 15-6-8.

Kaḍapangālu (*MMss.* 15-3-6 or), *maḷige*, (*EC.* iv. Ch. 37) *maṇḍi-sunka* (*EC.* xii. Gb. 32); *angaḍi-kaḍivāra*, (*EC.* xi. Mk. 1); *angaḍi-siddhāyam* (*LR.* 6 p. 324); *kōmaṭi-siddhāyam* (*LR.* 4 p. 426) are the names of taxes that occur in the inscriptions. Are they different names of the same tax? Or, are they names of different taxes? If they mean the same thing, as they very probably do, they must be classed under *angaḍi-siddhāyas*. The real nature of these, as well as several other taxes, current in Vijayanagara times can be ascertained only by future investigation.

† *LR.* 16 (Yaṟṟaguṇṭla) p. 460; *LR.* 37 (Cina Veṇuturla) pp. 33-4; *LR.* 40 Yaṟṟaguḍidinne) p. 220; *ibid* (Sirivoḷḷa) pp. 217-8.

‡ *MMss.* 15-3-6 p. 401. § *LR.* 14 p. 381. ¶ *LR.* 13 p. 74.

One peculiarity about the *daṇṇāyi-nivartana* should be noted. It makes its appearance in the inscriptions only of the Ceded Districts. No trace of this tax is seen in the records of Tamil and Canarese districts. But an inscription of Nagar in the South Arcot district mentions a tax called *daṇṇāyakara-magamai.** The word *magamai* originally meant a voluntary contribution made generally by merchants to a temple; but later it came to mean a contribution, voluntary or otherwise. Therefore, *daṇṇāyakara-magamai* may be taken to mean a contribution made for the maintenance of a *daṇṇayāka*. Again, a tax called *daṇṇāyakara-swāmya* is mentioned in some Mysore inscriptions. † '*Swāmya*' means a portion. Therefore, *daṇṇāyakara-swāmya* may be taken to be an equivalent of *daṇṇāyakara-magamai* and *daṇṇāyaka-nivartana*. It may be concluded from this that a military tax was collected from all the provinces for the maintenance of the commandants of the forts of the empire.

Other military taxes called *daḷavili* ‡ and *paḍaikāṇikkai* § are occasionally mentioned in the inscriptions. They were probably collected for the maintenance of the army; but the real nature of this tax can be determined only by future investigation.

The *kōṭṭai-magamai* mentioned in some of the Tamil inscriptions may also be noticed in this connection.¶ It was probably a tax collected for carrying on the necessary repairs in the forts, and keeping them in a defensible condition.

Taḷavārike‖ or *kāvalikaṭṇam*,** and *nāḍutaḷavārike* †† belong to the same class. Both of them were duties

* *MER.* 1911 para 51. † *MAR.* 1920 para 79. ‡ *ibid.*

§ *EI.* xvii. pp. 110-17. ¶ *MER.* 1922 para 43. ‖ *ibid* 106 of 1918.

** *ibid* 164 of 1913. †† *EC.* xi. Mk. 1.

levied on behalf of the police. *Taḷavārike* or *kāvalikaṭnam* was a tax which the villagers paid to the village *talāri* as a remuneration for his services. The *talāri* received from the villagers *mēra* and *mirāsi*. The *taḷavārike* seems to be an additional due collected by the villagers for the benefit of the *talāri*. It is not known whether the *taḷavārike*, which was a cash payment, was paid to the *talāri* directly, or to the government. According to an inscription at Kōṭakoṇḍa, half of the income at the *pēṭa* below the hill must be paid to the *kāvalgārs* of the place. * Probably the *taḷavārike* was paid to the *talāris* or *kāvalgārs* directly. The *nāḍu-talavārike* was a tax levied on the ryots in the interests of the district police officer, the *nāḍu-taḷavāra*. What has been said about *taḷavārike* is applicable to *nāḍu-talavārike* also. These two taxes were common to all parts of the empire.

(6) *Professional Taxes*:—It is not an exaggeration to say that the government of Vijayanagara exacted taxes from the people following almost every profession. Most of the *jāti siddhāyas* come under this head.† *Agasaru* ‡ or *cākala*, *mādārike*, § *mādige*, and *mangala siddhāyas* are the most typical. ¶ Some of the *jāti siddhāyas* are described in the *Aṭṭhavaṇa Tantram*. One of them which is frequently mentioned in the inscriptions is the barber's tax. In a record from Gaṇḍikōṭa dated A.D. 1550, it is said that Nandyāla Timmarāja, the governor of the place, laid down a rule that the barbers should pay a tax of one *vīsa* per day for plying their trade. || The reason why the barbers had to pay a tax to the government is made clear by

* *LR.* 41 pp. 22-23 (1523 A.D).

† cf. *LR.* 3 (Chadipirēla) p. 426.

‡ *EC.* xi. Mk. 1.

§ *EC.* iii. i. Ml. 95.

¶ *LR.* 40 (Poli) pp. 239-40.

|| *LR.* 14. (Puṣpagiri) p. 475.

the inscriptions thus. According to an epigraph of Guṇḍlakuṇṭa, barbers had to pay to the government taxes known as *pannu, khaḍḍāyam, kāṇike, nagari-kaṭṇam, kāvali, anuveccam, siddhāyam, dommari-pannu, veṭṭi*, and *vēmu.* * Two other taxes in addition to the above, the *hareṇam* and the *rājāvoli-pannu* are mentioned in a record in the village of Pōli near Kurnool. † The nature of most of these taxes is difficult to discover at present. They must have been paid by the other classes also.

The *agasaru* or washermen paid tax to the government, because the *rēvu*, where they washed dirty linen and dried it, belonged to the state. ‡ This tax, therefore, must be regarded more as land rent than a professional tax. The washermen had to pay a duty on *cavuḍu* and lime which they collected from the waste-land belonging to the state. Nandela Ahōbaḷa, the governor of Gaṇḍikōṭa, abolished it about A. D. 1585. He also remitted certain unspecified taxes which the washermen had to pay. §

The *agasālas* or the goldsmiths were similarly taxed. They were professional shroffs and money changers. One of their duties was to "shroff the money collected in the village in payment of revenue." ¶ Hence, they had to pay the tax. The government imposed a tax upon the executioners who invariably belonged to the *māla* caste. The reason why they paid the tax is this. It was the duty of all the members of the community to hang and behead criminals. The public executioners discharged their duties on behalf of the community to which they belonged. Every *māla* householder paid one *rūka* to the

* *LR.* 15 (Guṇḍlakuṇṭa) p. 133; 14 (Peṇḍlimaṟṟi) pp. 408-409.

† *LR.* 40 pp. 239-40. ‡ *MMss.* 15-6-8. § *LR.* 37 p. 8.

¶ *MMss.* 15-6-8.

executioner for performing this disagreeable work on his behalf. The executioner obtained a sum of money over which the government considered that they had a claim. Therefore, they exacted a tax called *jāyari gutta* from the executioners. The *rūka* which each *māla* householder paid to the executioners was called *mādārike.* * The Mādiga also had to make their own contribution to the imperial exchequer. † According to the *Aṭṭhavaṇa Tantram* he had a greater *āyam* or income than the others. His *āyās* were *horahallu*, *morabhatta*, *nijāyam*, *koltamigulu* and *mōtakūli.* Besides, as he supplied leather buckets and ropes for drawing water for the gardens, he would get grain from the ryots. As he had several sources of income, the tax which he paid to the government varied with the locality. He would offer several presents to the officials at the time of fixing the *gutta* or tax, so that they might assess his income favourably. When a *mādiga* failed to pay the tax, the government would attach his *amudāni* which they would subsequently sell in auction. Half the proceeds would be taken by the government, and the other half would be given to him.

Bōyi-sunkam is mentioned in an inscription of Kaṇḍlagūḍūr dated 1544 A.D. ‡ Two views are possible about the nature of this tax: (1) The *bōyi-sunkam* seems to be a tax paid by members of the *bōya* or the hunter community dwelling in the forests which, of course, belonged to the state. A tax must have been imposed upon them as they lived upon forest products belonging to the government. (2) The men and women of the *bōyi* class were professional bearers of palanquins which were the common means of

* *MMss.* 15-6-8; cf. *EC.* iv. Gu. 67.

† *MMss.* 15-6-8.

‡ *MER.* 362 of 1918.

conveyance of the aristocracy. "All the captains of the kingdom," says Nuniz, "make use of litters and palanqueens. These are like biers, and men carry them on their shoulders ..There are always at the court where the King is twenty thousand litters and palanqueens." * The presence of a large number of palanquins at the court is also mentioned in contemporary literature. †

The women of the community were employed in the imperial zenana as bearers. "Others are bearers (*bois*) who carry the King's wives on their shoulders, and the King also in the interior of the palace." ‡ The demand for the services of the men and women of the community must have been very great. Their income could not but be considerable. It is not unlikely that the *Aṭṭhavaṇam* must have imposed a tax upon them.

A few words may be said about the tax imposed on the earnings of the Brahmans. § No particulars pertaining to it are available. The Brahmans earned money in several ways. Some made their living by officiating at religious functions. Others entered government service. A large number of them, well-versed in the Vedas and literature, obtained the patronage of the emperor and his nobles from whom they obtained large sums of money. It is difficult to know whether this tax was collected from the Brahmans of all the three classes or only from some. Nor is it possible to state whether it affected the Brahmans only of a particular locality, or all those that lived in the empire.

* *FE.* p. 389.

† "మనుచరిత్రం బందు కొనువేళ పురమేగ పల్లకి దనకేల బట్టియెత్తె"

The Sources p. 153.

"తమ్ముమ్రోలనుండు నందలము గానక నాటి పేరెలుంగున బెస్త జీరువాడు"

Am: 4 : 7.

‡ *FE.* p. 382.

§ *MER.* 177 of 1913.

Some of the Tamil epigraphs * mention a tax which the government servants and people connected with the administration paid to the state. The tax paid by judges, tax-collectors, and members of village bodies belongs to this class. It is not possible to determine at present the various facts connected with this tax.

(7) *Social and Communal Taxes* :—

(*a*) *Social taxes* :—The *maduveya-sunka* or *peṇḍli-sunka* is the most important of the social taxes. It played an important part in the social legislation of the Tuluva period. It is not easy to trace its origin. The earliest mention of it in the Tuluva period is found in an inscription of Sāḷuva Timma at Tāḍpatri dated 1507 A.D. †

The marriage tax was imposed upon all the subjects of the emperor irrespective of caste or creed. The tax was payable by all classes of people at the time of the marriage. ‡ It affected all the people belonging to the eighteen castes, '*aṣṭādasa-varṇa*.' Probably, marriages in which widows were brides were exempted from the payment of the marriage tax.

Some of the inscriptions of the period mention the amount which the government exacted from the married couple. It was a sum of 3 *rūkas*, 1 *rūka* for the bride, and 2 *rūkas* for the bridegroom, as stated by an epigraph of Cadipirēla ; § but a different account is given in a copper-plate grant of 1546 A.D., according to which the *peṇḍli-varṭana* or the marriage fee which the members of *karṇagolla* community had to pay amounted

* *MER.* 59 of 1914.

† *SII.* iv. No. 803.

‡ *EC.* xii. Ck. 5 (A.D. 1535.)

§ *LR.* 33 pp. 201-2.

to 101 *māḍas* per marriage. * Beside the marriage tax properly so-called, several other dues were also collected. People celebrating marriages had to pay a tax for the marriage pandal or shed, and another for taking out the married couple in procession through the streets of the village. † Owing to the oppressive character of the taxes, several poor people, who could not pay them, remained unmarried until they became old. If the sense of universal relief felt by the people on the abolition of these dues be an indication of their unpopularity, it must be said that they were the most hateful taxes which the citizens of the empire were ever called upon to pay. The inscriptions invoke blessings upon those that abolished the marriage tax, and curses on those that might revive it. A few extracts are bound to be instructive in this context:

> "Cennarasa of Kṛṣṇarāya Mahārāya's *Aṭṭhavaṇam*, who had given up the marriage tax," says one, "shall govern the empire of all kinds, having acquired the religious merit due to the gift of one thousand cows and one crore of virgins, the performance of one crore of horse-sacrifices and one crore of *yajñas*; and he shall obtain eight sons and considerable wealth." ‡

> "He who takes the marriage fee," says another, "is (equivalent to one) who treats his mother as his wife." §

> "Whichever of the Oḍḍe, Karaṇa, and Telugu kings revokes this (edict abolishing marriage tax)," declares a thrid, "he shall go along the path of the sinner who has slain the Brahman and the cow." "The Turuka king shall suffer from the sin of having eaten the swine's flesh." ¶

The first attempt to abolish this evil tax was made by the Orissan monarch, Puruṣōttama Gajapati. ‖

* *LR.* 15 (Sanjīvipalle) pp. 213-14; *LR.* 41 pp. 52-3. † *EC.* xi. Hk. 17.

‡ *EC.* xi. Jl. 7. § *EC.* vi. Kd. 158.

¶ *LR.* 48 (Koṇḍavīḍu) p. 72. ‖ *ibid*

The abolition of this tax in the Vijayanagara empire, however, was due to the initiative taken by Timmarasa, while he was holding the office of prime minister under Vīra Narasimha.* He gave up the marriage tax in Gutti *rājya*, which was his *amara-māgāṇi*, in A.D. 1507. Although he was desirous that the reform should be introduced in every province of the empire, he did not find it possible to fulfil his desire until the accession of the great Kṛṣṇarāya to the throne of Vijayanagara. Timmarasa and two other officers *viz.* Ādepa Nāyaḍu, and Gauni Tātana made a joint representation to the Rāya, and convinced him that the tax was a social evil, and therefore should be abolished. Their efforts were crowned with success; for a few days later, a royal edict was published abolishing the tax in all the provinces of the empire that were then under the control of the emperor. † Copies of the edict were engraved on stones, and set up at important places in every province. The tax was not collected by the government once again until the end of the reign. It is true that an inscription of A.D. 1515 refers to the remission of the marriage tax by an officer of Kṛṣṇarāya; ‡ but it comes from Jagaḷūr in the Mysore State, a region which was subdued in A.D. 1511-12 *i.e.*, after the publication of the marriage edict.

The tax was apparently revived at least by the *amaranāyakas*, if not by the government, during the reign of Acyuta. A grant of A.D. 1534 mentions

* *SII.* iv. No. 803.

† *EC.* xii. Mi. 64.

Ghanagiri *Rājya*	Mulbāgal *Rājya*	Gaṇḍikōṭa *sthala*
Gutti "	Rāyadurga "	Siddhavaṭṭa "
Kandanavōlu "		Pottapi "
Candragiri "		Nāgamangala *sīma*

‡ *ibid* xi. Jl. 7.

madureya-kāṇike as one of the taxes which was granted to a certain Nārāyaṇayya together with a piece of land.* Another grant of A.D. 1539 mentions probably the remission of the marriage tax. † Similarly Bayakāra Rāmappayya remitted the marriage tax of Būdihaḷa *sīme* in A.D. 1535, ‡ and in the same year he also remitted it in the Kandikere *sīme*. § 'Hiriya Mallappaṇṇa remitted all the marriage tax in Jājūr *sīme*' in A.D. 1540. ¶ Similar remissions are recorded in other places. The latest records of the kind are dated in A.D. 1562. ‖ It is interesting to note that all these documents record the remission of the tax not only by the emperor himself but by the *amaranāyakas* as well as the *Seṭṭi-paṭṭaṇa-swāmis*, and the Ayyāvaḷi *nānādēśis*.

Although a few inscriptions of Sadāśiva's reign allude to the remission of the marriage tax, a copper-plate grant from Gaṇḍikōṭa** seems to mark the reversal of the policy adopted by Timmarasa and Kṛṣṇadēvarāya. As the marriage tax was very heavy and oppressive, Sadāśiva and his regent Rāmarāja are said to have reduced it from 101 *ma* to 16 *ma* per marriage. They are also said to have granted a charter to a certain Nārabōya, probably, to collect the tax from the *karṇagolla* community of which he was a member.

(b) Communal Taxes:—Some of the communal taxes such as *mādārike*, *agasaru*, and the tax upon barbers have already been dealt with under the professional taxes. The *samayaterege* or *sunka* has also been touched upon while explaining the meaning of the term '*sunka*', but it needs further elucidation.

* *EC.* ix. Cp. 155.

† *ibid* xii. Tm. 25.

‡ *ibid* xii. Ck. 5.

§ *ibid* xi. Ck. 44.

¶ *ibid* xi. Hk. 62.

‖ *ibid* xi. Hk. 111; vi. Kd. 158.

** *LR.* 41 pp. 52-53.

The term *samaya-sunka* is thus explained in the *Aṭṭhavaṇa Tantram.*

> "The government appoints a head over some of the low castes for the purpose of regulating caste rules and deciding caste disputes. When a dispute arises in a caste, the head of the caste holds an enquiry and imposes fines upon those who break the caste regulations. While enquiring into cases involving adultery by women, if he finds the accused person guilty, he sells her to some member of the caste, and paying a part of the sale money to the husband, pockets the balance. Moreover, on the occasions of marriages, and communal gatherings, the members of the caste should offer him a *tāmbūla* on behalf of the state, which he is empowered to receive. If, for any reason, the government *tāmbūla* were not offered, he would retire from the place, and none would preside over the function. Any one taking his place, contrary to the established custom, is punished severely by the government. Therefore, the members of these castes are obliged to satisfy the demand of the caste elder appointed by the government. In virtue of the monoply granted to him by the state, he derives much income from the community. He is required to pay a portion of this income to the government as a tax, which is known as *samayācāra* or *samaya-sunka*." *

A charter conferring the office of a caste elder is preserved in the inscriptions. Venkaṭa II appointed one, Peda Cennapa Reḍḍi, the *dēśāi* of Māyikollāpuram, as the head of the *kāpus* following the *samudra-kulācāra.* † According to this charter, the members of the community were thenceforward required to pay the dues such as *tappu*, *kāṇike*, *tāku*, *kappam*, *peṇḍli*, and *nōmulu* through Cennapa Reḍḍi. This charter is of considerable interest as it not only provides us with epigraphical evidence to prove the existence of the *samayācāra*, but specifies the various items of income for collecting which the emperor granted an exclusive right to Peda Cennapa Reḍḍi.

* *MMss.* 15-6-8.

† *EC.* xii. Tm. 51.

The *nālkusamaya-sunka* * is identical with the *samaya-sunka*. The *caudarige* † mentioned in a Mysore inscription is not altogether different from it.

(8) The Property Tax:—The most important tax of this kind is the *mane* or the house tax. ‡ It is identical with the '*illari*' of the Telugu epigraphs. § Besides the house-tax properly so called, taxes also were imposed upon verandahs ¶ house-sites ‖ and even on *vāsal* or the courtyard of the house.** The nature of the house-tax is described in the *Aṭṭhavaṇa Tantram*:

> (For the purpose of taxation) the people are divided into three classes, *jirāyati*, *bāgayir-jirāyati*, and *khuṣu-baṣu*. The cultivators belong to the first class; those that are not agriculturists, but who pay taxes indirectly, belong to the second; and those that do not come under these two classes, but lead a free life, belong to the third. The *bāgayir-jirāyatidārs* or the people belonging to the second class, pay a tax upon their houses according to their station in life. ††

The *illari* of Alavakoṇḍa during the time of Vīra Narasimha is entered as a separate item in the *Rāya-rēkha*:

> The ten houses of the community of Cillara Rājayya Lingayya paid 10 *ga*. The thirty houses of the community of Pagaḍāla Timmayya Appayya paid 15 *ga*. ‡‡

The houses belonging to the community of Rājayya Lingayya paid at the rate of 1 *ga* per house; whereas houses of Timmayya Appayya's community paid only ½ *ga* per house. The difference in the tax paid on the two classes of houses seems to bear out the statement of

* *EC.* iv. Hg. 35-36.

† *EC.* iv. Gu. 21.

‡ *EC.* iv. Ch. 30, Gu. 21; *EC.* iii. i. Nj. 118; *EC.* ix. Cp. 155.

§ *LR.* 13 p. 217; *LR.* 13 (Mārkāpūr) No. 8.

¶ *MER.* 59, 361, 364 of 1914.

‖ *ibid* 203 of 1921.

** *ibid* 335 of 1921.

†† *MMss.* 15-6-8.

‡‡ *LR.* 6 p. 324.

the *Aṭṭhavaṇa Tantram* that people paid house tax according to their station in life. The *Rāyarēkha* of Alavakoṇḍa corroborates the evidence of the *Aṭṭhavaṇa Tantram* in another respect also. It divides the taxes into four classes: (1) land tax (2) *siddhāyas* (3) *maṇiham*, and (4) *iṇḍlu* (houses). The last tax was collected from the members of only two castes, who correspond, in all probability, to the *bāgayir-jirāyatidārs*. This point, however, should be further investigated in the light of the evidence furnished by the inscriptions.

The owners of other kinds of property also had to pay taxes. The *aḍḍatere* or the tax on goats is mentioned in several inscriptions.* The taxes upon cows, buffaloes, and bulls are referred to in an inscription of Mysore.† Another inscription from Cadipirēla in the Cuddapah district describes the tax upon several domestic animals: ‡

She-buffalo	$\frac{3}{4}$ *rūka*	Cow	$\frac{1}{4}$ *rūka*
He-buffalo	$\frac{1}{4}$,,	Horse	$\frac{1}{2}$,,
Bull	$\frac{3}{4}$,,	Camel	$\frac{1}{8}$,,

It is very probable that taxes were levied on other forms of property also.

(9) The Religious Tax:—The only religious tax with which the government had anything to do, seems to have been the tax collected for the *mahārājaprayōjanās* or the great royal festivals. The word *mahārājatantu* occurring in an epigraph in the temple of Raghunāthaswāmi at Gaṇḍikōṭa is only a variant of the above, meaning the same thing.§ That this tax was due to

* *EC.* iv. Gu. 2, 21, 73; *LR.* 13 No. 8.

† *EC.* iv. Gu. 73.

‡ *LR.* 33 pp. 201-202.

§ *LR.* 15 p. 127.

the state is proved by the explicit statement of the inscription : " We have declared the *kāsuvīsālu*, due to the state from the *mahārājaprayōjanās*, *sarvamānya.* " * What was the purpose for which this tax was levied ? It appears to be closely connected with the worship of the *grāma-dēvatā* or the village deity. It is said in an inscription at Vēlpucerla that " out of the customary dues collected from certain villages for the *mahārāja-prayōjanās*, after paying the *maṇihāri* and *pambakāḍu*, the perquisites that accrued to the elders in the form of money, rice, betel, and nuts were granted to the goddess, Ankāḷaparamēśvarī of the place, for offering *dhūpa*, *deepa*, and *naivēdya*, and for celebrating the festivals of *parupu*, and *pārivēṭa* so that the merit might accrue to the Rāya and the chiefs governing the *sīma*." † It is obvious that the fees collected for *mahārājaprayōjanālu* were utilised for paying the salaries of the *maṇihāri* and the *pambakāḍu*, and the remainder was appropriated by the elders who probably managed the affairs of the temple. In another grant of Tāḷḷamārpuram, it is stated that a certain Irugajangam, the son of Rāmdēvarāya of Gaṇḍikōṭa and Irugalingam (the priest) of the shrine at Gaṇḍikōṭa, with all their *jñātis* granted to the shrine of Ankāḷadēvī erected by them at Tāḷḷamārpuram the 12 *rūkas*, which were collected from the villages of Tāḷḷamārpuram and Nangalūr for the *mahārājaprayōjanās.* ‡ Nandela Timmayadēva Mahārāja who was holding the Gaṇḍikōṭa *sīma* in *amaram* made a grant to the priests of Ankāḷaśakti in 1556 A.D.

" The *kāṇike*, and *kāsuvīsās* that are due to us ", says he, "according to the ancient custom from the *mahārāja-tantus* in all

* *LR.* 37 pp. 1-6.

† *MMss.* 15-3-6 p. 262.

‡ *LR.* 15 (Gaṇḍikōṭa) p. 127.

the villages of the Gaṇḍikōṭa *sīma* which our liege lord Sadāśivadēva Mahārāya granted to us, we have granted to Ankāḷaparamēśvarī. Taking (the *kāṇike etc.,*) you should regularly conduct in all the villages the festivals of *parupu* and *pārivēṭa* according to the custom, without violating this *dharma.*" *

Cinna Timmarāju Koṇḍayya granted in 1549 A.D. to Śrī Vīrabhadra of Jillēḷḷa the money that was collected as *kāṇika* and *kaṭṇam* for the *mahārājaprayōjanās* in the village of Jillēḷḷa. † Nandela Ahōbaḷēśvararāju granted in 1543 A.D. to Ankāḷamma of Koilakunṭla the rent and fees accruing from Ademala which were utilised for the *mahārājaprayōjanās.* ‡

The following points emerge from the foregoing epigraphical extracts:

(1) The dues for the *mahārājaprayōjanās* were collected from the villages of the Gaṇḍikōṭa and the Koilakunṭla *sīmas* both in coin and kind. It seems to be essentially a local tax.

(2) They were due to the crown, and the right of collecting them like that of the other taxes in the *amara* villages was delegated to the *amaranāyakas.*

(3) In all the cases excepting one, the dues were granted either by the *amaranāyakas* or by private individuals (to whom the *amaranāyakas* might have granted them) to the Goddess Ankāḷamma.

(4) The dues were granted to this deity, at least in one case, so that the merit might accrue to the Rāya and the chiefs governing the *sīma* under him.

The most important question, however, remains unanswered. What were the *mahārājaprayōjanās* for

* *LR.* 15 (Gaṇḍikōṭa) p. 127.

† *LR.* 36 (Jillēḷḷa) p. 468.

‡ *LR.* 33 pp. 370-71.

which dues were collected? It is not possible to give any correct answer to this question. However, the following suggestion may be taken for what it is worth. According to an ancient Indian belief, a kingdom is liable to be affected by evils the most important of which are famine and pestilential diseases. "From these," declares Kauṭilya, "shall the king protect his kingdom."* The village deities are generally believed to cause famines and epidemics, if they are not kept in good humour by offerings. As the dues collected for the *mahārājaprayōjanās* were, in almost all cases, utilised to carry on the daily worship and conduct the festivals of Ankāḷamma, it is not unreasonable to suppose that they were levied by the Rāya to protect his dominions from the wrath of the village deities. As the protection of the empire was the primary duty of the emperor, the dues which he collected from his subjects to secure this end came to be known as the dues for *mahārājaprayō-janās*.

(10) The Taxes on Mānya-grāmas:—The most important of the taxes which the holders of the *mānya* lands had to pay were *jōḍi (sōḍi)*, *kaṭṇam*, *kāṇike*, *khaḍḍāyam* and *araśupēṟu*.

The word *jōḍi* means 'a favourable quit-rent on *inām* lands.'† The *Aṭṭhavaṇa Tantram* defines it as "the money which the *gauḍ* and the *ṣānbhōg* pay to the government for their *mānyas*. Closely allied to this is the *mānya-kāṇike* which the holders of *inām* lands like Brahmans and fakirs pay to the state."‡ But the word *jōḍi* is used in the inscriptions to denote the quit-rent paid by the holders of all kinds of *inām* lands. *Sōḍi (jōḍi)* is said to be one of the taxes which was

* Kautilya: *Arthaśāstra* (Shama Sastri's translation) p. 253.

† H. H. Wilson: *Glossary* p. 241.

‡ *MMss.* 15-6-8.

due to the state from the lands belonging to the temples in Śōḷamaṇḍalam. * It is said, in a grant of 15 3 A.D., that *jōḍi* was paid by the holders of an *agrahāra*. † Another tax which is synonymous with *jōḍi* is *śrōtriyam*. According to an inscription of old Siruvoḷḷa, *śrōtriyas* were collected from all the *mānya* villages belonging to the gods and Brahmans, and other service *ināms*. ‡ No information is available at present for determining the exact proportion of the income of the *inām* lands which the state claimed as *jōḍi* or *śrōtriyam*.

In addition to the *jōḍi* or *śrōtriyam* the tax-free villages paid some other taxes also. These are *kappa*, *kaṭṇa*, *kāṇike*, *khaḍḍāya*, § (the four *ks*) which, however, were not peculiar to the *inām* lands. There is ample evidence to show that they were collected from other sources also. *Kappa* is one of those taxes which one usually meets with in the inscriptions. It is a different tax from the *jōḍi* or *śrōtriyam*; for they are mentioned together as two different taxes due to the state from an *agrahāra*. ¶ *Kappa* is also said to be one of the dues which the *kāpus* following the *samudrakulācāra* had to pay. ‖ It was collected from the barbers, washermen etc. It appears to be the same tax as *araśupēṟu* mentioned in a grant of the Tamil country.** The tax known as *kaṭṇam* was also exacted from the *agrahāras*. †† The word *kaṭnam* means a periodical present made to superiors by their subordinates. Probably the tax had its origin in the present made to a chief or king by his subjects, which, however, in course of time, was converted into a tax. It occurs in a slightly

* *MER.* 214 of 1926 (1517). † *EC.* v. i. Hn. 2. ‡ *LR.* 40 p. 215.

§ *MMss.* 15-3-6 (Gūbaguṇḍam); *EC.* iv. Gu. 67; vi. Hn. 2.

¶ *EC.* v. i. Hn. 2. ‖ *EC.* xii. Tm. 51.

** *MER.* 214 of 1926. †† *ibid* 700 of 1917.

different form, as *grāma-kaṭṇam*,* in several places, from which it is to be inferred that it was exacted from all the villages. *Kaṭṇam* was also paid by barbers and members of other lower classes. † *Kāṇike* is a similar tax. It means a present offered to a man of rank by a visitor. *Kāṇike* was collected not only from the villages but from communities such as the barbers and *kāpus*. *Kāṇike* occurs as a member of such compound words as *huraḷi-kaḍale-kāṇike*, *maduveya-kāṇike*, *dariśena-kānike*, and *kāvali-kāṇike*, ‡ in all of which it seems to mean a duty due to the state or some other body. It is not possible to state whether these have any connection with the simple word *kāṇike*. Lastly, the tax called *khaḍḍāya* must be mentioned. § It is translated by Rice in one place as a 'fine.' Kittel, however, understands it to mean 'force, compulsion.'¶ It is said to mean "forcing people to pay the price set upon articles, exaction." Nothing more about this tax can be known at present.

Section 4: *Psuedo-Taxes*:—*Psuedo* taxes, as their name indicates, are not taxes properly so called. They are dues which certain classes of people, or people residing in certain localities, paid, not to the government, but to private individuals or institutions. They fall under two heads (*a*) the religious, and (*b*) non-religious.

(*a*) The religious *psuedo*-taxes are :—

(1) *Gaṇākāra or Gaṇācāra-tere.* ‖

* *LR.* 14 (Moyiḷḷakālva) p. 426 ; *LR.* 3 (Cadipirēla) p. 426.

† *LR.* 40 (Nilicinameṭla) pp. 134-40.

‡ *EC.* iii. i. Ml. 95 ; *EC.* ix. Ma. 62 ; *EC.* v. i. Cn. 259 ; *LR.* 13 (Kattaragaṇḍla) p. 268.

§ *EC.* iii. i. Ml. 95.

¶ *Canarese English Dictionary* p. 347.

‖ *EC.* iv. Gu. 67.

(2) *Vīramuṣṭi-pannu.* *

(3) *Jīyar-terege.* †

(4) *Kūṭaderege.* ‡

(5) *Maṭha-terege.* §

(6) *Guḍipannu.* ¶

(7) *Tēre-kāṇike.* ‖

(8) *Jātre.* **

These eight dues or taxes may be reduced to three classes viz., (i) Śaiva (ii) Vaiṣṇava (iii) Common.

(*i*) *Śaiva* :—The *gaṇācāra-tere* was a tax paid to the *jangamas* or the Lingāyat priests by the Śaivas. It was known as *vīramuṣṭi-pannu* in the Telugu districts. It was payable by all the Śaivas including the Brahmans every year. The *guḍipannu* was paid by the *gaṇācāris* and the *tambaḷas* or *arcakas* of a Śaiva shrine for what purpose it is not known. †† The *jangamas* and *vīramuṣṭis* were attached to some one or other of the Śaiva *maṭhas*. They regarded themselves as the disciples of the head of that *maṭha* to whom they paid a part of the dues collected by them from the faithful. The head of a *maṭha*, or on his behalf his *kāryakarta*, had the right of remitting the tax in favour of any Śaivite temple. Thenceforward it was to be

* *LR.* 15 (Ayyalūru) pp. 353-4; (Gāḍidamaḷḷa) p. 377; (Bedadūr) p. 11; *LR.* 2 (Mācanūr) p. 271; (Peda Cappalli) pp. 371; (Koppolu) pp. 419-20; *LR.* 3 (Cadipirēla) p. 427; *LR.* 15 (Poṭṭipāḍu) p. 118.

† *EC.* iv. Gu. 67.

‡ *EC.* vi. Gu. 67.

§ *EC.* iii. i. Ml. 95.

¶ *LR.* 15 (Ayyalūru) pp. 353-54.

‖ *EC.* iv. Gu. 5, 6, 8.

** *EC.* v. Ag. 7.

†† *LR*, 15 (Ayyalūru) pp. 353-54.

paid to the temple and not to the *Jangamas* and the *Vīramuṣṭis.*

(*ii*) The *jīyaratere* was a tax paid by the Vaiṣṇavites to their *guru* or *jīyar* for maintaining his position in a becoming fashion. The *kūṭatere* must have been a contribution made by the laity for the maintenance of the *Rāmānuja-kūṭas* which were the usual places of meeting of the Rāmānujites.

(*iii*) The common taxes are those that might have been paid by both the Śaivites and the Vaiṣṇavites. *Maṭha* was an institution that was common to both. It was a tax which the followers of a *maṭha* paid for the purpose of maintaining the establishment of a *maṭha*. The *tēre-kāṇike* was a due which was collected from certain localities. It amounted only to two *haṇas* for a village. The money thus collected was probably used to pay the labourers employed in dragging the temple car on the day of the car festival. The *tēre-kāṇike* cannot be termed a sectarian tax, as both the Śaiva and the Vaiṣṇava shrines maintained cars of their own. *Jātre* was a non-sectarian tax. The worship of the village deity was common to all the Hindus to whichever sect they belonged. As *jātre* was a due raised by the villagers for celebrating the *jātra* or the periodical festival in honour of the village deity, it was payable by all the villagers whether they were Śaivas or Vaiṣṇavas.

(*b*) *The Non-religious Psuedo Taxes*:—These are wot in number: (i) the *vipravinōdi-pannu* and (ii) the *dommara-pannu.*

(*i*) *The Vipravinōdi-pannu*:—The term *vipravinōdi* means one who provides *vinōda* or amusement to the Brahmans. The *Vipravinōdis* are professional conjurers, who earn their livelihood by collecting annual contributions of money and rice from the Brahman households in the country. They narrate a story explaining the origin of the due. On one occasion, when there was a big religious disputation between the Brahmans and the Jains, the *Vipravinōdis* helped the former to win a victory over the latter by employing some of their tricks. In consideration of this timely help, the Brahmans are said to have gratefully promised to pay them a *varṣāśana* or annual contribution. This is how the *Vipravinōdis* explain the origin of their tax. Consistently with the legendary origin of the due, they only collect it from the Brahmans, and the other castes are free from it. The *Vipravinōdis* appear to have been a very wide-spread community in the 16th century, for according to an epigraph, they were living in "Vidyānagara, Beḍadakōṭa, Kaṭaka and Drāviḍa-dēśa." * Therefore, the Brahmans inhabiting all these countries had to pay the *vipravinōdi* contribution every year.

(*ii*) *The Dommara-pannu*:—The *Dommaras* are a tribe of professional acrobats who wander from place to place throughout the year. They earn their livelihood by performing wonderful feats, especially on the rope, in the streets of towns and villages. In the 16th century, it was obligatory on the part of every citizen to pay them some money or measure out some paddy in return for the entertainment. The *Dommara* acrobatic feats before the regent Rāmarāja are described at some length in the *Rāmarāyanabakhire.* † The *Dommaras* belonged to twenty four *kulas* ‡ and they collected their perquisites not only from the ryots but from the Brahmans also. It is said that the dues which they

* *MER.* 694 of 1917.

† *The Bhārati* x. p. 753.

‡ *LR.* 14 (Nosam) pp. 374-5.

collected from the cultivators of the Puṣpagiri *agrahāra* amounted to 1,000 *māḍas.* *

Section 5 : The Collection of Taxes :—How was the collection of revenue effected by the government? The collection of *dhānyādāya* or the land tax should be considered first. The *Aṭṭhavaṇa Tantram* says :

"The ryots in the villages pay the taxes to the *gauḍ* and *ṣānbhōg*. The *gauḍ* has to see that the ryots cultivate the village land for the money fixed by the government. He collects and pays the tax in due time, and at *jamābandi* would come to an agreement with the state on behalf of the ryots of his village regarding the rent to be paid the next year." †

Father Queyros gives a brief account of the method adopted by the government in collecting the land tax :—

"The manner which the Princes observe in renting land is the following. In June their Ministers go about in the villages and oblige the peasants to rent the lands for a certain sum. They return at the time of the harvest, because without their presence the husbandmen cannot reap, and they ask whether they are willing to give a further moiety or third of what was settled according to the abundance of the crop ; if they agree, a writing is made, they give sureties, and when they have threshed [the corn], they usually find that the produce is not enough to pay the King; if they refuse either to pay according to the contract or the increase they do not even then escape the ruin, for the Ministers who are present at the reaping, threshing and measuring, all of which is done at the cost of the farmers, after letting him take his share, which does not exceed 25 to 30 per 100, *compel the farmer to buy the King's share then and there at a price exceeding that current in the land*, as for instance giving him at nine what is worth six ; and he has not the wherewithal to support himself and his family [and] becomes indebted again for the coming year." ‡

* *LR.* 15 (Beḍadūr) pp. 112-13.

† *MMss.* 15-6-8.

‡ *The Conquest of Ceylon*, i. p. 92.

Sir Thomas Munro agrees with Father Queyros. According to him the land tax was paid in kind in proportion of half of the produce, and this half was converted into money at a rate unfavourable to the cultivator.* A similar opinion is expressed by Wilks.† According to these writers the ryots were compelled to purchase the government's share of the grain at a price fixed by the government themselves. The people who were responsible for the sale were the ministers or, more probably, the *pārupatyagārs* and other officers of the *Aṭṭhavaṇa* Department. If Kittel's interpretation of *kaḍḍāya* as 'forcing people to pay the price set upon articles' be correct, it must be admitted that there is a good deal of truth in the description given by Father Queyros and others. However, as their accounts are based on conditions obtaining in the *Nāyak* kingdoms subsequent to the dismemberment of the empire, they need not be taken as accurate descriptions of methods current in the sixteenth century. Moreover, there is reason to believe that the government's share of corn was not always sold to the ryots in the manner mentioned above; for the government themselves required large quantities of corn for their own purposes. Besides the quantity required for the daily consumption of the huge palace establishment consisting of 12,000 women and other attendants, the feeding of numerous horses and elephants which the emperor and his *amaranāyakas* maintained would have involved the expenditure of a large quantity of grain. Paes says:

> "Of the grain, there is a great quantity, because, besides being used as food for men, it is also used for horses since there is no other kind of barley." ‡

* *The Gazetteer of Cuddapah* pp. 146-147.

† *History of Mysore* pp. 169-70.

‡ *FE.* p. 237.

Barbosa says :

> " And daily(he) supplies (rations) as well for the horses and groom, which they fetch from the great kitchens kept up by the King to feed his elephants and horses. These are in many large houses where are many great copper cauldrons, and in these are many officials who look after the preparation of food, and others, who prepare it. The food is rice boiled with chick-peas and other pulse." *

According to another writer, Kṛṣṇadēvarāya towards the close of his reign, 'kept up at his own cost an establishment of 100,000 horses and 4,000 elephants.' † The number of horses is certainly exaggerated. Making allowance for exaggeration, the quantity of rice and other grain which was necessary to feed daily such a large number of beasts must have been enormous. It is extremely unlikely that the state would have sold away its share of grain completely, and purchased it again to feed the huge palace establishment, and the horses and elephants in the army. It is more reasonable to believe that the government had at least reserved a part of their share of grain which they stored up at convenient centres to be utilised according to their needs. This supposition is supported by a passage from the *Aṭṭhavaṇa Tantram* in which the government are advised 'to export their share of corn from provinces where it is plentiful to those suffering from scarcity so that they may sell it at a profit.' ‡ It is evident from this, that the government did not always compel the ryots to purchase their grain 'at a price exceeding that current in the land.' Instead, they preferred, at least on occasions, to store up the grain to be spent as they deemed fit.

A more popular method, however, was to farm the taxes. The *Aṭṭhavaṇa Tantram* refers to the contractors

* *Barbosa* i. pp. 210-11. † *FE.* p. 150. ‡ *MMss.* 15-6-8.

who bought the right of collecting taxes from villages. They had direct dealings with the *Aṭṭhavaṇam* or the Revenue Department who fixed the rent on which they were prepared to let the villages. What was done by the government was imitated by the *amaranāyakas*. This fact is revealed by an inscription at Vanipeṇṭa dated 1521 A.D., according to which that village was taken for *guttā* from Bukkarāju Timmarāju who evidently was the *nāyaka* holding the village under *amara* tenure.*

The taxes coming under the head *suvarṇādāya* were also let to the tax farmers. † In this connection, the definition of the term *sunkam* which is given in a former context should be remembered. The word was used in the 16th century in a loose manner, and several taxes which had no connection with tolls or excise duties were known by the name. The *sunka* should be broadly interpreted as a tax.

The country was divided into a number of fiscal districts or *sunka-ṭhāṇyas*, several of which are referred to in the inscriptions.‡ The *sunka-thāṇyas* or *sunka-kaṭṭes* are generally considered as places where tolls were collected on goods in transit. That this view is not correct is proved by the grant which three *sunkaris* belonging to the Cadipirēla *ṭhāṇya* made to a temple:

* The practice of farming the revenue is briefly alluded to by Nuniz. All the articles that were brought to the market of Vijayanagara had to pass through a single gate which was 'rented out for 12000 *pardaos* each year, and no man can enter it without paying what the renters ask, country folk as well as strangers.' *FE*. p. 366.

† *LR*. 18 (Vanipeṇṭa) p. 49.

‡ *MER*. 223 of 1913; *LR*. 14 (Cintakommudinne) pp. 393-4; *MER*. 557 of 1915; *LR*. 40 (Cippagiri) p. 384.

"We three, grant (the following items) included in our *sunkas* in the village of Cadipirēla in the Gaṇḍikōṭa *sīma* belonging to our *ṭhāṇya* * ":—

1.	*grāma-kaṭnam*	5.	*pinja-siddhāya*
2.	*magga-sthāvaras*	6.	*golla-siddhāya*
3.	*kōmaḷi-siddhāya*	7.	*uppara-siddhāya*
4.	*gānuga-siddhāya*	8.	*īḍiga-siddhāya*

The eight taxes mentioned above, as well as the *kaṭṇam*, *sunkasthāvarālu*, alluded to in an inscription at Koppōlu †, as having been collected by the *sunkamvāru*, do not come under tolls. It is obvious that *sunkaris* or *sunkamvāru* were not merely collectors of tolls but of several other kinds of taxes as well. The *sunka-thāṇya*, therefore, was not a place where tolls were collected, but a fiscal division of the empire.

The *sunkaris*, *sunkaravāru* or *sunkadavaru* may at first appear to be the members of a government department. They were mere tax farmers, and there is no evidence to show that they had anything to do with the government service. Their interest in the *sunka-ṭhāṇyas* was confined to the collection of as much money as they possibly could.

The Jamābandi:—The word *jamābandi* is defined by Kittel as 'the general assessment of land etc., settlement of the assessments.' ‡ Wilson gives a fuller definition of the term.

It is said to mean "settlement of the amount of revenue assessed upon an estate, a village or district, annual settlement of

* *LR.* 3 p. 426.

† *LR.* 33 p. 213.

‡ *Canarese-English Dictionary* p. 636.

revenue with cultivators or *ryotwari* settlement: an annual settlement modified according to the circumstances under which the revenue is paid whether by individuals or communities and whether to a zamindar or to the government." It also means "the annual tour of a revenue officer, village by village, for the settlement of assessment." *

There is no evidence in the inscriptions to show that *jamābandi* was known in Vijayanagara during the sixteenth century; but the constant enquiries made by the emperor and his officials about the condition of the ryots, and the frequent remission of taxes registered in the lithic records indicate that there must have been something corresponding to the *jamābandi*. This belief is confirmed by an explicit statement of the *Aṭṭhavaṇa Tantram* which refers to the *jamābandi* settlement several times. The *gauḍ* is said to make *jamābandi* settlement every year (with the government). Again the government are spoken of as preparing a consolidated list of all the *babs* (items of revenue) for *jamābandi*. If it were not possible to collect all the dues of the year completely, the arrears were entered in next *jamābandi* accounts under the head of *silusila-bāki*, which was collected with the taxes of the succeeding year. †

Section 6: *Oppressive Taxation*:—The government appears to have been very oppressive and tyrannical in its treatment of the peasants who tilled the soil. They were allowed, according to Nuniz, to retain only a tenth of the produce, the remaining being taken from them either by the government or the *amaranāyakas* as their share. ‡ Commenting on this statement, Sewell observes:

"Whether true or not, this statement, coming as it does from a totally external source, strongly supports the view often held

* *Glossary* p. 228. † *MMss*. 15-6-8. ‡ *FE*. p. 379.

that the ryots of South India were grievously oppressed by the nobles when subject to the Hindu government. Other passages in both these chronicles (Paes and Nuniz), each of which was written quite independently of the other, confirm the assertion here made as to the mass of people being ground down and living in the greatest poverty and distress." *

This view, although expressed in very strong terms, is corroborated by the inscriptions, literature, and the Local Records. A survey of the inscriptions of the period reveals the fact that the grasping hand of the tax-gatherer was, indeed, very active. It is stated in an inscription of 1512 A.D., that at Krottaceruvu, † taxes were collected from the *dēvādāya* and *brahmādāya* lands which were subsequently remitted by Kṛṣṇadēvarāya. The ryots of a village in the neighbourhood of Śrī Muṣṇam were obliged to emigrate from their native village owing to excessive taxation. Sinnappa Nāyaka, one of Kṛṣṇarāya's officers, fixed favourable rates in 1513 A.D., and persuaded the ryots to return to their homes. ‡ "The *sthānikas* of the temple of Perumāḷ-Kariyavar went on a deputation to the king, to Vijayanagara, and complained of the injustice done by the authorities (*rājagaram*) stationed at Dēviyakuricci village belonging to the temple. The chief *amaram*, Timmarasa, introduced them to the king, got their grievance redressed." § Instances of official oppression such as these were probably in the mind of the Rāya, when he wrote that a monarch, who entertained in his service an official who would not prevent the emigration of the ruined cultivators expecting to profit himself by their departure, could not be contented even with

* *FE.* p. 379, *n.* 2.

† *MER.* 180 of 1913.

‡ *ibid* 246 of 1916.

§ *ibid* 449 of 1913.

the sovereignty of the whole earth. * Kṛṣṇarāya was always ready to hear the miserable story of the unfortunate ryots, and alleviate their sufferings as far as possible.

The condition of the farmers became distinctly worse during the reign of Acyuta. Owing to the civil war, the authority of the central government was considerably weakened, and the *amaranāyakas* and petty chiefs behaved very tyrannically to the ryots. A *Kaifiyat* runs :

> " While Acyutadēvarāya was ruling at Vijayanagara, owing to the weakness of the central government, considerable disorder and insecurity prevailed in the country. The power of the *pāḷegārs* had so increased that they began to rule as independent princes, each in his own principality. The period of anarchy and confusion lasted for six years, when Aḷiya Rāmarāja overthrew the government, and installed Sadāśiva on the throne." †

The behaviour of some of the provincial governors was no better. Bācamarasa, the governor of Koṇḍavīḍu had attained such notoriety, that satirical writers made him the object of their lampoons. One writer declares :

> " The Turaka of Gōlkoṇḍa, eats cows ; but Bācamarasa consumes all the Brahmans of Koṇḍavīḍu. Which of the two is better, Turaka or Bācamarasa ? " ‡

* " ప్రజ నవసిచన్నఁ బిలువ కప్పసుల గొలుచు
నమ్మి యుండ్లింధనంబులకాయె ననెడి
కలని నక్కైౘన యధికారిగల నృపతికి
నేడుదీవులు గొన్న సమృద్ధిలేదు." *Ām.* 4 : 232.

† *LR.* 6 p. 40.

‡ గోలకొండ తురక గోవుల భక్షించు
గొండవీటి విప్రకులము నెల్ల
బాచమరసు చేరి భక్షించుచున్నాఁడు
తురక మేలో బాచమరసు మేలో ?

Palakalūri Gopana : ***Appakavīyam*** 3 : 230.

The story of misrule is confirmed by inscriptions. In front of the Hanumān's shrine at Kavutāḷam in the Ādōni tāluk of the Bellāry district, there stands a stone on which an important charter, which Salakarāju Cikka Tirumala granted to ryots of the Kavutāḷa *sīme*, is engraved.* The circumstances leading up to the grant of this charter are fully narrated in the *Kaifiyat* of Kavutāḷam.

> "Owing to the absence of orderly government the ryots of the Kavutāḷa *sīme* having deserted their native villages, migrated in a body to the Mānaveya *sīme* on the other side of the Tungabhadrā. While Acyuta was ruling at Vijayanagara, his brother-in-law, Salakarāju Cikka Tirumala Mahārāja, having visited Ādavāni, gave a fresh *kaul* to all the *gauḍas* of Kavutāḷa, and made concessions to them for reclaiming cultivable land from the jungle which had grown up during the period of desertion. Although these concessions were published by means of a *sāsana*, the *gauḍas* and *kulkarnis* alone returned, but not the cultivators who had lost all their faith in the government. Therefore, Tirumala Mahārāja had to open negotiations afresh. The ryots gathered near Hanumān's shrine at Kavutāḷa, where they came to an agreement with the government. They then returned to their old homes. The terms of the agreement were recorded on a stone slab which was set up at the place of meeting." †

According to another inscription, the *dēvādāya* and the *brahmādāya* lands, which had been tax-free since the time of Cikkavōḍeya, were 'assessed in corn and coin owing to the disturbances'; ‡ but Bhaṇḍārada Timma made them once again tax-free in 1533 A.D. A similar grant dated 1538 A.D., records that one Hanumeyadēva remitted to the temples of Pērusāmula the taxes in grain and coin. These taxes had been unjustly imposed by previous rulers on tax-free lands. § Bhōgarāju Timmayadēva granted a favourable *kaul* to the

* *MER.* 492 of 1915.

† *MMss.* 19-1-4.

‡ *MER.* 179 of 1913.

§ *ibid* 680 of 1917.

Reḍḍis and other people of Kaḍimeṭla to induce them to resettle in the village which they had formerly deserted.* An inscription in the Śrīrangapaṭṭaṇa *sīme* describes the extortion of the local officials serving under the *amaranāyakas*.

> "Whereas in the aforesaid *agrahāras*, and villages in the Śrīrangapaṭṭaṇa *sīme* granted to Ramābhaṭlayya as his *māgāṇi*, customs which did not before exist have been levied from all by Kāmappa Nāyaka while he held the *pārupatya*." †

The *sunkaravāru* or the tax-gatherers exacted without the knowledge of the government *kaṭṇam* and *sunkasthāvaras* from the villages of Koppōlu and Tippalūru, although they had been exempted from the payment of these taxes by Kṛṣṇadēvarāya. ‡ Finally, Vīrajiyya, the temple priest of Nandyāla ran away from his place, as he was not able to pay *kāṇike* and *kaṭṇam*. Although he was brought back, he consented to resume his office only after the taxes had been remitted. §

There is, therefore, ample evidence to show that during the reign of Acyuta, a good deal of extortion was practised by the *amaranāyakas* and the officials. When the hand of the oppressor became very heavy and ruinous, the ryots, no longer able to put up with tyranny, either formed voluntary associations to resist his extortions, ¶ or, more frequently, deserted their homes and farms and migrated to a neighbouring province where conditions governing life were less intolerable. The government made constant attempts to induce such ryots to return to their farms by offering them liberal concessions. The ryots were not always inclined to return, as they had completely lost their

* *MER.* 533 of 1915.

† *EC.* iii. i. Sr. 6.

‡ *LR.* 2 (Koppōlu) pp. 418-19.

§ *ibid* 40 pp. 209-10.

¶ *MER.* 92 of 1918.

faith in the promises made by the representatives of the government.

Matters did not improve very much after the accession of Sadāśiva. Inscriptions coming from different parts of the empire narrate the same tale of extortion and emigration.* It is evident from this that what was a normal evil became greatly exaggerated during the administration of weak monarchs such as Acyuta, owing to the rapacity of *amaranāyakas* and tax-gatherers whose nefarious activities the imperial government was not able to check.

Section 7: The Expenditure:—No satisfactory information is available about the way in which the emperor spent his revenues. The *Aṭṭhavaṇa Tantram* declares, that the money collected according to the *kistibandi* was deposited in the treasury, after deducting from it the expenditure incurred by the Revenue and the Military Departments.† It is difficult to test the accuracy of this statement, as the other sources give very meagre information on the subject. However, according to the *Āmuktamālyada* the income of the state should be divided into four parts, one to be spent on the palace establishment and charity; two to be devoted to the maintenance of the army; and the remaining part to be deposited in the treasury.‡ Does this division of the state

* *MER.* 2 of 1923; 62 of 1904; *LR.* 40 (Nilicinameṭla) p. 137; *LR.* 54 (Vellāla) pp. 112-13.

† *MMss.* 15-6-8.

‡ ఉరవొ చాగంబు భోగం బుభయము నొకపా లుగ్రసేనావనార్థం
బిరువా ల్లిబ్బండార బండారిలు చొర నొకపా లిట్లుగా నాయ మొప్పం
జరదృష్టి న్వైరి పక్షేక్షణము సచివవస్థ స్వపక్షేక్షణంబుం
ధరణీనాథుండొనర్పం దగుఁ దగుఁ దునుమన్ దస్కరాళిన్ నిజోర్విన్ ॥

Ām 4: 238.

income correspond to what was obtaining at Vijayanagara during the first half of the sixteenth century? Or, is it merely the restatement of an old theory which Kṛṣṇarāya found in some text book on *daṇḍanīti*? The fourfold division of the state's revenue seems to be based on fact. Both Nuniz and Paes give some valuable information concerning the public expenditure. Nuniz says:

"They (the nobles) also pay to him (the king) every year, "sixty *lakhs* of rents as royal dues......Of these sixty *lakhs* that the king has of revenue every year, he does not enjoy a larger sum than twenty-five *lakhs*, for the rest is spent on his horses and elephants and foot-soldiers and cavalry whose expenses he defrays." * "The king always gives large sums in charity; in the palace there are always two or three thousand Brahmans who are his priests, and to whom the king commands to give alms."†

"And now, I wish you to know", declares Paes, "that the previous kings of this place for many years past held it a custom to maintain a treasury, which after the death of each is kept locked and sealed in such a way that it cannot be seen by any one, nor opened, nor do the kings who succeed to the kingdom open them or know what is in them. They are not opened except when the kings have great need, and thus the kingdom has great supplies to meet its needs. This king (Kṛṣṇadēvarāya) has made his treasury different from those of the previous kings, and he puts in it every year ten million *pardaos* without taking from them one *pardao* more than for the expenses of his house." ‡

The state revenue, therefore, was utilised in three different ways; nearly two thirds of it was devoted to meet the expenses of the army; of the remaining third, a part was spent on charities and the palace establishment, and the remainder was stored up in the treasury. A similar account is given in the *Rāyavācaka*. At the

* *FE*. p. 373.

† *ibid* p 379; cf. *Ānandanidhi*.

‡ *ibid* p. 282.

commencement of the reign of Kṛṣṇadēvarāya, the gross income of the state was *ga* 10,8400000

The *dēvādāya*, *brahmādāya*, and *sarvamānya* ,,	8400000
Balance *ga*	10,0000000

The monthly expenditure on 24,00000 horses was	*ga* 24,00000
,, ,, 1500 elephants	,, 12,00000
,, ,, 2,00000 foot-soldiers	,, 4,00000
Total monthly expenditure	*ga* 40,00000

The annual military expenditure was *ga* 4,80,00000. Of the remaining *ga* 5,20,00000, a part was spent on the palace establishment and charities, the other being deposited in the treasury. *

Although there appears to be no agreement among our authorities about the exact proportion of money spent on various items, they are unanimous, or very nearly so, concerning the items themselves. The state revenue was spent either on the army, or the palace establishment and charity, or stored up in the treasury. The military expenditure consumed nearly 50 per cent of the state income. As the *Āmuktamālyada* and the *Rāyavācaka* almost agree about the proportion of military expenditure, the statement of the former, coming, as it does, from the pen of Kṛṣṇarāya himself, may be taken as correct.

Section 8: *The Ways of Increasing Revenue*:—The author of the *Aṭṭhavaṇa Tantram* suggests six methods by means of which a government may increase the revenue of the state. † These six methods fall into two classes. The government may increase the income by

* *ASPP.* iii. p. 29.

† *MMss.* 15-6-8.

introducing (i) agricultural, and (ii) commercial improvements. As there is epigraphic and literary evidence to show that almost all these methods were adopted by the emperors of Vijayanagara, a short account of them is given below. The *Aṭṭhavaṇa Tantram* says :

(i) Agricultural :—

(*a*) "The government may hand over to small farmers the uncultivated fields, and induce them to cultivate these fields, by offering *takāvi* loans. The ryots who are assisted in this fashion by the government extend the area of cultivable land, and thereby increase the income of the kingdom."

The offer of the *takāvi* loans is not supported by the evidence of the inscriptions, but there is ample evidence which proves the adoption of this method of increasing the state's revenue by the Vijayanagara emperors. The *Āmuktamālyada* lays it down as a duty of the king to destroy the forests in the interior of the kingdom. * The destruction of the forests extends the area of the cultivable land which he should provide with irrigation facilities, and offer, on very favourable conditions, to the poor ryots for cultivation. † The king, as a consequence of adopting this policy, not only enhances the income of the state, but acquires the credit for helping his poor subjects.‡ The Local Records preserve several instances of the destruction of the forest areas which were offered to the ryots for cultivation on very favourable conditions. Several inscriptions record

* *Ām* 4 : 256.

† cf. Nuniz. "This king (Kṛṣṇarāya) made in his time a lake for water which lies between two very lofty *serras* * * *. By means of this water they made many improvements in the city, and many channels by which they irrigated the rice-fields and gardens, and in order that they might improve their lands, *he gave the people the lands which are irrigated by this water free for nine years*, until they made their improvements, so that the revenue already amounts to 20,000 *pardaos*" *FE*. pp. 364-65.

‡ *Ām*. 4 : 232.

kauls granting the reclaimed areas to the ryots for cultivation by the government.* The most interesting document of this kind is the one which describes the arrangements made by one Doḍlonṭi Ranganātha for the cultivation of waste lands in the villages of Talamancipaṭṭaṇam, Mādhavāpuram, Vuppalapāḍu, Gollapalli, Voddirāla, Dannavāḍa Kambāladinne, Dugganapalle, Pedda-Kommerla, Bondulapalle, Ganganapalle, Mylāpuram, and Vyāparāla. According to these records the ryots cultivating the waste lands in these villages had to pay to the government during the first eight years a rent only of 2 *rūkas* per field, and ¼ *rūka* of *kāvali*.† At the end of this period, the ryots had probably to pay on these fields the same rent as on the neighbouring lands.

(*b*) "Owing to the ruined condition of tanks and other irrigation works, fields, which used to be cultivated at one time, might become fallow. If the government repair these tanks and irrigation works, the fallow fields can be brought once again under cultivation. Naturally the income of the government is bound to increase." ‡

Inscriptions frequently refer to the restoration of ruined and deserted villages. The village of Maleyabeṇṇūr which was in ruins was restored in 1528 A.D. by Ādiyappa Nāyaka who granted a *śāsana* to the ryots for improving its cultivation. § Hanakanahallu which was rapidly falling into ruins was similarly revived in 1531 A.D.¶ Cikka Nañjaya Arasu, the *pārupatyagāra* of Terakaṇāmbi *sīme* gave a charter in 1542 A.D. to certain people to rebuild a ruined *pura*:

"Whereas *pura* to the south of the hamlet of our village, having for a time been uncultivated, and uninhabited has gone to ruins, overgrown with..., the charter is written and given (so)

* cf. *MER.* 433 of 1920; 416 of 1920.

† *LR.* 36 (Talamancipaṭṭaṇam) p. 26.

‡ *MMss.* 15-6-8. § *EC.* xi. Dg. 105. ¶ *MER.* 333 of 1925.

that you may cut down the trees, fill up the ditches, renew the boundaries of the fields, rebuild *pura*, stock it with ryots, give out land, and collect the dues according to the former custom." *

One Dharmagōḍa Gauḍa built a fort at the village of Tūmukunṭe which was in ruins, excavated channels, and restored the village. †

(*c*) "The people of the districts having no orderly government are generally in an unsettled condition; they must be induced to migrate to any desired place through the influence of their relations residing therein. If the immigrants are given lands on favourable conditions, and offered *takāvi* loans to enable them to carry on agricultural operations much land will be brought under cultivation. In course of time, they strike root in the soil, and pay taxes like the ryots of the neighbouring villages. The income of the government is thereby considerably increased." ‡

Karaṇīka Mangarasa 'exempted the tenants colonising the Arasarakōyil from all taxes for one year, and fixed the rates of certain taxes leviable from the following year.' § During the reign of Acyutarāya, Paṇḍari Nāgappa, one of his agents, summoned before him the farmers of the *Neravāṭi* community who emigrated from Kurnool owing to bad times, and granted them in 1540 A.D. a *kaul* to build a village called Gunḍḷapāḍu, and settle down there. ¶ About the same time, some *Reḍḍi* families from the sea-side country migrated to Gaṇḍikōṭa *sīma* where they settled down permanently. ‖ These instances show that the author of the *Aṭṭhavaṇa Tantram* has stated what was traditionally the policy of the Hindu governments.

(*d*) "Those that have the supreme control of the affairs, having closely studied the condition of the market, should encourage the production of the commodities that sell dearly in such

* *EC.* iv Gu. 39. † *EC.* xii Pg. 39.

‡ *MMss.* 15-6-8. § *MER.* 307 of 1921.

¶ *LR.* 36 (Akkapalle) p. 163. ‖ *MER.* A 10 of 1912-13.

places that are suited for their cultivation, and market them in areas where they fetch the highest price, so that the profit may benefit the public treasury." *

No epigraphical evidence, which corroborates this statement, is available at present. It is not possible to ascertain how far it is true.

(ii) Commercial :

(a) "The government must invite the foreign merchants and *sowkārs* to establish trade relations with the kingdom, and grant them charters on favourable conditions. *Pēṭas* where they can remain in perfect security must also be built, so that they may import valuable articles of merchandise from abroad, and export such of the indigenous products that may be in demand in outside markets. The government can obtain much income from these merchants and the new shops that may be opened." †

This is fully supported by the evidence of the Portuguese chronicles, contemporary literature, and inscriptions.

Speaking of Kṛṣṇadēvarāya, Paes says :

"There live in this (Nāgalāpūr) many merchants, and it is filled with large population, because the king induces many honourable merchants to go there from his cities." ‡

The courteous manner in which he treated the Portuguese is referred to both by Paes and Nuniz.§ Kṛṣṇarāya briefly describes his commercial policy in the *Āmuktamālyada* :—

"The merchants who import elephants and horses from the countries across the seas should be treated kindly by the grant of villages and comfortable houses in the capital ; besides, they must have frequent audience with the king who should not only confer upon them honours and privileges but enable them to secure high profits (in their commercial transactions with the state), so that they might not go to the enemy." ¶

The Rāya and his officers used to build several *pēṭas* for the convenience of the merchants. A *pēṭa* was built at Kavuluṭla in 1523 A. D. || The weavers that

* *MMss.* 15-6-8. † *ibid.* ‡ *FE.* p. 244. § cf. *FE.* pp. 251, 343.
¶ *Ām.* 4 : 258 ; 4 : 245. || *LR.* 41 (Kōṭakoṇḍa) pp. 22-3.

settled in the place had to pay ½ *ga* as loom-tax to the government. It is stated that half of the income should go to defray the expenses of the *kāvalgārs* of the place. Another *pēṭa* was founded in 1524 A.D. in the village of Vērupaṭige,* and special concessions were granted to the 'officers and residents of the market place.' In 1554 A.D. a *pēṭa* was rebuilt in the Bāgūr *sīme* by an agent of Kṛṣṇappa Nāyaka, one of the *amaranāyakas* of Sadāśiva.† Those that settled in the *pēṭa* were exempted from all taxes for one year. Instances of the kind can easily be multiplied; but those that are cited are sufficient to illustrate the point.

(*b*) "Lastly, the government may open trade operations on their own account during times of scarcity. As they maintain large trains of pack-bullocks, they can transport corn and other commodities without expense to the regions affected by famine from places where the harvests are abundant. If, at the same time, the government prohibit the sale of articles in towns (and villages) by private merchants, until the government completely dispose of their wares, their profit is bound to be unlimited." ‡

Although such a step might easily have been taken by the government of the Rāyas, inscriptions and other contemporary records do not reveal any trace of trade by the government or any of their officers. §

* *MER.* 450 of 1920. † *EC.* xi. Hk. 112. ‡ *MMss.* 15-6-8.

§ There is evidence to show that the Bāhmani Sultāns maintained large numbers of pack-bullocks. It is said that Mahmūd Shāh (Bahmni) I, during a period of famine "employed 10,000 bullocks at his private expense, constantly going to and from Mālwa and Gujerāt for grain which was distributed to the people at a cheap rate." (*Ferishta* ii. p. 349) Syed Ali gives a slightly different account. "A thousand bullocks belonging to the transport establishment maintained for the court were placed at the disposal of those in charge of relief measures, and travelled incessantly to and fro between his dominions, and Gujerāt and Mālwa which have escaped the visitation, bringing thence grain which was sold at low rates in the Deccan, but to Muslims only." (*IA.* xlix.) Now, the most important point to be noted is that during a period of famine the government sold grain to its subjects. A less pious king than this Mahmūd would not have been deterred by any scruples to gain profit at the expense of his subjects. What was obtaining at Gulburga might not have been unfamiliar at Vijayanagara.

CHAPTER VIII

THE POLICE ARRANGEMENTS

Section 1: The Talāri:—When one thinks of the police, one usually pictures to oneself, a large body of officers organized into a department to exercise authority over the whole territory belonging to a state. The first thing, however, that one has to keep in mind when dealing with the empire of Vijayanagara is that there existed no state department of police. But it must not be supposed that the state had neglected its duties of preserving law and order, and of protecting the life and property of its subjects. The emperors of Vijayanagara, no doubt, made arrangements for policing their empire; but these were different from what one is acquainted with in a modern state. The police arrangements obtaining in all parts of the empire were not welded together so as to form parts of a well organized system; each district made its own arrangements which were more or less effective.

Here, as in many other cases, the study of the subject must begin with the village which was the unit of administration. One of the *āyagārs*, the *talāri* or *talaiyāri* discharged duties which were purely police in nature. He was regarded as the guardian of the village peace. It was probably for this reason that he was sometimes described as the village *kotwāl.* *

The origin of the office of the *talāri* cannot be traced easily. During the time of Manu, the *talāri* does not seem to have been in existence. The detection of crimes was one of the important duties of the village

* cf. *MMss.* 15-6-8. *Aṭṭhavaṇa Tantram.*

headman ; but later, the work of village administration became differentiated from mere police duties which were entrusted to a new officer called *yāmika*. The *yāmika* appears to be the earliest prototype of the *talāri*.* The *talavara* or *talayāri* had already come to prominence as early as the third century A.D. † He came to be regarded as one of *āyagārs* from the time of the Kākatīyas. At this time, he was one of the most important of the village servants whose duty it was to prevent quarrels among the villagers, and settle disputes when they arose by summoning the disputants before him. ‡ He seems to have lost his magisterial functions later, for he became a mere police official during the regime of the Vijayanagara emperors.

As a police officer, the *talāri* had to protect the life and property of the villagers who might be attacked by thieves and brigands. One of his duties was to watch the movements of the vagabonds, wandering bands of players, dancers etc. § He was held responsible for any property that might be stolen from the villagers ; and if he were not able to catch the thieves and restore the stolen property, he had to make good the loss sustained by the villagers from his own pockets.¶ In addition to his police duties, the *talāri* had to provide the government with labourers for repairing tanks and canals, specially for carrying the baggage of their civil and military servants. On all such occasions, he would seize whom he could lay hands on, as a

* M.S. Sarma : *Grāmarakṣaṇa* p. 15.

† *MER.* 200, 208 of 1927.

‡ M. S. Sarma : *Ugādi Sañcika of Dundubhi* (1922) p. 157 ff.

§ cf. *MMss.* 15-9-6 *Aṭṭhavaṇa Tantram.*

¶ "యిందుకు పొలిమేరలోఁగా యేమివస్తువులు పోయినా అచ్చుగలవారము."
MER. 9 of 1912-13 ; cf. Nuniz (*FE.* pp. 380-51).

consequence of which he was greatly dreaded by the villagers. *

The *talāri*, like the other *āyagārs* received no salary; but his work was not honorary. Like the other servants of the village, he received remuneration from two sources. A portion of the village land was permanently assigned to him on which he had to pay to the state a low tax called *jōḍi*. This permanent piece of land was called his *mirāsi*. In addition to this, he received from each ryot a few measures of paddy or other produce per *puṭṭi*. This was called his *mēra*. Moreover, he received sundry perquisites from villagers who were anxious to escape forced labour.

"The ryots," declares the *Aṭṭhavaṇa Tantram*, "offer the *talāri* food, curry, and ears of corn; the *kurubas* give him blankets and other things, bacause as a village *kotwāl*, he might single them out for forced labour, when the government stand in need of men to carry the baggage of their servants." †

A part of his emoluments consisted of the contributions of money made by the villagers which are frequently alluded to in the inscriptions as *talavārike* or *talavārike-haṇa*. ‡ The *talavārike* appears to have been a composite tax made up of a number of small dues coming from different sources. The *talāri* obtained some dues probably in the form of grain for guarding *dēvādāya* and *brahmādāya mānyas*. § He also collected dues from the houses of merchants ¶, barbers ‖, and weavers. ** At the time of marriages, he was entitled to fees, probably for protecting the guests and their property. ††

* *MMss.* 15-6-8. *Aṭṭhavaṇa Tantram*. † *ibid.*

‡ *EC.* v. Hn. 2; *EC.* vi. Kd. 158; *MER.* 164 of 1913.

§ *LR.* 24 p. 124; *LR.* 13 p. 288.

¶ *LR.* 18 pp. 407-409. ‖ *E.C* xi. Hk. 110.

** *LR.* 18 pp. 407-409. †† *EC.* xii. Ck. 5.

Section 2 : *Kāvalgārs* :—Sometimes it is asserted that the *talāri* was under the control of the *kāvalgārs* whose jurisdiction extended over the villages included in a *sthala*. And over the *kāvalgārs*, there were officers called *dēśa-kāvalgārs* or the superintendents of police. * It is very much to be doubted whether there was such a well co-ordinated system of police officers as the one described above. At any rate, the available evidence on the topic does not justify the inference.

Inscriptions, literature, and local records supply, no doubt, some information, which, however, is not sufficient for drawing a full and accurate picture. The villages seem to have been grouped into districts each of which was placed under a police officer called *kāvalgār*. The following inscriptions may be taken into consideration in this connection:

(1) In an inscription dated probably 1516 A.D., Kṛṣṇadēvarāya is said to have granted to Kūnapuli Peddi Nāyaḍu the right of policing the Mallela *samutu*. The *talāris* of all the villages in the *samutu* were his subordinates, and they were responsible to him. †

(2) Another inscription of Alattūr in the South Arcot records the grant "of the right of *kāval* of Alattūr and other villages by a certain Uyyālanallaṉ-Timmayyaṉ to the temple of Vēṭṭairāyaṉ." Allatūr was evidently the chief village of the group, and Timmayyaṉ must have been its *kāvalgār*. ‡

(3) Sadāśivarāya granted to one Kadirappanēni Lakki Nāyaḍu the right of policing the fourteen villages included in Ūṭukūr *(sthala)*. §

(4) A similar grant was made by the same monarch to Mahīpati Yaṟṟama Nāyaḍu, conferring the right of policing the

* M. S. Śarma : *Grāmarakṣaṇa* p. 15.

† *MER*. 9 of 1912-13.

‡ *MER*. 49 of 1919.

§ *LR*. 14 (Kāmpalle) pp. 404-405.

samuts of Yāḍaki, Tāḍpatri, Vellaṭūr, Singanamala, Siyyēḍuceruvu, Pāmiḍi, Konakoṇḍla, and Tarupūr with the territory of Gaṇḍikōṭa.*

(5) Aḷiya Rāmarāja made a grant of the *kāvaḷi* right of 14 villages included in the Vippapenṭa *sīma*, and 84 villages belonging to Siddhavaṭṭam to Namilinēni Peda Bucci Nāyaḍu of Guriginjakoṇḍa. †

Although these grants come almost exclusively from a single area, there is reason to believe that they indicate a system which was common to the whole empire. For maintaining peace and order, and keeping watch and ward, hereditary officers called *kāvalgārs* were appointed over districts consisting of several villages, the *talāris* of which were directly responsible to them. The districts, however, were not uniform in size; some contained only a few villages, whereas others consisted of nearly a dozen *samutus*. It is just possible that Mahīpati Yaṟṟama, who held the *kāval* right of several *samutus*, belonged to a higher cadre of police officials; he was, perhaps, a *nāḍu-kāvalgār*, an office whose existence is indicated by stray inscriptions here and there. ‡ Probably these higher police officials bore the distinctive title of *Mahānāyakācārya*. §

The *kāvalgār* like the *talāri* received no salary from the government. He was, however, given a *mānya* in every village within his jurisdiction. It is said that Kūnapuli Peddi Nāyaḍu was the owner of a *mānya* in one of the villages within his jurisdiction.¶ It is not unreasonable to infer that he was given similar *mānyas* in all the other villages. In the two grants which

* *MMss.* 15-3-43 p. 23.

† *LR.* 18 (Cintarājupalle) pp. 407-409.

‡ *MER.* A. 10. of 1922-23 ; *EC.* vi. Kd. 58.

§ *LR.* 14 (Kāmpalle) p. 404; *MER.* 297 of 1926.

¶ *MER.* 9 of 1912-13 ; *MMss.* 15-3-43 p. 23.

Sadāśiva made to Lakki Nāyaḍu and Yaṟṟama, it is explicitly stated that the *kāvali-mirāsi* consisted of a *mānya* in each of the villages under their respective jurisdictions.* The existence of similar *kāvali mirāsi mānyas* is also indicated by the *kaul* of Aḷiya Rāmarāja to Bucci Nāyaḍu. † In addition to the *mirāsi mānya*, the *kāvalgārs* were entitled to collect some other dues from the ryots. Sadāśiva's grant to Mahīpati Yaṟṟama refers to *kāvalgār's mēra* and *vartana* in addition to his *mānya*. The *mēra* is said to be one sheaf of paddy in every *tūm*, and *sunka-sūtras*. Further, they collected 2 *rūkas* for every loom and merchant's house. ‡ The *kāval-kaṭnam* or *rusum*, § of which one hears so much in the inscriptions, refers, probably, to these dues.

The *kāvalgār* had to supervise the work of the *talāris* in his district. His main duty was to see that no thefts or other crimes were committed within his jurisdiction. He had to make good any loss sustained by the people within his district from his own pocket. It is not possible to state definitely to whom the *kāvalgār* was responsible. It is said in the *Rāyavācaka* that the *daṇāikas*, when commanded to report on the internal condition of *rājyas* or the provinces, declared,

> "By the prowess of Your Majesty, in all the forts, mountain-fastnesses, and forest-strongholds *the police arrangements*, and fortifications are in perfect order." ¶

Nuniz also states that

> "If he (a person who suffers wrong) complains that he was robbed in such and such a province, and in such and such a road, the king sends immediately for the captain of the province, even though he be at court, and the captain may be seized and his property taken, if he does not catch the thief." ‖

* *LR.* 14 p. 404.

† *LR.* 18 pp. 407-409.

‡ *MMss.* 15-3-4 p. 23.

§ *MER.* 164 of 1913.

¶ *ASPP.* iii. p. 13.

‖ *FE.* p. 380.

From this it appears that the *daṇāiks* who were in charge of provinces were responsible to the Rāya for maintaining police arrangements within their respective jurisdictions. It follows, therefore, that the *kāvalgārs* who were in charge of *sthalas* or *samuts* and *nāḍus* were responsible to the *durga-daṇāika* or the provincial governor.

Section 3: *The Pāḷegārs*:—A slightly different arrangement was adopted for policing the areas in the outskirts of jungles and in the villages built within forest clearings. To ensure the safety of such places, *pāḷegārs* or adventurers of great daring and courage, were stationed at suitable centres, with a considerable body of retainers. They were given for their maintenance a *jāgīr* of one or two villages where they were given permission to erect a fort. The *Āmuktamālyada* lays down certain principles regarding the maintenance of order in forest areas which were rendered insecure by the frequent plundering raids of criminal tribes residing in inaccessible mountainous regions.

"To keep these *kirātās* in check, foreign military adventurers should be given villages temporarily as *jāgirs* in their neighbourhood. Until these criminal tribes are subdued, the distress of the people does not decrease." *

The Local Records describe several instances, where Kṛṣṇadēva and Acyuta are said to have followed the policy chalked out in the *Āmuktamālyada*:

(i) During the reign of Kṛṣṇadēvarāya, an adventurer called Yākarla Yarrama Nāyaḍu bearing the *biruda* of Basava Śankara, migrated from Bandar in the north, and settled down in the village of Rōḷḷamaḍugu. He made so much trouble to the Brahmans of the place by committing theft that they were obliged to abandon the *agrahāra*, and retire to the village of Rāyavara.

* *Am.* 4: 221, 222.

After sometime Yaṟṟama went to Vijayanagara, where he remained for a few months attending the imperial durbar regularly. On one occasion, while making a pilgrimage to the shrine of Tirupati, Kṛṣṇarāya broke his journey in the neighbourhood of Rōḷḷamaḍugu where he halted a few days. The Rāya learnt that the place was infested with thieves and robbers. He summoned Yaṟṟama before him and appointed him as the *kāvalgār* of the locality, commanding him to protect the people in the neighbourhood as well as the pilgrims travelling along the road from the fear of thieves and bandits. Yaṟṟama built a small fort on the banks of Ceyyēru to the north of Rōḷḷamaḍugu. A village sprang round the fortress which was granted to him as *jāgīr*." *

(ii) "On one occasion, when Kṛṣṇarāya, who was on a visit to the village of Munimaḍugu, was desirous of going to Gutti, the elders of the place represented to him that travelling on the road between Gutti and Munimaḍugu was not safe, as it was infested with bandits and wild animals. They requested him to spend a few days at the shrine of Narasimha which was built on a hill near the road, and clear the road of wild animals and robbers. The Rāya visited the shrine accordingly, and after spending a few days in worshipping the deity, appointed one of his officers called Kaulūri Buḍḍā Reḍḍi as the watchman of the road. He commanded Buḍḍā to station himself at the place, and make the road safe for travellers. Two villages, Kundenakōṭa and Kōnavuppalapāḍu, were granted to him as *jāgīr*; moreover, Buḍḍā was given permission to cut down the forests on the slopes of Yaṟṟamalais, and build a village there for himself. He obeyed the royal order and remained at Rācerla, the village which he had built for himself, according to the permission granted to him by the emperor." †

Later in the reign, this region again became the scene of activities of a bandit chief, Tupākula Cennama Nāyaḍu, a *māla* by caste. Probably Cennama was the original of the *māla* robber chief, Kākaśmaśru, whom the emperor describes graphically in his *Āmuktamālyada*.

(iii) Cennama, having gathered around himself a band of robbers, fixed his head-quarters in the Rācerla hills, and began to

* *LR.* 44 (Rōḷḷamaḍugu) p. 148. † *LR.* 6 (Rācerla) p. 236.

plunder the villages all round. His victims complained loudly to the emperor who commanded Vengaḷ Reḍḍi, one of the three sons of Kaulūri Buḍḍā Reḍḍi, to put an end to the career of the "*māla Nēyaḍu*." Vengaḷ Reḍḍi and his brothers proceeded against him with great caution. Having learnt that Cennama and his gang lay encamped in a palmyra grove in the midst of the forest, they marched to the place stealthily and fell upon the robbers suddenly. They were in no fit condition to resist their assailants, as they were already highly intoxicated with drink. Nevertheless, they fought so valiantly that Vengaḷ Reḍḍi lost both his brothers in the battle; but he prevailed ultimately against the robbers whose leader he slew. A temple was built in honour of the fallen *Reḍḍis*, where they are still worshipped as the emancipators of the country. *

(iv) "While Acyutadēvarāya was reigning at Vijayanagara, considerable trouble was caused to the travellers by robbers who lay concealed in the hills in the neighbourhood of the Jyōti Pass in the Nallamalais along the highway leading to the shrine of Ahōbaḷam. On account of excessive dread engendered by the highway men, merchants and pilgrims from Pōrumāmiḷḷa, Baddevōlu, Kambham &c., gave up visiting Ahōbaḷam even during the time when the annual *brahmōtsava* was celebrated. When this was brought to the notice of the Rāya, he appointed, on the advice of Salakarāju Timmarāju, an adventurer called Virnēyani Siddappa, who was attending the durbar for two years, as the guardian of the Jyōti Pass. The village of Dāsaripalle was granted to him as his *jāgīr*. Siddappa went to the place with all his retinue, and having settled down in his *jāgir*, he captured several robbers whom he sent to the Rāya." †

The conditions did not very much improve during the reign of Sadāśiva, as shown by an epigraph of Gōṭūr, recording the grant of a *netturu-paṭṭu* by the Brahmans of Puṣpagiri to one Perugu Basivi Nāyaḍu who lost his life while fighting against the robbers that plundered the village. ‡

* *LR.* 6 (Rācerla) p. 236 ff.

† *LR.* 5 pp. 79-80.

‡ *LR.* 18 (Gōṭūr) p. 513.

These extracts not only serve as a very good commentary on the verses from the *Āmuktamālyada*, but they give us a clear insight into the working of the police system in the forest and mountainous areas of the empire.

The protection which the state offered to its subjects and merchants was not adequate. Journeys along the public roads were risky and insecure. The forest regions were specially the haunts of bandits who not only plundered the travellers but neighbouring villagers also, causing thereby considerable alarm in the country side. Assassination by the robbers was so common that people generally expected to die as much in that way as in any other.* Yākarla Yaṟṟama, whom Kṛṣṇarāya appointed as the *kāvalgār* of Rōḷḷamaḍugu and its neighbourhood, started his career as a robber, although he carefully avoided direct participation in any one of his ventures.

The professional robbers had not infrequently to compete with the amateurs. The petty chiefs who rose up in rebellion against the emperor took to robbery and plunder partly to embarass the government, and partly to enrich themselves at the expense of defenceless villagers and harmless travellers. A few examples are sufficient to illustrate the statement:

(i) "When Sāḷuva Narasimha was governing the empire, Vīra Narasimha, a cousin of the Sambeṭa chief of Pernipāḍu, rose up in rebellion, and, making Maddiguṇḍāla in the Lankamalai Hills his head-quarters, began to plunder the country, and rob the pilgrims going to Rāmēśvara on the Bhāramārga of their belongings. Sāḷuva Narasimha sent against him Vankara Kumāra Basivi Nāyaḍu, who defeated and expelled him from the country." †

* *Ām* : 6 : 30.

† *LR.* 9 (Pathūrip[illegible]). 248-253.

(ii) During the reign of Kṛṣṇarāya, Musili Nāyaḍu rose up in rebellion and plundered the country. He was, however, defeated and driven into the hills; but later, he threw himself at the feet of the Rāya, who pardoned him and received him into favour once again. *

(iii) While Acyutadēvarāya was ruling at Vijayanagara, Cābrōlu Timmarāju, the chief of Puṭṭakōṭa on the Guṇḍlakamma, with the help of his brother Koṇḍarāju, and his friend Nāgarāju-Annarāju disturbed the peace of the eastern districts of the empire by committing dacoities on a large scale. He caused confusion in Ēruva; lifted the cattle of Palnāḍ and Gurujāla; smote thoroughly (?) Vinukoṇḍa *sīma*; plundered the Tangeḍa *rājya*; frightened Podile and Ammanavrōlu; burgled the houses (of the people) at Uddagiri; destroyed the Sagila Pāya by looting; held the people to ransom in Siruveḷḷa and Nandēla; prevented (the people of) Siddhāpura from sleeping by his constant attacks and dacoities; created much trouble at Toṇḍamārayaguḷḷa; and obstructed the travellers passing through the Nandikanama. Acyuta commanded Gani Timma, one of his subordinates, to destory the dacoit and his gang. Gani Timma marched upon him and killed him with all his followers in a fierce battle at Puṭṭakōṭa. †

The *kaul* of Aḷiya Rāmarāja refers to the rebellion of a petty chief called Tarigoṇḍa Rāmā Nāyaḍu ‡ which must be classed with the rebellions mentioned above. Such petty rebellions seem to have been frequent during the reign of Acyuta. There was considerable insecurity in the country during his time. It was owing to this insecurity that the merchants had to enter into separate agreements with the *pāḷegārs* or road *kāvalgārs*. A copper-plate grant in the possession of the descendants of Peda Cennama Nāyaḍu, the *pāḷegār* of Rōḷḷamaḍugu, registers an agreement between the merchants of "the fifty six countries," and the *pāḷegār* himself. It is said that the *pāḷegār* had recovered from the robbers some property of the merchants which was lost in the Rōḷḷamaḍugu pass. While

* *LR.* 9 (Pathūripāḷem) pp. 248-253. † *MM.* 14-4-3 p. 143. ‡ *LR.* 18 p. 407.

fighting with the robbers, some of the servants of the *pāḷegār* were killed. On this occasion the merchants, who assembled in the *mukhamanṭapa* of the temple of Śiva, agreed to pay to the *pāḷegār* tolls on specified articles for safely seeing them through the pass. And the *pāḷegār* agreed to pay the merchants half the value of the property lost within his district, if it were not recovered. This sum, however, should not be demanded in a lump; it should be realised gradually in instalments.* The insecurity of travel upon the roads might have been the reason for the joint grant of Gutti Timmarāju (the governor of the province) and the *agrahārikas*, *reḍḍis*, and *karṇams* of the Ūṭukūr fourteen villages to Lakki Nāyaḍu for guarding the *kanama* or pass. †

The *kāvalgārs* of roads, therefore, obtained much income from merchants and travellers. It is only natural that the government should levy some tax upon them. Probably the income from the road *kāval* was sold in auction to the highest bidder. Something of the kind is dimly indicated by the *kaul* of Aḷiya Rāmarāja

Section 4: Policing of Towns and Cities:—Much information is not available regarding the police system obtaining in the cities and towns. Each town had its own *taḷavaras*. The *kāvalgārs* or *taḷavaras* of *pēṭas* of whom one hears so much in the inscriptions belong to this class. ‡ The preservation of the peace in each town and city was entrusted to a band of *taḷavaras* headed by a prefect. § The movements of the people were strictly limited at night, when, after sounding the drum, it was illegal for any person to walk in the

* *LR.* 48 p. 341 ff.

† *LR.* 14 (Kāmpalle) pp. 404-405.

‡ *LR.* 41 (Kōṭakoṇḍa) p. 22.

§ *ŚS.* 2: 485, 494.

streets. * The *talavara* patrolled the streets holding torches in the hands, † and challenged suspicious characters whom they might find lurking in the thoroughfares and by-lanes. ‡ They apprehended thieves, and kept them in the stocks until the morning, when they were probably produced before the magistrate. § Another class of people whom the *talāris* kept under strict surveillance were lovers, who, under the cover of night, would resort to rendezvouses with the object of gratifying their lust. ¶ In order to avoid scandal and shame, people of this class always kept the *talāris* in good humour by a judicious distribution of bribes and favours. ‖ The *talāris*, therefore, seem to have taken much pains in safeguarding not only the property of the people, but their domestic peace also.

Regarding the police arrangements of the capital, there exists a good deal of information. The earliest account comes from the pen of Abdur Razāk. According to him, the police administration of the capital was under the control of a commissioner who was served by no less than 12,000 policemen, each of whom received a salary of 30 *paṇams* per month. The policemen had to patrol the city, and to acquaint themselves with all the events and accidents that took place within the seven walls, and to recover property that was lost or stolen. Failure on their part to trace the thieves or to recover the stolen property brought upon them the displeasure of their superiors which usually took the form

* *SS.* 4 : 111. † *SS.* 2 : 494.

‡ *Npm.* 2 : 93.
అనుచు జనయిత్రి నీతివాక్యప్రసన్న
హృదయు జేసితి సుతు నంచు నరిగె నతఁడు
ప్రొద్దుపోయిన దని తలారులకు వెఱచి
యొకవిధంబున నారాత్రి యుండఁ దలఁచె ॥

§ *SS.* 3 : pp. 222-23. ¶ *SS.* 2 : 482-94. *LR.* 12 (Krāsūr) pp. 268-69.

‖ *SS.* 4 : 111.

of a fine. They had to make good the value of the stolen property from their pockets. The police organization of the city was maintained by the state mainly from the dues collected from the dancing girls.*

This was in the time of Dēvarāya II who ruled half a century before the Tuḷuva usurpation. This system remained, however, almost unchanged in all essential features until the reign of Kṛṣṇadēvarāya, as shown by the *Rāyavācaka*. The city seems to have been divided, probably for the purposes of patrolling, into *pāḷems* or wards. There is reason to believe that the division of the city into *pāḷems* was made by Kṛṣṇadēvarāya himself.† Each ward, of course, consisted of several streets. A *talāri* with a staff of assistants was placed in charge of each ward. The watchmen had to patrol the streets day and night. There was a head *talāri* or commissioner called Jangamayya having jurisdiction over the whole city. The *talāris* in charge of the *pāḷems* had to report to the commissioner 'every minute' (క్షణ క్షణ) the happenings in their respective wards.‡

Very early in his reign, Kṛṣṇarāya issued an edict threatening to punish severely any one who exhibited riotous and disorderly conduct in the thoroughfares of the city. Therefore, people walked in the streets freely, without fearing molestation from any one, however high he might be. In order to see that his regulations were properly obeyed and respected, and

* *ED.* iv. p. 112.

† A *kaḍitam* dated Ś. 1526 or 1604 A.D., belonging to the *Aṭṭkavaṇam* of Venkaṭa II, is preserved in the Government Oriental Mss. Library, Madras. It describes the 77 *pāḷems* or wards into which Venkaṭa II divided the city of Candragiri. He is said to have taken the division of Vijayanagara effected by his ancestor Kṛṣṇadēvarāya as his model. If this statement be true, it must be considered that Kṛṣṇadēva effected a reform for the administration of his capital.

‡ *ASPP.* iii p. 27.

that the police were discharging their duties without negligence, he would wander through the streets in disguise mixing with the people, a habit which gave Commissioner Jangamayya not a little trouble. He had to lurk about the precincts of the royal palace after the dusk, watching the Rāya emerge from one of the gates in an unfamiliar disguise. He would stealthily follow the emperor to acquaint himself with all the untoward events which the emperor might witness, so that he might not be taken to task next day in the open durbar for neglecting his duties. * It is reasonable to infer that during the time of Kṛṣṇadēvarāya, the efficiency of the police force of the capital was greatly increased.

The system does not appear to have suffered alteration during Acyuta's reign. Penugoṇḍa Vīraṇṇa, who is often mentioned in the inscriptions at Lēpākṣi, was the *talavara* or the police commissioner of Vijayanagara. † If any person complained to the Rāya that he was robbed on such and such a road of the city, the king would send immediately for the chief bailiff who was obliged to give an account of the robberies in the capital; he might be seized and his property be taken, if he could not catch the thief. ‡ Acyuta, of course, did not go at night in disguise into the streets of the city to supervise the work of the police. Nevertheless, the police of the city discharged their duties so efficiently that only a few thefts were committed. Even if some were committed, the culprits could easily be caught by the help of the detectives whom Nuniz calls 'wizards.' §

* *ASPP.* iii. p. 27.

† *MER.* 785 of 1917.

‡ *FE.* pp. 380-81.

§ *ibid.*

Chapter IX

THE ADMINISTRATION OF JUSTICE.

Section 1: The Parāśara Mādhavīya and the Administration of Justice:—Some idea of the judicial system of Vijayanagara can be formed by a study of the *Vyavahārakāṇḍa* of the *Parāśara Mādhavīya*, a legal treatise by Vidyāraṇya, who is believed to have written it to provide the new empire with a fresh code of law. * It may be supplemented with the scanty material furnished by the inscriptions and the Local Records.

The emperor, as the head of the state, was the fountain head of justice; and he was expected, like all the Eastern monarchs, to settle the disputes of his subjects personally. However, as he could not personally attend to the judicial work of his extensive empire, he had to make arrangements for the efficient administration of justice by constituting a series of courts in all the provinces. A court of law was then

* "The minister and spiritual preceptor Vidyāraṇya, under whose auspices the new dynasty was erected, composed a work on law and government. It was intended as a manual for the officers of state; is founded on the text of Parāśara with a copious commentary by Vidyāraṇya..." Wilk's *History of Mysore*: p. 169.

Vidyāraṇya was not merely the spiritual guide of Bukka I, one of the founders of Vijayanagara. He was his prime minister. "Like Angirasa to Indra, Sumati to Nala, Medhātithi to Śaibya, Dhanuja to Rāma, Mādhava was *kulaguru* as well as *mantri* to king Bukka." Therefore, it is reasonable to believe that Mādhava-Vidyāraṇya wrote the *Parāśara Mādhavīya*, to provide the law courts of the kingdom with an authoritative code of law. This fact is brought out clearly by his treatment of the *Vyavahārakāṇḍa*. *Parāśarasmṛti*, on which *Parāśara Mādhavīya* is a commentary, does not contain a *Vyavahārakāṇḍa*, as Parāśara, according to tradition, died before finishing his work. Nevertheless, Vidyāraṇya supplied the omission by appending a chapter on *vyavahāra* or administration of justice, basing it on what other law-givers had said on the subject. It may, therefore, be assumed that the judicial institutions described in the *vyavahārakāṇḍa* were in use in the Vijayanagara empire, when Vidyāraṇya wrote his commentary.

known as a *sabhā* or assembly. The *sabhās* or courts were primarily divided into two classes, *mukhya* and *amukhya*. The *mukhya* class of courts shall be described first for the sake of convenience. A court which transacted business regularly was termed *mukhya*. It was further sub-divided into *pratiṣṭhita* and *apratiṣṭhita*; the former was stationary, and it was located in a particular place; whereas the latter was held in any place where the judge happened to find himself for the time being. Each of these two classes was again sub-divided into *śāstrita* and *mudrita*. A *pratiṣṭhita* or *apratiṣṭhita* court was *śāstrita* when it was presided over by the emperor himself. If, however, it was presided over by a judge appointed under the emperor's seal, it was known as *mudrita*.

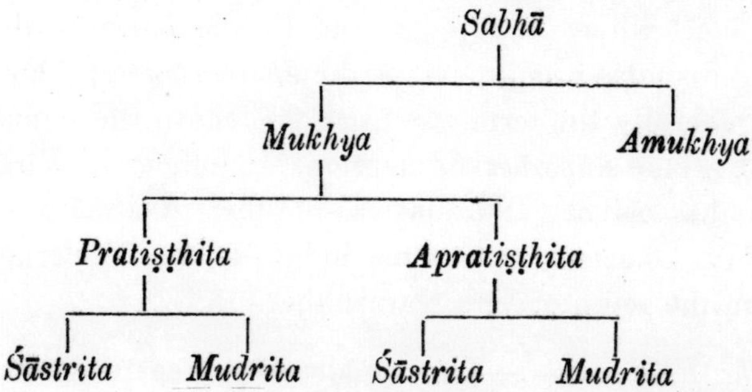

Section 2: The Imperial Court at the Capital:—The most important of these courts was, of course, the one at the capital. It had jurisdiction over civil as well as criminal cases. It consisted of the judge *(emperor)*, *prāḍvivāka* (his assistant), and two or more *sabhyas* (the assessors). These constituted the bench. In addition to these, there was a *lēkhaka* or the bench clerk who had to take down the oral statements made in the court by the parties, witnesses, &c. There was also a *gaṇaka* or accountant whose duty it was to calculate the sums of money involved in the suits pending before

the court. Lastly, there was the court bailiff *(sādhya-pāla)* who should produce before the court the parties, witnesses &c., concerned in the cases. He had also to preserve order in the court and execute its decrees.*

The Judge :—When the emperor presided over the court, he alone could decide cases, and pronounce judgments thereon. The *prāḍvivāka* and the *sabhyas* had to assist him. The judgment was to be issued over his signature and seal. The emperor, however, was not obliged to preside over the court always. If the business of the state demanded his personal attention in other branches of administration, he could appoint a *pratinidhi* or representative to take his place. The *pratinidhi* could discharge the judicial duties of the emperor as if he were the emperor himself. The place where the judge sat in the court while settling disputes was known as the *dharmāsana* ; † but more generally the term was used to denote the court itself. ‡ The *Rāyavācaka* mentions an officer of Vīra Narasimha called Dharmayya of the *dharmāsana*. Probably Dharmayya was the judge of the imperial court in the reign of Vīra Narasimha.

The Prāḍvivāka :—The *prāḍvivāka* was next in importance to the emperor and the judge. § He was

* cf. *JAHRS*. ii. pp. 105-108.

† *The Vaiśyavaṁśasudhārṇavam*, a work composed by the famous commentator, Mallinātha, at the instance of Dēvarāya I, refers to the *dharmāsana* at Vidyānagara. The *Vaidyarājavallabha*, a treatise on *Āyurvēda*, written by Lakṣmaṇa Paṇḍita, the *prāṇācārya* of Bukka II, also alludes to the *dharmāsana* at Vijayanagara.

‡ "విద్వాంసుల్ రాజమహేంద్ర పట్టణమునన్ ధర్మాసనంబుండి"

Śrīnātha.

§ " వంచనామతి ప్రాడ్వివాకులై పటువు లొజ్జల కొప్పగించిరి పదువులెల్ల ॥

Mc: 3 : 19.

This line is of importance as it shows that the judicial system of which the *prāḍvivāka* was a member was in existence during the 16th century.

required to help the judge by examining the witnesses with a view to ascertain the truth. The *sabhyas* or assessors explained the nature of the law applicable to the case under trial, and stated probably their individual views regarding the merits of the case. Neither the *prāḍvivāka* nor the *sabhyas* could decide a case, and pronounce judgment. *

The emperor could not take cognizance of any case that was not brought before him either by the parties themselves, or by some officer of government who was appointed for the purpose. The manner in which some of the aggrieved parties brought their complaints before the emperor Acyuta is graphically described by Nuniz. He says:

> "When any one suffers wrong, and wishes to represent his case to the King, he shows how great is his suffering by lying flat on his face on the ground till they ask him what it is he wants. If, perchance, he wishes to speak to the King, while he is riding, he takes the shaft of a sphere and ties a branch to it, and thus goes along calling out. Then they make room for him and he makes complaint to the King; and it is there and then settled without more ado, and the King orders a captain, one of those who go with him, to do at once what the suppliant wants." †

The captain whom the emperor commanded to do at once what the supplicant wanted was probably his *pratinidhi* or the judicial representative. The settlement referred to by Nuniz could be no more than an order to try his case.

The emperor could take congnizance of criminal cases without waiting for somebody to come forward with a complaint. He could summon an individual guilty of a crime before him and begin an enquiry;

* cf. *JAHRS*. ii. p. 113.

† *FE*. p. 380.

but generally criminal cases were brought before him by the *tālāri* whose duty it was to detect crime. *

The Procedure:—In civil cases when a party found it inconvenient to attend the court, he was permitted to employ a representative or *niyōgi* whom the party must authorise to act on his behalf in every matter concerning the case. The action of the representative was binding on the party employing him. However, this concession was not extended to the accused in criminal cases, who were required to attend the court in person and defend themselves.

When a person appeared in a court to lodge a complaint, he had to file a document called *pratijña* in which he had to describe his view of the case. Then the person against whom the complaint was lodged would be called upon to answer the charge. In civil cases, some time was granted to the defendant, if required, to file his answer or *uttaram* ; but a person accused of some crime should be ready with his *uttaram*, on the day he was summoned to the court; for no concession regarding time would be shown to him. When the *pratijña* and the *uttaram* were ready before the court, the trial would commence. The court examined witnesses and recorded their evidence. The evidence was of two kinds, human and divine. Human evidence might be personal or documentary. The divine evidence was afforded by ordeals and

* There is reason to believe that people accused of committing crimes were subjected to torture for extorting confession. The following lines of Tiruvengaḷanātha describe how people suspected of theft were tortured:

ఇడుముకట్టున వేఁడి ఎండలో మిగుల
జడియు వీపులమీఁద జాపరా లెత్తి
పొఁగడదండలు వైచి పోనీక యెదుట
బెగడ దిట్టుచు నడ్డపెట్టినవారి ॥

things of that sort. It was termed divine, because people believed that gods gave their testimony through the medium of the ordeals. The human evidence was always preferred to the divine. The latter was made use of only when the former was not available. When the examination of the witnesses was completed, the court decided the case on its merits, and pronounced judgment which was embodied in a document called *jayapatram* bearing the signatures of the judge and probably also the *prāḍvivāka* and the *sabhyas*. *

The punishments which this court inflicted upon the criminals cannot be described to be mild:

> "For a thief, whatever theft he commits, howsoever little it be, they forthwith cut off a foot and a hand, and if his theft be a great one, he is hanged with a hook under his chin. If a man outrages a respectable woman or a virgin, he has the same punishment, and if he does any other such violence, his punishment is of a like kind. Nobles who become traitors are sent to be impaled alive on a wooden stake thrust through the belly, and people of the lower orders, for whatever crime they commit, he henceforth commands to cut off their heads in the market-place, and the same was for a murder unless the death was the result of a duel....These are the common kinds of punishments, but they have others more fanciful ; for when the King so desires he commands a man to be thrown to the elephants, and they tear him in pieces." †

What has been said so far applies only to the *dharmāsana* or the regular, stationary court of justice in the capital which was presided over by the emperor in person or by his *pratinidhi*. When the emperor went on tour through his dominions, his subjects in the provinces would take advantage of his presence in their midst to place their complaints before him, and get his decision thereon. A court held by the emperor in the provinces would be called *apratiṣṭhita* in the language of *Parāśara-Mādhavīya*.

* *JAHRS*. ii. p. 114 ff.

† *FE*. pp. 383-4.

Section 2 : Justice in the Provinces :—The administration of justice in the provinces was not left entirely to the circuit court of the Rāya, which was not at all suited for the purpose. Permanent stationary courts must have been established at convenient centres to transact judicial business in every province of the empire. The governor of each province must have been entrusted with the same judicial and magisterial powers as exercised by the emperor, and he must have presided over the regular stationary court at his headquarters. The existence of such a court at least in one of the provinces is indicated by the inscriptions and the Local Records :

"A dispute arose between the *sthānikas* of the temple of Cennarāya of Gaḍḍamayyapalle *alias* Śrībhāṣyapuram, and the *āyagārs* of the village regarding the ownership of houses, gardens and fields. They approached Nandyāla Nārapa who was ruling at Gaṇḍikōṭa, and requested him to settle their dispute. Having held an enquiry, he decided the case, and had his decision engraved on a stone tablet which he set up in the temple at Sammaṭūr." * (A.D. 1551).

During the term of office of Rāmarāja Viṭṭhala, as the governor of the Tamil districts, a dispute arose between two sections of the *mahājanas* of Koṇḍagi, in Rāmnād district. The *mahājanas* of the village took the case before Timmappa Nāyaka, the agent of Viṭṭhala. He directed the parties to go to Sāḷuva Nāyaka, and the latter, having constituted a court of the learned pandits of Madura, settled the dispute. †

It is not unreasonable to infer that the governors of other provinces were similarly discharging judicial duties. The provincial court tried cases not only at the first instance but heard appeals also.

A certain Mallamrāju, son of Timmayya, having disputed the sole right of his cousins to hold the *karṇika-mirāsi* of Hanumatguṇḍam and other places, filed a suit against them before a *dharmāsana* at the *agrahāra* of Kāvērisamudram. The *dharmāsana* decided the case against Mallamrāju. Later,

* *LR.* 33 pp. 226-7. † *MER.* 2 of 1923.

Mallamrāju went to Gaṇḍikōṭa, and appealed to Nandyāla Nārasimharāju, who was then governing the province. Nārasimha commanded Telugucerla Gōpālācārlu, probably his *pratinidhi*, to constitute a *dharmāsana* for the purpose of hearing the appeal. The Ācārlu summoned a *dharmāsana*, which, having heard both the parties, came to the conclusion that justice was on the side of Mallamrāju. Therefore, they pronounced judgment in his favour, and gave him the *jayarēkha*." *

Each *amaranāyaka* was probably administering criminal as well as civil justice in the villages which were granted to him for *nāyakara*.

About 1537 A.D., the village of Tirukkalakūḍi was included in the *nāyakara* estate of a certain Timmā Nāyaka. A quarrel arose between the temple authorities and *taṇḍarimar* of the village in connection with the rehabilitation of the village. Siṭṭama Nāyaka, an agent of Timmā Nāyaka, enabled the parties to come to an agreement. †

The *nāyakara* holder had probably jurisdiction over criminal cases also. The people who were the victims of bandits lodged their complaints before the *reḍḍi* of the village where the dacoity was committed; and he took the matter before the *rāju* or the chief in whose estate the village was included. ‡

There is reason to believe that the temple trustees were permitted to try petty criminal offences such as theft, and punish the culprits; but their jurisdiction appears to have been confined to the servants in the service of the temple. §

* *LR.* 21 pp. 1-36. † *MER.* 49 of 1916.

‡ *Ām.* 7: 19. అనిశ లాఁతుక గొల్లోప్పయి యతఁడు రడ్డు
రాజు గను నని కొందయు దీర్పంగ మగిడి
యంత పరియును పై ప్రజ కలికి పాతి
పోవ వాఁడును వెడవోట్లు పొడిచి చనియె ॥

§ *MER.* 185 of 1894; *SII.* v. 479.

Section 3 : The Dharmāsana :—Most of the civil cases, however, were settled by the people themselves without any reference to the government. The bulk of the judicial work of the empire appears to have been transacted by the *amukhya* or the temporary courts. These were no courts in the modern sense of the term. As the administration of justice was thoroughly decentralised, almost all the disputes were settled by the people without seeking the assistance of government servants as far as possible. *

Each dispute, as it arose, was settled by a *sabhā* or court which was constituted for the purpose, and which was dissolved as soon as the judgment was delivered. Therefore, they were temporary, and were created only when there was a need for their existence. These courts were known by the name of *dharmāsanas* or seats of justice.† The judges presiding

* cf. *Parāśara Mādhavīya*: "The hill-men should be tried by courts composed of hill-men; the soldiers should be tried by courts composed of soldiers; merchants should be tried by the courts formed by the merchants; caste disputes should be settled by courts consisting of caste elders. The disputes among the villagers should be settled by the courts presided over by the village elders."

† That the *dharmāsanas* were popular during Vijayanagara period is proved by the evidence of literature. Śrīnātha's biting satire on the learned pandits of Rajahmundry is well-known. These pandits are said to have gathered together as a '*aharmāsana*.' Vallabhāmātya, who was a subordinate of Harihara II of Vijayanagara, gives a satirical description of *dharmāsana* in his *Krīḍābhirāma*. A Brahman of Toṇḍamaṇḍalam went to Warangal on some business. Desirous of spending the night in the embraces of a famous courtesan in the suburb known as Akkalavāḍa, he went thither, and struck a bargain with the mother of the courtesan under consideration. The crafty old hag substituted her servant for her daughter and congratulated herself on her cleverness. Next morning, however, the Brahman discovered the fraud and lodged a complaint with the *talāris* of the ward. They arrested the old woman and dragged her before a *dharmāsana* which hastily met in the porch of the temple of Bhairava in the neighbourhood. The people who were well versed in the intricacies of the *kāma-śāstra* were chosen as judges. Both parties stated their respective versions of the facts; and the woman pleaded not guilty. While the judges were considering the facts, Gōvinda Śarma (the hero of the poem), who was one of the great doctors of *kāma-śāstra*, passed by that way. He was eagerly invited to join the *dharmāsana*; and when he took his seat, he was requested to pronounce his opinion on the merits of the case. He said that according to strict laws of *Kāma*, the head of the old woman should be shaven: but he requested his fellow judges to temper justice with mercy.

over them were drawn from the rural population and most of them were personally acquainted with the facts of the case.

The judges worked hard to discover the truth and administer justice rather than to satisfy the requirements of the law. Consequently, there was no encouragement for litigants to pursue a case from court to court in order to get a favourable decision of a higher tribunal by the help of some clever lawyer. These temporary courts were courts of arbitration. Their character can be clearly understood by a study of a few cases. The *pratijñā-patrika* in the case of Jūpalli Vengubhaṭlu *vs.* Cennubhaṭlu may serve as very good example.* The parties, after filing their respective *vyavahāra-patrikas* before the *dharmāsana* that met at the village of Tāḷḷamārpura, were called upon by the judges to submit their *pratijñā-patrikas*. The *pratijñā-patrika* runs thus :—

> "The *pratijñā-patrika* which is given by Jūpalli Cennubhaṭlu on Bhādrapada ba 2 of the (cyclic) year, Nala, to the learned *mahājanas* of Gōpālapura who observe the six *karmas*, *yajana*, *yājana* etc: Jūpalli Vengubhaṭlu and myself having a dispute (about the right of *paurōhitam*), approached you for *dharma*. I promise to abide by your decision. He who goes against your verdict is a *hīnavādi*."

A similar *patrika* was given by Vengubhaṭlu, the defendant. It is obvious that the parties agreed to abide by the decision of the court before the commencement of the enquiry. The court had no means of enforcing its judgment; but public opinion was on its side, and generally nobody dared to go against it. Occasionally, however, some litigants would altogether ignore the judgments of the dharmāsana; but, by such an action, they placed themselves in the

* *LR.* 1 pp. 106-17.

wrong.* The *sabhās* which met to decide boundary disputes were essentially arbitration courts. Therefore, it appears that most of the disputes during the Vijayanagara times, were settled by arbitration.

The composition of the *dharmāsana* seems to have varied according to the nature of the case it had to deal with. When the decision of the case depended upon the correct interpretation of law, naturally the case was tried by a panel of Brahman judges proficient in the Hindu Law.† The cases involving *mirāsi* and *mēra* rights were tried by courts consisting of people whose knowledge of facts specially qualified them for trying the case; ‡ but such cases were also taken before the *mahājanas* of an *agrahāra*. The disputes among the villagers involving probably the breaches of village rights were settled by an assembly of the village elders. § Caste disputes were generally settled by an assembly of the *gurus* and leaders of disputing castes. ¶ The boundary disputes were usually decided by a single judge in whom the people of the disputing villages had confidence either on account of his probity or special knowledge of the village tradition regarding its boundaries. ||

Procedure :—Generally, the parties involved in a civil case approached the *mahājanas* of an *agrahāra*, or the members of a merchant guild and requested them to hear their case and settle their dispute. They might either take up the case themselves; or,

* *LR*. 21. pp 1-36. † *LR*. 36 p. 445 ff. ‡ *LR*. 37 p. 312 ff.

§ *ibid* 13 of 1912-13; *LR*. 48 (Iṭimārpuram) p. 443 ff.

¶ *MER*. 687 of 1917.

|| *LR*. 37 p. 248 ff; *LR*. 36. p. 25; *LR*. 1 pp. 13-14.

Occasionally, however, some of the boundary disputes appear to have been settled by the government officials. (*MER*. 582 of 1926).

if they found it inconvenient to go into the case, they might send the parties to a neighbouring *agra-hāra* or merchant guild with a letter of recommendation requesting that the *mahājanas* of that *agrahāra* or the members of that merchant guild, as the case might be, should try the case and do justice to the parties. * Sometimes the parties approached a government servant (a governor of a province, or the *kāvalgār* of a *nāḍu*) with a request to hear their case. † He summoned a *dharmāsana* or *sabhā* and entrusted the trial of the case to that body. Boundary and caste disputes were seldom taken to the outsiders.

The *agrahāra* or town from which the litigants were so sent was technically know as '*sthala.*' The letter of recommendation or introduction was known as *priya-patrika*. It contained the names of the litigants, and a brief description of their case; and it ended with a request to the *mahājanas* or merchants, as the case might be, to try the case.

When a *dharmāsana* was duly constituted, both the parties, the plaintiff and the defendant, had to submit an affidavit called *vyavahāra-patrika* each describing his side of the case. Then they were called upon to submit their *pratijñā-patrikas*, pledging their word to abide by the decision of the court.

The enquiry would then commence. The parties and their witnesses would be examined. In several cases, the witnesses were required to take a most solemn oath before they made their depositions. ‡

* *LR.* 1 pp. 106-7; *LR.* 37 p. 312 ff.

† *MER.* 2 of 1923; *LR.* 13 (Cillāvāripalle) pp. 270-72.

‡ *LR.* 55 p. 283 ff.

The person taking the oath should bathe in the temple tank without removing the garments; and he should stand facing the god with the dripping clothes still clinging to his body and make his statement. This was the usual method. The process of taking the oath might assume a more complicated form. Sometimes, as in the case of Cennamarāju *vs.* Mallamrāju, the witnesses might be required not only "to bathe in the temple tank according to the prescribed fashion, but to drink the *tīrthas* and hold in the hand the *prasādas* of the three deities of Tirupati, Śrīsaila and Ahōbala," * while giving evidence standing in front of the God Siddhēśwara of Siriverla. When the examination of witnesses was completed, the court would deliver the judgment. Lastly, they would send a *priya-patrika* to the *agrahāra* or town from which the litigants were sent, giving a brief account of the enquiry and the judgment of the court. A document embodying the judgment called *jaya-patrika* or letter of victory addressed to the *karṇam* and *reḍḍi* of the village to which the parties belonged would also be given to the party in whose favour the court decided. The *dharmāsana*, having completely transacted the business for which it was constituted, would then dissolve itself.

The procedure adopted in settling caste and boundary disputes was different. In the case of caste disputes, the leaders of the disputing castes would request their respective *gurus* to meet together and decide the matter. † Tradition would be restated; old records would be examined, and sometimes supernatural aid would be invoked. On such occasions, a government servant of high rank might be requested to be present. ‡ In the case of boundary disputes, the

* *LR.* 55 pp. 283-93. † *MER.* 13 of 1912-13. ‡ *LR.* 48 p. 443 ff.

people of the disputing villages would first agree to end their quarrel by means of arbitration.* They would then select a person in whose honesty and knowledge of village affairs, they had great confidence. An auspicious day would be fixed for 'treading the boundary.' Invitations would be sent to the *karṇam*, *reḍḍi* and the elders of the neighbouring villages to attend the function.† On the morning of the day on which the boundary had to be 'tread', the person selected for the purpose should take a bath with his clothes on, and in one of the folds of his nether garment, he should carry 'the nine grains.' In addition to this, he should bear on his head an unbaked pot containing milk.‡ Then he should visit all the temples of the village, and salute their inmates. Lastly, he should walk along the boundary, which would be marked with stones by the assembled *reḍḍis*, *karṇams*, and the elders of villages present to witness the function.§ Usually the villagers rewarded the boundary treader by granting him a *mānya*.¶

These village courts, although unacquainted with lawyers, knew law books which were constantly used.

* *LR.* 36 (Cina-Kommerla) p. 25.

† *ibid.*

‡ "In all disputes regarding the boundaries between any two villages, neighbours or elders of five or ten villages shall investigate the case on the evidence to be furnished from natural or artificial boundary marks.

"Elders among cultivators and herdsmen or outsiders who have had the experience of former possession in the place or any one or many persons (not) personally acquainted with the boundary marks under dispute, shall first describe the boundary marks, and then *wearing unusual dress* (*viparīta vēṣah*), shall lead the people to the place. If the boundary marks just described are not found, a fine of 1000 *paṇas* shall be imposed on the misleading or the guilty person. If, however, they arrive at the exact spot, the party who have either encroached upon the boundary or destroyed the boundary marks shall be similarly punished. Kauṭilya : *The Arthaśāstra* p. 257 ; cf. *The Parāśara-Mādhaviya*.

§ *LR.* 1 p. 280 ff.

¶ *LR.* 37 p. 248 ff ; *LR.* 41 pp. 14-15.

The judges who presided over the *dharmāsanas* were familiar with the *dharma-śāstras*. The one book which appears to have been usually consulted was the *Yājña-valkya smṛti*.* *Manu* and other *smṛtis* are occasionally mentioned. Custom and usage played an important part in deciding communal disputes. Inscriptions containing a record of grants of privileges and titles would be cited and examined.† The *rāyarēkhas* were invariably consulted in the case of boundary disputes.

The *dharmāsanas* met usually in the hall of the village temple. In nineteen out of the twenty cases which have been culled from the Local Records, the *dharmāsana* or the *sabhā* is said to have met in the *maṇṭapa* of a temple. In one place, however, it is said to have met on a pial under the huge margosa tree in the village.‡ As the holy margosa is the usual place of residence of the village deity, the pial under it must be considered as her shrine. The court was held within the precincts of the temple, because it was the most convenient place where several people could meet without any discomfort. A more important reason, however, was the belief that people would not perjure themselves in the very presence of the deity. The belief was not groundless. To the South Indian Hindu of the sixteenth century, the house of God had a greater significance than to us. Nobody was believed to be capable of uttering lies in the temple. That was why the village courts were held in the halls of the village temples.

Occasionally the decision of the village court was not accepted as final. Some dissatisfied litigants

* *LR.* 55 p. 129.

† *MER.* 13 of 1912-13.

‡ *LR.* 9 p. 177 ff.

appealed to the court of the provincial governor * or even to the Rāya. Generally, the governor or the Rāya did not personally go into the matter, but entrusted the trial of the case to a *dharmāsana*. † The procedure in the appellate court was the same as that obtaining in the other courts.

* *LR.* 21 p. 1 ff

† *MER.* 2 of 1923.

CHAPTER X.

TRADE AND COMMERCE.

Section 1: Classes of Merchants:—Trade, both external and internal, was in a flourishing condition. The Rāyas who drew a good part of their revenue from the sea-port towns and *sunka-thāṇyas* fostered trade by adopting a definite policy towards merchants trading with the empire. The policy which found favour with the emperor Kṛṣṇadēvarāya has already been noticed. His policy was continued by all his successors.

(*I*) *Foreign Trade*:—Almost the whole of the foreign trade passed through the hands of (*a*) the Arabs, and (*b*) the Portuguese.

(*a*) *The Arabs*:—The relation between the Arabs and South India is ancient. The Arabs imported commodities from the European markets which they sold in India, and purchased Indian products such as pepper, ginger, spices, cloth etc., to be sold in Europe. Since the advent of the Muhammadan conquerors, cavalry became the most efficient instrument of warfare; and horses were in great demand both at the Muhammadan and Hindu courts all over India. As horses did not flourish on Indian soil, they had to be imported from abroad mainly from Persia and Arabia; and the trade in horses consequently became very lucrative. The Arab merchants naturally took advantage of this demand, and pocketed large profits by supplying the Indian monarchs the kind of horses they wanted. The Arab merchants who enjoyed the virtual monopoly of the horse trade, however, showed considerable partiality to their co-religionists, and they did not supply the horses to the Rāyas of Vijayanagara. The behaviour of the Arabs had so exasperated Virūpākṣa II that he ordered a general massacre of the merchants who had settled down at Goa. * The situation, however, did not improve. The Hindu monarch had only succeeded in scaring away the Mussalman merchants from his ports; and consequently he had to go without foreign horses. Sāḷuva Narasimha who, succeeded Virūpākṣa on the throne of Vijayanagara, was anxious to restore the prestige of the empire and turn the tables upon his Muslim neighbours. He knew that he could realise his ambition only by increasing the efficiency of his army. Therefore, he attempted to induce the Arbas whom Virūpākṣa scared away to return by offering them extravagant terms. Nuniz declares:

> "He caused horses to be brought from Oromuz and Adeem into his kingdom, and thereby gave great profit to the merchants, paying them for the horses just as they asked. He took them dead or alive at three for a thousand *pardaos*, and of those that died at sea, they brought him the tail only, and he paid for it just as if it had been alive." †

So long as there were no competitors in the field, the Arabs could regard themselves as the masters of the situation; but they were not destined to remain for long the sole purveyors of horses to Indian princes. During the last decade of the 15th century, the Portuguese made their appearance in India; and they succeeded in driving out the Arabs almost completely from the Indian markets.

(*b*) *The Portuguese* :—The accession of Kṛṣṇadēvarāya marks a new epoch in the commercial policy of the empire. He was determined from the day of his accession to invade the dominions of his neighbours, and to recover from them the territories which they had wrested from his predecessors. As soon as he ascended the

* *FE.* p. 99.

† *FE.* p. 307.

throne, he introduced a reform in the army which was calculated to strengthen his position. He was aware of the value of horses and elephants in his wars with his enemies, and spared no effort to secure as many animals as possible. The merchants who imported horses and elephants from abroad were given special consideration, so that they might not sell them to his enemies.* By this time, the Arab merchants were almost completely driven out of the Indian market by the Portuguese, who enjoyed practically the monopoly of the horse trade. Kṛṣṇadēva, therefore, found it advisable to open negotiations with them in order to induce them to sell him all the horses which they imported from abroad. He was so far successful in his attempt that the Portuguese Viceroy promised to 'send him all the horses available at Goa rather than to the Sultān of Bijāpūr.' †

The nationality of the merchants who supplied the Rāya with the elephants is not known. All or most of the beasts were imported from the island of Ceylon. Barbosa says:

> "And in this island are reared many wild elephants which the King has caught and tamed. These he sells to the merchants of Charamandel, of *Narsingua*, Malabar, Daquem, and Cambia, who come hither to seek them."‡.........."These elephants are a valuable merchandise among them, they are worth much, and are greatly esteemed by the Kings of India who keep them for war and to labour on various tasks." §

It appears that the elephant dealers were the native merchants of India.

* సింధుర మహాశ్వముఖ్యముల్ చేర్చు దాల।
దీవివణిజుల కూళ్లు సద్గృహములుపురి।
గొలువుఁ దేశంబు వెలమేలు గలుగ బ్రాత
హారిగాఁ జేయు నరి నవి జేరకుండ॥ Ām: 4: 258.

† Heras: *The Āraviḍu Dynasty* p. 59.

‡ *Barbosa* ii. p. 113. § *ibid* pp. 114-5.

The policy laid down by Kṛṣṇadēva was continued by Acyuta, who bought 'thirteen thousand horses of Ormuz' every year; * and by Sadāśiva who concluded a formal treaty with the Portuguese. By this treaty the governor of Goa agrees to "allow Arab and Persian horses landed at Goa to be purchased by the King of Vijayanagara, none being permitted to be sent to Bijāpūr, nor to any of its parts; and the King of Vijayanagara will be bound to purchase all those that were brought to his ports on quick and proper payment." †

The Portuguese merchants did not confine themselves to the horse trade. Caesar Frederick says:

> "The Merchandise that went every year from Goa to Bezeneger, were Arabian Horses, Velvets, Damaskes, and Sathens, Armesine of Portugal, and pieces of China, Saffron and Scarlets: and from Bezeneger they had in Turkie for their commodities, jewells, and pagodies which be Ducats of gold." ‡

The Portuguese merchants were equally busy in the other parts of the empire, where they had warehouses at Mangalore, Barçalore, Negapatam, St. Thome, and other places. The *Āmuktamālyada* mentions horses, elephants, precious stones, sandals, and pearls that were imported into the ports. § According to the *Aṭṭhavaṇa Tantram*, the principal commodities that were imported were glass, broad-cloth, indigo, lead, nutmeg, mace, silk, China cigars, damask, camphor, quicksilver, and cloves. ¶

* *FE.* p. 381.

† Heras: *The Āraviḍu Dynasty* p. 62.

‡ *Purchas His Pilgrims* x. p. 99.

§ రేవు లాన్నవు మతంగజంబును మణి శ్రీఖండముక్తాదియుఁ
రా వాణిజ్యముఁ బెంచి యేలఁగ నగుఁ .. *Ām*: 4: 245.

¶ *Mss.* 15-6-8.

Section 2: The Sea-Ports:—It is said that during the reign of Dēvarāya II, there were in the empire of Vijayanagara, three hundred ports, each of which was equal to Calicut.* Since that time, however, the Rāyas of Vijayanagara lost some important ports like Goa, Chaul, and Dabul, which ultimately passed into the hands of the Portuguese early in the sixteenth century. The Tuḷuva emperors made extensive conquests in the north-east and the extreme south. Kṛṣṇadēva re-conquered the provinces of Udayagiri and Koṇḍavīḍu, and subdued the kings of Kāyattār and Quilon. The number of sea-ports must have correspondingly increased. Some of the Tuḷuva emperors, especially Kṛṣṇadēvarāya, took great interest in improving the ports. He made them suitable places for importing foreign commodities; and offered protection to the foreigners who migrated thither owing to famine, pestilence or strife in their own land. †

A brief description of a few of the most important sea-ports will not be without interest in this context.

Goa was the largest port on the west coast:

"In this port of Goa there is a great trade in many kinds of goods, from the whole of Malabar, Chaul, Dabul and the great kingdom of Cambaya, which are consumed on the mainlands, and from the kingdom of Ormuz come every year ships laden with horses, and great numbers of dealers from the great kingdom of Narsyngua, and from Daquem, come hither to buy them." ‡

"The Ormuz merchants take hence in their ships cargoes of rice (great store), sugar, iron, pepper, ginger and other spices of diverse kinds, and drugs, which they carry thither." §

* *ED.* iv. p. 103.

† "..............................వర్షంపు లేవ్వేఁ రుజఁ
పావళ్లఁ దిగు నన్యభూప్రజల రాజా యాయి జాత్యోచితిఁ
బ్రోవంగాఁదగు; ..." *Ām*: 4: 245.

‡ *Barbosa* i. p. 178. § *ibid.*

This great port, however, was not included within the dominions of the Rāya of Vijayanagara. At the commencement of the reign of Kṛṣṇarāya, it was wrested from the Muhammadaṇs by the Portuguese who made it their capital.

(1) Honāwar was the first important Vijayanagara port on the West Coast. It had a flourishing trade:

> "Here the Malabares carry on a great trade, taking away great store of black rice..., and bringing in return coconuts and oil obtained therefrom and palm-sugar, and palm-wine, and everything in great abundance, and yearly a multitude of *zambuquos*, both great and small, come for this trade, for much rice is consumed in Malabar by reason that it is their chief diet." *

The port of Honāwar deserves notice for another reason. It was the head-quarters of Timōja who 'was practically and in effect the commandant of the Vijayanagara fleet.' † And he was assisted in the office by his brother Raogy (Mihr or Mihr Roa). They were entrusted by the Rāya 'with the task of waging perpetual war with Goa.' ‡ Until 1540 A.D., the port appears to have been governed by a subordinate *rāja* paying tribute to the emperor of Vijayanagara, when it was annexed to the neighbouring kingdom of Bhaṭakal.§

(2) Bhaṭakal stood further to the south along the coast.

> "There is great traffic in goods of diverse sorts. There dwell both Moors and Heathen, all given to trade. Many ships come hither every year from Ormuz to get cargoes of white rice (great store), and powdered sugar (of which this land has great plenty). They know not how to make it into loaves, and they wrap it up in small packets, as it is in powders....... They also take

* *Barbosa* i. pp. 185-6.

† Heras: *The Āraviḍu Dynasty* p. 57.

‡ *ibid*

§ *ibid* p. 186.

many cargoes of iron, and these three kinds of goods are the principal cargoes they get here. There is also some pepper and spices which the Malabares bring hither from India. Here is great store of myrobalans of good quality, and of these they make a conserve in order to sell them to the Moors of Arabia and Persia, who buy them at a good price. The Ormuz ships, which...come hither every year, bring horses in great numbers, and many pearls which they sell here to the Kingdom of Narsyngua, but now on account of our armies they take them to Goa, with many other kinds of merchadise. A few ships belonging to the Moors of Meca also venture to come to this spot to take loads of spices, notwithstanding that by the rules and orders of our people, they are forbidden so to do. The *zambucos* of Malabar come hither yearly for loads of iron and sugar, and themselves bring palm-sugar, coconuts (and the oil got therefrom), palm-wine, pepper (great store), and sundry other drugs." Besides, "much copper is also used and taken inland for coinage, also for cooking pots and other vessels used by the country people. Much quicksilver, vermilion dye, coral, alum and ivory (which is here of great value) are also dealt in at this place." *

(3) Bacanor and Braçalor :—

"Many ships from abroad, and many as well of Malabar take in cargoes" of husked rice. "Great store thereof they carry hence to Ormuz, Aden, Xaer, Cananor and Calecut and barter it for copper, coconuts (and the oil thereof) and molasses. †

(4) Mangalore :

"Many ships take cargoes of black rice, which is better and more wholesome than the white, to sell in the land of Malabar, and it can be got good cheap. Cargoes of this rice are likewise taken in many ships of the Moors to Aden; and of pepper as well,...which the Malabares take thither in small craft." ‡

(5) Cumbola :—

"Here is garnered a great abundance of very bad black rice which the Malabares come hither to purchase, and to take

* *Barbosa* i. pp. 188-91. † *ibid* p. 194.

‡ *ibid* pp. 195-6; cf. Varthema: *Itinerary* p. 51.

away in their *zambuquos*, to sell to the lower sort of people who, buy it readily, as it is good cheap, and by it they make more than by the good rice. They also take much thereof to the Maldive Islands, which lie over against Malabar, as the inhabitants are poor Moors, who, by reason of its lower price, would rather have the black than the white. They give it in exchange for *cairo*, which is a thread used for making cables and ropes ; it is made out of the husks of the coconut, and much of it is made here." *

(6) Quilon was 'a very great city with a right good haven.' The king of Quilon was very often at war with the king of Narsyngua ; and he defended himself well. He seems to have been defeated by Kṛṣṇadēvarāya, and Quilon became a tributary state of Vijayanagara empire. It was a great commercial centre, and pepper its staple product, attracted the merchants of many nationalities.

"Hither come Moors, Heathen and Christians in great numbers. The Moors and Heathen are great traders and possess many ships dealing in goods of diverse kinds, in which they sail in all directions to *Charamandel* and *Ceilam*, to the *Isles* of *Benguala*, *Malaca*, *Çamatra*, *Peeguu*, but they trade not with *Cambaya*. Here there is great store of pepper, and there is a great river." †

(7) Kāyal :—This port belonged to the kingdom of Quilon until 1514 A.D. ; but subsequent to this date, it seems to have passed into the hands of the king of Kāyattār from whom the Rāya of Vijayanagara wrested it. It was inhabited by 'Moors and Heathen merchants of importance.'

"It has a very good haven, whither every year sail many ships from Malabar and others from Charamandel and Benguala, so that here there is traffic in goods of many kinds coming from diverse regions. The *Chatis* of this land are men of high standing dealing in abundance of precious stones and of seed-pearls also for the right of fishing for these belongs to the King." ‡

* *Barbosa* i. pp. 196-7. † *ibid* ii. p. 97. ‡ *ibid* p. 123.

(8) Negapatam was the port of Cōḷamaṇḍalam. Although Caesar Frederick speaks of it as 'a countrey of small trade,' * Barbosa does not belittle its importance. He says:

"Numbers of ships from Malabar sail hither every year, most of them to take cargoes of rice by which they make great profits: and they bring hither abundance of goods from Cambaya, copper, quicksilver, vermilion, pepper and goods of other kinds. In this Province of Charamandel are also found many sorts of spices and drugs which come from the kingdoms of Malaca, China Benguala in Moorish ships for they dare not pass Malabar through fear of our fleets." †

"The more part or all of the Heathen merchants or *Chatis*, who live throughout India, are natives of this country, and are very cunning in every kind of traffic in goods. At the sea-ports are also many Moors, natives of the land; who are great merchants and own many ships." ‡

(9) Mailāpūr:—It was a growing port and merchants brought goods to it from other places. Its pilgrim traffic appears to have been considerable. §

(10) Pulicat:—This port was inhabited by both the Moors and Heathen, great traders. Pulicat may be described without exaggeration as the eastern port of the city of Vijayanagara.

"It has a very fair sea-haven whither resort ships of Moors in great numbers conveying goods of diverse kinds. By land also from the Narsyngua kingdom come many traders to buy goods of many kinds for which reason they bring hither from Peguu...great store of rubies, spinels, and abundance of musk [which precious stones are good cheap here, for him who knows how to buy and to choose them.]

"Here are made great abundance of printed cotton cloths which are worth much money in Malacca, Peguu, Çamatra and in

* *Purchas His Pilgrims* x. p. 108.

† *Barbosa* ii. p. 125.

‡ *ibid* pp. 125-6.

§ *ibid* pp. 126-9.

the kingdom of Guzerate and Malabar for clothing. Here also copper, quicksilver and vermilion as well as other Cambaya wares, dyes in grain [Meca velvets and especially] rose water." *

Most of the maritime trade passed through the hands of three classes of merchants: (*a*) The Portuguese, (*b*) the Arabs, and (*c*) the Indians. Almost all the trade between India and the West was in the hands of the Portuguese and the Arabs; but the Indian merchants also competed with them in the Eastern markets. They frequented Peguu, Tenasserim, Malay peninsula, the Archipelago and even China. The Indian merchants belonged to two classes: (*i*) the *Labbais* (Mussalmans), and (*ii*) the *Chatis* (the Hindus). In the markets of Malabar, the Christian and Jewish merchants made their appearance. All the coastal trade was entirely in the hands of native merchants.

Section 3 : The Pirates :—The merchants trading with foreign countries carried on their ventures at very great risk. The seas were infested with pirates who attacked the merchant men and robbed them of their cargoes. As the pirates had the support of powerful states on the mainland, it was not an easy task to suppress them. Barbosa records two instances of piracy.

(i) Honāwar, as noticed already, was the seat of two brothers, Timōja and Raogy who were commissioned by the emperor of Vijayanagara to wage perpetual war on the port of Goa.

Each of them maintained, "five or six large ships with crews of well-armed men in great numbers : these issuing forth to the sea took all the ships they met (saving only those of Malabar) and robbed them of whatsoever they carried, leaving men alive ; and they shared the stolen goods with the lord of the land to obtain

* *Barbosa* ii. pp. 130-2.

his favour ; and in this wise they lived, gathering great riches, and established in the land." *

Timōja and his brother cannot be strictly termed pirates; for they were commissioned by the Rāya to wage war against the Mussalmans who were the natural enemies of the Hindus. They attacked only the Mussalman ships which they robbed. The fact that they did not molest the Malabar ships which belonged to the Hindus shows that they were not pirates by profession.

(ii) The second instance seems to be a genuine case of piracy. Pōrkāḍ in the kingdom of Quilon was another nest of pirates. There lived many fishermen who earned their livelihood in winter by fishing; but in summer they lived by robbery of everything they could find upon the sea.

> "They are great oarsmen and a multitude of them gather together all armed with bows and arrows in plenty, and thus they surround any vessel they find becalmed with flights of arrows until they take and rob it. Those who are taken therein, they put ashore. Thus with these boats of theirs which they call *catures*, they take much spoil, part whereof they give to the lord of the land." †

The Indians were not the only people who took to piracy. The Portuguese, not being satisfied with the profits obtained from honest trade, joined the ranks of the pirates, and made sailing upon the sea utterly unsafe. A passage in the *Kēraḷa Pazhama* runs thus :

> "Besides these cruelties perpetrated on the land, the Portuguese were also responsible for unmentionable atrocities on the sea. The Feringi ships alone did not keep the peace. The Muhammadan ships were the special objects of their fury. Every ship had to carry safe-conduct issued by the Portuguese captain. But even with that they were not safe. The Portuguese seamen

* *Barbosa* i. p[illegible] 7.   † *ibid* ii. pp. 95-6.

demanded heavy bribes and *bakshish*, and if whatever they asked for was not given, the ships would be confiscated." *

The Portuguese seamen whose object seems to have been to suppress competition forcibly, could not restrain on occasions from laying hands upon non-Muslim merchantmen, although they carried the necessary safe-conduct from the Portuguese authorities.

Section 4 : Inland Trade :—The internal trade of the empire appears to have been in a satisfactory condition. Large quantities of articles were transported from one part of the empire to another. Some idea about the movement of goods may be had from a careful study of the lithic records of the time :

Place.	Reference.	Date.	Articles in transit.
1. Rôḷḷamadugu.	*LR.* 48 p. 341.	1521 A.D. ?	*Perikas* of *rasavargas*, and bales of cotton passing along the Ancient Road.
2. Bukkapaṭṭaṇam.	*LR.* 37 p. 116.	1530 A.D.	*Perikas* of pepper, jaggery, pulses, cholam, nuts, fruits, vegetable baskets, and bales of silk.
3. Animala.	*LR.* 14 p. 415 ; *LR.* 7 p. 77.	1531 A.D.	Bales of cotton, *perikas* of *rasavargas*, nuts, pepper, jaggery, yarn, cloth, cloaks, rice, cholam, ragi &c.
4. Udayagiri.	*LR.* 42 No. 23.	1546 A.D.	Various kinds of grain, *rasavargas* (ghee, sugar, oil &c.), perfumes like sandal, camphor, musk, pilli roots &c.

Besides, an inscription dated 1516 A.D., refers to the commodities that were taken to Śrīśailam by various

* Paṇikkar: *Malabar and the Portuguese* p. 94.

means of transport.* Rāmarāja's *kaul* dated 1526 A.D., alludes to *perikas* of nuts, *nagās* of *rasavargas*, cloth &c., that were passing along the Tirupati Road. † The *Kaifiyat* of Dāsaripalle speaks of merchants going to Ahōbalam. ‡ These references are enough to show that, during the period under consideration, there existed active trade relations amongst the cities and the provinces of the empire. The *Aṭṭhavaṇa Tantram* gives a more detailed account of the internal trade relations. It is said that pepper, nuts, cardamoms were imported from the districts of Nagar into Bālaghāṭ; opium, asafœtida, cotton, shawls, musk, horses and pearls were imported to Bālaghāṭ from the north; woollen blankets, nuts, iron, grain, and sandal were exported to other places from Citradurga; sandal which was available at Nagar, Ambāpura, Garḍanagiri &c. in Bālaghāṭ was purchased by the merchants for exportation to China; cotton which grew plentifully in the district of Ādavāni was sold in Kōlār and Sidlagaṭṭa; copra which was produced in Sīra and Gubbi was sold elsewhere; ghee, oil and tobacco which were obtained in large quantities at Dharmāvaram, Cirumana and Rācerla were exported to the neighbouring provinces where they were sold; cloth, and silk fabrics that were manufactured at Dharmāvaram, Tāḍpatri, Ādavāni, Gutti, Bellary, and the black pulse growing in these localities, were exported to Śrīrangapaṭṭaṇam, and its neighbourhood where they were marketed with very high profits. §

Trade Routes:—The road between Bhaṭakal and Vijayanagara is described by Paes. ¶ It passed through Zambuja, Recalem, Darcha &c. Inscriptions frequently

* *MER.* 18 of 1915.

† *LR.* 18 p. 407.

‡ *LR.* 5 pp. 79-80.

§ *MMss.* 15-6-8.

¶ *FE.* pp. 236-43.

mention an 'Ancient Road' connecting the Deccan with places in the East Coast. An inscription of Rōḷḷamaḍugu alludes to the 'Ancient Road' which passed through the mountain pass at the place; * the same road is said to go through hill passes at Pulivendala, Gaṇḍi, Peṇḍḷimaṟṟi &c. † The Kāśī-Rāmēśvaram Road mentioned in the *Kaifiyat* of Pattūripāḷem,‡ and the Tirupati Trunk Road mentioned in the chronicle of Cuddapah § and Rāmarāja's *kaul* ¶ probably refer to the same road. The *Śukasaptati*, a work probably of the early seventeenth, century, describes a road connecting Vidyānagara with Conjeevaram. ‖ The *Kaifiyat* of Rācerla gives an account of the road between Gutti and Munimaḍugu;** and another road connecting Ahōbalam with Pōrumāmiḷḷa, Baddevōlu, Kambham &c., is mentioned in the *Kaifiyat* of Dāsaripalle.†† Barbosa hints at a trade route connecting Vijayanagara and Pulicat. ‡‡ Raffi-ud-Din Ibrāhīm Shīrāzi alludes t two roads, one going from Masulipaṭam to Kōvilkoṇḍa and another from Kōvilkoṇḍa to Kampili. §§ Lastly, a trade route is said to have passed from Kāyamkulam to Tinnevelly; it went through the kingdom of Quilon. ¶¶

* *LR.* 48 p. 341.

† *LR.* 14 p. 415.

‡ *LR.* 9 pp. 248-53.

§ *LR.* 18. pp. 462-3.

¶ *ibid* p. 407.

‖ జగతిఁ బొగడొందు విద్యా । నగరంబున బరమధూర్త నాయకు లగుచున్
నెగడుదు రిద్దరు భూసురు । లగణితులై విందుఁడనఁగ ననువిందుఁ డనన్
వారలంతట నల కంచివరదరాజు । గరుడ సేవ నిరీక్షింప నరిగిపోవు
పరుస వెంబడి జని యన్యభామినీ వి । లోకనాపేక్ష నెమ్మదిలోన హెచ్చ ॥

SS. pp. 102-3.

** *LR.* 6 p. 236.

†† *ibid* 5 pp. 77-8.

‡‡ *Barbosa* ii. pp. 130.

§§ *JBBRAS*. xxii. p. 28.

¶¶ Paṇikkar: *Malabar and the Portuguese* p. 96.

The Means of Transport :—The internal means of communication were not at all suitable for the rapid transport of commodities. The roads were bad, and probably, no better than mere tracks. Although wheeled carts were used for agricultural and military purposes, they were not employed for transporting articles of merchandise. An inscription of the time of Kṛṣṇadēvarāya gives us what seems to be an exhaustive list of vehicles used for trade purposes : (1) *kāvaḍis*, (2) head-loads, (3) pack-horses, (4) pack-bullocks, and (5) asses. * That is to say, men and animals were employed to carry the articles of merchandise from place to place, but no wheeled carriage seems to have been in use. This is corroborated by the evidence of foreign writers, literature, and Local Records.

Barbosa speaks of the asses and pack cattle on which pepper was brought from Malabar to Vijayanagara. † Paes mentions laden oxen that crowded the streets and markets of Vijayanagara. ‡ An inscription of Rōḷḷamaḍugu alludes to the trains of laden oxen ; § and a Nanjangūḍ grant refers to bullock loads. ¶ The *Āmuktamālyada* describes horses that were hired to carry loads. ||

* *MER.* 18 of 1915.

† *Barbosa* i. p. 203.

‡ *FE.* p. 257.

§ *LR.* 48 pp. 341-50.

¶ *EC.* iv. Nj. 266.

|| " లావుగల యద్దెగుఱ్ఱపు । జావడనుల మీద మా,తసంచులు దూలఁగ "
Ām. 2 : 96.

The author of *Śukasaptati* narrates a story containing a dialogue between a fox and a pack-horse. As the story graphically describes the miseries of the poor beast of burden, a rough paraphrase of it may not be out of place in this connection :—

The horse approached the stream neighing feebly to quench his thirst. On his spine was a sore which attracted crowds of flies; the hair of his tail was a source of amusement to the youngsters of the village. As his front legs were

TRADE AND COMMERCE

The journey along the roads, as noticed elsewhere, was not safe, as they were infested with robbers, especially in forest and hilly tracts. The merchants generally preferred, therefore, to travel in company, very well protected. The caravans are referred to in several contemporary works. The *Āmuktamālyada* describes the progress of a caravan which was robbed of its belongings on the road by highway men.* Rafi-ud-Din Shīrāzi states that the caravans were plundered by the dacoits on the Kampili-Kōvilkoṇḍa and Kōvilkoṇḍa-Masulipatam Roads during the reign of Muhammad Shāh IV. † Owing to the plundering raids of the Portuguese captain Rodrigues, 'all the traders who

tied together, he moved by hopping. He was bleeding profusely on account of the wounds caused by the blows which he received from his cruel master. Swarms of flees hovered over his neck, ears and belly.

As the horse was about to drink water, Buddhisāra (a fox) accosted him and asked him to explain the cause of his miserable condition. The horse replied, "you know that I was purchased by a *Reḍḍi* of the yonder village who used to treat me kindly. As he fell on evil days, being unable to maintain me, he sold me to a *Bēri*, the robber of other peoples' fortune. It is not possible for me to describe to you satisfactorily the manner in which he treated me. He would always drive me to the fairs held in all places in the neighbourhood laden with *perikas* or loads. He would show no consideration for the sufferings of my poor body. The weight of the *perika* was enough to break my back; to add to its weight, he would not only mount on the top of it, but cudgel me mercilessly to make me run fast. May his hands be blasted by Cengāḷammā! He would let me to bulky persons going to *tirunāḷs* in the neighbouring villages, and extract from them money for tolls, fare &c. In order to satisfy his insatiable greed, he would drive me to all and sundry places, but would never give me any feed. Instead, he would allow me to graze on grass wherever available on the roadside, after securing my legs with a rope. He would never apply the *gorapa* to my body, nor would he wash it with water. I had no grass to eat, no covering over my body to protect me from inclement weather. When I returned home at night after a day's wandering, I had no stable to retire, but to remain tied between two plough buffaloes with unusally long horns. Alas! although a horse by birth, I had to put up with this miserable plight. That stony-hearted man would give a spade to his daughter, whom he commanded to fetch grass for me; but that wanton would throw away the instrument, and spend the day in the company of her lovers; and when she returned home, she would bring the grass picked up from the excreta of the elephants.

A similar tale is narrated in the *Hamsavimśati*. These show that the horses were common beasts of burden and their owners trea ed them cruelly.

* *Ām* 7: 7-21.

† ?AS. xxii. p. 26.

carried on a great land commerce between Tinnevelly and Kāyamkulam' stopped their commercial activities.* Similar happenings are described in the Local Records. A *maghava-sādhaka* dated 1531 A.D., records the death of the men of the *Reḍḍi* community while defending the *Balija* merchants against robbers near the pass of Rōḷḷamaḍugu. † The activity of the freebooters is also recorded in the *Kaifiyat* of Dāsaripalle. ‡

It is obvious that the merchants carried on trade under adverse circumstances. They embarked on their ventures at the risk of their lives and property. As the government did not make adequate provision for the protection of their life and property, they had to pay money to private persons to keep guard over dangerous zones on the road. Moreover, the vexatious tariff walls, which the government set up all over the land, acted as so many barriers in the path of trade. The country was honey-combed with *ṭhāṇyams* or tariff districts where the merchants had to pay duties on all articles. Duties were collected not only on the exports and imports but also on those that were in transit. Under these circumstances, trade could not have flourished unhampered.

Nevertheless, the government appears to have taken some interest in promoting trade. According to Paes, Kṛṣṇadēvarāya induced the merchants to go to Nāgalāpore from his other cities. § The example of the Rāya was copied by his *nāyakas*. They encouraged the merchants by offering them concessions, because the merchants were a source of income to them. They set up fairs in new places, and revived them where they were in decay. Almost every big village seems

* Paṇikkar: *Malabar and the Portuguese* p. 96

† *LR.* 48 pp. 341-50.

‡ *LR.* 5 pp. 79-80.

§ *FE.* p. 244.

to have had a fair of its own to which flocked the men and women of the neighbourhood for purchasing articles of domestic consumption, and probably for marketing what they had produced. *

*ఊరూరి సంతసంతకుం 'దిరుగఁ బెద్దలింట సంతరించిన పిలుకువాటి గోడగల,etc.''

Ām. 4 : 35.

The *Hamsavimśati*, a work of the eighteenth century gives a list of places, where merchants gathered for the sale and purchase of commodities. The commercial conditions of the sixteenth century could not have undergone much change. The list is given below. It may be taken for what it is worth.

1. Rāyadurgam, 2. Gutti, 3. Rāyavēlūru, 4. Ānegondi, 5. Muluvāya, 6. Śrirangapaṭṭaṇam, 7. Gingee, 8. Coñjeevaram, 9. Kappara, 10. Gagara, 11. Gaḍag, 12. Lakṣmēśvar, 13. Bankāpūr, 14. Madura, 15. Ādavāni, 16. Māsūr, 17. Vinukoṇḍa, 18. Koṇḍavīḍu, 19. Koṇḍapalli, 20. Podili, 21. Tañjāpuram, 22. Udayagiri, 23. Kaisūr, 24. Mysore, 25. Penugoṇḍa, 26. Mangaḷagiri, 27. Basavapaṭṇam, 28. Sirpi, 29. Wandavāsi. 30. Kundurpi, 31. Bellamkoṇḍa, 32. Dēvarakoṇḍa, 33. Rācerla, 34. Munimaḍugu, 35. Dūpāḍu, 36. Rāparti, 37. Mācerla, 38. Rācavīḍu, 39. Kambham, 40. Banagānipalle, 41. Pōrumāmiḷḷa, 42. Dhārāpuram, 43. Cini, 44. Tāḍpatri, 45. Nandyāla, 46. Ciruvalli, 47. Nandavaram, 48. Kandukūr, 49. Rāmayapaṭṇam 50. Ārubaṇḍa, 51. Hampi-Virūpākṣam, 52. Āraṇi, 53. Venipalli, 54. Kampili, 55. Kandanūr, 56. Kaḍapa, 57. Siddhavaṭam, 58. Gaṇḍikōṭa, 59. Kāsūr, 60. Puttūr, 61. Cintaguṇṭa, 62. Gaṇḍavaram, 63. Damanaceruvu, 64. Vellatūr, 65. Kullūr, 66. Kalavāyi, 67. Nellore, 68. Vellore, 69. Rāicūr, 70. Cadumūr, 71. Rācakoṇḍa, 72. Kadiri, 73. Kutaguḷḷa, 74. Gangēru, 75. Śringēru, 76. Rāmaḷakōṭa, 77. Vajragiri, 78. Nūgūr, 79. Nuṣum, 80. Cōbada, 81. Bāgūr, 82. Kollāla, 83. Gudibaṇḍa, 84. Bellary, 85. Kottakōṭa, 86. Gummilēnipāḷem, 87. Gobbūr, 88. Baḷḷāpuram, 89. Punganūr, 90. Āku, 91. Rāmaṭenki, 92. Manava, 93. Kautāḷam, 94. Mānukoṇḍamūr, 95. Kumbhakōṇam, 96. Kōṭakoṇḍa, 97. Peravali, 98. Duvvūr, 99. Bangalore, 100. Vottūr, 101. Cittoor, 102. Huni, 103. Ciratanāpali, 104. Rājōle, 105. Gadwāl, 106. Kācanagar, 107. Tiruttani, 108. Kāḷahasti, 109. Sinūr, 110. Madhyārjunam, 111. Trināmali, 112. Nāmukoṇḍa, 113. Pākāla, 114. Kāvēripāka, 115. Mōhanagiri, 116. Cadukūr, 117. Mallūr, 118. Cādukoṇḍa, 119. Sāgoṇḍa, 120. Vāvili, 121. Nāgore, 122. Taḷḷūr, 123. Mylāpore, 124. Peddamangaḷam, 125. Rāmasamudram, 126. Rāmāpuram, 127. Vellāla, 128. Bhuvanagiri, 129. Koṇḍāpuram, 130. Gaurī-Mayūram, 131. Harpanahaḷḷi, 132. Bedanaravāri, 133. Naḍigallu, 134. Kokkallu, 135. Kaḍavakolanu, 136. Veligōḍu, 137. Tangeḷḷa, 138. Darsi, 139. Kangundi, 140. Tanugoṇḍa, 141. Kaḍavapettam, 142. Doosti, 143. Sivanagāḷḷavalandi, 144. Singalam, 145. Mannārukōvela, 146. Sonnagallu, 147. Cidambaram, 148. Vāgenagar, 149. Purānpura, 150. Woḍayārpāḷem, 151. Uḍipi, 152. Mujjangi, 153. Māḍuva, 154. Mōsavagallu, 155. Rāmanādhapuram, 156. Beḍanda, 157. Dharmavaram, 158. Dāḍigoḷḷa, 159. Mandam, 160. Māvanike, 161. Mārkāpūr, 162. Kumbhi, 163. Haranga, 164. Majjhari, 165. Haḷikēhaḷḷi, 166. Rattipalli, 167. Kuranji, 168. Revaṇi, 169. Sannaki, 170. Pāluvāyi, 171. Gujjari, 172. Āmūru, 173. Bezwāḍa, 174. Koṇḍūru, 175. Kaṇḍēru.

Section 4: *Industries* :—Agriculture was the most important industry of land. As rice was the staple food of the people, it was grown extensively at all places. White rice was consumed by richer classes; but the red rice (the black rice of Barbosa) was used by the lower classes. It was cultivated almost everywhere, because it was needed not only for domestic consumption but for export. The state bestowed special attention upon rice industry and created special facilities for agriculturists. Tanks were excavated, canals were dug, and *takāvi* loans were advanced, and heavy taxes were remitted during seasons of scarcity. Besides rice, people in the interior subsisted upon *ragi*, and *cholam*. Although the ryots took very great pains to cultivate these grains, the government did not offer any sort of encouragement to improve their cultivation. The same remark applies to the cultivation of pulses of different varieties. The sugar-cane was grown wherever water could be had in plenty. The cane was cut in summer, when the mills became busy pressing the juice. *

The sugar-cane plantations gave birth to two other industries, the manufacture of jaggery and sugar. Jaggery was consumed all over the country by people of all classes; but sugar appears to have been less common in the houses of humbler folk. Barbosa describes the kind of sugar that was manufactured in the country. It was in a powdery condition, as the people did not know how to make it into loaves; † but Varthema, who visited Vijayanagara a decade earlier, states that at Bhaṭakal, there was 'a great abundance of sugar, and especially of sugar candied, according to our manner.' ‡ Besides sugar manufactured from

* *Ām.* 2 : 70. † *Barbosa* i. p. 188. ‡ Varthema : *Itinerary* p. 49.

sugar-cane, palm sugar was produced in plenty.* Although the industry is smothered to death, it still lurks in the out of the way corners of the country. It might have been consumed largely by people in the past; and it formed an important ingredient in the preparation of some *Āyurvēdic* medicines.

The country is said to have been filled with groves of fruit growing trees.† The Portuguese writers state that fruits could be had abundantly everywhere. Mangoes, jack fruits, pomegranates, *karbuse*, grapes and plantains of different varieties were available at the capital and in the great cities of the empire.‡ It is said that on the Ānegondi side of the Tungabhadrā there were 'many orchards and gardens with many fruit trees, for the most part, mangoes and areca-palms, and jack trees and also many lime and orange trees.' There were also white grapes. The fruit gardens grew 'so closely one to another' that they appeared 'like a thick forest.' § All kinds of kitchen vegetables were cultivated in gardens. But the one product of the garden which attracted the attention of the foreigners very much was the betel leaf. ¶ The betel gardens are frequently mentioned in the inscriptions and the *rāya-rēkhas.* ‖ The cultivation of the plantain was undertaken in areas where water was available in plenty. It was entered in the records of the *Aṭṭhavaṇam* as a *nīrārambha* crop. ** The plantain fruits and leaves were so much in demand that people took to its cultivation extensively. The flower gardens attracted much attention. The city of Vijayanagara is said to have had a

* *Barbosa* i. p. 189. † *FE.* p. 237. ‡ *Ām.* 2: 75.

§ *FE.* pp. 256-7. ¶ *ibid* p. 242.

‖ *EC.* iv. Gu. 67; *LR.* 13 (Mārkāpūr No. 7) pp. 230-1.

** *LR.* 6 (Alavakoṇḍa) pp. 324-48.

plentiful supply of flowers, especially roses, at all times in the year. The desire of the people for sweet-scented flowers appears to have been insatiable. They wore them as garlands on their heads and around their necks. Women decorated their hair with different kinds of flowers. The rich people strewed their beds with flowers. Every nobleman kept a flower garden of his own; and so did every temple.

The most important of the textile industries was the weaving of cotton cloth. The weavers seem to have divided themselves into several classes. An inscription of Andirāju-Kōḍūr mentions two classes of looms, *togaṭa-maggas*, and *sāle-maggas.* * The same classification is alluded to in the *rāyarēkha* of Alavakoṇḍa. Of the 411 looms that were at work in the village, 230 were *togaṭa-maggas*, and the rest were *tella-maggas.* † *Togaṭa - maggas* were looms specially set apart for weaving red cloth, whereas the *tella-maggas* wove only white cloth. In addition to the weaver castes such as the *padmasāles*, *sāles*, *jāṇḍras,* ‡ etc. the *mālas* or the *pariahs* took to weaving as a profession all over the country. § The *Aṭṭhavaṇa Tantram* divides the weavers into two classes, the *kurubas* and the *sāles.* The *kurubas*, who were shepherds by profession, took to weaving as a by-industry. They wove woollen blankets and sold them to the merchants trading with different parts of the empire. The *sāles* evidently busied themselves with the manufacture of the cotton and other kinds of

* *LR.* 1 pp. 11-13. † *LR.* 6 p. 324 ff.

‡ cf. *Ām.* 4: 35.
"అప్వేటి మేటి సాలె పటుసాలె వాన్వైజాతి సాతులేతుల."

§ The common Telugu proverb సగము సాలె నేతా సగము మాల నేతా? shows that the *sāles* and the *mālas* were the two principle weaving communities of the Telugu country.

cloth. The *kaikkōlars* were the weavers par-excellence of the Tamil country. They figure often in the inscriptions of the time; and they are said to have been enjoying certain privileges such as *taṇḍu* and *sangu* conferred upon them by the government; * but the *kaikkōlars* were not the only people who were 'professional weavers.' The *pariah* looms were busy in manufacturing cloth in almost every *cherry*.

Cotton fabrics were manufactured largely in Dharmāvaram, Tāḍpatri, Adavāni, Gutti and Bellary; woollen blankets in Citradurga and Jarimela; and silk cloth in Bangalore, Gutti, Molatāyitūr, Bellary and Rāyadurga. Coarse cloth was, of course, manufactured at all places. †

The carding or combing of cotton, and spinning it into yarn were, of course, dependent upon the weaving industry. Although no information is available about them, they are occasionally mentioned in the inscriptions. *Pinjaṇigaru* or *pinja-siddhāyam* ‡ presumes the existence of the combing industry; yarn which was one of the commodities for sale must have been produced in the country itself. § The salt industry engaged

* *MER.* 473 of 1921; 41 of 1922.

† *Aṭṭhavaṇa Tantram*: *MMss.* 15-6-8.

‡ *EC.* xi. Mk. 1; *LR.* 3 (Cadipirēla) p. 426.

§ The *Śukasaptati* (2: 416-19; 421.) describes spinning in the houses of the farmers. Women of several houses joined together, bringing with them their spinning wheel, combed cotton, and proceeded to spin narrating scandalous stories.

గీ॥ దివసమంత వితాపోయె నవుర రారె ।
గుంపునంపున లేకుండ గుండుపోగు।
గాఁ బదాఱింటి తరమును గాఁగ నూలు।
వడకరే యంచు నొండొరు లొన్నడివి కొనుచు ॥

క॥ వడి దారము చెవులుం ద్రో ।
కుక్కడు పలుకయు దిండు కదురు గుంజలునుం ద్రో॥
కుక్కడు బొమ్మయునుం ద్రిప్పుడు ।
పుడకయునుం గలుగు రాట్నముల నై కొనుచుఁ ॥

the attention of several people not only on the sea-coast but also in the interior. The information available on the subject pertains to the manufacture of salt in the inland districts of the empire. Two Markkāṇam grants record gifts of salt-pans to a temple;* two more grants from the Canarese districts register the remission of taxes which the salt makers had to pay to the government.† One of them contains regulations subject to which the salt makers had to remove the saline earth.‡ The reference to saline earth is interesting, as it gives us a hint about the manner of manufacturing salt in inland places. The salt makers used to remove saline earth from the waste land belonging to the government. They spread them on the surface of pans specially prepared for them, and let into the pans water which was allowed to evaporate slowly. Finally, the salt which remained in crystals on the surface of the pans was collected and marketed.§ The same method was probably employed with the necessary modifications, in manufacturing salt on the sea-coast.

గీ॥ ఎడమ దెస దొడ్డుగా వైచి యేకులెల్లఁ । గెలనఁబలువుగ వేఁపుచు గింజ లునిచి ।
చేప పీఁటల మీద నాసీనులైన । వారలై వావివరుసలు వదరి కొనుచు ॥

సీ॥ గుంపునంపును లేక కొనసాగ బ్రోగువెంట మెఱుంగుజూపు పేరెములు వార।
బ్రాయంపుపడుచుల పనిగొంటివే దూదియనెడి పాటలదేనె చినుకు లీనఁ ।
నేకుతోఁ జెలఁగు కేలెత్తుచో భుజమూలకాంతులు బయలు బంగారు సేయ ।
బుడుకఁ ద్రిప్పెడు రయంబునఁ బైటజారుచో మినుకుగుబ్బలు తళుక్కని రహింప
మడిచికొన్నట్టి తెలిగంజి మడతచీర లరిది తొడనిగ్గుచే పసు పంటినట్లు
పొసఁగఁ జరణాభ్ర త్రొక్కుచు బొమ్మమీద బచ్చెన ఘటింప వడికి రప్పద్మముఖులు

గీ॥ ఎన్నికలు పట్టిపుంజంబు లేర్పరించి । పంటకఱ్ఱలు మఱి తోడుపడగ లూచ
కండె లొనరించి చాలించి కాపుటింతు । లున్న యవ్వేళ యద్భుతం బుట్టిపడఁగ

* *MER.* 41, 46 of 1919.

† *EC.* xi. Mk. 8, 9.

‡ *ibid* Mk. 8.

§ cf. *Aṭṭhavaṇa Tantram* : *MMss.* 15-6-8.

The iron that was needed for all purposes was produced within the empire itself. It was not one of the articles that was imported from abroad. On the contrary, it was produced in such large quantities that the people not only satisfied their own wants, but exported it to foreign countries. * Iron is said to have been one of the articles exported from Citradurga. It was extracted from two sources. Stones containing iron ore were brought and pounded into powder which was then smelted in large furnaces. Another method appears to have been more popular. Fine particles of ore deposited on the beds of streamlets in the hilly tracts were collected ; and the ore so collected was smelted in huge furnaces erected for the purpose in jungles where fuel could be had abundantly. †

The principal mineral that was dug out of the earth was the diamond. The most important mines were 'in the Kurnool and Anantapūr districts, notably at Vajra Karūr.' Linschoten says :

> "They (diamonds) grow, "in the countrie of Decam behinde Ballagate, by the towne of Bisnagar, wherein are two or three hills, from whence they are digged, whereof the King of Bisnagar doth reape great profitte ; for he causeth them to be straightly watched, and hath farmed them out with this condition, that all diamonds that are above twenty-five *Mangellyns* in weight are for the King himself." ‡

According to Nuniz diamonds came from the country of Gutti. Adapanayaque, the lord of the country, paid to the emperor forty thousand *pardoas* every year ; but he had to hand over to the imperial treasury 'all diamonds which exceed twenty *mangelins*.' §

* *Barbosa* i. p. 188. † cf. *Aṭṭhavaṇa Tantram* : *MMss.* 15-6-8.

‡ *FE.* App. A. p. 399 ; *Linschoten* p. 136.

§ *FE.* p. 389.

Section 5: *The Guilds*:—The merchant guilds played an important part in the commercial life of the people. Most of the internal trade of the country passed through their hands, and their activities seem to have extended all over the empire. These guilds were generally known by the name of 'the several *Ayyāvaḷi Cālumūlas* of the fifty six countries.' They also styled themselves occasionally as "the several *Ayyāvaḷi Cālumūlas*, both native and foreign *Nānādēsis*, of the fifty six countries." * The occurrence of this name in the inscriptions in different parts of the empire may, at first sight, seem to indicate the existence of a huge mercantile corporation doing business everywhere; but this is not the truth. 'The several *Ayyāvaḷi Cālumūlas* etc.,' was a common name by which the merchant guilds were generally known everywhere. The existence of a guild of this name in almost every town of the empire is indicated by the letter which 'the several *Ayyāvaḷi Cālumūlas*' of Yāḍaki addressed to 'the several *Ayyāvaḷi Cālumūlas* of Tāḍpatri.' † The *Vīra-Baṇjigas* probably constituted themselves into a separate guild, and had their organizations in all the important commercial centres. Although the information supplied by the inscriptions is meagre, it is still possible to form an idea of the constitution and the functions of these corporations. The merchant guild of each city had a president called *paṭṭaṇaswāmi* or *seṭṭi-paṭṭaṇaswāmi*, who appears to have been its executive officer. The members met usually in the front-hall of a temple whenever they had any business to transact. The full insignia of the guild was paraded, specially the diamond *baisāṇige* without which no meeting of the guild could be valid.

* *LR.* 55 (Sirivoḷḷa.) p. 286.

† *LR.* 37 (Niṭṭūr) p. 313.

Each merchant guild had certain powers of taxation, as it was directly responsible to the imperial government for the payment of taxes due from its members. Therefore, the president collected the dues from the members and remitted them to the Rāya or his officers. When the Rāya and his officers desired to alienate these dues in favour of a temple or some other religious institution, they had to obtain the consent of the guild or the *seṭṭi-paṭṭaṇaswāmi.* * Moreover, the guild had the right of imposing taxes on its members, whenever there was a need for it to do so. Generally, it imposed duties on the goods sold by its members for the benefit of some temple or *maṭha*, and granted a charter called *maghava-sādhaka* or *paṭṭa* † describing the nature of the gift, to the donee. The guild was not infrequently obliged to enter into agreements with the road *kāvalgārs*, in order to protect the life and property of its members who happened to be trading with the distant parts of the empire. In order to remunerate the *kāvalgār*, the guild granted him a *maghava-sādhaka* or charter, promising to pay him dues on the goods in transit. Lastly, the merchants were also required to discharge certain judicial duties. The several *Ayyāvaḷi Cālumūlas* were frequently required by the officers of the king to constitute themselves into a court of justice and try cases involving disputes about the ownership of property. Generally they seemed to have tried cases and settled disputes, without the assistance of any outside body; ‡ but on occasions, when the settlement of a dispute required an expert knowledge of law, they used to refer the case to the provincial governor who would entrust its trial to a *dharmāsana* of the *vidvan-mahājanas* of one or more *agrahāras*.

* *MER.* 681 of 1922.

† *LR.* 18 (Vāmanūr) pp. 63-4.

‡ *LR.* 55 (Pērūr) p. 283.

The Mahānāḍu:—It is stated in an inscription of Hospet dated 1535 A.D., that the *seṭṭi-paṭṭaṇaswāmis* of certain suburbs of Vijayanagara viz., Tirumaladēviyār-paṭṭaṇa, Vardājammanapaṭṭaṇa and Kṛṣṇāpura, and the *Mahānāḍu* gave their consent to a grant of the *mūla-vīsas* to the shrine of Tiruvengaḷanātha made by Abbarāju Timmappa. * It is evident that each of the suburbs of the capital had its own merchant guild; and what is of greater interest is that the donor had to obtain its consent as well as that of another body called *Mahānāḍu Dēśvara.* The meaning of these terms is not quite intelligible. *Dēśvara* may denote the class to which the merchants belonged; and *Mahānāḍu* may be understood as the conference or the meeting of all the merchants belonging to that class. It is only reasonable that the donor should have obtained the consent not only of the presidents of the guilds, but of the general body of the merchants in order to secure permanence to his benefaction.

Craft Guilds:—The artisans engaged in each industry had their own separate organizations. The existence of the craft guilds in Vijayanagara is attested by the evidence of Abdur Razāk, the earliest of the foreign writers, who left behind him an account of the city. "The tradesmen of each separate guild or craft", says he, "have their shops close to one another." † Paes, another foreign writer, alludes to the confraternity of craftsmen and merchants. ‡ Kṛṣṇarāya perhaps alludes to the guilds of weavers, goldsmiths, weavers of silk-cloth, *Kōmaṭis*, *Vaijātis*, gunny-bag makers, basket makers, etc. § Inscriptions frequently allude to another craft guild called the *Pāñcālas*

* *MER.* 681 of 1922. † *ED.* iv. p. 107.

‡ *FE.* p. 256. § *Ām.* 4: 35.

or the *Pāñcahaṇamvāru* *; the *Uppararu* or the manufacturers of salt † had also probably organized themselves into a guild. A careful study of the inscriptions, may reveal the existence of many more.

No information is available about the regulations according to which these guilds conducted business. Probably they collected dues from the members, and spent the money for promoting the common welfare. They might have been also allowed to make laws for the guidance of the members, and punished the offenders by the imposition of fine or excommunication. These are only conjectures about the probable nature of the activities of these guilds, and they may have to be modified in the light of future research.

There is reason to believe that these craft guilds were subordinate to the merchant guilds. An inscription at Vāmanūru in the Cuddapah district dated 1536 A.D., records the grant of some dues on the looms of the Pennabaḍi, Mulkināḍ, Rēnāḍ, Sakilisīma, Awuku, Kōilkunṭla, Pedanandēla and Pulivendala by 'the several *seṭṭis* of the fifty six countries' to the presiding monk of the *maṭha* at Śrīsaila. ‡ This epigraph seems to indicate that there existed a merchant guild having jurisdiction over a wide area, comprising nine sub-divisions of the district of Gaṇḍikōṭa. However, it is not possible to assert definitely that the craft guilds were controlled by merchant guilds, until more evidence of a reliable character is brought to light.

* *LR.* 18 (Vonṭimiṭṭa) pp. 404-5.

† *EC.* xi. Mk. 8, 9.

‡ *LR.* 18 (Vāmanūru) pp. 63-4.

PART III

RELIGIOUS AND SOCIAL CONDITIONS.

Chapter I

RELIGIOUS CONDITIONS.

Section 1: The Religious Policy of the State:—The religion which found favour with the emperors of Vijayanagara during the 16th century was Vaiṣṇavism; but it never became the religion of the state, which, however, did not assume an attitude of neutrality in religious affairs. The state did not divorce itself from the religious and social activities of its subjects; on the contrary, it identified itself with all the communities of the empire, and extended its patronage to all sects alike.

The foundation of the religious policy adopted by the emperors in the 16th century was laid down by Bukka I about the middle of the 14th century. The spirit of fanaticism which had a strong hold upon the popular mind as a consequence of the Vīra Śaiva, and Vīra Vaiṣṇava propaganda was still vigorous. And the religious dissensions emphasizing separatist tendencies which proved disastrous, at the time of Mussalman invasions, appeared to revive. Only a few people could rise above the sectarian prejudice, and they protested against the intolerant tyranny of the narrow-minded theologians. It was fortunate that the founders of the Vijayanagara empire came under the influence of the eminent Advaita philosopher, Mādhavācārya-Vidyāraṇya. As a true Advaitin he had the breadth of vision to comprehend that all religions were so many ways leading ultimately to the supreme reality, the *Brahman*. He understood the true import of the *Gīta*, and had sympathy with the expression of genuine religious feeling, wherever he found it. He made his influence felt by his imperial disciples whom he taught to regard all sects alike. They built temples to Śiva and Viṣṇu, and extended their patronage even to the Jains. They set their face resolutely against religious strife, and did not suffer one sect to persecute another. Taking advantage of a quarrel between the Vaiṣṇavas and the Jains, Bukka I laid down the religious policy of the state in an edict, the copies of which he had engraved on stone in several important places :

> " The Jainas of all the nāḍs of Ānegondi, Hosapaṭṭaṇa, Penugoṇḍe, and Kalyaha, made petition to him (Bukka I) that the *bhaktas* (*Vaiṣṇavas*) were unjustly killing them,...... the king, thereupon, summoned before him representatives of the Śrī Vaiṣṇavas of Eighteen nāḍs, including the *Ācāryas* of Kōvil (Srīrangam), Tirumale, (Tirupati), Perumāḷkōvil (Kāñci), Tirunārāyaṇapuram (Mēlukōṭe) with the other members of the sect ...and, proclaiming that he would not countenance their unjust proceedings against the Jains or allow themselves to shelter themselves under the plea of religion, —— passed the following decree :—That to the Jains the use of certain musical instruments customary among them was to be confined to the five bastis (not mentioned), and disallowed in others." *

In another version of the same edict, the king declared that there was no difference whatever, ' between the *Vaiṣṇava-darśana*, and the *Jaina-darśana.*' He ' took the hand of the Jains, and placing it in the hand of the Vaiṣṇavas issued his decree.'† This edict laid down the fundamental principles on which the religious policy of the state was to be based. The spirit of the edict was liberally interpreted by the later monarchs so as to include within its scope all the creeds including Islam. Although the Muslim rulers bitterly persecuted their Hindu subjects, on account of their religion, no instance of a Vijayanagara emperor or his subordinate illtreating Muslims

* *EC.* ix. Intr. p. 24; cf. *EC.* ix. Ma. 18. † *ibid* ii. SB. 344.

for religious differences is recorded. The attitude of the emperors was not one of passive indifference. They extended their patronage to Muslim religious institutions. Dēvarāya II built a mosque in his capital for the benefit of his Mussalman soldiers. * The policy which the state followed in religious matters was so shaped as to secure the concord of all the religions of the empire; and this policy was completely in harmony with the views of the rulers of the 16th century. Kṛṣṇadēvarāya, the greatest emperor of Vijayanagara, allowed perfect liberty to all his subjects. Although a staunch Vaiṣṇava, he showed considerable regard for the Śaiva religion. One of his earliest acts was to repair, and partly rebuild, the temple of Virūpākṣa at Hampi. He made several gifts to the Vaiṣṇava as well as the Śaiva temples. The temples of Tirupati, Kāñci, Simhācalam and Ahōbalam as well as those of Tiruvaṇṇāmalai, Cidambaram, Kāḷahasti, Śrīśailam and Amarāvati received liberal grants of land from him. He employed the Vaiṣṇava as well as the Smārta Brahmans in his service. The Jains found in him a monarch who offered them protection. A Vīra Śaiva chief of the Lingāyat community called Śānta Linga, massacred several Śvētāmbara Jain priests with the object of paving his way to the Kailāsa. † Kṛṣṇarāya did not, however, like the shedding of blood in the name of religion. At his instance, the Velugōṭi chief, Gani Timmā Nāyaḍu, attacked the bigotted Lingāyat and slew him. ‡ This must have taught the necessary lesson to all the religious propagandists that the days of violence were over. The Hindus were not the only people who reaped the benefits of his religious policy. The Muhammadans, Christians and Jews,

* Brigg's *Ferishta* ii. p. 431. † *MER.* 1915 p. 93 Appendix C. 16.

‡ *VV. MMss.* 15-4-3.

who resided in his dominions, were treated in the same way. Barbosa says:

"The king allows, such freedom that every man may come and go, and live according to his own creed without suffering any annoyance, and without enquiry, whether he is a Christian, Jew, Moor or Heathen. Great equity and justice is observed by all." *

The policy of Kṛṣṇarāya was continued unaltered during the reign of Acyuta. Like his brother, he made gifts to Brahmans of all sects. He did not show any partiality to the temples of Viṣṇu of whom he was a sincere devotee. The temples of Śiva at Kāḷahasti and Kāñci were enriched by his gifts of land. That the spirit of toleration pervaded the whole Hindu community is shown by an epigraph recording the construction of a mosque by a pious Hindu for the benefit of the Mussalmans. † The most enlightened person of the age was the famous Rāmarāja, the son-in-law of Kṛṣṇarāya. Like most of his contemporaries he was a very devoted Vaiṣṇava. In order to reconcile his Muslim soldiers, "to the act of making obeisance to him, he caused the *Korān* to be placed before him, when they came to pay their respects." He allowed them to build mosques, and to observe all their religious rites, as if they were residing in a Mussalman state. The pursuance of such a liberal policy towards the Muhammadans created a strong opposition to Rāmarāja. On one occasion, when the Muhammadans sacrificed cows in a mosque in the Turukavāḍa of the city, the nobles and officers became so excited over the matter, that, led by Tirumala, a brother of Rāmarāja,

* *Barbosa* i. p. 202.

† *EC.* iv. Kp. 72 (date 1537) "Rangai-Nāyak-ayya, in order to endow the stone *masiti* (mosque) which Bābu Seṭṭi had erected in the inner street of Sindaghaṭṭa, made a grant for it of the village of Śivapura, and Habība's house."

they made very strong representations to Rāmarāja exhorting him to prohibit the Muhammadans from slaughtering the cows. Rāmarāja, however, did not yield to them ; but told them that he was the master of the bodies of his soldiers, and not of their souls. Further, he pointed out that it would not be wise to interfere with their religious practices.* The firmness, which he exhibited on this occasion, was indeed remarkable, as the opposition was led by one of his own brothers. The nobles, who wanted to show Rāmarāja the foolishness of his attitude towards the Muhammadans went away convinced that there was wisdom in it.

The religious begotism, which temporarily took possession of the Hindu mind in the 12th and 13th centuries, began to wane even before the foundation of Vijayanagara, and it completely disappeared before the first Tuluva monarch seized the throne of the city of victory. The 16th century may be justly described as the age of enlightened rulers.

Section 2: Religious Conditions:—The most active form of Hindu religion during the 16th century was Vaiṣṇavism. The accession of Sāḷuva Narasimha to the throne of Vijayanagara gave a great impetus to the expansion of Vaiṣṇavism over the whole of South India. Sāḷuva Narasimha was greatly devoted to the God Venkaṭēśa of Tirupati which became the most important centre of Vaiṣṇavism in the 15th and 16th centuries.

The Vaiṣṇavas of this period fall into two classes : (i) the Śrī Vaiṣṇavas or the followers of Rāmānuja ; and (ii) the Mādhwas or the followers of Madhwa, the famous dualist philosopher. There was much in com-

* *JBBRAS*. xxii. p. 28.

mon between the two sects, although there were some differences between them in their theology, dogmas of faith, and rules of conduct. Of the two sects, Śrī Vaiṣṇavas may be said to be more liberal in their general outlook and principles. Therefore, their creed had greater attraction for the masses than Madhwaism, which never became popular outside a small section of the Brahman community.

At the commencement of the 16th century, the Śrī Vaiṣṇavas had able leaders who were men of considerable learning. They were men of great tact, and possessed much skill in carrying on religious propaganda. According to the Telugu literary tradition, a Śrī Vaiṣṇava teacher called Tātācārya was the *guru* or spiritual adviser of Kṛṣṇadēvarāya. * Who this Tātācārya was, it is difficult to say. The *jīyars* of the Ahōbalam *maṭha*, appear to have played an important part in extending the influence of Vaiṣṇavism. Vān-Saṭhakōpa *jīyar*, the founder of the *maṭha* seems to have

* cf. *LR.* 7 (Cintaguṇṭa) p. 47.

యీ ప్రకారం వుండగా విద్యానగర సింహాసనాధీశ్వరులయిన వీర శ్రీ కృష్ణరాయ మహారాజులు రాజ్యము యేలుచూవుండి రాయలవారికి ఆచార్యులయిన శ్రీవైష్ణవులు శఠమర్షణ గోత్రోద్భవులయిన ఆపస్తంబ సూత్ర యజుశ్శాఖాధ్యాయులయిన తాతాచార్యుల అయ్యవార్లగారికి సర్వాగ్రహారంగా పాలూరు గ్రామం దత్తం చేసినారు.

There appear to have flourished two or three people bearing the name of Tātācārya during the first half of the 16th century. A copy of a copper-plate grant noticed in the *Mys. Arch. Rep.* for 1918 p. 52 mentions Venkaṭa-Tātārya [of *Śaṭhamarṣaṇagōtra Āpastamba sūtra, yajus śākha* son of Ahōbaḷācārya son of Śrīraṅgadēśika] on whom Kṛṣṇarāya conferred some privileges in 1522 A. D. A Kumāra Tatācārya of the same *sūtra, gōtra* and *śākha* figures in an inscription of Sadāśivarāya at Tirupati dated 1542. A. D. (*Tirupati-Dēvasthānam Epigraphical Report* p. 259). The sons of a Nala Tātācārya are mentioned in a grant of Sadāśiva's time dated 1569. A. D. Probably, the first two records refer to the same person.

been closely in touch with the religious life in the court. He was the *guru* of the great poet Allasāni Peddana, the poet laureate of Kṛṣṇadēvarāya. It is said that this Saṭhakōpa *jīyar* was 'an asylum of all learning', and 'dispeller of the thick darkness of sins of his disciples through the moonlight of his looks'.* According to a passage in the *Āmuktamālyada*, he carried on vigorous propaganda in the Āndhra country, where he firmly established the *Vaiṣṇava* faith. † But the work of spreading the gospel was not performed exclusively by great teachers like Saṭhakōpa *jīyar*. Several Śrī Vaiṣṇava families made the preaching of the religion of Viṣṇu their life-work. Of these the Kandāḍai and the Paravastu families appear to have secured a greater number of disciples than the others. ‡ As a consequence of the proselytising activity of the teachers, Vaiṣṇavism became the most influential religion of the country.

Although the influence of the Mādhwas was not so widespread as that of the Śrī Vaiṣṇavas, it was by no means negligible. Brahmaṇyatīrtha, Vyāsatīrtha and their disciples attempted to popularise the teachings of Madhwa. They were considerably helped in this by the great saint Purandaradāsa, who is said to have been one of the converts of Vyāsatīrtha. The greatest exponent of Mādhwaism was, no doubt, the famous Vyāsatīrtha himself, who may be considered as the second founder of that religion. According to tradition Vyāsa was in his early days attached to the *maṭha* at Mulbāgal, whence he migrated to Candragiri, the capital of Sāḷuva Narasimha, on the advice of his *guru*

**Mc.* 1: 6. † *Ām.* 6: 66.

‡ Several Telugu writers of this and the succeeding periods claim members of one or other of these two families as their *gurus*.

Brahmaṇyatīrtha. He stayed at Tirupati, probably at the bidding of Sāḷuva Narasimha, for a period of twelve years, during which he is said to have functioned as the *pūjāri* of the temple of Venkaṭēśa. When Narasimha usurped the imperial throne and removed the seat of his government to Vijayanagara, Vyāsatīrtha followed him thither. After the demise of Narasimha, he became the spiritual adviser of the succeeding emperors. He is said to have acquired much influence over Kṛṣṇadēvarāya. It is said that, on one occasion during Kṛṣṇarāya's reign, there occurred a conjunction of stars known as the *kuhuyōga*. It was believed that the Rāya would die, if he occupied the throne at that time. In order to avert this calamity, Kṛṣṇarāya is said to have placed on the throne Vyāsatīrtha, who became for the time being the emperor of Vijayanagara. To commemorate this event, Vyāsa assumed the title of *rāya* and consequently he became known as Vyāsarāya. *

No authentic information is available regarding the early career of Vyāsa. No doubt, he figures in half a dozen inscriptions all of which unfortunately belong to the reign of Kṛṣṇadēvarāya. They throw little or no light on the events connected with his early history. The inscriptions, however, leave no room for doubt regarding the place which he occupied in the estimation of Kṛṣṇarāya. The Rāya had a very great regard for him on account of his vast learning, skill in debate, and his saintly character. He granted him some villages to meet the expenses of a *maṭha* which he established in one of the suburbs of the capital. Vyāsa survived Kṛṣṇarāya ; and he is said to have retired from Vijayanagara to some village in the neighbourhood, owing, probably, to the changed atmosphere at the court ; but he returned to the city in 1532 A.D., in order

* B. Venkoba Rao : *Vyāsayōgicaritam* Introduction : p. 87 ff.

'to set up the image of Yōga-Varada Narasimhaswāmi in the court-yard of the Viṭṭhala temple at Hampi.'* He appears to have breathed his last a little later. "Even to-day," says the epigraphist, "the pious pilgrim who goes to the Pampākṣetra (Hampi) is shown the tomb of this great religious teacher, and scholar on an island called '*Navabṛndāvana*' in the Tungabhadrā river about half a mile to the east of Ānegondi." † In spite of the efforts of Vyāsatīrtha, Mādhwaism did not evoke popular enthusiasm. The only contribution which it made to popular religion was to give an exaggerated importance to the worship of Hanumān. A few Brahmans and fewer nobles ‡ accepted the teachings of Madhwa; and although the latter had long ago disappeared, the former still uphold the tenets of the faith with great zeal and enthusiasm. The influence which Mādhwaism wielded declined rapidly after Kṛṣṇarāya's death; and it does not appear to have played any prominent part in the religion of the subsequent period.

The reigns of Acyuta and Sadāśiva were very favourable for the growth of Śrī Vaiṣṇavism; kings, ministers and nobles vied with one another, in extending their patronage on a lavish scale to Vaiṣṇavas and their religious institutions. It is no wonder that as a

* *MER.* 710 of 1922. † *MER.* 1923 para 84.

‡ Periya-Rāmappa, Acyuta's governor of Madura, was a disciple of Vyāsatīrtha.

"ప్రియబంధు వ[illegible]చైత్ర పిప్పాలగోత్ర
దయ సత్య దాక్షిణ్య ధర్మస్వరూప
తగమించు వ్యాసతీర్థ ప్రియశిష్య
విలసిల్లు పెదరామ విభవ సుత్రామ"

CC. (Triennial Catalogue of Telugu Mss.)

consequence of this support, it became the most dominant faith in the empire of Vijayanagara.*

The support of the state, however, was not monopolised by Vaiṣṇavism. A large majority of the emperor's subjects were Śaivas or Smārtas. The emperors assumed, as noticed already, a tolerant attitude towards them, built temples for them and endowed them with grants of money and lands.

One aspect of the religion of the age is not usually touched upon. The part played by the *maṭhas* and the temples in the religious life of the people is generally ignored by writers on Vijayanagara history. The *maṭhas* may be broadly divided into three classes (1) the Śaiva, (2) the Vaiṣṇava and (3) the Jain.

(1) The *maṭhas* belonging to the Śaivas may be further divided into two classes: (a) the Brahmanic, and (b) the non-Brahmanic. (a) A section of the Brahmanic *maṭhas* traces its origin either to the great philosopher Śankara, or to one of his disciples. The most important *maṭha* belonging to this class was, of course, the *maṭha* at Śṛṅgēri which had very close and intimate relations with the state. Branches of this *maṭha* were established at Puṣpagiri, Virūpākṣam, and Kumbhakōṇam. The monks attached to these *maṭhas* studied exclusively the Brahmanic or the Vēdic literature. They were strict Advaitins in philosophy; and they taught their disciples to follow the *ācāra* approved by the *Smṛtis* and *Śrutis*. Several Brahmanic Śaiva *maṭhas*, especially in the Tamil districts, were not devoted to the study of the Advaita philosophy. The monks who resorted to these *maṭhas* studied a species of Śaiva theology called *Pāśupata-siddhāntam*, hence they were generally known

* cf. *MER.* 1915 para 48; *ibid* 1923 para 85.

as the Pāśupatas. One of their important centres was Dēvikāpuram where three of their establishments, the Bhikṣāvṛtti *maṭha*, the Mallikārjunayyan *maṭha*, and the Gōḷakī *maṭha* flourished in the sixteenth century.* A branch of the Bhikṣāvṛtti *maṭha* called the *Kallār maḍam* also flourished in the extreme south of the peninsula at Pīrānmalai in the Ramnad district. † It is not unlikely that the Pāśupatas had similar monasteries in many other places in the empire.

(b) The non-Brahmanic Śaiva *maṭhas* belonged to two types (i) the Lingāyat and (ii) the non-Lingāyat.

(i) Several *maṭhas* belonging to the Lingāyats were in existence all over the Telugu and the Canarese districts, the most important of them being those at Śrī-śailam, Sangamēśwaram and Ummattūr. These *maṭhas* were constituted specially to propagate the tenets of Lingāyatism as propounded by the Vīra Śaiva reformer Basava in the 12th century. The monks of these *maṭhas* spent their time in the study of the *āgamas*, and allied literature which came into being since the days of Basava. They chose the vernacular languages rather than Sanskrit in preaching the gospel of Basava.

(ii) Nothing is known from the inscriptions of the non-Lingāyat Śaiva *maṭhas* which exercise a good deal of influence in the religious life of the Tamil country at present. The *maṭhas* at Tiruvāḍuturai, Dharmāvaram and Tiruppanandal which are said to be the most ancient Śaiva monasteries in the Tamil country must have existed during the age of the Rāyas. The monks of these *maṭhas* must have concentrated their attention more or less exclusively on the Śaiva *āgamas*, Śaiva *purāṇas* and the hymns composed by the *Nāyanmārs*

* *MER.* 354, 375, 400 of 1912. † *ibid* 193 of 1924.

or the Śaiva saints. They must have specialised in and taught the *Śaiva siddhānta*, which is said to approximate very nearly to the Pāśupata system. The study of the Sanskrit language and literature could not have had much attraction for them as for the inmates of the other *maṭhas*. They must have encouraged the study of Tamil which they chose as the vehicle of their thought.

(2) The *maṭhas* belonging to the Vaiṣṇava sect fall into two classes: (*a*) The Śrī Vaiṣṇava, and (*b*) the Mādhwa.

(a) The Śrī Vaiṣṇava, *maṭhas* can be divided into two classes, corresponding to the two main sects of the Śrī Vaiṣṇava community, the *Vaḍahalai*, and the *Tengalai*. The *Vaḍahalai maṭhas* were found at Ahōbalam,* Tirupati, † and Śrīrangam; Mēlkōṭe, ‡ and Vānamāmalai § were the most influential of the *Tengalai maṭhas*. There is not much difference between the two sects of the Śrī Vaiṣṇavas. The *Vaḍahalais* give greater prominence to the Vēdas than to the hymns of the Āḻwārs, whereas the *Tengalais* prefer the *Prabandhas* to the Vēdic literature. Consequently, in the *Vaḍahalai maṭhas*, Sanskrit language and literature, Vēdic hymns and the *Upaniṣads* were largely studied, although the study of the *Prabandhas* was not altogether neglected. In *Tengalai maṭhas* the study of the hymns and *Prabandhas* of Āḻwārs engrossed the attention of the religious.

(b) As the Mādhwas exclusivey followed the *Vaidika ācāra*, a study of the Vēdas, the *Upaniṣads*, the *Dharma śāstras*, and the *Purāṇas* became incumbent on

* *MER*. 534 of 1915. † *TDER*. pp. 211, 248.

‡ *ibid* p. 276. § *MER*. 258 of 1927-28.

them. In this respect they differed very much from the Śrī Vaiṣṇavas. Their principal *maṭhas* were found at Uḍipi, Mulbāgal, and Vijayanagara.

(3) Although Jainism was already a religion of the past, it still lurked in certain localities in the country. The Tuluva *rājya* had the largest Jain population in the empire; Śrāvaṇa Beḷagoḷa, the most popular religious centre of the Jains, was situated in this province. There was a monastery here, the monks of which studied the scriptures and the allied literature pertaining to their faith. Another Jain *maṭha* was also found at Conjeevaram in the Paḷaivīḍu *rājya*, though it was in a decadent condition.

The constitution of the *maṭhas* to whichever sect they might have belonged was strictly based upon the monarchic principle. The head of the *maṭha* was the absolute ruler of the institution, and his authority was not subject to any kind of check. The monks belonging to the *maṭha* had no voice in its government, and they were completely under the control of the head. They had no hand even in choosing a successor to the *mathādhipati*, as he had power to nominate his own successor from among his disciples.

All the *maṭhas* were centres of learning. The monks studied and taught not only the scriptures of their respective creeds but also secular literature. They not only taught laymen to read and write, but gave them instruction in arts, literature, and medicine. The burden of educating the community partly rested on the *maṭhas*; and they seem to have given satisfaction to the people in discharging their duties. The emperor extended his patronage to all institutions alike, irrespective of the sects to which they belonged. The learned of all the communities were treated with equal respect, and no partiality was shown in rewarding them on the score of their faith.

The *mathas* may be said to have catered to the intellectual needs of the community. The monks who spent their lives in the study and contemplation of theological and philosophical problems must have given satisfaction to the head rather than the heart. Although the monks came frequently into contact with the masses, they could not completely satisfy their religious needs. Therefore, the people turned to another important religious institution *viz.*, the temple which gave full scope for the expression of their religious emotions.

Section 3: The Temple:—The rise of religions like Vaiṣṇavism, and Lingāyatism which inculcated the belief in a personal god whose service was considered one of the chief means of obtaining salvation, gave a fresh impetus to temple building. The emperors of Vijayanagara and their subordinates built hundreds of new temples, repaired several old ones, and endowed them richly with lands and money so that the daily worship might be carried on in them without interruption. The gods in whose honour these temples were built, were believed to have the same needs as persons occupying exhalted stations in life such as kings and princes. Therefore, the person who built a temple made careful provision for satisfying all the wants which its divine resident might be supposed to feel. As at the palaces of kings and princes, musicians were required to sing songs in praise of the deity and play upon their instruments in the early hours of the morning to rouse him or her from slumber. The *arcaka* had to give the idols a bath, and dress them properly, before he offered them food. In the evening, the musicians were required to entertain the deity by their music both instrumental and vocal; and the courtesans had to dance before him. Flowers, sandal paste, and scents were needed for his worship; and very fine and costly jewels were required for adorning him and his consort. Even to carry on the ordinary daily worship of the temple, the services of several people were needed. The pipers who were invariably drawn from the barber community, * the dancing women, † the *arcaka*, ‡ the flower gardener, § the sandal paste grinder, ¶ the lamp lighter, ‖ and several other menial servants had to co-operate in looking after the comforts of the deity presiding over a temple. Besides, there were monthly festivals ** during which the god and his consort had to be taken in a procession through the principal streets of the city or the village. The *Brahmōtsava* or the annual festival had to be performed for ten days continuously on a grand scale. All these involved heavy expenditure of money. The service in the temple was costly; but, as it made a direct appeal to the imagination of the people owing to its impressive character, many came forward to pay willingly the expenses of the gods, however heavy they might be. The temple endowments did not always come from the Rāya and his nobles. Ordinary men and women made grants of land and money to gods in order to acquire merit for

* *LR.* 13 (Pedakōḍūru) p. 295.

† *TDER.* p. 225.

‡ *LR.* 15 (Pulimadya, Nandyāl Tq.,) p. 370; *LR.* 40 (Nandyāl) pp. 209-10.

§ *TDER.* p. 32.

¶ *LR.* 15 (Ayyalūru) pp. 353-4.

‖ *ibid* 14 (Puṣpagiri) p. 475; *ibid* 15 (Dommara Nandyāla) p. 82; *ibid* 2 (Pedaceppalli) p. 371.

** *LR.* 40 (Bētamcerla) p. 195.

themselves and their relations in the next world. The professional jugglers, the acrobats, and the courtesans surrendered willingly land and valuables to gods so that they and their kinsmen might enjoy the bliss of heaven.* The endowments, therefore, came from several sources. Mostly, they took the form of landed property, but money was also frequently donated. † The bigger and more famous the temple was, the richer were its endowments.

Now the endowments had to be properly managed by somebody on behalf of the gods, because they could not manage them without assistance. The property of the temple was managed by a board of trustees known as the *sthānikas*. The *Āmuktamālyada* mentions the *sthānikas* who were managing the temple at Śrīvilliputtūr. ‡ A record of Gaḍigirēla in the Kurnool district dated 1542 A.D., refers to the *sthānikas* of the local temple ; § the temple of Cennakēśava at Mārkāpūr was also managed by a board of *sthānikas* ; ¶ and properties of the temples of Śiva and Viṣṇu at Puṣpagiri were similarly under the control of the *sthānikas*. ‖ The *Srī Bhaṇḍāramvāru* mentioned in a Conjeevaram inscription dated 1535 A.D., must be regarded as the *sthānikas* of Varadarāja temple.** Examples of temples governed by a board of *sthānikas* may easily be multiplied. These, however, are enough to show that the temple properties were managed by trust boards.

* *MER*. 689, 694 of 1917 ; *LR*. 2. (Pedaceppalli) p. 372 ; *LR*. 2 (Koppōlu) pp 419-20 ; *LR*. 54. (Tāḷḷamārpuram) p. 6 ; *LR*. 15 (Beḍadūr) pp. 112-3 ; *LR*. 14 (Nosam) pp. 374-5

† *MER*. 1925 : *The Kāḷahasti Inscriptions* 152-3, 156, 160, 164, 166, 171, 180 ; 183 of 1924.

‡ *Ām*. 4 : 35.

§ *MMss*. 15-3-6.

¶ *LR*. 13. (Mārkāpūr) No. 7.

‖ *LR*. 14 (Puṣpagiri) p. 439

** *LR*. 55 (Kāñci) p. 424.

How did these trust boards originate? Were they appointed by the government or by the person or persons who built or endowed the temples with lands? The latter appears to be the way in which some of the boards had come into being. According to a record of 1523 A.D., the lands which were granted to the temple of Vīrabhadra at Hattalakōṭe were placed under the management of one Allappa, who became the permanent manager of the temple. * The office of the *sthānika* came to be regarded, in certain cases at least, as the hereditary property of the family. If the trustee, who had originally secured the office, had a number of sons, his office, after his death, was regarded as common property, and was divided equally among his sons. Thus, the place of a single trustee would be taken by a board of trustees within a generation or two. It is said in an inscription at Dēvaguḍi that the *sthānikas* were the six sons of one Cinnajiyya, who probably had held the trusteeship of the temple. † Although the trust boards of some of the temples had sprung up in this fashion, it is extremely unlikely that all of them have had a similar origin. Most of them probably were created by the government, one of whose principal duties was to look after the well-being of the temples.

It is not possible, at the present stage of our knowledge, to state the exact number of *sthānikas* comprising a board. The Dēvaguḍi epigraph, it is true, states that there were six *sthānikas* managing the affairs of the local temple; but, as they were sons of the same father, Cinnajiyya, its evidence cannot be relied upon in fixing the normal strength of the board of the *sthānikas* of the time. Each board of *sthānikas* had a president known as *sthānapati* or *sthānācārya*. The *sthānācāryas*

* *EC.* iv Ch. 99.

† *R.* 15 p. 82.

of Mārkāpūr, Ahōbalam,* and several other places are mentioned in inscriptions. No information is available regarding the duties of the *sthānācārya*, although it is reasonable to infer that he must have presided over the deliberations, and guided the general policy regarding the management of the temple property.

The Functions of the Sthānikas:—The *sthānikas*, administered lands and other properties belonging to the temple. They received gifts of money and land on behalf of the god.† They extended the temple estate by the acquisition of fresh lands by purchase; ‡ they disposed of the temple property when the ceremonies of the temple demanded ready money. § They gave loans probably on the security of lands, ¶ and also cancelled the debts by purchasing the mortgaged property.‖ They leased the temple properties to the ryots; ** and made *dasabandha* grants either for repairing or for rebuilding the temple. †† They invested the money deposited in the temple treasury by donors and others in a manner profitable to the temple. ‡‡ Lastly, the *sthānikas* had some judicial functions also; they investigated into cases involving the theft of temple properties and punished the culprits. §§

The *sthānikas* of temples were not completely free to manage the temple properties as they liked. They

* *LR.* 13 (Mārkāpuram) No 7; *LR.* 15 (Ahōbalam) pp. 434-5.

† *The Kāḷahasti Inscriptions*: *MER.* 1925

‡ *MER* 7 of 1922, *LR.* 36 (Vanipeṇṭa) pp. 485-6.

§ *ibid* 446 of 1921; 32 of 1921.

¶ *EC.* iv. Gu. 4.

‖ *MER.* 179 of 1924.

** *LR.* 55 (Kāñci) p. 424.

†† *LR.* 15 (Dēvaguḍi) p. 80.

‡‡ *The Kāḷahasti Inscriptions*: *MER.* 1925.

§§ *MER.* 185 of 1894; *SII* v. No. 479.

seem to have been under the control of the *sīma pāru-paiyagāra*, although exemption was occasionally granted in certain cases. * Officers called the overseers of the temple are mentioned in a Kambadūr grant of 1556 A.D. † The nature of the work which they performed is nowhere stated. It is not unlikely that they were government officials, probably belonging to the Religious Endowment Department, supervising the work of the *sthānikas* in administering temple properties.

The Temple Cāvaḍi:—Every temple had its own *cāvaḍi* or office, where one or more *karṇams* kept the accounts of its properties. The office of the *karṇam* was hereditary, although the appointment was made at first by the emperor or his provincial representative. For instance, Rāmarāja-Kōnēṭi-Timma, who was the governor of Udayagiri about 1552 A.D., appointed one Vīragangayya, as the hereditary *karṇam* of the temple of Raghunāyaka at Udayagiri. According to the grant recording his appointment, he was to maintain the accounts of the villages belonging to the temple, and of the dues on articles that were sold therein. In addition to these, he had probably to draft leases which the temple authorities granted to its tenants, and to keep the duplicates of the deeds in the temple office. He had also to keep a register describing the various kinds of taxes due to the temple treasury. His salary was fixed at 1 *varāha* a month or 12 *varāhas* in a year. Besides, he was entitled to get from the temple four *paḍis* of *prasādam* every day. ‡

The Income of the Temple:—The income of the temple was derived from two sources: (1) The grants of money made by pious donors from time to time; and

* *EC.* iv. Ch. 99. † *MER.* 94 of 1913.

‡ *LR.* 42 (Udayagiri) No. 13.

(2) Income from the landed estates which the founders, and renovators had given. The temple authorities seem to have claimed, at least in some places, three-fourths of the produce as the share of the temple, leaving only a fourth to the cultivator. * This may not indicate the exact proportion of the income in all the places in the empire. Their *dhanādāya* consisted of a number of dues which they collected from their tenants. They fell under eleven heads in the Mysore country. †

(1) *Tiruṇāla-kāṇike.*	(7) *Sollega.*
(2) *Haḷudu.*	(8) *Avudu.*
(3) *Hostu.*	(9) *Bēḍige.*
(4) *Grāmavecca.*	(10) *Bījavari.*
(5) *Biṭi.*	(11) *Solage.*
(6) *Birāḍa.*	

Roughly the same number of dues must have been collected by the temples in the other parts of the empire also. The temple authorities, at least in certain places, appear to have been considerate to their tenants. The trustees of the Varadarājaswāmi temple at Coñjeevaram reduced the temple share of the produce from three-fourths to two-thirds in 1535 A.D., owing to famine. ‡

The Pārupatyagār or Maṇiagār:—The executive officer of the temple was known as *pārupatyagāra.* Sometimes he is also spoken of as the *maṇiagār*. His duties are nowhere clearly stated. He probably supervised the servants of the temple, and distributed the *prasādas* among them. In addition to this, he might have been required to look after the cultivation of the temple lands, the repairs of irrigation tanks belonging

* *LR.* 55. (Kāñci) p. 424.

† *EC.* x. Mb. 172.

‡ *LR.* 55 (Kāñci) p. 424.

to the temple villages, and the collection of dues payable to the temple.

The Śrī Bhaṇḍāra :—The treasury of every shrine was known as the *Śrī Bhaṇḍāra*. The *Śrī Bhaṇḍāra* of the temple at Śrīvilliputtūr is mentioned in the *Āmukta-mālyada.* * The *Śrī Bhaṇḍāra* of other temples is alluded to in the inscriptions. † All the money which accrued to the temple from its estates and other 'sources' was deposited by the temple authorities in the vaults of the treasury. The money, however, was not allowed to remain idle. It was invested, as described already, by the *sthānikas* in a manner most profitable to the temple.

The temple was usually the place where the *dharmāsana* met. It appears to have been also the place where caste gatherings were held, for settling caste disputes. The caste elders also made money grants to the deity in the *maṇṭapa* of the temple. It is obvious that the temple played an important part in the social and religious activities of the people of cities and villages during the sixteenth century.

Section 4 : *The Village Deity* :—The worship of the village deities was as popular then as it is at present. Inscriptions give us occasionally a glimpse into this aspect of the religion of the people. A few taxes such as the *jātre* ‡ and the *mahārāja-prayōjanāla pannu* § were collected from certain localities to conduct the daily

* *Ām.* 2: 95.

† The *Śrī Bhaṇḍāra* of Varadarāja of Kāñci, *LR.* 55 p. 424 ; 1535.
The *Bhaṇḍāra* of Triambakadēva at Bommanahaḷḷi, *EC.* iv. Gu. 2; 1494.
The *Bhaṇḍāra* of Triambakadēva at Bommanahaḷḷi, *ibid* Gu. 4 ; 1535.
The *Bhaṇḍāra* of Cennarāya of Mārkāpūr, *LR.* 13 (Mārkāpūr) No. 7, 1515.
The temple treasury of Kāñci, *MER.* 472 of 1919 ; 1532.
The temple treasury of Tiruvāmattūr, *MER.* 7 of 1912 ; 1485.
The temple treasury at Kāḷahasti referred to in general *MER.* 1925 ; 1530-40.

‡ *EC.* v. Ag. 7.

§ *LR.* 15. (Gaṇḍikōṭa) p. 127.

worship and annual festivals of the village deities.* The worship of some of them was conducted in such a striking fashion that it attracted the attention even of the foreign travellers. In the capital there was a temple where several sheep were slaughtered every day. Paes states :

> "At the door of one of these (temples) they kill every day many sheep; for in all the city they do not kill any sheep for the use of the Heathen, or for sale in the markets, except at the gates of this pagoda. Of their blood they make sacrifices to the idol that is in the temple.......There is present at the slaughter of these beasts a *jōgi* who has charge of the temple, and as soon as they cut off the head of the sheep or goat, the *jōgi* blows a horn as a sign that the idol receives that sacrifice." †

The temple was evidently the home of one of the Seven Sisters; for no other deity could have been so very fond of blood and the services of a *jōgi*. The greatest festival at Vijayanagara was also celebrated in honour of Durgā whose manifestations, the Seven Sisters are. A large herd of buffaloes, and thousands of sheep and other cattle were butchered during the nine days of the *Mahānavami* festival to propitiate Durgā, ‡ and this butchery took place in the presence of the Rāya and his nobles.

The *jātra* of the village deity caused much excitement among the rural population. The women having anointed their heads in lukewarm oil, bathed in water mixed with the powder of turmeric. They put

* The tax for the performance of the *mahārāja-prayōjanālu* is invariably associated with the worship of Ankāḷammā or Ankāḷaparamēśvarī. The existence of Tallakanṭīśvarī, the famous goddess presiding over the destinies of the village of Dēvaguḍi in the Cuddapah district, is proved by a series of inscriptions ranging from the time of the Kalyāṇi Cāḷukyas to the eighteenth century.

† *FE*. p. 255.

‡ Nuniz gives an account of the number of beasts slaughtered during the *Mahānavami* festival :

"The first day," says he, "they kill nine male buffaloes and nine sheep and nine goats, and thenceforward they kill each day more, always doubling the number." (*FE*. p. 377). The following table gives an idea of the large number of cattle slaughtered during these festivals.

on new clothes, and visited the temple built in the fields outside the precincts of the village. The *Reḍḍis* of the neighbouring villages came to see the festival accompanied by their spouses. Goats were slaughtered on a liberal scale; liquor could be had in large quantities and the uproar caused by the low caste people filled the whole atmosphere. Several women came to the shrine to fulfil their vows; one of them swung by a hook which passed through her muscles fastened to a '*siḍle*-beam'; another plunged in a '*fire-river*' (*i.e.*, a long narrow pit filled with blazing coals); a third entered a *panḍirigunḍa* or circular pit of fire over which a temporary shed was put up; one woman danced upon a tender plantain leaf; and another offered the deity bits of flesh cut off from her shoulders. *

Some of the Portuguese travellers were so struck with the manner of fulfilment of these vows that they considered it worth their while to record their observations. Barbosa appears to have been present at a hook-swinging ceremony. He says:

"The women of this land are so bold in their idolatry, and do such marvels for the love of their gods, that it is a terrible

DAY.	BUFFALOES.	SHEEP.	GOATS.
1	9	9	9
2	18	18	18
3	36	36	36
4	72	72	72
5	144	144	144
6	288	288	288
7	576	576	576
8	1152	1152	1152
9	2304	2304	2304
Total	4599	4599	4599

The grand total:—13797.

These figures seem to be greatly exaggerated; for, they do not tally with the figures supplied by Paes. He refers to the slaughter of only buffaloes and sheep. The number of buffaloes sacrificed every day is said to be 24 and the sheep 150. On the last day, two hundred and fifty buffaloes and four thousand five hundred sheep were slaughtered.

* *Prm.* 3: 73-79.

thing......If any young maiden would marry a youth on whom she has set her fancy, she makes a vow to her god that if he will arrange for her marriage, she will do him a great service before giving herself to her husband. If her wish is fulfilled, and she obtains him for her husband, she tells him that before giving herself to him she must offer sacrifice to such and such a god to whom she has promised to make an offering of her blood. Then, appointing a certain day for the ceremony, they take a great ox-cart and set up therein a great water-lift like those used in Castille for drawing water from wells, at the end of which hang two very sharp iron hooks. She goes forth on the appointed day in the company of her relations and friends, men and women, with much music played and sung, also dancers and tumblers. She is naked from the waist up, and wears cotton garments below. When she arrives at the gate where the cart stands ready, they let down (the long arm of) the lift, and push the hook into her loins through skin and flesh. Then, they put a 'small dagger'....into her left hand, and from the other end cause (the arm of) the lift to rise with much outcry and shouting from the people. She remains hanging from the lift, with the blood running down her legs; but shows no signs of pain, nay, she waves her dagger most joyfully, throwing limes at her husband. In this manner they conduct her to the temple wherein is the idol to whom she has vowed such a sacrifice, on arriving at the gate whereof, they take her down and attend to her wounds, and make her over to her husband, while she, according to her station in life, gives great gifts and alms to the Brahmans and idols and food in abundance to all who have accompanied her." *

The temple of Durgā was the place where such daring deeds were usually performed. It is said that in some of the shrines dedicated to her, there were a few implements such as nail-parers, arrows, swords, and huge scissors with the help of which people desirous of securing gifts immediately from the goddess should demonstrate the faith before her. A person must pull out his eyes with the nail-parer, if he wanted to secure the gift of seeing distant objects; he

* *Barbosa* i. pp. 220-2.

must pierce his ears with the arrows, if his object was to hear what was said in distant places; he must cut off his tongue with the sword, if he expected to obtain knowledge and learning; and he must thrust his head between the two blades of the scissors, and chop it off, if he desired to kill his enemies without receiving any injury.*

People believed that they could obtain miraculous powers by the grace of Durgā who would yield to the wishes only of the most daring and adventurous spirits. There were probably several who blinded, maimed and even killed themselves in vain attempts to possess gifts which were not bestowed upon them by providence.

Section 5 : Pilgrimage and Travel :—The people of the sixteenth century, like the Hindus of all ages, were fond of making pilgrimages to holy places. The Muhammadan conquest of Northern India made pilgrimages to the holy shrines in the Āryāvarta, very risky. This did not, however, damp the enthusiasm of the pilgrims. This aspect of the question does not pertain to the present study. The empire of Vijayanagara was full of holy shrines and *tīrthas*, which the pious pilgrims usually visited. The most important of them are enumerated in several copper-plate charters of the 16th century. † These were:

* *Kpm.* 3: 106-8.

† नानादानान्यकार्षीत् कनकसदसि यः श्रीविरूपाक्षदेव:
स्थाने श्रीकाळहस्तीशितुरपि नगरे वेङ्कटाद्रौ च काञ्च्याम्
श्रीशैले शोणशैले महति हरिहरेऽहोबलेसङ्गमे च
श्रीरङ्गे कुम्भकोणे हततमसि महानन्दितीर्थे निवृत्तौ
गोकर्णे रामसेतौ जगति तदितरेष्वप्यशेषेषु पुण्य-
स्थानेष्वारब्धनानाविधबहुळ महादानवारिप्रवाहैः ॥

EC. ix. Ch. 153.

Cidambaram, Virūpākṣam, Kāḷahasti, Tirupati, Kānci, Śrīśaila, Tiruvaṇṇāmalai, Harihar, Ahōbala, Sangamēśwar, Śrīranga, Kumbhakōṇam, Mahānandi-*tīrtha*, Gōkarṇa and Rāmēśvara. They include both the Śaiva and the Vaiṣṇava places of pilgrimage.

As the holy shrines which the pilgrims visited were scattered all over South India, the pilgrims had to travel long distances generally on foot. The travel was very difficult and risky. The roads were mere tracks, and, as the innumerable rivers, streams and channels were not spanned by bridges, travel during the rainy season was out of the question. People appear to have preferred the summer, in spite of the scorching heat of the tropical sun, to make long journeys, specially pilgrimages to holy places. As the roads were infested with robbers, it became well nigh impossible to travel on the roads without company. Therefore, the travellers, whether they were pilgrims, businessmen or private individuals, were obliged to travel in company. Any person intending to make a journey was to be on the look-out for finding a suitable company of travellers. The unscrupulous Brahman traveller of the *Āmuktamālyada* had to ask his fellow travellers, "Where do you go? When do you start?" * The two Brahman adventurers of *Śukasaptati* had to join at Vidyānagara a band of pilgrims proceeding to Conjeevaram to witness the *Garuḍōtsava* of Varadarāja. † A company of ordinary travellers or merchants was known as a *sātu*, and a band of pilgrims, as *parṣa*. The road from Vijayanagara to Tirupati was called *parṣa-dōva* or the pilgrim road, probably on account of the innumerable pilgrims that travelled along it.

* *Ām.* 7 : 7.

† *ŚS.* ii. pp. 102-3.

Means of Conveyance :—Although the palanquin or *andaḷam* was commonly used by the nobles and officials, it was not employed by the common travellers making journeys either long or short. As the use of palanquin was a privilege which the government granted to men of distinction, it was beyond the reach of the common wayfarer. But when men of rank travelled they were carried in palanquins by *bestas*. It is said that Kṛṣṇarāya lifted with his own hands Peddana's palanquin, when the latter was going to his village after dedicating his poem the *Manucaritra* to the Rāya.* Viṣṇucitta is said to have travelled from Śrīvilliputtūr to Madura in an old palanquin lent to him by the *sthānika* of the temple. † Although wheeled carts were employed by the ryots in their agricultural operations, there is no evidence to show that they had been used by travellers. This was probably due to the impracticability of driving the carts on the roads on which the travellers performed their journeys. The common wayfarers had to foot their weary way; and they constituted the bulk of travelling population. The richer sort, however, usually rode on horses or bullocks which were available for hire at all places.‡ The hired horse is mentioned in the *Āmuktamālyada* ; Viṣṇucitta is said to have hired them for the purpose of carrying his luggage. The hired horse is also mentioned in Rāmāraja's *kaul* : § the

* మను చరిత్రం బందుకొనువేళ పురమేగ పల్లకి తనకేల బట్టెరాయుత్తె

† అనతిబహు శ్రీఖండా
గానన్నంబడసు నడుప్రాంతంబులయుక్
స్థానికు డొసంగి పనుపగ్
గా నానతిబడిన నిమిత్తకాంద్రుడు వహింపక్ ॥ *Ām.* 2 : 95.

‡ లావుగల యుద్దె గుఱ్ఱపు జావడములమీఁద మాత్ర సంచులు దూలన్
Ām. 2 : 96.

§ *LR.* 18 p. 407.

kāvalgār of the Tirupati Road was permitted to collect a toll of 4 *nebs* for every horse carrying a pilgrim.*

Under these circumstances, it was impossible for the ordinary foot passenger to carry any luggage with him. He could not, however, entirely dispense with it; for he had to take with him some of the necessaries to keep body and soul together on the way. Although there were hotels in cities and towns, † they had no attraction for the common travellers. Notwithstanding the fact that rice could be purchased at all places, they usually carried with them a small quantity of rice which might last for the first few stages. Another indispensable article was ghee which formed a necessary ingredient in the preparation of food. Besides, they had their clothing, and a woollen shawl or two to protect themselves from the cold

* The hired horse whose lament is described in the 17th tale of the *Hamsavimśati* informs his friend the he-buffalo that he was let frequently to men going to the fairs.

'సంత సారెకులందు స్వారినడిచి' *HV.* 5: 40.

The same thing is referred to in the *Śukasaptati* Canto iii. p. 153.

పౌరగూళ్ల న్దిరునాళ్లు సాగిన భరంపు న్నానిసినోన్నయ ని
ష్ఠుర వృత్తిఁ నను జూపి సుంకము లటంచుఁ గూలియంచు న్వరా
లు రయం బారగ ప్రోచి నన్ను దరుముఁ లోభా ప్తిమై......

The bullock in the 17th tale of the *Hamsavimśati*, in enumerating the cruel actions of his master, informs the buffalo that he was let to the travellers.

"ఎకిరింత దోలి" *HV.* 5: 35.

† The hotels of the city are spoken of in the *Āmuktamālyada* 7: 7.

వంటపూటింటి కెప్పంటికంటెను బాలుపెరుగునే గూరలం పెడు తెగువలు"

The existence of hotels even in the villages on the way is referred to in the *Tārakabrahmarājīyam,* Canto ii.

పల్లెకు నల్లన జనియొక । యిల్లాలికి దగిన విలువ యిచ్చి నయమునన్
దల్లీ నా ప్రియురాలికి । యుల్లం బలరంగ జేయు మోగిర మనినన్ ॥
అయ్యా నిమిషములోనను । నయ్యోడు నెచ్చటుకు దెత్తు ననవుడు నతడుం
నెయ్యమున మత్తిక్రిందికి । సయ్యన గొని రమ్మటంచు జనియెన్ ప్రీతిన్ ॥

weather. If, however, like the greedy Brahman of the *Āmuktamālyada*, the travellers were returning home from the city, they would in addition purchase fine sarees for their wives. The bag containing the betel leaves, nuts &c., formed an invariable adjunct to the travellers' outfit. All these were packed in a bag having two compartments called *mātra* or *asimi-sañci* which the travellers swung on their shoulders while travelling. If the traveller were a teacher, having one or more *brahmacārins* studying the Vēdas under him, he would shift the burden on to his or their shoulders.* If he were wealthier, his luggage would necessarily increase, and fill several bags which were carried by pack-horses accompanying his train.†

The travellers usually started on their journey long before daybreak so that they might cover as much distance as they possibly could before the sun's heat became intolerable.‡ The roadside was studded

* సంబెళ విదళించి తాంబూల దళపూగ నివహంబు జాలఁగ నుంచు నబ్బ
బ్రహ్మచారి భుజంబు మాత్రకు సడింపు
బ్రాలు నాలికి మేలు చీరలు గొనియెడు
సంభ్రమంబును............" *Ām.* 7: 7.

† The articles which Viṣṇucitta carried with him, when he started on his journey to Madura consisted of several delicacies and condiments to season his food on the way. Several *kāvaḍis* of delicacies such as *ariśas* were carried by people who accompanied him:

భక్తి ద్రోవకు సాధ్వి బరికరంబులు వెట్టికట్టిన పొరివిళంగాయ గమియు
నెసటి పోతలుగాఁగ నేర్పరించిన చిరంతనపు శాలిక్షేమ తండులము లు
వడిబెట్టి లోఁజెరకడము సాబాలూన్న జెలఁగు సంబారంపు చింతపండు
పెల్లులో హండి కావళ్ల కొమ్ములఁ బ్రేలు గిడ్డి మొత్తపు నేతి లడ్డిగలును
బెరుగు పడియుంబులును బచ్చివరుగు బేడ... *Ām.* 2: 97.

‡ ....దా
దిత్తి యొకటి గొని త్రేణి మ
రుత్తర మత్తర మటంచు నొక ప్రొద్దు కడక్ ॥
లేచి పోవంగ దత్తరమేచి తోడి
వారు నన నేను ముడె మోపు వటున కత్తి
పోవ................ ॥ *Ām.* 7: 8, 9.

with groves of shade giving trees, and tanks containing cool water. These served as suitable camping grounds for merchants and travellers. Paes describes the road connecting Baticala with Vijayanagara.

"You walk for two or three leagues under the groves of trees ; and behind cities and towns and villages they have plantations of mangoes, and jack-fruit trees and tamarinds and other very large trees which form resting-places where merchants halt with their merchandise. I saw in the city of Recalem a tree under which we lodged three hundred and twenty horses, standing in order as in their stables, and all over the country you may see many small tress." *

Sewell is of opinion that 'the great tree was, of course, a banyan.' † The banyan, no doubt, offered plenty of cool shade to the travellers ; and it appears from a reference in the *Tārakabrahmarājīyam* that they usually rested under its spreading branches. ‡ Those that liked to get their food from the hotel in the neighbouring village ate it there ; and those who preferred to prepare their food cooked it on temporary hearths constructed with loose stones picked up from the roadside. §

* *FE.* p. 237. † *ibid*

‡ అప్పుమప్పవతీ పట్టణం బిచటికి పదియోజనము లున్నది. దానిమార్గం బెఱుంగుదు పదమనిన, సంతసిల్లి యవ్విప్రుండు... దాని పిరుదం జనియె. మరునాడు లేపగలింటికి యోజనత్రయంబు గడచి తెరువున నొక్కపల్లె యున్న దాని సమీపంబున నీళ్ల వాగుకడ నీడల గుజ్జుమఱ్ఱిక్రింద నిలిచిరప్పుడు. *Tbm.* Canto ii.

§ *The Śukasaptati* (Canto iii p. 158) describes a traveller's camp under the banyan tree : " The women having fed their babies rocked them to sleep in cradles of bamboo suspended to the boughs of the banyan tree. Some of the travellers who fell asleep while their maid-servants were preparing the food, having been awakened from their slumbers, went to the neighbouring tank to bathe in its cool water. They returned after finishing their ablutions wearing their respective caste-marks. When they sat before their leaf-platters to eat their dinner, some of their fellow travellers begged them for a meal, which was, of course, given. Some of the way-farers having quenched their thirst in the cool waters of the tank, divided themselves into two groups and began to discuss with considerable heat the current political problems. The shepherd women of the neighbouring villages who came to the camp to sell curds, buttermilk, ghee &c. having disposed of their articles quickly, began to flirt with the amorous type of travellers."

The travel along the roads was, no doubt, difficult and risky; but it had also a lighter side. The camps at the end of every stage offered some relaxation to the weary traveller. Charitable people erected sheds along the road where water and other drinks were served free to the passers-by. * The water shed contained huge pots filled with cool water, which young damsels served out to the thirsty people. The water was delicately scented with powdered camphor, cuscus grass and *kuru*-roots. † The water sheds appear to have offered other attractions. The young women distributing water and other drinks feasted the ears of their customers with amorous prattle. ‡

The greatest danger which every traveller had to face on the road was the encounter with the bandits.

* *LR.* 18. [In the temple of Tiruvengaḷanātha at Cuddapah] [A.D. 1552]. pp. 469-473.

"తిరుపతి దోవన" చలివెంద్ర పెట్టేటందుకు దశవంద మాన్యం.

† ఇసుక మెదువు నెలవులం బన్నిన పసుపుటాకులం జప్పరంబులలోనం గుప్పిలించిన కప్పురంబుతోడి కురువేరు పరిమళంబులును, జాజివిరుల వలపును, వట్టివేళ్ల వాసనలుం గల ప్రపాపాలికాప ఘనవ్రజతంబులగు కలశోదకంబులు గ్రోలి సేదదేఱి తెరువరులు తాలవృంతానిలంబులం బలుపుకొలిపి... *Prm.* 4: 16.

‡ The *Āmuktamālyada* describes the '*prapa*' or the water shed in canto 2, verses 57-9. The amorous actions of the damsels are described in verses 58 and 59. *The Hamsavimśati* (2: 158-160) gives a more vivid description of the attractions of the *prapa*:

It was a temporary shed built every summer for the purpose of distributing water to the thirsty wayfarers. On one of its sides, it had one or more apertures through which water was poured into the hands, probably, of the untouchables. Huge earthenware vessels filled with watery-buttermilk (నీరుమజ్జిగ) mixed with the powder of dry-ginger and lime juice, were arranged in a row on one side. Vessels containing water, scented with the crushed cardamoms were kept on another side. Small pots of thin *rāgi* gruel spreading the odours of commin seed and *karivēmbu* leaf were placed in a corner; huge pots containing *ganjee* mixed with powdered salt and the juice of onions were in another corner. The chief attraction, however, is said to have been the Brahman woman who was in charge of the shed.

The nefarious activities of the highwaymen of the time have already been described.

The *Caṇḍālas* usually infested the highways and robbed the travellers of all their belongings; but they were not the only people who depended on the king's highway for their living. Another class of people who were given to thieving and robbery were the *Bōyas*, * living on the outskirts of the forests. The *Caṇḍālas* and *Bōyas* were not the only people who preyed upon the travellers. Sometimes, men of nobler castes were also attracted by the prospects which the highways offered. The activities of the robber bands appear to have been very vigorous during the reign of Acyuta, when, taking advantage of the unsettled condition of the empire, the ***pāḷegārs*** plundered towns and villages.

The Methods of the Robbers :—The methods which some of the robber bands employed to ensnare their victims had strong affinities to the manner of attack which the thugs adopted much later. One of the gang, sometimes the leader, would mix with the population of a town or city in search of travellers ready to start on a journey. He would announce his intention of joining the party as a fellow traveller. Like the other travellers, he would bring his ***mātra*** or *asimi* bag with him, and sleep in their company in a convenient place. He would arouse the company from their sleep long before the break of day, shouting that it was already

* " తనమగఁడు బోయవీటంగల వెలఁగవారి నెల్లం గూర్చికొని కొల్లగొళ్లకు దూరంబు పోయినాఁడు..." *Tbm.* Cantc ii.

" తీర్థయాత్రాపరులం బ్రాహ్మణులఁ దలలువగులం జెరవాటులు గొట్టి పుటుకలు గోయఁ కరవాతిం గంద్రదగొడ్డలియుం...... గొని." *ibid.*

late and that they should hurry up. On hearing him, the whole company would begin the march, the robber leading them in the wrong path. When they arrived at a chosen place, where the other members of the gang awaited their arrival, he would whistle as arranged beforehand. Then the robbers would fall suddenly upon the travellers and plunder them.*

Kṛṣṇarāya gives a graphic account of an encounter of a party of travellers with robbers on the highway. When a few arrows and stones fell upon them, several travellers took to their heels, realising that the bandits were near at hand. Some of the travellers, who became disgusted with the behaviour of their companions cried out, " O cowards! What do you expect to gain by your flight; the robber gang is not so strong as you imagine it to be; it can be put to flight with ease." Having, by these words, rallied a few of the party, they attacked the robbers by pelting them with stones, clubs etc; some, having bundled up their valuables, threw them into the midst of thick bushes with the hope of recovering them later, and took to flight in order to escape the blows of the club. Others, made of sterner stuff, placing their luggage on the ground drew their swords to defend themselves against the attack of the robbers. Some begged the bandits not to pollute the box of domestic deities, parcelled in their upper garments, promising that they would themselves untie the parcel and surrender the garments. A few who were conscious of their family pride, desirous of protecting the honour of their women, said, " Gentlemen, we shall give you everything belonging to us, including the jewels worn at present by our ladies provided that you do not offer them any violence by wresting the jewels from them."

* *Ām.* 7 : 8, 9, 10

Having said so much, they handed over to the robbers all their belongings and departed. *

"The robbers did not molest such travellers that boldly marched along the road with drawn bows in their hands, ready to strike down any one that dared to approach them; but they overpowered those that opposed them by stabbing them rapidly. They did not torture the miserly traveller, but obtained from him as much as they could by letting his blood flow freely from his wounds. They did not attempt to recapture those that made a sudden dash for freedom at a convenient moment; and did not interfere with the poor wayfarers that had nothing to lose; but they were searched by some robbers who were posted at some distance. Some of the travellers who concealed themselves in the bushes, were forced to come out of their hiding places at the point of the lance. They were stripped almost naked, and their belongings were appropriated; their sandals were ripped open by the sharp but delicate arrow heads shaped like olyander leaves in order to lay bare anything that might lie concealed therein; the tufts of their hair were untied and examined for the same purpose." †

Having finished their work, the highwaymen departed. The travellers had to shift for themselves as well as they could. Those whose shoulders were very nearly severed by the blows of the robber's sword had to go in search of a surgeon, holding the wounded limbs with the fingers of the other hand, to get the wound dressed. The soot of the burnt cloth was thrust into the gaping wounds in the heads of others, caused by blows of the bandit's bludgeon. They dragged themselves painfully from village to village feeding on the gruel of *rāgi* and rice which they begged on the way. Those that were robbed even of their garments had to dress themselves in old, worn-out clothes which the compassionate householders offered them. The misfortune of the poor travellers was taken advantage of by unscrupulous men who

* *Ām.* 7: 14. † *Ām.* 7: 21.

quartered themselves indefinitely on their relations, narrating stories of the imaginary riches which they had to surrender to the dacoits. *

Such were some of the difficulties which the travellers, whether merchants or pilgrims, had to face while journeying on the king's highway. In spite of these dangers, people seem to have frequently gone on pilgrimages and business to places even in the remotest corners of the empire.

* *Ām*. 7 : 21.

Chapter II

THE SOCIAL CONDITIONS

Section 1: The Four Castes:—The bulk of the population of the empire consisted of Hindus. No doubt, there were a few Muhammadans, Christians and Jews, who lived mainly in the commercial centres. They enjoyed considerable freedom of action, as the state pursued a liberal policy towards them.

The Hindu community was, of course, divided into the traditional four castes: the Brahmans, the *Kṣatriyas*, the *Vaisyas* and the *Śūdras*. In fact, the castes were far more numerous than the four suggested by tradition; but most of them were regarded as the sub-divisions of the fourth caste. Besides, the *Caṇḍālas* formed a caste by themselves, and they lived in hamlets exclusively set apart for their habitation, away from the abodes of the men of superior castes.

The Brahmans:— The Brahmans did not busy themselves exclusively with the performance of the six *karmas* enjoined by the *śāstras*. They were divided into several classes. The Portuguese travellers, who sojourned at Vijayanagara, give some interesting information about the Brahmans with whom they came into contact. Barbosa says:

"Among them, is another class of people whom they call Bramenes, who are priests and rulers of their houses of worship... Among them, all these men hold the greatest liberties and privileges, and are not liable to death for anything whatsoever which they do. The king, the great Lords, the men of rank give them much alms on which they live; also many of them have estates, while others live in the houses of worship, as in monasteries, which possess good revenues. Some are great eaters, and never work except to feed well; they will start at once on a six days' journey...only to get a good bellyful, their honey and butter, rice, sugar, 'stews of pulse and milk.' *

Paes declares:

"These Brahmans are like friars with us, and they count them as holy men—I speak of the Brahman priests and lettered men of the pagodas—because, although the king has many Brahmans, they are officers of towns and cities, and belong to the government of them; others are merchants, and others live by their own property and cultivation, and the fruits which grow in their inherited grounds. Those who have charge of the temples are learned men." †

Nuniz says:

"And in this kingdom of Bisnaga, there is a class of men, natives of the country, namely Brahmans, who the most part of them never kill or eat any live thing, and these are the best that there are amongst them. They are honest men, given to merchandise, very acute and of much talent, very good at accounts, lean men and well formed, but little fit for hard work. By these, and the duties they undertake, the kingdom is carried on." ‡

From the point of view of these foreigners, the Brahmans were divided into six classes: (1) the priests or men living in the pagodas, (2) the estate owners, (3) the inmates of monasteries, (4) the government servants, (5) the merchants, and (6) the eaters.

(1) The worship of the idols in a temple was, and is, not a respectable calling for a Brahman to follow. The *Nambis* the *Śiva-Brahmans*, were only *brahmabandhus*, and no respectable Brahman, would even consent to dine with them. The *Tambaḷas*, who officiated as priests in several temples of Śiva, were classed with the *Śūdras*. § But, with the advent of Rāmānuja, the

* *Barbosa i.* p. 217.

† *FE.* p. 245.

‡ *ibid* p. 390.

§ *LR.* 37 (Hanumadguṇḍam) pp. 246-48.

worship of idols was considered a legitimate duty of a Vaiṣṇava; and the Rāmānujites captured the priesthood of as many temples of Viṣṇu as they could. As the Rāmānujite Vaiṣṇavism became a dominant force in the religious life of South India during the 16th century, the Brahmans of this sect became the priests of almost all the shrines of Viṣṇu. Several of them, indeed, were very learned. Therefore, the Brahmans whom the Portuguese travellers speak of as priests of temples, must be regarded as the members of the Śrī Vaiṣṇava community.

(2) Although monastic life was not popular, there were several monasteries in the land, as all forms of Hinduism recognised the need for their existence. The monasteries were not exclusively Brahmanic institutions; several of them, specially those belonging to the Vīra Śaivas were essentially non-Brahmanic. Most of the dependents and servants of the monasteries were not monks but married men. As the monasteries were centres of learning, they maintained several scholars who were not called to take upon themselves the vows of monastic order. The number of Brahmans that lived in monasteries during this period could not have been very large.

(3) The estate owners were the holders of tax-free land granted to them or their ancestors by kings and nobles as a reward for their learning. Their holdings consisted of *agrahāras* or shares in them as well as *mānyas* in several places and some hired pieces* of land from the government, on condition of paying

* "గుడ్డ వృత్తులు వృత్తులు గొలుచు గుత్తి
చేలు గ్రామాంశములు సాధినేల లెల్లఁ
జనవరుల కమ్మఁజూపు" *Prm.* 3:16.

an annual rent. An ideal Brahman of this class had several fields with crops ready for harvest, and herds of cows whence milk was brought in pails to his house every day. He performed in his house marriages and *upanayanams* from time time; and satisfied the beggars by giving them alms. He acted in such a manner that all his fellow-villagers regarded him as an embodiment of truth and virtue; he was served by several servants, and his house was usually thronged with his relations. He performed his *karmas*, both *nitya* and *naimittika* with great care, and ate the food, offered to Viṣṇu, served by his wife.* If such a person happened to be learned, he maintained an establishment of students whom he taught the Vēdas, the *śāstras* or literature in which he was proficient. Such a man would not accept gifts from any other, because acceptance of gifts was considered sinful. He spent most of his time in retirement in his village, and never troubled himself about life in the cities. Yet he could save money which he advanced as loans

* సీ॥ కీలారమున నుండి పాలింటి కేతేర
బహుధాన్యములు చేలఁ బండియొరఁగ
నెడనెడఁ బెండ్లిండ్లు వడుగులు వొడమఁ
గ్రాతార్థులై యర్థించు నర్థులలరఁ
బరిచారికా కోటి పనిపాటు పాటింపఁ
జుట్టంపు సంపది నెట్టుకొనఁగ
గ్రామమంతయు నిజ ప్రాభవంబున మన
సత్యనిష్ఠుఁ డన్న సాక్షిగాఁగ
నిత్య నైమిత్తికములు నిర్లిప్త బుద్ధి
నాచరించుచు హరిభుక్త మాత్మభార్య
భక్తి నిడ భుక్తి గొను చున్కి సుకృతిగాని
నిదురవంటిది రాతివంటిదియుఁ గాదు॥ *Prm.* 5 · 216.

to the needy on interest. He was hospitable, and offered food to all those that came to his house.*

Such was the life which was regarded as most proper for a *śrōtriya* Brahman to lead. From the fact that this kind of life was praised by several contemporary writers, it appears that the position of land-owning Brahman was coveted by many.

The *mahājanas*, who play a prominent part in the legal documents of the age, belonged to this class. Their services were frequently utilised by the government in the administration of justice. The trial of almost every civil case was entrusted to the *mahājanas* of the numerous *agrahāras* who constituted themselves into temporary courts or *dharmāsanas*. The fact, that the Rāya, his governors, and *amaranāyakas* would invariably command the *mahājanas* to form *dharmāsanas*, shows that they occupied an important place in the body politic.

(4) The majority of the educated Brahmans sought to enter the government service which offered them bright careers. They were specially trained to become good accountants and administrators. The imperial secretariat was almost entirely manned by men of this class. In the Telugu country, they separated themselves from the other Brahmans, and formed a sub-caste known as the *Niyōgis*. There is

* " తండ్రికి నిడ్డ పత్రములు దొంగిలిపోయి పోయినంతకు నిచ్చు
పారయువిత్త "
Prm. 3: 16.

" గికురించి రిచ్చి పుచ్చుకొనుచోటులవార లాఁకవులోనుగా కప్పు లీక "
Mc. 3: 129.

" సరసాహారము లింటఁబెట్టి బహు శిష్య శ్రేణికిన్ దెల్పు శా
స్త్రి రహస్య స్థితిఁజెప్పు నధ్యయన సంధ్యల్ హవ్య కవ్యంబులన్ "
Rc. 3: 11.

reason to believe that Brahmans of this class were not very orthodox in the observance of their religious rites*. They became ministers, commanders of armies, and governors of provinces. Every Brahman mother wished that her son should become a *durgādhipati* or

* బ్రహ్మ వక్త్రమున నుద్భవమైన బ్రాహ్మణుల్
కొందఱాచార్యులై యుందు రెపుడు
వరుసతో గొందఱు వైదికమార్గంబు
జెన్నొందు చుందురు సిద్ధముగను
నియోగులై కొంద ఱయ్యెడ నుందురు
నీతికార్యము లెల్ల నెగడు కొఱకు
వాసిగా లెక్కలు వ్రాసిన మాత్రాన
శూద్రులుగారు భూసురులుగాని
విప్ర సంహతి చేలను వీసమైన
పట్టనని మున్ను సత్యంబుఁ బలికినావు
గణిక భూసుర నివహంబుఁ గరుణ బ్రోవు
రామభూపాల చినతిమ్మ రాజచంద్ర॥

LR. 54 pp. 112-113. [From an inscription at Vellāla dated Ś 1470 (1584 A.D.).]

मकः—सखे, मिलिन्द, इत एव सकलविद्यानिषध्यायमानं विद्यानगरम् ।
अस्मिन् किल महानयं वेषो राजनियोगव्यापारशालिनाम् ।
यज्ञोपवीतं मलिनं तदेकं, श्मश्रूणि कृत्तानि चमत्कृतानि ।
उष्णीषशाटी धवलातिसूक्ष्मा वासस्त्रिकोणं द्विपटी विशाला ॥

मिलि—एतेषां कोऽयं प्रातःकालीनो विधिः—
उत्थायोषसि धूमपानकलनात्ताम्बूलिकाचर्वणं
पश्चाद्विश्लथकेशपाशनहनं शारीरशुद्धिस्ततः ।
प्रक्षाल्याननमच्छदर्पणधृतिः पुण्ड्रप्रकारस्ततो
लेखं लेखनिकां पिधाय च पटे कार्याद्बहिर्निर्गमः ॥

एते वैदिकं कर्म परसात्कृत्वा सुखेन वर्तन्ते—
सन्ध्याविधिं भावनयैव कृत्वा
होमं जपं दैवतपूजनं च ।
पुरोहितायत्ततया विधाय
यभन्त्यहो निद्रति भुञ्जते च ॥ *Keraḷābharaṇam.*

the governor of a fort. Some of the most eminent men of the age, such as Sāḷuva Timma,* Koṇḍamarasa, Ayyaparasa, Sāḷuva Narasingarāya Nāyaka, Candragiri Sōmarasa, and Dēmarasa, belonged to this class. They were honest, intelligent, and industrious ; and these qualities greatly contributed to their success.

(5) Both Paes and Nuniz refer to a class of Brahmans who adopted trade as their profession, but Barbosa was not aware of their existence. Although nothing prevented a Brahman from keeping a shop or trading with other countries, contemporary literature and inscriptions have nothing to say about the Brahman merchants. It is possible that some Brahmans attempted to open for themselves mercantile careers ; but their number must have been very limited.

(6) The eaters must have been the poorer members of the community ; and they must have formed the majority. They could not have been as idle as the Portuguese writers represent them to be ; for they had to work hard in their own way to earn money. In an age, when feeding a Brahman and offering him largesses of money were considered meritorious actions, the Brahman of this class rendered a distinct social and religious service to the community, and he was adequately rewarded for it. But he was unscrupulous and greedy. He exposed himself to some risk in earning money. In the palace of Acyutarāya who was fond of distributing large sums of money in charity, there were always two or three thousand Brahmans.

* గుత్తిం బుల్లెలు గుట్టి చంద్రగిరిలోఁ గూడెత్తి పెన్గొండలో
నాత్తిం సత్రమునందు వేడి బలు దుర్గాధీశ తాంబూలపుం
దిత్తుల్ లోన్నసి పదస్థులైన ఘనలన్ దీవింప ; దీవించెదన్
మత్తారాతి యయాతి నాగమసుతున్ మంత్రీశ్వరున్ దిమ్మరున్ ॥

Rāmarājabhūṣaṇa *Cāṭu*

"The Brahman priests", says Nuniz, "are very despicable men; they always have much money, and are so insolent that even by using blows, the guards of the door cannot hold them in check."* The emperor Kṛṣṇadēvarāya, who seems to have specially studied their ways and character, describes their activities vividly. They would agree for the sake of money, to perform light purificatory rites and dine with outcaste Brahmans; they would wrangle and fight with the *purōhits* of the merchants for a share in the rice, which they got at the time of performing purificatory rites; they would wait in the court-yards of noblemen, offering them the religious merit which they acquired by meditation and penance, at the time of solar and lunar eclipses; they would attempt to establish a monopoly for accepting gifts of sandals made of the leather of buffalo, goat, and cow; they would secure invitations to dine at the *śrāddhās*; failing that, they would accompany such Brahmans that officiated at the *śrāddhās* to eat the *pitṛiśēṣa*; when they could not get a free meal, they would attempt to appease their hunger by purchasing half a meal in the street where the cook-maids lived. The money which they accumulated in this way, they invested with the *Kōmati*; and if he declined to give them as much interest as they asked for, they would loudly complain against him in a court. †

This is, no doubt, an exaggerated picture; all the Brahmans belonging to this class could not have been so bad or so unscrupulous as the type described by the Rāya; but some of the qualities described by him must have been present in several members of this class.

* *FE.* p. 379.

† *Ām.* 7: 5, 6.

To whichever of the six classes a Brahman might belong, his diet was simple; his food consisted of grains, vegetables, milk, curds and ghee. His dress, except when he happened to be rich, was simple. His needs were few. In that age, when polygamy was almost universal, he remained monogamous. His love of monogamy was partly due to his economic condition. It was not an easy task for a man of ordinary means to maintain more than one wife; the majority of the Brahmans being poor could not afford to enjoy the luxury of marrying several wives. Even the rich Brahmans preferred to be satisfied with a single wife. Persons like Sāḷuva Timma, Koṇḍamarasa and Rāmābhaṭlayya could have easily married a dozen; but they were content to remain monogamous. Although the law permitted a Brahman to marry as many women as he could maintain, he showed a positive distaste to polygamy; probably the practice of polygamy did not appeal to his imagination.

The Kṣatriyas:—The *Kṣatriyas* were a flourishing community. They still formed the ruling class, although they had to compete with members of the other castes, specially the *Śūdras*. The Solar and the Lunar families were both fairly represented. The chiefs who claimed descent from the Cōḷas belonged to the Solar race; the Gajapatis of Orissa, with whom the Tuḷuva emperors intermarried, and the Mādrāju chiefs were the scions of the same race. The Lunar dynasty was numerically stronger than the other. The Sangamas, the Sāḷuvas, the Tuḷuvas, the Āravīḍus and the Pāṇḍyas all traced their origin from the Moon. The one interesting feature of the *Kṣatriya* caste of this period is the total disappearance of the *Agnikulas*. The numerous inscriptions and literature are totally silent about this branch of the *Kṣatriya* caste.

The Vaiśyas:—Although agriculture, cattle-rearing, and trade are said to be the legitimate professions of the *Vaiśyas*, they had no connection with the first two. They confined themselves to trade, which was considered to be the only profession that they could enter in strict conformity with the rules of the caste. All the *Prabhandhas*, that were written during the century, refer to the *Vaiśyas* as mere tradesmen.* It is very much to be doubted whether there was a *Vaiśya* community properly so called in South India. The *Kōmaṭis* of the Telugu and the Canarese countries claimed to be *Vaiśyas*, and their claim was admitted by other communities. The *Bēris*, the chief mercantile caste of the Tamil districts, made a similar claim; but the *Kōmaṭis* would not recognise them as *Vaiśyas*. Consequently, there arose bitter quarrels between the two castes. The dispute between the two communities became so acrimonious during the reign of Dēvarāya I, that he appointed a commissioner to examine the problem and decide whether the *Kōmaṭis* and the *Bēris* were *Vaiśyas*. † Although the *Kōmaṭis* claimed to be the only mercantile community properly so called, they had to do business in the teeth of keen opposition. The Muhammadans, and the Lingāyats were skilful traders. Besides,

* వెచ్చము వెట్టు మన్న బదివేలకు నుద్ధరు వోల్ల రర్థము
దెచ్చిన శేషు నాదలల దివ్యమణుల్ వలెనన్న విల్వలన్
హెచ్చును గుండునాడుకొన కిత్తురు లాభముగోర కెన్నఁగా
నెచ్చట గోటికిన్ బడగ యెత్తని వైశ్యులు గల్గ రప్పురిన్ ॥ *Skp.* i. p. 10.

వలె నన్నన్ వెలయిచ్చి కొండ్రు మురజిద్వక్షస్థలీ రత్నముల్
బులిజున్నే నియు నమ్మ జూపుదురు తప్పుల్ పట్టి బేహారమే
వలనన్ జేరడటంచు బల్కుదురు సర్వజ్ఞాప్తునిం దత్పురిన్
గలిమిం జే రెలమిన్ దలిర్చిన వణిగ్వర్యుల్ యశోధుర్యులై ॥

Sdp. 1 : 82.

† *MAR.* 1927 p. 26.

the Brahmans, *Baṇijagas*, *Balijas* etc., took to trade as a profession; and many of them seem to have been very successful and prosperous.

The Śūdras :—The *Śūdra* caste was a heterogeneous body comprising several sub-castes both higher and lower. Agriculture was their main occupation. The *Reḍḍis*, the *Vakkaligars* and the *Veḷḷālas* usually tilled the soil. They formed the back-bone of the nation; and the prosperity of the state depended upon them to a very great extent. Several of them entered the army and eked out a living by serving the state. Some of the *Śūdra* communities should be termed, strictly speaking, military. The *Kammas* and the *Velamas* of the Telugu country were military communities par excellence. No doubt, members of these castes cultivated the soil and owned extensive estates; but their main occupation was fighting; the *Balijas* also emulated to some extent their example, although the main occupation of the caste appears to have been trade. They appear to have been a very enterprising community during the sixteenth century. The leaders of these military castes were appointed as *amaranāyakas;* and they became, in course of time, rulers of small principalities.

Several classes of people following diverse professions were included in the *Śūdra* caste. The *Kurubas*, the *Gollas*, and the *Iḍaiyans* who were shepherds by profession, the washermen, the barbers, the courtesans, and the *Dommaras* were all reckoned as *Śūdras*. Every caste or sub-caste married within itself; and inter-dining was permitted within certain limits. In the Tamil districts the *Śūdras* divided themselves into two factions, the right hand and the left hand castes. The quarrels between these two factions were so bitter and chronic that the state had to intervene from time to time to restore peace and order.

The *Caṇḍālas* were recognised as the fifth caste. They may be divided into two groups: *(a)* the *Māla*, the *Hoḷeya* or the *Pariah*, and *(b)* the *Mādiga* or the *Cekkili*.

(*a*) The *Mālas*, the *Hoḷeyas* or the *Pariahs* constituted the bulk of agricultural labourers in South India. Spinning and weaving served them as important by-industries. These peaceful occupations, however, had no attractions for the spirited and enterprising men of the community. As they were debarred by their birth from entering into the civil and military service of the state, they took to highway robbery. An enterprising leader would gather around him a band of allied spirits and organise expeditions of robbery and dacoity, until the government moved its lethargic machinery to put him and his followers down. Therefore, the *Mālas*, the *Hoḷeyas* or the *Pariahs* became one of the principal criminal tribes of the empire.

(*b*) The *Mādiga* or the *Cekkili* was more an artisan than an unskilled labourer. Shoe making was the legitimate trade of this caste. He also supplied the cultivator with ropes, leather-buckets etc., needed to carry on agricultural operations; and he also joined the weaving industry to increase his income.

CHAPTER III

THE SOCIAL LIFE

Section 1: *The Idea of Bhōga* :—The ideal of social life may be said to be epicurean. The people, specially the upper classes, were desirous of extracting the maximum *bhōga* or enjoyment from life. They did not pause to consider whether the enjoyment, the pursuit of which was their supreme object in life, involved their fellow-creatures in hardship, pain or misery. They aimed at securing pleasure, and so long as they obtained what they wanted, they cared little for the rest. However, it must not be inferred that they were materialistic in their outlook on life. They paid considerable attention to spiritual things also.* As Vaiṣṇavism, the most popular faith of the country, encouraged a sort of refined sensualism, the indulgence in the *bhōgas* was not regarded as incompatible with leading a spiritual life.

The ancients who were fond of classifying everything divided *bhōga* into eight kinds, which were together known as the *aṣṭabhōgas*. These were habitation, dress, ornament, perfume, flower, *tāmbūla*, bed, and women. Three other kinds of *bhōga* may be added to the list *viz.*, bath, food, and drink. The social life of the people, specially of the upper classes, can be described under these eleven heads.

Section 2: *Habitation* :—The people were familiar with three kinds of houses. The Portuguese writers give a fairly good description of the houses in the cities, especially in the capital. (*a*) The emperor,

*R. Anantakrishna Śarma: *Rāyalanāṭirasikata* and other essays pp. 5-7.

his nobles, merchants, 'and other rich and honourable men' lived in beautiful houses built of stone. The houses in which the courtesans lived also belonged to the same class.* These differed in certain respects from the modern houses. They had only one floor 'with flat roofs and towers.' They stood on pillars, and were 'all open with verandahs inside and out,' where several people could easily be accommodated. There were several palaces in the city after the same fashion in which dwelt the great noblemen, and governors of provinces.† The royal palace as well as the mansions of nobles and governors had their own gardens full of aromatic herbs.‡ These palaces and the houses of the rich were adorned with 'many figures and decorations,'§ which may be assigned to two classes: they were either carved images on stone or wood, or figures painted in brilliant colours on the walls. The Portuguese visitors to the royal palace saw many sculptures on the walls which were gilded so that they might seem to have been made of gold.¶ Even the wooden door jambs were covered with carved images of peacocks and doves. The profusely sculptured temple of Hazāra Rāma is the only surviving example of the graceful art, which gives some faint idea of how the sculptured palaces might have looked. The figures which were painted on the walls represented

* "These women are of loose character, and live in the best streets that are in the city; it is the same in all their cities, their streets have the best rows of houses." *FE*. p. 242.

† *ibid.*

‡ కేళీ సౌధము గేళిడోలికయునుఁ గేళీవనశ్రేణియుఁ

* * *

బోలఁ లేని గృహంబు లేదొకటియుఁ

Kmm. 4 : 145; cf. *Barbosa* i. p. 202.

§ *FE*. p 254.

¶ *ibid*. p. 287.

mythological stories and scenes from the contemporary life. One of the halls of the imperial palace was painted with pictures, depicting 'all the ways of men' including the Portuguese, which were so designed as to give the inmates of the zenana an idea of how each one lived in his own country.* This was probably the *citraśāla* or the picture gallery of the palace, which is frequently alluded to in contemporary literature. The paintings were not, however, confined to the *citraśālas* alone. It was customary for almost all classes of people to adorn their houses with painted pictures.† The favourite subjects which attracted the attention of the artists were usually stories from the Hindu mythology, *e.g.*, the churning of the Milk Ocean for nectar and the celebration of the marriage of Viṣṇu with Lakṣmī; the burning of Kāma by Śiva and the latter's marriage with Pārvatī; the marriage of Nala and Damayantī; and the ways of such birds as swans, parrots etc.‡ These

* *FE.* p. 286.

† ఒకచాయ చిత్రభిత్తికగా యనుచు సోయగమున బాయక డాయగాఁ దలంతు.

Vc. 4: 73.

చందన గంధు లిందుమణి సౌధతలంబుల గొండ్లి సల్పగా
నందలి దివ్యచిత్రముల యం దొకరై యని మేచభామినుల్
కందళితాద్భుత స్ఫురణ గన్గొని తన్నటనాంతగీతని
ష్యంద సజీవ చిత్రముల సందడి నేగుదు రప్పురంబునన్ ॥

ibid 1: 105.

‡ ఆదినారాయణుం డమృతాబ్ధి మథియించి యబ్జవాసిని బెండ్లియైన కథలు
చంద్రశేఖరుఁడు పుష్పశరాస్త్రుఁ గెల్చి హిమాచలతనయు బెండ్లైన కథలు.
శ్రీరామచంద్రుండు శివధనుర్భంజన మడరించి సీత బెండ్లైన కథలు
నలచక్రవర్తి వేల్పులు సిగ్గువడఁగ భీమాధీశు కన్య బెండ్లైన కథలు
గీ॥ చిత్తభవ కేళిబంధవిచిత్రగతులు హంసకలరవకీరరథాంగగతులు
వ్రాసి రలవడ తత్స్వయంవర మహీస్థలాంతిక స్వర్ణకుడ్యముల నెల్ల॥

Rm. Canto iv. p. 198.

The only surviving instances of the painting of this period are seen in the ruined Cennakēśava temple at Sōmpāḷem in the Madanapalle tālūk of the Chittoor district, and at Lēpakṣi in the Anantapūr district.

furnished themes for the artists to work upon, probably because the people loved to have the visible representations of these stories in their houses. But these had little or no attraction to the courtesan women whose company was sought by all fashionable and cultured men. They filled their drawing-rooms, and bed-rooms with amorous pictures representing the love scenes from the stories of Ratī and Manmadha, Rambhā and Nalakūbara, Ūrvasī and Purūrava, Mēnakā and Viśwāmitra, Gōpikas and Kṛṣṇa etc. Obscene pictures, depicting the eighty four postures of sexual intercourse, were painted not only in bed-rooms but in public places. As these did not offend the popular sense of decency, they were also carved in temples and other structures of the kind. *

It is not possible to form a clear idea of the plan of the palace, or the mansions of the nobles. The Portuguese writers, no doubt, give elaborate descriptions of some of the imperial palaces; but as their accounts are confused and imperfect, they are not helpful in forming definite notions about the ground plan and design of these structures. One important feature of the residences of the Rāya and his nobles

* రతివధూ మదనుల రంభా కుబేరపుత్రకు లూర్వశీ పురూరవులు మేన
కా కౌశికులు గోపికా ముకుందులు ధాన్యమాలినీ రావణుల్ మత్స్యలోచ
నర్ష్యశృంగులు దాశనలినేక్షణా పరాశరులు తారా నిశాకరులు గౌత
మాంగనా దేవేంద్రు లమరవేశ్యా జయంతులు ద్రౌపదీ పాండవులు పృథా బ్జ

గీ॥ హితులు నడచిన గతులాత్మ సుతుల బెంచు
నింటిగోడల వ్రాయించు నిందువదన
వనితలకు సరసత కల్మి వావి వరుస
లేమియును లేమి వారల కెఱుకపఱుప॥

క॥ వనిత చతుర్జాతి వయో । వనజాక్షుల బంధవైభవము భద్రుని ద
త్తుని గూచిమారుఁ బాంచా। లుని వ్రాయించెన్ గృహంబులోపలి గోడన్॥

Khm. **4: 14, 15.**

was the enclosing wall,* which surrounded them, resembling very probably the high wall around the 'Zenana Enclosure' at Ḥampi. Within this wall were several streets of well-built houses and mansions where the emperor or the nobleman and the inmates of the zenana lived. The terraces of these palaces were decorated with *kalasas*, and flagstaffs on which fluttered multi-coloured pinnaces.† The enclosure appears to have been divided into several *kakṣyāntaras* or inner courts. These courts, each containing rows of houses and mansions were inter-connected with one another by means of *kakṣas* or gates.‡ Over the first *kakṣa* or the gate stood a *gōpura* or tower surrounded by a pillared verandah. This may be called the clock

* హరిపదమార్గలంఘనము లన్నియు నన్నియు హేమపత్రము
లుపరి భవనంబు లందు నృపపుంగవు మంగళ ధామమెద్దియో ?
Vc. 4: 67.

అని చింతించుచు నొక్క ధామమునకున్ యక్షాంగన లుపహార
ధ్వనితోఁ జారణకన్యక ల్పటుల వాగ్వైచిత్రితోఁ బన్నగాం
గన లుద్యన్మణిదీపమాలికలతోఁ గంధర్వకాంతల్ సుకంఠని
నాదాతిశయంబుతోఁ బ్రహరి చుట్టం గంటి చిత్రంబుగాన్ ॥
ibid 4: 48.

† अध्वश्रान्तामिव निजचमूमग्रतो वीजयन्तीम्
वारम् वारम् भवनवलभी वैजयन्तीसमीरैः ॥
Abm. Canto xii.

పోవఁ బోవఁగఁ దోఁచె బురరమామకుటమాల్యంబులై భర్మహర్మ్యధ్వజంబు
లేగ నేగఁగఁ దోఁచె గృహదేవతామౌళికలితాబ్జకళిక లై కలశతతులు—"
Vc. 4: 61.

హరిత మణి ప్రకల్పితము లన్నియుఁ నన్నియుఁ జిత్రకేతువుల్" *ibid* 4: 67.

కక్ష్యాంతర ద్వారదేశంబుల మంగళార్థంబుగా నిడిన పూర్ణకలశముకురాది
పదార్థంబులం గనుంగొనుచు" *Mc.* 5: 75.

"కక్ష్యాంతరంబులు గడచి యేతెంచు సొంపు దెలుపు" *Vc.* 3: 154.

tower, as in or near it was placed the sand clock tended by a sentry or two, who struck a metallic gong to indicate the *gaḍiyas* and the *yāmas.* * This gate opened on a court known as *mogasāla* "with its verandahs round it," † which served as an anteroom, where people desirous of having audience with the emperor or the nobleman, as the case may be, waited. At the other end of the court, there was another gate which opened on a second court-yard, where stood a portico on pillars. It was here, where the Rāya despatched business with his ministers and gave audience to his subjects. Another gate led into the interior of the zenana of which it is not possible to give a correct idea. In addition to the apartments of the Rāya, his queens, and their numerous attendants, certain parts of the palace are referred to in literature. These are *citraśāla* (picture gallery) *nāṭyaśāla* (dancing hall) *majjana-gṛha* (the bath) ‡ *bhōjanaśāla* (the dining hall), *candraśāla* or the roofless chamber on the top of the palace where the inmates went to enjoy the moonlight, the *arcana-gṛha*, the ivory chamber, the

* (ని) ర్భర కౌతూహల వృత్తినుండ ఘటికా పర్యాప్తి ఘంటారవాం
తర నిర్ణీతములై వినంగ బడియెఁ మధ్యాహ్న శంఖ ధ్వనుల్ ॥
Phm. **2: 3.**

క్రోసె న్గడియారమున మ । హా సంకులరవము గాఁగ యామద్వయ సం
ఖ్యా సూచక ఘంటాధ్వని । వాసర మద కేసరి ప్రవరగర్జితమై ॥
Spm. **2: 48.**

† *FE.* **p. 246**; *Prm.* **4: 153.**

‡ కేళిగతి మీఱ మజ్జనశాల కరిగి ।
శాతమన్యవమణిమయాసనమునందుఁ
గౌస్తుభాది విభూషణోత్కరము నెల్ల ।
నొయ్య నొయ్యన సడలించి యున్న యంత ॥ *Phm.* **2:8.**

drinking hall, the *gariḍi*, the *bhuvanēśvara*, the *jalayantradhāma* (room with water-spouts) and the nursery.*

Birds such as swans, peafowls, doves, and parrots were domesticated and taught to amuse the inmates of the palace, specially the womenfolk. Swans strutted about the palace; doves lived in its eaves; peafowls stood on square planks attached to long bamboo poles and danced; and the parrots prattled in their golden cages. †

These characteristics were not peculiar to the imperial palace; most of them were common to the houses of the nobles and wealthy persons who generally imitated the manners of the court. The domestic comfort was not considered perfect without a pleasure-house, probably situated in the pleasure garden, attached to the residence, containing swings, bathing tanks, and artificial hillocks. These were regarded necessary for making life tolerable. ‡

* తళుకు పసిండి యోవరులు దంతపుచావడు లర్చనాగృహం
బులు గుడినీరుమేడలును భోజనశాలలు కెంపుటోడుబి
ళ్లలగరిడీలు శీతలశిలాతలముల్ భువనేశ్వరంబు లు
జ్వలజలయంత్రధామములు సజ్జలు దాటి ధరాపతీర్ణనై ॥ *Vc.* 4 : 72.

† కనకపంజర శారికలకుఁ జక్కెర వెట్టి చదివింప రేలొకో సకియ లిపుడు
కరతాళ గతుల మందిర మయూరంబుల నాడింపరేలొకో యతివ లిపుడు
కలికి రాయంచ బోదల నెల్ల నెలయించి నడిపింప రేలొకో పడతు లిపుడు
Phm. **1** : 106.

పలుకులు నేర్చువేళ కలభాషిణి నీవిటు లుండ బంజరం
బుల నరగన్న వెట్టి ముఖముల్చరణాగ్రనఖాళి గోకుచున్
నిలుగుచు నావలించుచు వనీవిహగోత్కర మెట్లు పల్కెన
ప్పలుకులె యట్టులెత్తి విని పల్కెడు కంటివె కీర శారికల్ *Mc.* 3 : 58.

‡ కేళీసౌధము గేళిడోలికయునుఁ గేళీవన శ్రేణియుఁ
గేళీశైలము గేళిదీర్ఘికయునుఁ గేళీమరాళంబులుఁ
బోలం లేని గృహంబు లేదొకటియుఁ బూఁబోండ్లు ప్రాణేశులుఁ
శ్రీ లక్ష్మీ హరిమూర్తి భేదములు వర్ణింపంగ నింకేటికిఁ ॥ *Vmn.* 4 : 145.

The middle class people lived either in tiled houses * or in terraced structures built of mud. The latter caused much annoyance to their owners during the rainy season. † The bulk of the population in the capital as well as the country resided in thatched houses, which were built strongly. ‡ People belonging to a profession lived in a single locality specially in towns.

Section 3 : *Dress* :—Much information is available about the dress of the people specially belonging to the upper classes. The foreign travellers describe only the dress of the nobility and the courtiers. Although the contemporary writers are mainly interested in depicting the life of the court and the nobility, they offer valuable information occasionally about the life of the lower classes also. It is possible from these to form a fairly accurate idea of the kind of dress, which the common people wore in the 16th century. Barbosa says:

> "Their men wear certain clothes as a girdle below, wound very tightly in many folds, and short white shirts of cotton or silk or coarse brocade, which are gathered between the thighs but open

* *Vasucaritra* (4 : 72) refers to కెంపుటోడుబిళ్లలగరిడీలు. If the *gariḍis* had roofs of ruby-coloured tiles, it is not unlikely that at least some of the dwelling-houses should have been similarly roofed.

† మట్టి మిద్దెలవారికి మరు పనులకు
నెలఁతఁ బాసిన వారికి నిదుర చెడియె ॥ *Ām*. 4 : 123.

‡ పిడుగుల కల్కి లోఁ దొలఁచి భీరులు కంచముఁ జల్లు దీ ధితు
ల్గడపల వెళ్లి రాఁ బొగల కావిరి గ్రుంగిన పుల్గృహంబు లె
ల్లెడఁ గనుపట్టె నీళ్ల నిల యెల్లను ముంచి రసాతలంబు పై
విడియఁగ దండు డిగ్గిన సవిద్యుదురస్తన యత్నులో యనన్ ॥
ibid 4 : 128.

cf. *Barbosa* i. p. 202.

"The other houses of the people are thatched, 'but none the less are very well built, and arranged according to occupations, in long streets with many open places."

in the front: on their heads, they carry small turbans, and some wear silk or brocade caps, they wear their rough shoes on their feet [without stockings]. They wear also large garments thrown over their shoulders like capes." *

Nuniz describes the dress of the Rāya; it was like the dress of any other nobleman, only richer and more gaudy.

"His clothes are silk cloths of very fine material and worked with gold...; they wear at times *bajuris* of the same sort, which are like shirts with a skirt, and on the head they wear caps of brocade which they call *culaes*." †

Paes gives an account of shoes which the people wore:

"The shoes have pointed ends, in the ancient manner, and there are other shoes that have nothing but soles, but on the top are some straps which help to keep them on the feet. They are made like those which of old the Romans were wont to wear." ‡

It is evident that *dhōti*, *kabāyi* or *bujari*, cap or turban and *uttarīya* were the garments in which the courtiers were usually dressed. This is corroborated by the evidence of the poet, Śrīnātha, who refers to *kullāyi*, *kōka*, and laced *kurpāsa*. § Although the majority of the people wore no shoes, sandals with or without pointed ends were in use among the rich and the courtiers. The shoes which the rich wore were, according to several contemporary writers, provided with *gilakas* or devices for the purpose of producing creaking sound. ¶

* *Barbosa* i. p. 205. † *FE.* p. 383. ‡ *ibid* p. 252.

§ కుల్లా యుంచితి కోక సుట్టితి జరీ కూర్పాసముఁ దొడ్గితిఁ

* * *

తల్లీ కన్నడరాజ్యలక్ష్మి దయలేదా యేను శ్రీనాథుఁడఁ ॥

Vīdhināṭakam.

¶ *Spm.* 2 : 40.

The dress of the *rasika* who frequented the salons of the fashionable courtesans differed from the above in certain particulars. He wore knee-breeches which he tightened with a white *daṭṭi* or sash. He wound round over the breeches a thin muslin *dhōti*, and stuck a long dagger in the waist; over his shoulders was another fine muslin worn in a careless fashion; and on the head was a *rumāl* or turban covering the chignon. Such was the sartorial equipment of the dandy, who frequented the salons of dancing-women.* The dress of the respectable *vaidīka* Brahman was simple in the extreme. He put on only two garments, the *dhōti* of *nīrkāvi* colour and an *uttarīya* or the upper cloth, which was replaced in the case of the learned by a shawl.† The men of the cultivating class were usually satisfied with a loin-cloth; but the well-to-do farmers put on one or two garments of home-spun cloth.‡ The dress of the artisans such as weavers of silk and cotton cloth, the goldsmiths, and the oil-mongers was probably more pretentious. They put on white clothes to which the younger members applied scented oil of the clearing nut with brushes.§ The shepherds wore only a loin-cloth, and a woollen blanket, which they carried either on their shoulders or on the head. The *Bōyas* had only a *kāse* around the loins, the

* చల్లడ మా మీఁదఁ చలువఁ బట్టినదట్టి దలిమంపు దుప్పటి దానిమీఁద
మొల జముదాళిచాయల పిడియంబు చేఁ బడగ సూరియుఁ జిల్లబటువు చేత
వలకారి సిగతాయతులు దానిపై జాజివిరు లందుపై నొంటి పారరుమాలు
Npm. **2 : 20.**

† *Npm.* **2 : 16.**

‡ *Śs.* **2 : 410.**

§ చిల్లతైలంబును వాసన కొడుపులం బూసి మణుంగు చంద్రిక చేలలె
రవణంబులుగా నెదురుగాఁ వేడుకం జూడ వచ్చిన యవ్వీటి మేటి
సాలె యగసాలె పటుసాలె వానె వైజాతి సాతులేతుల కొమరులు...
Ām. **4 : 35.**

rest of the body remaining naked.* The *Mālas* or *Pariahs* put on a *kāse* of blue colour; † the more respectable among them dressed themselves in a dirty leather *kabāyi*, and a cap of the same material, ‡ whereas all tied a towel over the head so as to form a sort of turban.

More information is available regarding women, as almost all contemporary writers take special delight in describing their limbs, dress, ornaments etc. Barbosa gives an account of the way in which the women at the capital were dressed.

> "The women wear white garments of very thin cotton, or of silk of bright colours, five yards long: one part of which is girt round them below, and the other part they throw over one shoulder and across their breasts in such a way that one arm and shoulder remain uncovered." §

The dress of the women at court has been described by several writers. It consisted of a *pāvaḍa* (a sort of petticoat), *paiṭa* (mantle), and a *ravika* (bodice). These three were the principal garments constituting a lady's dress. The petticoat of saffron colour, and thin muslin *paiṭa* were very popular among the ladies of aristocratic birth. They liked the bodice to be as close-fitting as possible. They wore shoes made of soft leather lined with velvet and ornamented richly. ¶ The queens and the numerous women of the zenana, as well as the courtesans, dressed themselves more or less

* మొల నిరుగడల పొరల కాశకోకయుఁ బొరల బిగియించి. *Tbm.* Canto ii.

† కటి నుండి చనుమఱ గడిగాఁగ బిగియించి కట్టిన నిడు నీలికాసె మెఱయుఁ
... ...
బూది బ్రుంగిన మొగంబున గాదకట్టుమైనపు మైల బ్రాఁజౌతు నాఁజెలంగఁ
Ām. 7: 18.

‡ "చమురైన తోల్కు బుసంబు టెక్కియును" *ibid* 6: 6.

§ *Barbosa* i. p. 207.

¶ cf. *ibid* p. 209. "They wore leather shoes well embroidered in silk."

in the same fashion. But the common women wore only a long *sāri* and a bodice. The *sāris* of the women of the cultivating class had on them squares and other designs printed in bright colours. * Similarly the *Bōya* women dressed themselves in simple garments, but it was of white colour and fine texture. They wound half of it around their loins, the other half passing over their breasts and shoulders so as to form a sort of hood covering the head. †

People had, on the whole, a partiality for coloured garments. The common folk had to be satisfied with cotton cloth only. The rich, however, loved to dress themselves in silk fabrics with borders of gold lace. They were great connoisseurs of dress, and paid particular attention to the texture of the cloth they wore. The coarse cloth was considered fit only to be worn by rude people, who were low in the scale of civilization.

Section 4 : The Ornaments and Perfumes :—The love of ornaments was common to all people of both the sexes. Necklaces, anklets and armlets were worn by men and women alike. Jewelled belts, and ear rings might be included in the same class, although there must have been some difference between those worn by men and women. Such ornaments as the *mungara* (nose ring), the *kammalu* (ear rings) and the jewellery pertaining to the coiffure were peculiar to women. Each caste had a certain type of ornaments peculiar to itself.

The people, specially men, attached great value to a particular kind of anklet known as the *gaṇḍapeṇḍēra*, not so much on account of the material of which it

* cf. *Prm.* 3 : 74. "కట్టిరి చిరుత చౌకముల క్రొం బుట్టముల్"

† *Tbm.* Canto ii.

was made as from considerations of honour. Originally it appears to have been worn by soldiers of distinction as a symbol of their valour on the battlefield; but, in course of time, it lost its special significance, and came to be regarded as a badge of honour with which the Rāya decorated his soldiers, ministers, men of letters and others. * The *gaṇḍapeṇḍēra* was worn olny on one anklet, and the Rāya personally put it on the ankle of the person whom he desired to honour specially. † Ample material exists for a detailed and systematic study of the jewellery of the period, which, if undertaken, is bound to reveal the artistic taste of the people.

Perfumes:—The love of scents and perfumes seems to have been only second to that of ornaments; but it was only the rich that could satisfy their desire in this direction; for, the poor had no money to purchase the costly stuffs that were manufactured in the country or imported from abroad. The perfumes used by them varied according to the season. In summer men besmeared their bodies with sandal, camphor, musk, civet, all ground together and kneaded into a paste. ‡ This is confirmed by Barbosa, who alludes to this habit of the inhabitants of Vijayanagara.

* ముద్దుగ గండపెండియరమున్ గొనుడంచు బహూకరింపగా
నొద్దిక నాకొసంగుమని యొక్కరు గోరగలేరు లేరొకో ?
పెద్దన బోలు పండితులు పృథ్విని లేరని నీ వెరుంగవే ?
పెద్దన కీఁదలంచినను పేరిమి నా కిడు కృష్ణరాణ్ణృపా ॥

† "బిరుదైన ఘనగండ పెండేరమున కీవ తగుదని తాన పాదమున దొడిగె"

‡ వలరాచకేలి సలుపు నెడల నంగంబుల చకచకలు వెలి వోవకుండ నిండారు లేపంబులు సేయుచొప్పున కర్పూర కస్తూరికా సంకుమద మిళిత చందన పంకంబులొ కళ్ళొకళ్ల మేనులం గలయనలందుకొని చలువ చప్పరంబులం దీర్చిన పుప్పాడి తిన్నెల విశ్రమించు సతీపతులును" *Phm.* 2: 52.

"The substances with which they are always anointed are these: white sandars-wood, aloes, camphor, musk and saffron, all ground fine and kneaded with rose water. With these they anoint themselves after bathing, and so they are always very highly scented." *

Aloe wood was made use of in the place of sandal, in cold weather. Women also anointed themselves with the same substances, but very frequently they applied saffron or musk to their breasts. † In winter, chafing dishes containing bits of burning aloe wood were kept in convenient places in the mansions of the noblemen, so that they might spread the perfumed smoke throughout the building and protect the inmates from chillness. ‡ People made use of rose water, specially in the summer, on a large scale. They showered it on their bodies from small spouted leather bottles. § Civet, camphor, and several other kinds of perfumes and their compounds were in great demand. ¶

* *Barbosa* i. p. 205.

† ధౌత గంధామోద శీతల స్తనములు వొందఁ గౌఁగిళ్లతోఁ బోరగిల్ల
Ām. 2: 60.

"వనితకుచద్వయంబుఁ పయి వ్రాసిన కుంకుమ పత్ర భంగముల్
జనితనితాంత ఘర్మకణ జాలము చేత గరంగి......" *Phm.* 1: 113.

నీ చనుదోయి సంకుమద నిర్భరవాసన మేననూన న
య్యో చిర సౌఖ్యముల్ గనుట యుండె ... *Mc.* 3: 105.

చనుదోయిం గొనబౌ కురంగ మదచర్చల్ జారిపో" *ibid* 3: 136.

‡ దళముగా సాగరు వాసంతి వెలుఁగ సౌధ
శిఖర వాతాయనాగతా చిరరుగంతు
నతదృగవరోధముల తోడ నగరిన్నృపులు *Ām.* 4: 135.

§ "పన్నీరు నించిన తన్నీరు తిత్తులొత్త వియత్తలంబునం బారికై వారు
ధారల వాద్యంబులు దుడిచిన" *ibid* 4: 35.

¶ సద్యో వినిర్భిన్న సారంగనాభికావృతమై పిసాళించు మృగమదంబు
కసటువో బీరెండ గరగి కల్జల నంటి గమగమ వలచు చొక్కపు జవాజి
పొరలెత్తి ఘనసార తరువుల దనుదాన తొరగిన పచ్చకప్పురపు సిరము
గ్రొజ్జంగి పూఁ బొదల్ గురియంగ బటికంపు దొనల నిండిన యట్టి తుహినజలము॥
Mc. 2: 55.

The Āndhras are said to have been specially skilled in the art of compounding the scents.* Sometimes, thin solution of sandal-paste was sprinkled in front of the mansions to make the atmosphere balmy.†

The love of sweet scents also manifested itself in other directions. The water which the rich people used for bathing and washing purposes, and the clothes which they put on, were also perfumed; ‡ and they even sprinkled powdered camphor in the liquor they drank. §

The people of this age had an insatiable love of sweet smelling flowers. Among the flowers that had no fragrance, they liked only the lotus, the others were treated with contempt. Rose, jasmine, *campak*, *jāji*, *virajāji*, *molla*, *kētaki* etc., were some of the favourite varieties for which people had special fondness. Men wore flower garlands on their heads and around the necks. Persons belonging to both sexes allowed their hair to grow luxuriantly, which they carefully combed with ivory or wooden combs having applied perfumed oil. They stuck small wreaths of flowers in their chignon. It was customary to hang flowers across the doorways. Very often, during the summer, flowers were spread on couches, on which men and women slept at night. Each respectable house had a flower garden of its own, where several varieties of flower bushes were grown

* గంధకలనా కుసుమస్రగ్గ్రథనాదులనాంధ్యంబులే
కలరు నంధ్రదేశీయులగు గంధకారులు... *Ām.* 4 : 35.

† అనుచుం జందన పంకపంకిల తలంబై ...యొప్పు నప్పురంబు సొచ్చి" *Mc.* 5 : 53.

‡ మజ్జన మాడె రాజు కృశమధ్యమ లింపున నంపుగుంపులై
గొజ్జగ నీటి వెల్లువలు గోవజవాజులు నిగ్గుజూప " *Mc.* 5 : 57.

§ కలధౌత మాణిక్య కనక పాత్రికలందు వాసిత మధుర పుష్పాసవంబు
వోసి కర్పూరపు పొడి మీద వెదజల్లి" *Rm.* 4 : 186.

by trained gardeners, whose loud songs, while baling out water from wells, filled the atmosphere of the city in the morning. * One of the favourite resorts of the *rasikas* appears to have been the flower-market, where all kinds of flowers were offered for sale. The flower vendors were women of questionable character, who indulged in vulgar conversation and low badinage. †

Section 5: *Tāmbūla and Bed*:—One of the most common practices of Indians of all castes and creeds is the eating or chewing of the *tāmbūla*. In the sixteenth century, it appears to have been more popular than it is at present. An Indian, who did not chew the *tāmbūla* in that age, must indeed have been a rare creature. The betel leaf, the areca nut, and lime are the principal, and among the common folk, the only ingredients that enter into its composition. The well-to-do people add cardamoms, cloves, nutmeg etc., to make it fragrant. In the sixteenth century, however, people were accustomed to consume with the *tāmbūla* some other substances such as musk, camphor etc., which have gone

* ప్రాతర్వేళల నట్టి వెట్ట సాఁగస్సై పాటిల్లె గుంభోంభ నో
ద్భూతాంబు ధ్వని వాద్యమై మరుదధః పుంజీ భవత్పాటల
వ్రాతామ్రేడిత సిక్త భూసురభిళారామంబు కుల్యా బహు
స్రోతస్సంధుల నంధు యంత్ర నధికృతోప్తోద్గీత గేయాఘముల్॥
Ām. 2: 55.

† పద్మాస్య పురి ననుభవితకు నీవ యెత్తులు వెట్టెద నఁగ రావలసె నిటకుఁ
తెలుపుమా జాముండు నలరింపా ఘటికాద్వయంబుండు నలరింపా కంబుకంఠి
యే వేడుటకు నీవు ఋతువేల చెప్పెద వువిద మే మందాక నోర్వఁగలమె
చేరఁగా రాదె బాసికము గ లోఁకిన యంతనే చెడునె యేణాయతాక్షి

యనుచుఁ బరిభాషఁ బోలెఁదమ్మాన దొరల
నాడఁమోవిఁ జెరంగిడి యాగు నవ్వు
కంట నిగుడ విరుల్నాన్పు కరణిఁ జల్లు
సరసపు జలంబె జాణల మరులు కొల్పు॥ *Ām.* 2: 21.

out of use since.* It was customary with people in those days to offer visitors betel, nuts, and a few slices of camphor. The *tāmbūla* was considered not only as a luxury but as a mild tonic, which stimulated the digestive organs. It excited the curiosity of the foreigners, who visited India, to such an extent that several of them took pains to describe it at length. Paes says:

> "The betel, is a herb which has a leaf like the leaf of pepper, or the ivy of our country; they always eat this leaf, and carry it in their mouths with another fruit called areca. This is something like medlar, but it is very hard, and it is very good for the breath and has many other virtues." †

Some of these virtues have been described by 'Abdur Razāk.

> "It relieves hunger, stimulates the organs of digestion, disinfects the breath and strengthens the teeth." ‡

The *tāmbūla* acquired a definite place in the social customs of the country. Custom enjoined that every householder should offer *tāmbūla* to all those that visited him. To receive it from the king was considered a special honour. Therefore, one of the ways in which the Rāyas manifested their favour was to give *tāmbūla*, camphor, etc., in addition to jewels, robes of honour, palanquins, and *cowries*. Moreover, it was also regarded as a sign of ratification of a commission or appointment. When the Rāya or some other man of high rank entrusted to a person the performance of some work, say the writing of a book, the capture of a thief, or the defeating of an enemy, he offered the person so selected a *tāmbūla* without which the appointment was not considered as formally made.

* మృగమద సౌరభ విభవ । ద్విగుణిత ఘనసారసాంద్ర వీటీ గంధ
స్థగితేతర పరిమళమై । మగువపొలుపు దెలుపు నొక్క మారుత మెలసెన్ ॥
Mc. 2 : 24.

† *FE.* p. 242.

‡ *ED.* iv. p. 114.

Bed :—Two kinds of furniture may be conveniently considered in this connection, the swinging-cot and the ordinary bedstead.

The swings and swinging-cots appear to have been specially popular among the upper classes. The poets of the time frequently describe damsels rocking themselves in swings made of ropes or creepers suspended to the branches of trees in pleasure gardens. The swing-cot, however, was an article of domestic furniture, which gave not only the pleasure of a swing but also the comfort of a bed. Hence the popularity which it enjoyed. Paes saw some swing-cots in the palace of the Rāya at Vijayanagara. One of them, which was intended for the use of the queens, was hanging on four silver chains from a cross beam on two pillars in the midst of an open court-yard within the palace. Another swing-cot with feet made of gold bars, and gold plated cross-bars was suspended by silver chains in a corridor. A third was suspended by chains of gold in a chamber. It had feet of gold with much setting of precious stones; and the cross-bars were covered also with gold. * The feet of some of them were of finely cut coral, set with precious stones so as to resemble parrots and swans. They had flowers of gold and other beautiful designs painted on

* *FE*. pp. 286-87; cf. *Kpm*. 2 : 15.

"బంగారు గొలుసులు పవడంబు దరిమెన కోళ్లును వింతబాగుల బొగడలు
రత్నంపు జిలుకలు రాయంచ ప్రతిమలు పసిండి పువ్వుల వ్రాతపనుల సొబగు
వివిధంబులగు చిత్ర విరచనలును దసిలీ నూలుపట్టె యల్లిక బెడంగు
పలుదెఱంగుల పట్టు తలగడ బిల్లలు మవ్వంపు గుంకురుపువ్వు పఱుపు
గలిగి మెఱుగులు దిక్కుల గడలుకొనఁగ
మించు దంతపు టుయ్యాన మంచమునను"

them. The bottom was interlaced with tape of *dasili* silk, on which quilts and silken pillows were placed so as to give maximum comfort. Although the common folk were not able to furnish their houses with swing-cots made of gold, suspended on gold and silver chains, they provided themselves with those made of wood hanging on iron chains or ropes. The poet, Peddana, expressed the opinion that a swing-cot was one of the articles necessary to make human existence comfortable and inspire poetry.*

The ordinary bedsteads were similar to the spring cots in construction, although they were more solidly built. The cots of the palace, especially those reserved for the use of the Rāya and his queens, were made of costly material. The feet were made of ivory, set with precious stones and mounted with the figures of such birds as parrots, doves etc., which were so designed as to produce sounds resembling the notes of those birds when touched. The bottom was interlaced with white silk tape, over which extended a canopy richly set with pearls.† Paes who had an opportunity of entering the Rāya's bed-chamber observed a cot which was covered with work of rubies, diamonds, and all other kinds of precious stones. The

* నిరుపహతి స్థలంబు రమణీప్రియదూతిక తెచ్చి యిచ్చు క
ప్పుర విడె మాత్మ కింపయిన భోజన ముయ్యాల మంచ మొప్పు త
ప్పురయు రసజ్ఞు లూహ తెలియం గల వాచక పాఠకోత్తముల్
గలిగినగాని యూరకఁగృతు ల్రచియింప మనంగ శక్యమే॥

† మొలక మెఱుంగు కెంపు మొనముక్కుల నిక్కు కిరీటి పచ్చరా
చిలుకల కోళ్లతోఁ జికిలి చంద్రిక వన్నియ పట్టుపట్టెతోఁ
దొలకు పసిండి వ్రాల తెఱతో నెఱతావుల మేలుకట్టుతోఁ
జలువలు చిందు ముత్తియపుఁ జప్పర మంచముపై మహోన్నతిన్॥
Vc. 4 : 78.

cross-bars were covered with gold; 'it had all round it a railing of pearl, a span wide.' In another chamber, which was 'all of ivory,' the chamber as well as the walls, he noticed two thrones, covered with gold, and a cot of silver with its curtains. * According to Nuniz, the cots in which the wives of Acyuta slept were 'covered and adorned with silver plates,' whereas his own cot, which had legs of solid gold, was 'plated and lined' with gold. † While camping, he would carry a bedstead kept in a box made of pieces of iron. The mattresses and pillows were made of silk stuffed with softest material. ‡ The *hamsatūlikā talpa* or the bed stuffed with swan's down was specially valued on account of its softness. Beds stuffed with saffron § also seem to have been in use. In addition to these, the *ciguru pānpu* (bed made of tender herbs), and *pūbānpu* (bed of flowers) are alluded in contemporary literature. The latter is not still uncommon among the very rich who spread in summer flowers, especially jasmine, over their beds. The bedsteads of the royal palace were provided with curtains to keep off the mosquitoes; they seem to have been made of costly material containing beautiful designs painted in golden colour, ¶ and mounted on frames of silver. The mosquito curtain was used not only by the members of the imperial household but by all the well-to-do citizens also. || People were accustomed to keep in winter braziers containing glowing fire under the cots to keep off the cold.

* *FE.* p. 285.

† *ibid* pp. 369-70.

‡ *ibid.*

§ పలుదెఱంగుల పట్టుతలగడబిల్లలు మువ్వంబు <u>గుంకుమ పువ్వుపఱుపు</u>.

Kpm. 2 : 15.

¶ *Vc.* 4 : 78.

|| *Ām.* 5 : 104.

The cots used by the nobility, although not so magnificent as those of the emperor and his queens, were costly enough; for, the nobles imitated the life of the court in almost every particular. But the poor folk had then the same cots as now, which were constructed with wood and bamboo interlaced with cords. That this was the kind of cot commonly in use all over the country is amply proved by the satires of Śrīnātha who lived half a century earlier. * Probably the same kind of furniture is alluded to by Kṛṣṇarāya in his *Āmuktamālyada.* †

Section 5: Women:—From the fact that women were regarded as objects of enjoyment or *bhōga*, it is evident that our forefathers did not regard women as their equals. No doubt, women were necessary to make life worth living; but the same might be said of some other articles of enjoyment. Although the people of the age could very well imagine a state of existence, where men could live without women, they could not conceive of the possibility of women living apart from men. They believed that the whole creation was intended for the enjoyment of men. As women, like several other things, were regarded as playthings to amuse men's fancy, they surrounded themselves with as many of the fair sex as they could maintain; but they liked young damsels; middle aged women of over forty years, not to speak of older women, had no attraction for them; ‡ for they could not offer them any pleasure. Therefore, they married as many damsels as they liked, and

* మలినపుఁగుడ్డలున్ నులకమంచపుఁ గుక్కియుఁ జీకటిల్లునున్. *Cpr.* p. 10.

† *Ām.* 4: 135.

‡ నలువదియేండ్లపై నరసిన వనితలు... భోగయోగ్యములు గారు. *Nītiśatakam.* 64.

kept others as maids to wait upon their wives. They found in each of them a potential wife, or more generally, a concubine. They dispensed with the services of men-servants altogether within the walls of the zenana. The imperial household, on which the nobles modelled their own, was a huge establishment consisting entirely of women from six to twelve thousand in number. These women were either in the service of the emperor himself or his wives. Nuniz says:

> "Some are dancing-girls, and others bearers who carry the King's wives on their shoulders, and the King also in the interior of the palace...He has also women who wrestle, and others who are astrologers, and soothsayers; and he has women who write all the accounts of expenses that are incurred inside the gates, and others whose duty it is to write all the affairs of the kingdom and compare their books with those of the writers outside; he has also women for music, who play instruments and sing." *

The emperor spent most of his time, excepting the hours when he had to transact the state business, in his own apartments within the precincts of the palace, when he was waited upon by several women each of whom had a special duty to perform. The casket of musk, the white *cowry*, the spittoon, the sword, the perfume casket, the mirror, the fan, the golden pitcher, the betel pouch, and the camphor box were each held by a single woman who stationed herself about the emperor. † Not that he wanted to make use of these articles, but court etiquette demanded that he should keep them, as they were the insignia of royalty. ‡

* *FE.* p. 382.

† *Spm.* i. pp. 179-188.

‡ కుకురుకాశకురుకరూశకోసలాంధ్ర సింధుబా ।
హ్లీకశకాంగవంగసింహళేశకన్యకామణి ।
ప్రకరపాణిఘటితరత్నపాదుకాకలాచికా ।
ముకురవీటికాకరండ ముఖ్యరాజలాంఛనా ॥ *Mc.* 1 : 183.

cf. *FE.* p. 269. "And around him stand his pages with his betel, and ι i; sword, and the other things which are his insignia of state."

When, however, he sat in the audience hall, men seem to have taken charge of them.* The wives of the emperor were permitted to enjoy the same privilege.† Women also helped the emperor to bathe ; they dressed him, served him food, and narrated stories of love to amuse him. They sang, played on musical instruments, and danced before him.‡ When he went to the chamber of any one of his wives, he was again surrounded by a batch of her servants. Thus, he spent most of his time in the company of women, who did everything in their power to please him. He was not free from their company even when he went to war or toured through the provinces of his realm. According to Nuniz, thousands of women accompanied the Rāya, when he went to war.§ This is confirmed by Barbosa who alludes to the numerous unmarried women accompanying the army. "Among these," declares he, "are many women who are reserved for the king,

* హరి యంతఃపురినుండి వచ్చుటయునయ్యై సేవకై యున్నవా ।
రురువేగంబున వామదేవశుక ముఖ్యుల్ చేరి కాళాంజియు ।
క్కరుఁడొక్కండ డపం బొకండు నిజఖడ్గంబు న్వహించంగనొ ।
క్కరుఁడొప్పారఁగఁబట్టె నుజ్జ్వలత ముక్తచ్ఛత్ర మగ్రంబునన్ ॥
Vmn. **4 : 185.**

That men were also employed for the purpose is revealed by inscriptions which mention Haḍapada Cina Nāgama, Goḍugu Pōla etc.

† కాళాంజి పట్టు నిక్కలికి గాండేంద్రదనం। దన దీని లెస్సగా మనుప వమ్మ।
కుంచియ వైచు నీ కోమలి చోళక । న్యక దీనిమన్నన నడపవమ్మ ।
యడపంబుబట్టు నీ యతివ మాళవరాజ। సుత దీనిజులక గాఁజూడ కమ్మ ।
పావడ పట్టు నీ పడతి మాగధుకూర్మి । బిడ్డదీని దలంచి పెంచ వమ్మ।
పసిడిపావలు వెట్టు నీ పద్మగంధి। పాండ్యభూపాలు గారాపుఁ బట్టి దీని।
ననుదినంబున నరసి కాపాడ వమ్మ । వలయు వరములఁ దగురీతి
[మెలప వమ్మ ॥ *Rc.* **3 : 202.**

‡ ***Spm.*** ii. p. **41** f ; cf. ***FE.*** pp. 382-3.

§ ***FE.*** p. 328.

and these travel in great state for they have great riches.*

People were not averse to imitate the manner of court. The great popularity of polygamy, which was such a marked feature of the age, might be partly attributed to the example set by the Rāya and his nobles.

Section 6 : Bath :—Hindus, especially those inhabiting the south of the peninsula, attach considerable importance to bathing. No one belonging to the upper classes takes his food without bathing first. The importance of bath in the social and the religious life of the people was far greater a few centuries ago than it is at present. Three kinds of baths are known to have been popular in the 16th century : (1) The ordinary bath in cold or warm water. This was the most common kind of bath, as it could be taken by every person without incurring any expense. Although the lower and the middle class people bathed daily, the first place should be given to Brahmans, as they, both men and women, bathed several times a day for ceremonial purification. They would rise up in the early hours of the morning, and repair to a neighbouring river or tank to take a plunge in the cold water, and wash their clothes. † All people, however, took *abhyangana* or oil bath once a week, preferably on a Saturday, ‡ although its nature varied according to the wealth and the position of persons. The common people went to a river, tank, or well carrying with them the necessary articles

* *Barbosa* i. pp. 225-26.

† *Mc.* 1 : 54.

‡ కదళిగర్భరప్రభవ పుటికాచ్ఛటఁ జేతులనిప్ప పిండిపైఁ ।
గుదురుగనిల్పి యోపుగతి గూనల నూనియ నించి త్రాటము ।
న్నదికిన శాటిత్రేవల నదినొక్కటఁ గ్రుంకిడి వత్తు రెండఁ జే ।
వదలక యాతనింట శనివారమునన్ బరదేశి వైష్ణవుల్ ॥

Ām. 1 : 83.

which would enable them to take the *abhyangana*. Having reached the place, they anointed the head and body with gingelly oil. Next, they rubbed themselves with the powder of *mahuva* seed to remove the oil. Lastly, they entered into the water, if they happened to be bathing in a river or a tank; or had it poured on them from pails drawn from a well, in order to wash themselves clean. The middle class people bathed at home in warm water. They employed the services of professionals. Usually, men of the courtesan class, * not only massaged the body but anointed it with oil, while entertaining the bather with their humorous conversation. The *abhyangana* of the princes and nobles was a more elaborate process. It was customary for them to take the *abhyangana* daily just before they sat at dinner. Young damsels anointed the head with fragrant oil of *campaka* flowers; then they proceeded to carefully disentangle the hair with their finger nails, sprinkling rose water over the head now and then. Next, they applied the paste called *aṭakali*, prepared from sandal wood and *usirika* (phylanthus emblica) seeds. Rose-water perfumed with Goa civet was poured over the head without interruption. Finally, the moisture over the body and the head was dried with a *valipa* or thin muslin cloth. It must not be supposed that a single women assisted the bather throughout; for it is said that each process was to be performed by a separate person † The *abhyangana* of women was analogous to that of men except that it differed in one particular: just before the close of the bath they besmeared their bodies with the paste of turmeric and

* పండువ తలంటులకు నింటికిం దెచ్చు పణ్యాంగనా భ్రాతల పరిహాస చేష్టలయందు. *Ām.* 4: 187

† *Phm.* 2: 8-13.

washed themselves clean. * The importance which the people attached to *abhyangana* was due probably to the belief that it would promote the luxuriant growth of hair which they—men as well as women—valued highly. In summer people bathed in cool water to mitigate the severity of the heat. The rich and the nobles spent a good part of their time with their women in *dīrghikas* or long oblong baths provided with steps to facilitate descent into water. † The princes and the Rāya sported similarly with the women of their zenanas in large artificial reservoirs or tanks. Barbosa alludes to this practice in a brief passage: He says:

> "They (the women of the Rāya's zenana) bathe daily in the many tanks of which I spoke above, as kept for that purpose. The king goes to see them bathing, and she who pleases him most is sent for to come to his chamber." ‡

It is, however, the contemporary literature that gives graphic account of the *jala-krīḍa* or the water sport as it was called. The prince or the Rāya was not always accustomed to sit on the bank eagerly observing the fair bathers. Very often he joined them and enjoyed the sport for hours. Each bather had to provide himself or herself with a bathing costume, consisting of a thin silk garment, which when wet would so stick to the body as to show no distinction between itself and the skin. § On reaching the tank, they put on the bathing

* *Ām.* 1 : 56.

† పవలెల్ల దీర్ఘికాంబువుచల్లుపోరాట నలసి మృణాళికా జడములైన
బాహువుల్ తమదుకూర్పరముల కెదురుగా మలఁచి మూపుల గరతలము లునిచి
....కలసి
రెలమి ధన్యులు దఱిపి వెన్నెలబయళ్ల ॥ *Ām.* 2 : 61.

‡ *Barbosa* i. p. 208.

§ తడిసి తనువులఁ భేదంబు గాన్పింప కుండఁ ।
గడు నడఁగిన చేలల్ గల్మి స్రుక్కళ్లపట్టె ।
ర్పడఁ దెలుప ఘనాంభో భారతం గుంతలంబుల్ ।
మడమల పయి వ్రేలఁ మత్తమాతంగయానల్ ॥ *Kpm.* 6 : 233.

costume and removed all the jewellery from their bodies. Then they entered the tank, several of them carrying syringes made of leaves and metals. * Some of them stood in rows and threw water on each other's faces ; others squirted water, perhaps coloured, from their syringes upon their neighbours. Some others played the exciting game of *ōla* or hide and seek in water. Having thus sported until they were completely tired, they left the tank and repaired to their chambers. †

Food :— According to Paes, " rice, wheat, grains, Indian-corn, and a certain amount of barley and beans, moong, pulses, horse-gram, and many other seeds " were the food of the people. ‡ The staple food-stuff of the empire was, of course, rice, which was cultivated on a large scale. The rice grown in Tulu *nāḍu* belonged to four varieties *viz.*, *garaçal*, *açal*, *quavagas*, and *pachary.* § There must have been many more. All these varieties may be classified under two heads : the white rice, and the black (red) rice. The former was considered superior and it was consumed only by the well-to-do people. The Rāya, the princes and the nobles ate only the best kind of white rice known as the *rājana*. The ' black ' rice was cheap and it was very much in demand among the poor. All the people, however, were not rice eaters. The Muhammadans ate wheat.¶

తొడవులటు వెట్టి పలిప పావడలు గట్టి।శృంగములు వట్టి నీరాడఁ జేరునపుడు
Vc. 3 : 155.

చిగురుంజిమ్మనగ్రోవిలో నొక తెరాజీ వాసవం బుంచి పై । నిగిడింపఁగ
ibid 3 : 158.

" బంగరు కొమ్ము పూని యొక ప్రౌఢ రయంబున నీరుచల్ల
ibid 3 : 160.

† *Vc.* 3 : 155-166.

‡ *FE.* p. 257.

§ *Barbosa* i. p. 192.

¶ *FE.* p. 257.

The *Reḍḍis* and probably the other cultivating classes of the inland districts subsisted upon *chōḷam āriga*, *rāgi* etc. Several kinds of vegetables and herbs entered largely into their diet whether they were vegetarians or meat eaters. * Pulses of all kinds were articles of common consumption. The meat eaters enriched their diet by the addition of many meat dishes. According to Nuniz, the Rāyas of Vijayanagara, and with them the meat eating section of their subjects, ate "mutton, pork, venison, partridges, hares, doves, quail, and all kinds of birds." † Fish might be added to the list, and a special dish consisting of slices of fresh fish from the river and half ripe mangoes appears to have been very popular. ‡ It is said that "even sparrows and rats and cats and lizards" § were sold in the markets of the city; but it is very unlikely that these were eaten also. Sugar, oil, and spices formed the necessary ingredients in the preparation of several dishes; and ghee was as much in demand among the upper classes as it is at present. *Hayyangavīna*, or the ghee melted from the butter of the previous day, was specially liked. ¶ Pepper

* గురుగుం జెంచలిఁ దుమ్మిలేఁదగరిసాకుం దింత్రిణీపల్లవో ।
త్కరముం గూడఁ బొరంటి నూనియలతోఁ గట్టావికుట్టారుగో ।
గిరము ల్మెక్కి తమిం బసుల్వొలము వోఁ గ్రేవు ల్మెయి నాన్చ మే ।
కెరువుం గుంపటి మంచ మెక్కరి ప్రభుత్వైకాప్తి రెడ్లజ్జడిన్ ॥

Ām. 4 : 134

† *FE.* p. 375.

‡ తారుణ్యాతిగ చూత నూత్న ఫలయుక్తైలాభి ఘారస్వన ।
ద్ధారా ధూపిత శుష్యదంబుహృత మాత్స్య చ్ఛేద పాకోద్గతో ।
ద్గారంపుం గన రార్చు..." *Ām.* 2: 68.

§ *FE.* p. 375.

¶ "జాంగలామిషముతో శాల్యన్న మధిక హైయ్యంగవీనంబుగా నారగించి ॥"

Ām. 4 : 135.

was used in the preparation of all the curries, as chillies were either not known or had not yet become popular.* Fruits such as mangoes, jack, grapes, cucumber, plantains, etc., were taken along with rice at the table of the rich. †

Section 7 : Drink :—The common drink which was within the reach of all was, of course, water to which the rich added several aromatic substances to make it agreeable and refreshing. Two other drinks which the well-to-do took specially in summer were *pānaka*, a beverage made of sugar and water, and *nīru-majjiga* or watery-buttermilk. To the same class may be added the juice of crushed sugar-cane and the water of the tender cocoanut. The former could be had either free or for a small consideration at the sugar-cane mills to which people flocked on summer evenings. ‡ The latter were probably available for sale in the markets of towns and cities. To keep the water cool, the cocoanuts were buried under heaps of sand under the shade of trees in the garden. § These drinks did not

* పునుఁగుఁ దావి నవోదనంపు మిరియంపుం బొళ్లతోఁ జట్టిచు ।
య్యన నా దాలని కూరగుంపు..." *Ām.* 1 : 82

† పరిపక్వసురభిరంభాఫలంబులతోడ దళమెక్కు పనసపెం డొలలతోడ।
ఘృతపిండనిభ కర్కరీఖండములతోడ। బలు దెరంగుల మావిపండ్లతోడ ।
గోస్తనీమృదుగుళుచ్ఛస్తోమములతోడ..." *ibid* 2 : 73.

‡ తోఁటఁ బగలుండి మల్లెలు దుఱిమికావు ।
లమర మాపైన నిక్షుయంత్రముల కొయ్యఁ ।
జేరు ప్రజవోల్చె భావివృష్టికి నిగ్గుడ్డు ।
తో మధురిమేచ్ఛ డిగు నెఱ్ఱచీమలనఁగ ॥ *ibid* 2 : 70.

§ ...గనరార్చు భోగులకు సంధ్యావేళలం గేళికాం ।
తారాభ్యంతర వాలుకా స్థిత హిమాంత ర్నారికేళాంబువుల్ ॥
ibid 2 : 68.

involve much expense, and they caused no harm to any one.

The same, however, cannot be said of the alcoholic drinks which seem to have been very popular among the rich. The *bhōgis* or the cultured persons of both sexes considered drinking liquor as a special mark of refinement. The most common beverage which they drank appears to have been the toddy drawn from the cocoanut palm.* The taverns, with pandals of cuscus grass † in their front, appear to have been the usual resorts of lovers, where they spent the moon-lit nights in each other's company.

The nobles, however, did not frequent the taverns, although they were more addicted to drink than the common people. There is reason to believe that a portion of the mansion of each nobleman was specially set apart for celebrating Bachchanalian festivities.‡ In the summer season, they would adjourn to the *candraśāla* allured by the brilliant moonlight. The *candraśāla* was probably decorated for the purpose. The maids of honour, who played a prominent part on such occasions, took particular care in arranging wine pots brimming with liquor and cups of gold and silver set with precious stones. Dishes containing delicious *upadamsanas* § of meat were also placed by their side so

* నారికేళాసవపుఁజీఁపు టూరు పొలయ ।
వలిపె యొుం టాల్లెతో నురస్థలులఁ గూర్చి ..॥ *Ām* 2:61.

† 'పానశాలాపురోభాగ భాసమాన నలదకాయమానంబులం' ॥ *Vc.* 4:23.

‡ *Vc.* 4 : 72 refers to ***kuḍinīrumēḍaḷu***, which may be interpreted as halls set apart for drinking (water); but in another place in the same work it is stated that liquor was drunk in these drinking halls.

§ వలపల కేల నామిషము వామకరంబున మద్యపాత్రయుఁ ॥ *Rm.* Canto iv.
మంచి యుపదంశనంబులు మానవతుల ।
ముద్దకెమ్మోవి తేనెల నుమ్మరములు ॥ *Spm.* 2 : 152.

that the revellers might nibble at them as a relish to drinking. Some of the popular varieties of liquor were *puṣpāsava*, *tāḷamadhu*, *aikṣava madirārasa*, *mairēya* and *drākṣāsava*, beside *narikēḷāsava* which has already been mentioned. The liquor was sometimes taken in a raw condition; but it was customary to subject it to a process of concoction by adding some ingredients such as powdered camphor, in order to remove the disagreeable odour and make it more pleasant to the taste.*

The convivial party would usually begin rather late in the night. The people comprising the party squatted on the ground in a circle around the wine pots, and sipped the wine slowly from the cups, nibbling at the relish every now and then. Sometimes, lovers exchanged their cups, probably to feel more at home in each other's company.† Song and dance enhanced the gaiety of the occasion. They drank until they became thoroughly intoxicated. The behaviour of the young women attending the festivities of the *candraśāla* is vividly described by a contemporary writer.

"One young woman who lost her balance completely tumbled down muttering words in an incoherent and indistinct fashion ; another laughed loudly and uttered obscene words and phrases causing delight to her lover ; one lost all sense of shame and strutted like a pigeon ; a few sang and frolicked, whereas several joined in a game of hide and seek. One of the young

* కలధౌత మాణిక్య కనక పాత్రికలందు వాసిత మధుర పుష్పాసవంబు।
పోసి కర్పూరంపు పొడిమీద వెదజల్లి ...॥ *Rm.* Canto iv.

† మండలాకృతి గూర్చుండి మంచిదనుచు।
గ్రుక్కగ్రుక్కకు తలలూచుకొనుచు నొకరి।
కొకరి కందిచ్చి చూపుచు నుబ్బియుబ్బి।
త్రావఁదొణగిరి యుల్లాస రసముతోడ॥ *ibid.*

women in whom intoxication reached the highest pitch, having stripped herself of her clothing, went about the place in a naked condition." *

Such seem to have been the pleasures which allured the people to the moon-lit *candraśālas*; but they did not wound the popular sense of decency, as they were strictly confined to the high-walled zenanas.

* లాహిరి యెక్కంగ దేహము ల్వడబార పరఁగ నర్థోక్తులు పలుకువారు ।
వాసవామృతగంధ మాస్యంబు వలువంగ నలిరేగి పకపక నవ్వువారు ।
ధవులకుఁ గర్ణామృతంబుగా పెడ యుల్కి యరుదందఁ జిరుబూతు లాడువారు ।
పారావతాదుల భంగి సిగ్గరుగక కొందరు తెరంగులు గులుకువారు ।
పెల్లదిరి పాడువారు కుప్పించువారు । కోరికనుమూసి గంతాడువారు నెలమి ।
తివిరి మొలకోకలూడంగ దివుచువారు । నగుచు మధుపాన రతిఁదేలి రబ్జముఖులు ॥

Rm. Canto iv.

CHAPTER IV.

THE POSITION OF WOMEN

Section 1 : The Family Women :—The attitude of men of the sixteenth century towards the women has already been explained in a previous context. The women, as mentioned already, were regarded as objects of enjoyment, like dress, vehicles, houses etc., and in this view, strangely enough, the women themselves acquiesced. Therefore, the woman of the sixteenth century had no independent existence; and she was taught to believe that she was created only to cater to man's needs and keep him in good humour. For the convenience of the present study, women may be divided into two broad classes: the family women and the courtesans; but before proceeding to describe the position which each of them occupied in the society of the day, a few remarks must be made about the sources of information. Much of the information that has a bearing on the subject is culled from the works of contemporary writers, who were interested in depicting only the sunny side of the life of the nobility. They do not provide the historian with any information about the condition of the humble and the poor. A few, however, lift the veil, affording us a glimpse into the lives of common folk, which, it must be admitted, is not very pleasing. In describing the condition of the women of the age, therefore, we have necessarily to confine our attention to the position of the women of the upper classes.

The women of this class, if they happened to be members of the aristocratic families spent the major portion of their lives within the seclusion of the zenana. They did not participate in the public functions where men were likely to gather. The large bulk of the Hindu women, however, did not care to retire behind the purdah, and they moved freely with men in ordinary activities of daily life

The Education :— Girls born of all families were strictly under the control of their parents ; those belonging to the aristocratic houses were carefully educated. They were taught to read and write not only the vernaculars but Sanskrit. Music and dancing played a very important part in their educational curriculum. Skill in music, both vocal and instrumental, appears to have been one of the necessary accomplishments of cultured women. Considerable care was bestowed on teaching the girls to sing and dance. Kṛṣṇarāya employed the famous musician Lakṣmīnārāyaṇa to teach music and dancing to the ladies of his zenana. Acyuta and Rāmarāja engaged Bayakāra Rāmappaya for the same purpose. The noblemen emulating the example of the Rāya offered patronage to musicians. The popularity of music and dancing was so great that it was noticed even by the foreigners. "They teach their women," says Barbosa, "from childhood to sing, play and dance, and to turn about and take many light steps." * In the palace of the Rāya, there was a dancing hall where he sent 'his women to be taught to dance.' It was a structure of 'stone sculpture on pillars,' so designed as to help the dancers to correct themselves, if they had gone wrong in dancing. Between one pillar and another, there was a cross-bar which was like a panel, the designs on which represented 'the positions at the end of dances' so that on each panel, 'there is a dancer in the proper position at the end of a dance.' † They were intended to remind the women, if they forgot,

* *Barbosa* i. p. 208. † *FE.* pp. 288-9.

the correct position which they had to assume at the end of a dance. It is needless to point out that similar dancing halls must have existed in the houses of the ministers and the *nāyakas*. There is reason to believe that there were public dancing halls,* where probably professionals entertained the people by their performances.

Each nobleman of any consequence had a pleasure garden attached to his palace, where he grew fruit trees, and flower bushes. The women of his household, especially the girls went thither, accompanied by their maids, to divert themselves. They seated themselves under the cool shades of trees and sang to the accompaniment of the *vīṇa*; they rocked themselves in swings made of creepers; they plucked flowers from the bushes which they strung into wreaths and garlands. They swam in the tank and sported in the water.

The parents regarded their daughters as burdens from which they should free themselves at the earliest opportunity. They were, therefore, anxious to marry them to suitable persons as early as possible. Among the Brahmans the marriage of a girl was usually celebrated before the girl attained maturity. † The marriage after maturity was common among most other communities. It is very much to be doubted

* అన్నగర నాట్యశాలలఁ ।
జెన్నగు మురజముల రవళిచే నటియించున్ ।
గన్నియలకన్న మున్నగఁ ।
పన్నగ భుక్తతులు దృష్టిపాత్రము లగుచున్ ॥ *Vc.* 1: 103.
చిలుకలకొల్కి కల్కి యొకచేడియ నాటకసాల మేడపై ।
నిలువున నాడుచుండి ॥ *Mc.* 5 : 63.

† " ఇంతనాడు కరగ్రహవంతురాలిఁ జేసి తోడ్కొని వచ్చితి॥ "
Npm. 2 : 58.

whether a girl was allowed to select her own husband; for custom ordained that he should be selected by her parents or elders. As the women of the noble class were confined within the four walls of the zenana, it was not possible for them to mix with men, let alone the choice of a husband. Moreover, as the polygamous habits of the people prompted men to marry many women, it is highly improbable that the element of love could have been present in most marriages. That, at any rate, is the opinion which the greatest writer of the age had expressed on marriages of this type. He declares:

> "It is not possible that one man should love several women, and several women one man. I believe that he has no love for them, nor they for him." "Don't speak to me of these women, who dare not even get angry with their husband, although he has intercourse with other women in their very presence." "The feelings which he manifests towards them should not be termed love but regard which a master condescendingly shows to his servants." "If all the women are really in love with him, not one of them, if she has self-respect, can cherish any more that feeling towards him, when she sees him making love to another. These women, therefore, surround him just as his maid-servants do, influenced by considerations of his attainments, wealth, and position in society." "That is love which binds a man permanently to a single woman and vice versa; and it is a lie that one person can love several women." *

It is no wonder that the women considered it to be the result of the religious merit obtained in the past births for man and wife to entertain even feelings of love towards each other. † Indeed, it was a rare fortune for a woman especially of the higher classes to secure a husband who would concentrate his

* *Mt.* 6 : 69-75.

† కలకాల మొక్కగతిఁ బూ । సలలో దారంబు మాడ్కి సతిమదిలోనన్ ।
మెలఁగెడుపురుషులు గలుగుట । తొలిజన్మము నోముఫలము తోయజనేత్రా ॥
Phm. 1 : 93.

affection entirely upon her. Under these circumstances, conjugal life could not have been very happy. The literature echoes the agonising cries of women writhing with pain caused by the cruel treatment of men. * That was, however, an evil which was considered necessary.

Marriages were celebrated with great pomp and show; much money was spent, and many guests were entertained for several days. Custom demanded that the marriage should be performed in the house of the bride's parents. In the case of Brahmans the bride's parents demanded and obtained *araṇa* or the nuptial present; † but among other communities, the bride's father had to give at the time of marriage several gifts to the bridegroom. If he happened to be a man of consequence, say a great nobleman or a king, he had to offer his son-in-law jewels, horses, elephants, palanquins, villages, and above all servant maids. ‡

The activities of the women of the noble class were mostly confined to the zenana. They never worked but spent most of their time in luxurious sloth. They diverted themselves with intrigues against their

* పతిప్రాణ సదృశబంధువు ।
పతిదైవం వేడుగడయుఁ బతి సతులకు న ।
ప్పతియు కడు మేరఁదప్పిన ।
గతి కులకాంతలకు వేఱు గలదే చెపుమా ॥ *Phm.* 1 : 96.

నాకేమి దేహసుఖము పు ।
రాకృతమేకాక నేడు గాఁబోనే యీ ।
లోకమున నేనె యరుదా ।
మాకోడలు గాదొ పొరుగుమంచము గాదో ॥ *Npm.* 2 : 56.

† అప్పచెల్లెంద్రపై నాదరంబులుసూపి । యరణముల్ గొనిపోయి యుపహరించు ॥
ibid **2 : 26.**

‡ ***Mo.*** 5 : 98-102.

co-wives to secure the fleeting affection of their inconstant husbands. Of the women of the middle class nothing is known. However, it is possible to infer from the few stray references in contemporary literature that the Brahman house wife was the mistress of her household, though she had to perform most of the domestic work herself. The lower class women had to work hard all the year round; they had not only to attend to domestic work but to assist their men in the fields.

The family woman, to whichever community she might belong, was strictly under the control of her husband, whom she was taught to regard as her lord and master. * She was required to conduct herself in a manner which might enable her to become a *satī* or ideal wife. A *satī* was she who remained faithful to her husband, under all circumstances, although he might ill-treat her cruelly. † She was taught to believe that her husband was her life itself. ‡ She should

* All the women were not submissive to their husbands. The people of the time knew the rebellious, pugnacious and termagant women who made the married life a curse instead of a blessing: the advice which Peda-Tirumalayya gives to women tells its own tale: *Nitiśataka* 32.

పతికి మాఱాడక పలుమారు నేడ్వక । యలుగక మిగుల గయ్యాళి గాక
తను దిట్టికొనక తాతాలించి గొణుగక । మ్రుచ్చిలించక పాపమునకుఁ జొరక

* * * * *

కాపురము సేయు కామిని కలిగె నేని । పలుకులేటికి పురుషుని భాగ్యమహిమ ॥

The perverse interpretation of this verse by the poet, Rāmakṛṣṇa, is too well-known to need any quotation here.

† పతి కొట్టినఁ బతి దిట్టినఁ ।
బతి నిర్దయుఁడగుచు నెట్టిపాటుఁ బఱచినఁ ।
మతి నన్యథాత్వ మొందరు ।
పతి దేవత లతివ! నీకుఁ బ్రతియగు వారల్ ॥ *Prm.* 4: 201.

‡ *Phm.* 1: 96. పతిప్రాణసదృశబంధువు etc.

regard him as her god and saviour without whom she had no business to exist.

It was in this belief that one of the most cruel customs of the age had taken deep root. As women believed that their salvation was dependent upon their personal services to their husbands, they did not like to commit any breach of the *satī dharma*, by allowing them to suffer, even after death, any discomfort in the other world. In their zeal to be good *satis*, therefore, they plunged enthusiastically into the blazing funeral pyre, where the remains of their departed lords were burnt, or allowed themselves to be buried alive in the same grave. There is reason to believe that most of the women that committed *sati* had done so willingly; for the widow who did not do so was treated in a most inhuman fashion. Barbosa declares:

> "Those who do not so, they hold in great dishonour, and their kindred shave their heads and turn them away as disgraced and a shame to their families. And as far as some who have not done it, to whom they wish to show favour, if they are young they send them to a temple there to earn money for the said temple with their bodies...They are forced to play and sing before the idols for certain hours every day, and continue to earn money for these for most of the time left them." *

It is evident that the position of widows in the Hindu society was not enviable. Most women would have preferred death to leading dishonourable lives. It is not unlikely that on occasions physical force was employed by the kindred of the widowed women, who showed their excessive zeal for *sati* by casting into the funeral pyre, many pitchers of oil and butter, and 'much wood,' † so that the unhappy widows might be quickly reduced to ashes.

* *Barbosa* i. p. 216.

† *ibid* p. 215.

Section 2 : The Courtesans :—The courtesan women played a very important part in society. They were regarded as a respectable community by the people. So much is evident from the place which the poets assigned to them in the social order described in their poems. According to the rules of composition of the new form of literature known as the *prabandha*, they were required, while describing the capital city of their heroes, to give an account not only of the four castes but also of the courtesans. Therefore, the courtesan community was, in the opinion of the *prabandha* writers and probably also of the public for whom they wrote, as important as the four great castes.

The courtesans may be divided into two classes: (*a*) those that were attached to the temples, and (*b*) those that lived independently of them. To whichever class a courtesan might belong, she plied the trade of the caste quite regularly. No blame was attached to it; and she did not suffer from any social disabilities on account of it. *

The caste was not homogeneous; it was open for the women of any community to join the sisterhood. Some women of good families were forced to adopt the profession by tyrannical social customs. Parents in poor circumstances either sold or handed over their young daughters to the rich courtesans, who brought them up so as to make them ornaments of the profession. †

The girls of this class were carefully educated. All of them were taught tc read and write. Several

* cf. *FE.* p. 242. "They are very much esteemed, and are classed among those honoured ones who are the mistresses of the captains; any respectable man may go to their houses without any blame attaching thereto."

† cf. *Barbosa* i. pp. 216, 226.

acquired a very sound knowledge of the Sanskrit and the vernacular literatures. Great emphasis was laid on the training for the professional work. Considerable importance was attached to singing and dancing.* Parrots, doves, minas, swans etc., were reared in cages in the courtesan houses in order to teach young girls to modulate their voices in imitation of the sweet notes uttered by these birds. They were taught to sing to the accompaniment of *vīṇa*, *paravādini*, *kaḷānāda* etc., and to dance according to the rules of *nāṭya* as laid down by Dattila, Bharata, Matanga, Āñjanēya, Kāhaḷa and others. The education which was imparted to them was such that it developed in them sex-instinct at a very early age.

Pictures representing the clandestine love stories from the *purāṇas* were painted on the walls of the rooms, where they played and moved about. They were made to worship Ratī and Manmatha. † The final conclusions of Kūcimāra, Manōja, and Ghōṇikāputra on the *kāma-sāstra* were explained to them. They were made to learn *kaḷas*, *pramāṇas*, looks, *jātis*, *bandhas*, embraces and *avasthas*, so that they might give satisfaction to cultured customers of fastidious tastes. The most important lesson which the courtesan girls had to learn was to evoke love in their customers without loving any of them in return. ‡ Good looks

* " ఎన్నడు నేర్తురో చదువ నెన్నడు నేర్తురో యాడ పాడగా "

Khm 4 : 26.

† *ibid* 4 : 14-15.

‡ సీ॥ కూచిమార మనోజ ఘోణికాపుత్రాది కానీత కామసిద్ధాంతములను ।
నిరుపమ కలనాద పరవాదినీ వీణ లాదిగాఁ గల గానయంత్రములను ।
గీర పారావత శారికా సారస హంసాదు లైన విహంగములను ।
దత్తిల భరత మతంగాంజనేయ కాహళమతప్రముఖ లాస్యాగమముల।
తే.గీ॥ సంతరించె గృహంబులో జలజనేత్ర । రతులఁ జతుర గాన ధురంధరతల ।
గంధరవ నిపుణతల నాట్యకౌశలముల। చిన్నిపడుచుల ప్రౌఢలఁ జేయఁదలఁచి॥

ibid 4 : 16.

alone were not enough to ensure success in the profession. A courtesan should indeed be very accomplished in several fields to capture men of wealth and distinction. According to a contemporary author, the most successful courtesan had to employ several arts in keeping her lover firmly moored. If he were a scholar, she discoursed with him upon the beauty of the classics; if he had no taste for learning, she sang melodiously; on occasions when song did not please him, she entertained him by playing upon the *vīṇa*; when that did not arouse his interest, she played dice with him; and when dice ceased to have attraction, she engaged him in witty conversation; for she was a learned scholar, a skilful musician, a clever gambler and a brilliant conversationalist.*

A rich and influential courtesan took early steps to open a career to her daughters by introducing them into the palace, and obtaining a foot-hold for her in the imperial household establishment, where the women of this class were very much in demand to discharge several duties.† A fortunate girl might on occasions rise to the position of a queen;‡ the majority of them, however, had to exercise all their wits in ensnaring men and earning money.

* సాహిత్యమార్గంబు చాక చేసిననాఁడు సంగీతమున ప్రీతి సల్ప నేర్చు ।
సంగీతవైఖరి సమ్మతింపనివేళ నింపుగా వీణ వాయింప నేర్చు
వీణావిరావంబు వెగటుదోఁచినయప్డు సొగటాల వేడుక సూప నేర్చు ।
సొగటాలపైవేడ్క సుదకువచ్చినయంత వింతమాటలఁ గారవింప నేర్చు ।
చదువఁ బాడంగ నింతింత చతుర గాదు। వీణవాయింప నింతింత జాణ గాదు ।
జూదమాడంగ నింతింత జూటగాదు। ప్రతిభఁ బల్కంగ నింతింత ప్రౌఢ గాదు॥

Npm 2 : 40.

† cf. *Barbosa* i. p. 226.

‡ cf. *FE*. pp. 247-48.

As soon as a courtesan girl attained maturity the *kannerika* ceremony was usually celebrated.* That was a great event in her life. The *kannerika* was a ceremony analogous to marriage of the girls of good families. The courtesan girl should undergo the ceremony with a man seated together like the couple in a wedding. The occasion was celebrated with great eclat, and it involved heavy expenditure. As the man had to finance the whole show, the elders of the girl took advantage of the occasion to exact from him as much money as they possibly could. Unless the *kannerika* was performed, no courtesan should have sexual intercourse with any person. In that age, when a man of any consequence kept a mistress, it was not a difficult task for a courtesan to secure a suitable man for the purpose. She was not, however, bound by any vow to be faithful to him. All that was required of her was to give him preference over her other customers.

The courtesans that were attached to the temples had certain specific duties to perform. Every day they had to sing and dance before the deity during the time of worship and accompany the processions conducted in his honour dancing in front of him. † The girls born of these women also belonged to the temple, and they should perform the same duties as their mothers, when they attained womanhood. Those that were not bound by temple service had no other duty than earning their living. If they were resident in

* ఏనెఱజాణలైన గమలేక్షణలన్మణిమంత్రతంత్ర వి ।
ద్యానవ చాతురీమహిమనైనను మందులనైన నీశ్వర ।
జ్ఞానము మాన్పి కామ సుఖసక్తులఁ జేసియేని యిత్తుగా ।
నైనను బుచ్చుకోక కమలాస్యల కన్నెరికంబు వారికిఁ ॥ *Khm* 4: 49.

† *FE.* p. 241.

the capital, they had to visit the palace every Saturday to dance before the deity whom the Rāya personally worshipped.* The country courtesan had not even this obligation. During the celebration of the *Mahānavami* festival, all the courtesans, whether residents of the city or the provinces, had to go to the palace, and actively participate in the various functions on the occasion. †

Many of the courtesans were extremely rich, and most of them were beautiful. The profession which they followed was not, as already noticed, condemned by public opinion. Prostitution was regarded as the lawful profession of the community; and no blame was attached to it so far as the members of the caste were concerned. On the contrary, they were highly respected. Their company was sought after and obtained by captains and great noblemen of the court. Kings and princes visited them in their houses, and summoned them to their own residences, when they were disinclined to visit them.‡ On great occasions, they carried on with the courtesan women clandestine transactions in the public streets which passed unnoticed. §

* *FE*. p. 379. † *FE*. p. 262.

‡ మెలఁత యడపము దేఁ జరన్మొరు వనఁగ దలవరులు గొంద ఱాలసి యుంగలఁ [జనంగ ।
నర్థిరథ్యాన్త రాంతఃపురాంతరమున । భోగినీసంగతికి రాజు వోవుచుండి ॥
Ām. 2 : 75.

రాకుమారులయిండ్ల కేకతంబునఁ దదాప్తుల వెంట బుడిబుడి వోవువారు ।
* * * * *
నైన వెలయాండ్రచే నప్పురాధిరాజు। వేశ్యవాటిక చూడ్కికి వేడ్క యొసఁగె॥
Vc. 4 : 66.

§ తద్రాజకదంబకం బచ్చటి పడంతుకులకుం దమకుం బురికిం జనుదెంచు నప్పుడెల్ల నెడకాం డ్రగుట మేలమాడఁబోలు నప్రోలి మేళంపుఁగళావతులవై చు నెపంబునం గ్రామద్రామ గ్రామణులొసంగు నారంగ మాతులుంగ జంబీర కుంద కందుకాదులం బూర్వానుభుక్తలగు నక్తంకరముఖులవై వ॥
Ām. 4 : 35.

The courtesans enjoyed certain privileges. They lived in the best houses of the most fashionable streets in the cities; they had free access to the zenana of the emperor, where they chatted with the queens and chewed betel in their presence. * The same privilege they enjoyed even in the presence of the emperor himself. † During the time of war, the presence of the courtesans was considered indispensable. Thousands of them could be seen in the camp filling the tents of the emperor and his officers. They were paid by the emperor, because he believed that those who were enamoured of these women would fight better for their sake. ‡

When a courtesan grew old, she retired from the profession; but she never abandoned the business which was productive of so much wealth. She had to take care of the interests of her daughters whom she taught all her wiles. She kept guard over them to protect them from impecunious customers. One of the most reviled women of the age was the courtesan's mother. The poets heaped curses upon her; and no term seems to have been strong enough to express their feelings of loathing and detestation.

* *FE*. pp. 241-2.

† *FE*. p. 269.

‡ *Barbosa* i. pp. 225-26.

Chapter V.

EDUCATION AND AMUSEMENTS.

Section 1 : *Educational Institutions* :—The state did not take an active interest in imparting education to the public. Some of the *maṭhas* which the Rāyas patronised, no doubt, held schools, where religious and secular education was given to all who were inclined to study; but the patronage was extended to the *maṭhas* not so much as educational institutions but as centres of religion. The Rāyas of Vijayanagara did not continue the policy of previous Hindu sovereigns such as the Pallavas, the Cāḷukyas, and the Cōḷas, who founded schools and colleges to afford educational facilities to their subjects. Although no inscription of the period recording the foundation of a school, or college has been discovered so far, it cannot be said that the Rāyas were totally indifferent to the promotion of learning; for they seem to have helped to improve the education of the people in an indirect manner. The innumerable *agrahāras* which they founded were so many centres of learning. In some cases, provision was made for the maintenance of a school at the time of the foundation of an *agrahāra* itself. * Such schools were intended to teach the Vēdas to Brahman youngsters, and admission must have been denied to pupils of other communities. Each *agrahāra*, however, had a few Brahmans noted for their scholarship in some branch of learning; and they usually attracted several pupils from the neighbourhood. † An

* *The Bhārati* ix. p. 234.

† एतेषु किलाग्रहारेषु केचिज्जपन्ति । अपरेपाठयन्ति । कतिचित्पठन्ति । अन्येतत्त्वविद्यामुपदिशन्ति । इतरे अध्यापयन्ति । पश्य पश्य ।

Kēraḷābharaṇam.

ideal *śrōtriya* Brahman was a learned and wealthy person owning tax-free lands in several villages; he was hospitable and generous, and surrounded himself with several students whom he taught the branch or branches of knowledge in which he was proficient.* The students were usually unmarried, and they were fed freely by the teacher himself.† They stayed in the teacher's house serving him in such a manner as to win his affection. As a single teacher could not be learned in all the branches of knowledge, it was customary for ambitious young men of parts to study under several teachers. Though teachers of this class generally taught the Brahman youth, they did not set their face against young men of other communities. It would have been impossible for such great writers as Rāmarājabhūṣaṇa to become prominent, had they not received their early education and training under some learned pandit of an *agrahāra*. The influence of Vaiṣṇavism liberalised the outlook of men in several fields. Most of the writers who became famous in the sixteenth century received their education from some distinguished Vaiṣṇava teacher or other. The Paravastu and the Kandāḍa families claimed several of the sixteenth century poets as their disciples. The Vaiṣṇava teachers were probably responsible for enabling the young men of non-Brahman communities to study the works of great Sanskrit writers, and to model their own productions on them.

* ... .మాన్యక్షేత్రముల్ పెక్కుచం ।
దాలంబండు నొకప్పుడున్ దఱుఁగ దింటన్ బాడియుం బంటయున్ ॥
Mc. **1: 55.**
కెడఁ దోడునీడలై క్రీడించు సచ్ఛాత్రు లింతకు నెంత చింతింతు రొక్కొ
ibid **2: 17.**
పంచనామతి ప్రాడ్వివాకులై వటువు లొజ్జల కొప్పగించిరి చదువులెల్ల
ibid **3: 129.**

† సరసాహారము లింటఁ బెట్టి బహుశిష్యశ్రేణికిన్ దెల్పు శా ।
స్త్ర రహస్యస్థితి చెప్పు నధ్యయనసంధ్యల్ హవ్యకవ్యంబులన్ ॥ *Rc.* **3: 11.**

EDUCATION AND AMUSEMENTS

The curriculum of studies was narrow. The only subjects taught in the *agrahāra* Vēdic schools were probably the Vēdas and the allied literature; but a wider choice was offered by individual teachers who seem to have taught the *Trayi*, the *śāstras*, the *purāṇas*, the *itihāsas*, the *kāvyas* and the *nāṭakas*, besides music and the art of writing poetry. * Another subject, the study of which appears to have been popular was the *Āyurvēda* or medicine consisting of eight *angas* or branches. †

When the education was completed, the young men generally married, and most of them settled in their village homesteads, where they led unobtrusive lives. But the more ambitious went to the court of a neighbouring chief or even that of the Rāya, where, by attaching themselves to some influential man, they attempted to come to the lime-light. The emperors of

* చదివినారలు పెక్కు సంథలఁ గించుత్తుఁ దప్పకయుండ వేదత్రయంబు ।
పఠియించినారలు ప్రతిభాసమున్నిద్ర సౌష్ఠవంబున మూలశాస్త్ర వితతి ।
శోధించినారలు శుద్ధమతిస్ఫూర్తి నఖిల పురాణేతిహాస సమితి ।
చూచినారలు బుధస్తోమంబు గొనియాడఁ గావ్యనాటక ముఖగ్రంథ సీమ॥
Rc. 3: 21.

చదివించెం ద్రయివాక్యముల్ గఱపె శాస్త్రింబుల్ పఠింపించె సా ।
మ్యదవిష్ఠప్రతిభం గవిత్వము రచింపంజేసె గాన క్రియా ।
విదురుంగా నొనరించె......................॥ *Npm.* 1: 94.

† ....బ్రహ్మమిత్రుండు శి।
ష్యులకున్ గంటను వత్తిఁ బెట్టుకొని యాయుర్వేద మారంతప్రా ।
ద్ధులఁ జెప్పన్ వినుచుండి మానసము నందున్ దజ్జిఘృక్షారతిన్॥
Mc. 5: 7.

కాయబాలగ్రహోర్ధ్వాంగకములు నాల్గు ।
శల్యదంష్ట్రాజరా వృష సంజ్ఞ నాల్గు ।
నైన యష్టాంగకము తావు లారఁ గల్గు ।
వైద్య మెనిమిదినెలల సర్వమును నేర్చి ॥ *ibid* 5: 15.

the Sāḷuva and the Tuluva families were patrons of learning. Their courts served as academies to test the erudition of scholars and the creative genius of poets. The subordinates of these emperors acquired their love of art and letters from their masters. Consequently, pandits and poets were held in great esteem. Ambitious scholars often joined the learned discussion in the royal *sabhā*, and, if they pleased the Rāya, they obtained rewards of costly garments, jewels, palanquins, and horses.* If they were specially lucky, they even obtained gifts of tax-free lands. Such was the ordinary course which the careers of most scholars followed.

The education of a large section of people was so designed as to enable them to enter the government service. Probably, there were schools in almost all villages, where pupils were specially trained for service under the government. Young men were usually admitted into such schools in the autumn. They began their studies by learning to write upon oblong planks of blackened wood with pencils. † The boys were also taught to write well both on the *kaḍitam* and the palm-leaf. A knowledge of mathematics, especially arithmetic, was considered indispensable for a person to become a qualified *karṇam* or accountant. He should also acquire a knowledge of several scripts,

* కొడుకులు సర్వవిద్యల నకుంఠితులై సభలందు శాస్త్రముల్ ।
దడయ కుపన్యసించి వసుధాతలనాథులచేత గుఱ్ఱముల్ ।
గొడుగులు గాంచి సత్యగుణకోవిదులై విహరింప సంపదన్ ।
బొడవగునట్టి గేహినులె పుణ్యశరీరలుగా కుమారకా ॥ *Npm.* 2 : 87.

† ఫలకగ్రహణముఁ జౌపదముల గరిమంబుఁ బరఁగె బాలకులుకు గురువు లిండ్ల॥
Prm. 4 : 44

particulars of the calendar, and of the history of the kings who ruled the country formerly.*

The *karṇams* fell into two classes: those that became the village accountants, and those that entered the *cāvaḍis* of the various government departments. The portals of the imperial palace were thrown open to the latter class; and, if fortune favoured them, they rose to be the *rāyasams* and the *avasarikas* of the emperor. If the emperor or his ministers were impressed with their ability and capacity in the discharge of their duties, they were taken into the ministerial cadre. The governorship of a *durga* or province was not regarded as too high which an ambitious young man could legitimately aspire to get. Several men of ability came into prominence in this fashion.

Section 2: Amusements: The Theatre:—One of the chief means of diversion was the theatre. The popularity of dramatic representations is attested by an

* సరులు గ్రుచ్చినయట్లు వెరసులు చక్కఁగా విశదమయిన లెక్క వెసగనిడుచు
నెలమి నేకస్థానములు దశస్థానముల్ చెదరిపోవకయుండఁ జిరువపుచ్చి
తలఁపులో మఱవక తరవాయిఁ దప్పక కుఱుచలు ద్రొక్కక కుంటుపడక
యెదిరివారు వినఁగ నెన్నక బలపంబు మోపక పెనువ్రేలు దాఁపుగొనక
తెలివిపడఁగూడి తలఁపులోపలను వెరసు ।
నిశ్చయముచేసి వ్రాయంగ నేర్చునతని ।
గణితశాస్త్రజ్ఞు లిలమేటి కరణమంత్రు ।
మంత్రిమందార యబ్బయ మంత్రికంద ॥ *Snm*: 297.
కరణంబుకొడుకు ముండఅ । కరణిక ధర్మంబునందుఁ గడుఁ గుశలుండై ।
ధరణిఁ గల విద్యలన్నియుఁ। బరువడి నెఱుగంగ వలయుఁ బని లేకున్నన్ ॥
శకకాలంబును వత్సరంబు నెల పక్షంబున్ దిథి న్వార ము ।
నొక్కదేశంబును దాని నేలువిభు నయ్యార్యున్ నిజస్థానమున్ ।
సకలార్థంబును నామనిశ్చయముగా సాక్షిసమేతంబు వ్రా ।
యక కాదంబరి వ్రాల వ్రాయు కరణం బజ్ఞాని గా కుండునే ॥
ibid: 301-2.

inscription of 1514 A.D., which refers to *Naṭṭuva* Nāgayya, son of Cēgaya, who acquired reputation in enacting a drama called *Tāyikoṇḍanāṭaka*. It also mentions a daughter of *Naṭṭuva* Timmayya of Pōtavara who was a *pātri* or actress. * Literature teems with allusions to players and play-acting. Youth is compared in the *Nirankuśōpākhyānam* to a player who reveals herself dancing as soon as the curtain is withdrawn. † In the *Prabhāvatīpradyumnam*, the city of Dwāraka is compared to an actress, who enters the stage behind the curtain *viz*, the sea. ‡ The *Manucaritra* and the *Vasucaritra* refer to the *nāṭakasālas* or theatres, where plays were probably enacted. These references show that one of the chief means by which people diverted themselves as by attending dramatic performances.

The plays that were written during the period fall into two classes: (1) *The Sanskrit Plays*:—Some plays were written in the Sanskrit language. A few specimens of this type of drama have come down to us; and so far as their technique is concerned, they do not differ from the typical classical dramas. One such play is the *Jāmbavatīkalyāṇam*, attributed to the emperor Kṛṣṇarāya himself. The plays of this class were usually enacted on important occasions, when large numbers of people gathered together at the capital. The *Jāmbavatīkalyāṇam* is said to have been put on boards for the first time before people, who had assembled at Vijayanagara to witness the spring festival celebrated in honour of

* *MER.* 556 of 1916.

† ....తరుణ యౌవన లక్ష్మి నర్తనము సూపె
నధికతరమైన తెరతీసినంతలోనె చిత్రరచనఁజూపు పాత్రకత్తెఁబోలె
Npm. 2: 9.

‡ జడనిధి యను తెరమఱుఁగట వెడలి నిలిచినట్టి యాట వెలఁదియ పోలెన్
Pp. 1: 57.

God Virūpākṣa.* It was customary for poets and scholars from all lands to flock to the court of Kṛṣṇarāya during the celebration of the *vasantōtsava* to participate in the learned discussions on poetry, religion, philosophy, etc., of which the Rāya was very fond. †

Though it is said that *Jāmbavatīkalyāṇam* was played before the people, it is very doubtful whether the common folk could have taken any interest in it; for it was written in the Sanskrit and the Prākrit languages, which could not have been understood by any one except the pandits.

(2) *The Yakṣagānas* :—The masses, however, were attracted by another kind of drama written in the vernacular languages. Although no specimen of the sixteenth century vernacular drama has survived, the names of a few plays, such as the *Tāyikoṇḍanāṭaka* and *Gangāvatāra* are preserved in the inscriptions and literature. They seem to be the earliest representatives of the modern *yakṣagāna*. The *yakṣagāna* is a dramatic composition set to music and sung and acted upon the stage, accompanied by instrumental music such as the *vīṇa*, flute, *mṛdanga*, cymbals etc.

The plays of this type were enacted by the actors, and actresses belonging to the courtesan community, who formed into itinerant companies and wandered from place to place, staging plays usually

* *The Sources* p. 142.

विजयनगरनिवास वासनावधीरित धनदनगर विहारदोहलस्य हेम-कूटगिरिकटक वास्तव्यकुटुम्बिनः कर्णाटराज्य रक्षामणेः श्रीविरूपाक्ष-देवस्य चैत्रोत्सवावलोकनाय सङ्गता परिषत् ॥

† ప్రతివర్ష వసంతోత్సవ । కుతుకాగత సుకవినికరగుంభిత కావ్య
స్తవైతిరోమాంచవిశంకిత । చతురాంకః పురవసూప్రసాదనరసికా ॥

Phm. 1 : 140.

connected with some *purāṇic* story. A group or band of players constituted itself into a *mēḷa*, and each *mēḷa* contained in addition to the actors and actresses several others such as songsters and players of instrumental music. *

The plays were generally staged on important occasions such as festivals, and *brahmōtsavas* of temples, or during the performance of sacrifices. Some interesting details of the stage have been given by contemporary writers. The curtain is, as already noticed, frequently alluded to in literature; and the characters are said to emerge from behind it. It is said that rivers like the Ganges and mountains like the Kailāsa, forests, wild beasts and birds were represented in such a realistic manner as to produce an impression on the audience that what they were witnessing were real objects and not artificial creatures. † It appears from this that the stage paraphernalia were not simple; and the scenic arrangements must have given much trouble to the stage manager. The actors put on clothes and ornaments suitable to the rolls which they assumed. The ornaments were made of chips of wood so painted and gilded as to give them the semblance of gold and precious stones. ‡

The performance commenced with the songs of women accompanied by the play on all musical instruments. The *sūtradhāra* or the stage manager then appeared on the stage and recited the *nāndi* verse; next, he announced the name of the play which was about to be enacted, and of the author who was responsible for its composition. As soon as he retired, the characters of the play came upon the stage one

* *Pp.* 4 : 90-93.

† *ibid* 4 : 101.

‡ *ibid* 1 : 107.

after another. They danced and sang as they proceeded to act. * At the close of the performance, they received presents from the audience whom they praised in eulogistic language. †

Occasionally, a *mēḷa* or company might be invited to the palace of the Rāya or one of his grandees in order to entertain the members of the zenana. The Rāya might grace the occasion with his presence, if the performance took place within the precincts of his palace. His relations, officers and other nobles would be invited to witness the play. Separate arrangements were made for the accommodation of the queens, princesses, and other ladies of the zenana so that they might see the actors without being seen. ‡

The histrionic talents of these actors and actresses probably perished with them. The names of a few prominent members of the profession have come down to us through literature and the inscriptions. Peṇḍela Nāgi, Buccigāḍu or *Naṭṭuva* Nāgayya are only names to us; but to their contemporaries they must have been the embodiment of the dramatic art which they seem to have cherished fondly.

The *bommalāṭa* or shadow-play appears to have been popular. One of Kṛṣṇarāya's confidential servants was Kāḷa, the son of a certain Bommalāṭa Virūpākṣa. § Now, the surname or family name of Kāḷa, probably derived from the profession which his father followed, is of considerable interest, as it indicates that the people of the sixteenth century were familiar with *bommalāṭa* or the shadow-play. The *bommalāṭa* like the *yakṣagāna* was staged at night in

* *Pp.* 4: 98-100. † *ibid* 4: 101.

‡ *ibid* 4: 96; *LR.* 56 (Mācupalle) p. 66 ff. See: Appendix C.

§ *The Sources* p. 157.

a temporary shed open in front, and closed on the other sides. A screen of white cloth covered the front or the open side. The interior of this building was illuminated by lamps, and the shadow of the pictures made of leather or other material was projected on the screen by the interception of light. According to the requirements of the play, enacted at any given time, the *prasangi* (expounder) and the *pāṭhakas* (songsters) moved the pictures by means of strings. They also supplied the appropriate conversation and songs for the edification of the audience, seated outside in the open air.* The performance of the shadow-play lasted throughout the night, and it came to an end only at day-break. †

Wandering bands of *Dommaras* and *Vipravinōdis* roamed over the country visiting towns and villages to collect the customary fees due to them from the citizens of the empire. The *Dommaras* were professional acrobats, and, according to some inscriptions, they belonged to twenty-four *kulas* or clans. They usually exhibited their feats in the open air. When they visited a town or village, they set up the poles for rope-walking in the main thoroughfare, and attracted the people by beating the drum. They collected an annual fee from the people, which they frequently granted to temples and other religious foundations. Occasionally they gave a performance in the presence of the Rāya and his courtiers, when they were richly rewarded for their skill. The

* నికటక్షోణికఁ బువ్వుపీడఁ దెరయై నీడల్ సభాసీనులై
శుకరాజంబు ప్రసంగియై కిసలయస్తోమంబు దీపంబులై
పికముల్ పాఠకులై యళుల్ ప్రతిమలై పెంపొందఁ జైత్రుండు ద
ర్పకుఁ డీక్షింపఁగ బొమ్మలాటఁ గనుపింపన్ జూచితే నెచ్చెలీ॥
Cgc. 4 : 207

† వేగినదాఁక బొమ్మలాటలుగన్న భోగిపగిది. *Pcp.* Canto 1.

Vipravinōdis were professional jugglers; and, like the *Dommaras*, they used to visit towns and villages, for the purpose of showing their tricks, and collecting their annual *vartana* or fee which was fixed by custom. The *Vipravinōdis* collected their *vartana* only from the Brahmans, and it is not known whether they derived any income from the other communities.

There were other means of diversion. The *vanavihāra* or strolling in the pleasure garden, and the *jalakrīḍa* or sporting in water are two other forms of amusement which were very popular among the rich. As these have been described already in another context, it is not necessary to dilate upon them once again. Games also appear to have played an important part in the social life. Although the information available on the subject is only scanty, it is sufficient to give us an idea of how people, specially the Rāya and his nobles, spent their leisure hours. The games may be conveniently described under two heads: the outdoor, and the indoor.

The Outdoor Games:—The common people took considerable interest in cock-fighting.* Whether they interested themselves in any other amusement, it is not possible to say. A kind of game resembling polo was played by princes and the nobles. The player of the game, mounted on a charger, had to beat a ball lying on the ground with a long staff held in one of his hands, while the animal closely followed the movements of the ball.† It seems to have been a military game probably introduced by the Muhammadan soldiers, whom the Vijayanagara emperors employed in their army in large numbers. The most exciting outdoor

* "కాసెకట్టుటయుఁ గత్తిదాల్చుటయుఁ గృకవాకుల కలహంబుల యంద" *Ām.* 4 : 187.

† *Pp.* 2 : 29-36.

amusement, however, was the chase in which the emperor and his courtiers were greatly interested. Several varieties of chase such as *teravēṭa*, *edduvēṭa*, *ganṭavēṭa* etc., are mentioned by contemporary writers;* but it is not easy to make out the difference.

The Rāya seems to have maintained a large establishment of falcons and hounds, which he lodged in that part of the palace which was opposite to the stables. † The hounds helped the hunters in tracking the wild animals to their lairs; the falcons pursued the birds. No firearms were employed in shooting the game. Bows, arrows, daggers, short swords and spears were the only weapons with which the hunters armed themselves. Foot-traps and nets were also made use of to capture the animals alive. The tiger, the elephant, the bear, the wolf, the hyena, the deer, the bison, the boar, the wild goat etc., were some of the animals which the hunters usually killed in the chase. At the close of the hunt, the hunters brought together the game which they shot down, skinned the animals and cut the fat parts of their carcases, which they cooked and ate, having at first offered it to the presiding deity of the forest. ‡

The wealthy people appear to have sought diversion in playing the chess and the dice; chess was a popular game which occupied the attention of the upper classes. The emperor Kṛṣṇarāya was an expert

* *Rbm.* 2: 29.
"యెచ్చరిక మించి తెరవేఁట యెద్దువేఁట గంటవేఁటయు మొదలుగాఁ గలుగువేఁట"

† ముంగిస మోరలుఁ బోని మోరలు సారెసారెకు నెత్తి బయలు ప
ట్టుచుఁ గట్టెదుటివాజిశాలలఁ గట్టిన పొట్టేళ్ళకై యాదిగాని
నీల్గికాలుఁద్రవ్వు... జాగిలంబులునుఁ ..." *Mc.* 4: 27.

‡ cf. *Mc.* 4: 37.

in playing the game. He seems to have shown as much respect to good chess players as to poets and philosophers. The most famous chess champion of the age was a certain Timmana of the Boḍḍucerla family, who, it is said, constantly won the game while playing with the Rāya. It was probably in recognition of his skill in playing the game that the Rāya granted him the village of Koppōlu as an *agrahāra.** Rāmarāja also was fond of chess. The Mādhwa tradition reproaches him with showing disrespect to Brahmans and regard for gamblers. The game of dice was more popular than chess. The part which it played in social life may be inferred from the place assigned to it at the imperial court. One of the ladies-in-waiting carrying the symbols or insignia had to hold a board of dice while waiting on the emperor. From the constant allusions to the game by the contemporary writers it is evident that gambling was a fashionable pastime in the aristocratic circles. Women were as much addicted to gambling as men; and they often played the game for stakes. There might have been other means of diversion besides chess and dice; but we know nothing of them at present. The future investigator of the social history of the sixteenth century may have to say more about them than what is possible at present.

* శతసంఖ్య లెక్కలైనను । సతతము శ్రీకృష్ణరాయ జగతీపతితోఁ
జతురంగ మాడి గెల్చును । ధృతిమంతుఁడు బొడ్డుచెర్ల తిమ్మన భళిరే॥

" చిన్నతిమ్మన్న అనే ఆయన కవీశ్వర దిగ్దంతి అనిపించుకొని కృష్ణరాయలవారియొద్దకు పోయి రాయలతో చదరంగం ఆడుతూ వుండేవాడున్నా, ఆట గెలిస్తే వెయ్యార్లు పందెంచేసి గెలుస్తూవుండేవాడున్న. అప్పుడు కృష్ణదేవ మహారాయలు చాలా సంతోషించి కొప్పోలుగ్రామం సర్వాగ్రహారంగా ధార వోసి యిచ్చి "

LR. as quoted by Mr. V. P. Sastri in his introduction to the Vāviḷḷa edition of the *Manucaritra.*

CHAPTER VI.

LITERATURE AND ART.

Section 1: Literature:—The sixteenth century is characterised by an outburst of great literary activity. Several authors of eminence flourished during this century, and produced works of lasting importance, not only in the Sanskrit language but in all the principal vernaculars of South India. The Rāyas of Vijayanagara fostered the growth of the literatures of all the languages that were spoken in their extensive empire, from the very beginning; but the imperial court did not become the general resort of men of letters before the commencement of the sixteenth century.

The reign of Kṛṣṇadēvarāya marks the dawn of a new era in the literary history of South India. Himself a scholar, a musician, and a poet, he loved to gather around him poets, philosophers, and religious teachers whom he honoured with munificent gifts of land and money. He was so much attached to the company of learned men that he spent most of his spare time, when he was at the capital, in hearing their learned discourses and discussions. He took them with him, when he started to tour through the provinces or to conduct a military campaign. Although he loved poetry in whatever language it was written, he had a special partiality for Telugu, which he considered the best of vernaculars. He showed greater regard for Telugu poets and scholars, towards some of whom he entertained genuine personal affection. Very early in his reign, he constituted an academy of Telugu poets, the members of which were known as the

*Aṣṭadiggajas.** Peddana, Timmana, Dhūrjaṭi (senior), Mallana, Rāmarājabhūṣaṇa Rāmakṛṣṇa, Pingaḷi Sūranna, and Rudra are said to have been the members of this academy, over which the Rāya himself presided. There were also others, who, though not admitted to this learned body, belonged to the Rāyā's literary circle. The court of Vijayanagara became a place of pilgrimage to all men of letters, especially to those who chose Telugu as the medium of their expression. The approval of the Rāya and his pandits was considered by many writers of distinction a sufficient reward for their labours. Here as in other things the nobles and captains, who considered it highly desirable to walk in the footsteps of the Rāya, imitated his example by extending their patronage to poets and scholars, so that no writer suffered any hardship for the want of a patron. This gave a tremendous impetus to the development of South Indian literature in general and the Telugu in particular. As Acyuta, Rāmarāja and Tirumala, the successors of Kṛṣṇarāya inherited some of his love of letters, the progressive movement which commenced in his time continued without any interruption until the end of the century.

In attempting to trace the development of literature, one has to face a difficulty, which cannot be overcome completely, as matters stand at present. Although several poets must have written during this period, it is not easy to discover who they were, as the chronological order in which they lived is almost totally unknown. The difficulty is greatest regarding the Sanskrit and Tamil writers; for, no systematic attempt appears to have been made so far to arrange them in their chronological order. This obstacle, however, does not beset the path of the historian of the

* *LR.* 2. (Tippalūru) p. 357 dated 1528 A.D., records that Tippalūru was granted as an *agrahāra* by Kṛṣṇadēvarāya to the *Aṣṭadiggajas.*

Telugu and the Canarese literatures. Thanks to the efforts of some modern scholars, we have before us a fairly settled chronology, which helps us in studying these literatures in their historical setting. In spite of the absence of a settled chronology of the Sanskrit and the Tamil writers, it is just possible to notice briefly the activity of some of them, as, by their contact with the court, they are known to have flourished during this period.

Section 2 : Sanskrit :—The study of the Sanskrit language and literature was pursued with as much enthusiasm during the sixteenth century as in the previous ages. Although several new treatises were written by eminent scholars on a variety of topics, it is not possible to ascertain their value, as most of them remain still unpublished. Of the Sanskrit writers of this age, Kṛṣṇarāya appears to be the earliest. The composition of several poems, such as the *Madālasacaritra*, the *Satyāvadhūpariṇaya*, the *Sakalakathāsārasamgraha*, the *Jñānacintāmaṇi* and the *Rasamañjari*, is attributed to him; but none of them is extant. However, a play called the *Jāmbavatīkalyāṇam* ascribed to him is preserved in some of our mss. libraries; and this does not seem to be a work of great merit. One of the prominent scholars of Kṛṣṇarāya's court was Lolla Lakṣmīdhara, a *vaidika* Brahman of Koṇḍavīḍu. Lakṣmīdhara spent his early days in the court of the Gajapati king, Pratāparudra, at Cuttack. It is believed that he had a hand in the composition of the *Sarasvatīvilāsa*, ascribed to that monarch. He wrote commentaries on several works including the *Sivānandalahari* of the philosopher Sankara. The most important of his works is the *Daivajñavilāsa* which he wrote in collaboration with another scholar, Kencam Yellaya, by name. The *Daivajñavil*[illegible] is an encyclopaedic work of the class of Basavarāja's *Sivatatvaratnākara*, containing much useful information on a variety of topics, which, if properly exploited, is bound to enrich our knowledge of the history of the sixteenth century.

Another scholar who migrated from the court of Cuttack was the musician Lakṣmīnārāyaṇa. He easily won a footing at the Vijayanagara court owing to Kṛṣṇarāya's fondness for music. In his youth, it is said, the Rāya learnt to play upon the *vīṇa* from an eminent artist of the name of Kṛṣṇa, one of the ancestors of the Mādhwa *guru*, Rāghavēndra. When he ascended the throne, he appointed as the music master of his harem, Lakṣmīnārāyaṇa, who composed a treatise on music called *Sangītasūryōdaya* probably for the benefit of his pupils. Though the book is not yet published, it is believed to be a valuable contribution to the literature on the subject.

The great minister Sāḷuva Timma, and his nephew Nādiṇḍla Gōpa were eminent Sanskrit scholars. The former commented on Agastya's *Bhārata*, and the latter on the well-known Sanskrit allegorical drama the *Prabōdha Candrōdaya*. Gōpa was not only an author but a patron of men of letters. The poets Mallana and Rāmakṛṣṇa first won recognition at his court in Koṇḍavīḍu.

On the religious side, the activity was even greater. Some of the most eminent religious teachers of the time either came, or were invited, to Vijayanagara, where they were asked to expound the doctrines of their respective creeds before the Rāya. The religious reformer Vallabha and the Jaina theologian Abhinava Vādi Vidyānanda claim victories over the pandits of the Rāya's court. There is reason to believe that Caitanya also paid a visit to Vijayanagara. One of the lithic records of Acyuta's reign refers to a tax-free village which was granted to Caitanya.* The disputations of these itinerant scholars led to the birth of much religious literature of a controversial character. The most prolific writer on religious and theological problems was Vyāsatīrtha, the head of the Mādhwa sect. He wrote a series of books on theology, logic etc., in order to condemn the tenets of the rival sects and establish those of his own. He wrote *Tarkatāṇḍava*, *Nyāyāmṛta*, *Sudha*, *Mandāramañjari* and *Madhwatātparyacandrika*, and commented on several *Upaniṣads* such as the *Cchandōgya*, the *Māṇḍūkya* etc. Only two writers of the time of Acyuta are known to us at present. Rājanātha Ḍiṇḍima, Acyuta's poet laureate wrote two poems, the *Acyutarāyābyudayam* and the *Bhāgavata Campu*. The former is an historical *kāvya*, in which the author describes the early career and achievements of his master. Though Ḍiṇḍima clothes the events in a poetical garb, they are nevertheless genuine. Therefore, his poem should be regarded as the most valuable contemporary document of Acyuta's reign. The *Bhāgavata Campu* is a composition of a different species; and its literary value cannot be assessed until it becomes available in print.

The other writer was a lady, Tirumalāmbā by name. She was probably one of the ladies-in-waiting in the Rāya's palace. She wrote a *Campukāvya* called the *Varadāmbikāpariṇayam*, in which she describes the marriage of Acyuta with his queen Varadāmbikā. The *Varadāmbīkāpariṇayam* seems to be important not so much for its literary merit but for its value as a source book of history; for the authoress appears to narrate the events of which she herself was an eye-witness. As an artist, Tirumalāmbā is far inferior to Gangādēvī whose

* *EC.* ix Cp. 1.

Madhurāvijaya, though fragmentary, must be regarded as a perfect literary gem.

Not many Sanskrit works of Sadāśiva's reign have come to light so far. Some of the great Śrī Vaiṣṇava teachers such as Doḍḍayācārya flourished at his court. It is not unlikely that Tātācārya who later on became the spiritual preceptor of the Āravīḍu monarchs, should have risen to prominence during Sadāśiva's reign. The works of the Śrī Vaiṣṇava teachers, however, have not yet been published, though they are said to be numerous. The Mādhwa *guru* Vijayīndra appears to have been a person of considerable learning; and he is said to have written works on various religious subjects. What these works are is nowhere stated.

Rāmarāja like his great father-in-law, Kṛṣṇarāya, was a lover of music. He extended his patronage to Bayakāra Rāmappaya or Rāmayāmātya, whom he appointed as the music master of his daughters. He composed a treatise on music called the *Swaramēḷakaḷānidhi*, which became during the subsequent period a subject of bitter controversy between two opposing schools of Karṇāṭic music. Cina Timma, a cousin of Rāmarāja, utilised the services of the famous Śaivite scholar and philosopher Appaya Dīkṣita, whom he commissioned to write a commentary on Vēdānta Dēśika's *Yādavābhyudaya*.

Section 3: Tamil:—The growth of the Tamil literature was less due to the patronage of the court than that of the other languages. Nevertheless, several authors were dependent on the emperor or one of his nobles. The connection of the Tamil poets with the Vijayanagara court appears to have begun with the reign of Dēvarāya II. The Śaivite author, Aruṇagirinātha, was one of the principal men of letters at his court.

The poet Kālamēga is said to have been a protége of Sāḷuva Gōpa Tippa, one of Dēvarāya's officers governing a part of the Tamil country. These writers and their patrons, however, belonged to the past. During the sixteenth century, several scholars and poets seem to have flocked to Vijayanagara, attracted by the munificent gifts of Kṛṣṇadēvarāya. The most prominent among them was perhaps the *Veḷḷāla* poet, Haridāsa, the author of the *Irusamaya Viḷakkam*, a work in which he describes the comparative merits of Śaivism and Vaiṣṇavism. Haridāsa was honoured by the Rāya with the grant of several gifts including an entire village free of all taxes. Kumāra Saraswati, some of whose verses are included in the *Nāvalār Caritai*, was probably at the court. He describes the conquest of Kaḷinga, and Kṛṣṇarāya's marriage with the daughter of the Gajapati. The Jain lexicographer, Maṇḍala Purudar Jñānaprakāśar, the author of *Mañjarippa*, and Tatvaprakāśar of Tiruvārūr appear to have received encouragement from the Rāya. One of the Pāṇḍyan chiefs wrote a *Kalambaka* which he dedicated to Aramvalarta Mudaliar, one of Kṛṣṇarāya's ministers.

Though no information is available regarding the interest which Kṛṣṇarāya's successors took in the Tamil literature and poets, there is reason to believe that Rāmarāja Viṭṭhala, who was the viceroy of the Tamil country during Sadāśiva's reign, offered asylum to Tamil men of letters. Nevertheless, the growth of Tamil literature seems to be more due to the activity of *maṭhas* than to the patronage of the kings and princes. In the absence of a settled chronology, it is not possible to describe this activity, however considerable it might have been.

Section 4: Canarese:—Nearly fifty poets flourished between A.D. 1500 and 1570. Not one of them, however, can be described as a writer of outstanding merit. They are usually divided into four classes: the Brahmans, the Vaiṣṇavas, the Jains and the Vīra-Śaivas. Most of them wrote without any encouragement from the imperial court; but some of the Canarese chiefs, especially those of Gersoppa, Haive, Konkaṇa, and Nuggihaḷḷi, who were the subordinates of the Rāya took much interest in their mother-tongue and promoted learning by offering patronage to poets and scholars. The Lingāyat *maṭhas* made also their own contribution by maintaining scholars who devoted their time to the pursuit of letters.

Of the Canarese poets of this age, the Brahman and Vaiṣṇava writers alone received any encouragement from the Rāya. Timmaṇṇa completed Kumāra Vyāsa's Canarese *Mahābhārata* at the command of Kṛṣṇarāya. His work, however, is not of a high order, and it does not bear comparison to that of Kumāra Vyāsa. Nevertheless, it is read with much devotion by a large majority of the Canarese people. Cāṭu Viṭṭhalanātha appears to have flourished during the reigns of Kṛṣṇarāya and his successor; and probably he wrote his *Bhāgavata* at their suggestion. The contribution of the Vaiṣṇava writers to the Canarese literature took the form of popular devotional songs, which were better suited to communicate the tenets of Vaiṣṇavism to the common people. The earliest Vaiṣṇava psalmist was Vyāsatīrtha, the supreme pontiff of the Mādhwa sect. The most famous of them was Purandaradāsa, who appears to have been a familiar figure in the streets of Vijayanagara during the reigns of Acyuta and Sadāśiva. His songs are characterised by great fervour and sincerity of feeling.

They teach *vairāgya*, and devotion to the cult of Viṣṇu, and are popularly sung all over Kannaḍa even at the present day. The most important Vaiṣṇava poet was the *Bēḍa* (hunter), Kanakadāsa, who wrote several works such as *Mōhanatarangiṇi*, *Nalacaritra* and *Kṛṣṇacaritra* etc., besides a number of songs extolling the greatness of Viṣṇu.

Mangarasa III appears to have been the earliest Jain poet of this period. He was a contemporary of Vīra Narasimha, and Kṛṣṇadēvarāya, and probably a subordinate of the Cangāḷva chiefs. His *Jayanṛpakāvya* seems to be the most important of his works. His style is said to be lucid and natural. Abhinava Vādi Vidyānanda was a contemporary of Kṛṣṇadēva and Acyuta, the former of whom is said to have honoured him by performing the *ratnābhiṣēka*. He was a native of Gersoppa, and probably wrote a treatise on poetics called *Kāvyasāra*, which is considered important as it preserves extracts from ancients whose works are not extant. Sālva was another writer of some importance. His *Bhārata*, though not comparable to Kumāra Vyāsa's work, is said to be a work of considerable merit. He was "the court poet of Sālvamalla, the king of Tuluva, Haiva and Konkaṇa countries." He lived about the middle of the century. Notwithstanding the controversy regarding the date of Ratnākaravarṇi, he should be included among the poets of this age. He was a man of great learning, and he wrote two *śatakas* and a voluminous poem of nearly 10,000 verses called *Bharatēśvaracarita*. In addition, he seems to have composed a few songs which teach morality and truth.

Gubbi Mallaṇārya, who lived about 1518 A. D., was probably the first Vīra-Śaiva writer of considerable importance. He produced several works of which

Vīra Śaivāmṛtā and *Śivabhaktapurāṇa* appear to be noteworthy. His works appear to have exercised some influence over Vīra-Śaiva writers of the succeeding generation, as Cēramānka and others acknowledge their indebtedness to him. Nanjuṇḍa who lived about 1525 A. D., wrote in the *sāngatya* metre, the *Kumārarāmanacarite*, the story of Kumāra Rāma, the prince of Kampili. It deserves to be studied more on account of its historical value than its literary merit. Cēramānka was a contemporary of Nanjuṇḍa, and he is remembered on account of his poem, the *Cēramanakāvya*. Lingamantri, who was the court poet of Rāyaṇarāja of Nuggihaḷḷi, a subordinate of Acyutadēvarāya, wrote a lexicon called *Kabbigara-kaipiḍi* about 1530 A.D. Vīrabhadrarāja, who seems to have flourished about the same time, was a prolific writer of several poems. His *Vīrabhadravijaya*, written in a melodious and pleasing style, appears to be the best known of his works. Emme Basava is to be remembered not so much for what he had written but for his association with Salakarāju Cina Tirumala. The composition of a *kālajñāna* or a prophetic account of future events is attributed to him, and it furnishes the historian with some useful information. Sadāśivayōgi wrote his *Rāmanāthavilāsa* about 1554 A.D., and Virakta Tonṭārya compiled the *Karṇāṭakasabdamañjari* besides several other works about 1560 A.D. Although there were many writers other than those mentioned above, they do not seem to be so important as to deserve mention here. The age was certainly one of incessant literary activity; but no work of outstanding merit appears to have been produced.

Telugu :—The sixteenth century is rightly regarded as the Augustan age of the Telugu literature. The age of translations and adaptations came to an end with the close of the fifteenth century, though a few writers here and there still continued to abridge some *purāṇa* or other. The poets Haribhaṭṭa and Vennelaganṭi Sūranna appear to have been the only genuine representatives of the old school. Haribhaṭṭa adapted several *purāṇas* such as the *Matsya*, *Varāha*, and *Nārasimha* and translated a considerable portion of of the *Bhāgavatapurāṇa*. His style is chaste, and elegant reminding the reader frequently of the compositions of some of the best writers of the epic poetry. Vennelaganṭi Sūranna was a protége of Bavaya Rāghava, a subordinate of Kṛṣṇadēvarāya; and he adapted the *Viṣṇupurāṇa* which he dedicated to his patron. Although his poem is characterised by simplicity and elegance of style, it lacks the vigour and dignity of Haribhaṭṭa's works. Kōnērinātha, who lived about the middle of the century, may be conveniently considered in this context. His *Bālabhāgavata*, written in an easy and attractive style, appears to be a work of some literary merit. The authoress Molla, who is assigned to this century, reproduced the story of *Rāmāyaṇa* in charming verse. These writers, however, represented a school which was dying fast. Their work was not as popular as it would have been, had they lived in an earlier age. This was due to a great change that came over the public mind. The people were no longer satisfied with *purāṇic* translations. They expected something new, something original from the authors, if not in their themes, at least in their treatment and presentation. Therefore, the age saw the birth of a new type of *kāvya* known as the *prabandha*.

What is a *prabandha*? It means literally a poetical composition, and in this sense, it may be applied to any *kāvya* or *purāṇa*. The Telugu *Mahābhārata* is sometimes referred to as a *prabandha*; and the poet

Śrīnātha styles his translation of *Kāśikhaṇḍa* a *pra bandha*. In course of time, the connotation of the term appears to have undergone a change, and its scope became restricted by the commencement of the sixteenth century. A *prabandha* came to mean a *kāvya* of an erotic type which, while narrating the story of a hero and a heroine, must contain descriptions of eighteen set topics. These are: (1) a king, (2) his capital, (3) a mountain, (4) a river, (5) the sun-rise or sun-set, (6) the moon-rise, (7) the seasons, (8) a lake, (9) a garden, (10) a damsel, (11) *viraha* or love sickness, (12) *dautya* or negotiation, (13) marriage, (14) wine drinking, (15) coition, (16) birth of a son, (17) war, and (18) pilgrimage. A *prabandha*, in order to be classed as perfect, should deal with all the eighteen topics. There are but three or four perfect *prabandhas*, the rest forfeiting their claim to perfection, as they fall short of the requirements in certain respects. Therefore, a concession has to be made so that the name *prabandha* must be applied to all, although strictly speaking, they should be regarded as imperfect specimens.

The *prabandhas* have been divided into three classes, according to the source from which their theme or story is drawn. These are: (1) the *prakhyāta*, (2) the *utpādya* and (3) the *miśrabandha*.

(1) A *prakhyāta prabandha* is one, the theme or story of which is taken from some well-known source such as the *Rāmāyaṇa*, the *Mahābhārata*, or one of the *purāṇas*, and described without any alteration whatever. The author is expected to show his originality in describing the details. The *Śṛngāra Śākuntalam* of Pina Vīrabhadra may be taken as the most familiar example of a *prakhyāta prabandha*. However,

no author of the sixteenth century excepting perhaps Rāmabhadra seems to have followed Pina Vīrabhadra.

(2) The theme of an *utpādya prabandha* is drawn from the imagination of the author himself. He is free to create his own plot, and arrange his characters in whichever way he likes. Only three poets seem to have composed *utpādya prabandhas* during this period. Mallana wrote his *Rājaśēkaracaritram*, which he dedicated to Nādiṇḍla Gōpa, Kṛṣṇarāya's governor at Koṇḍavīḍu. His style is simple and elegant, although it is considered faulty in certain respects. Rudrayya, a learned goldsmith of Kandukūr in the Nellore district, wrote the well-known *Nirankuśōpākhyānam*, which he dedicated to the god of his place. His work is held up as a model for the elegance of its style, though it is scoffed at by ultra-puritan critics who denounce it as an immoral poem. The greatest *utpādya* writer of the age was, no doubt, Pingaḷi Sūranna, the court-poet of the Nandyāla chief, Kṛṣṇarāja, who lived about the middle of the century. He produced two works of great beauty, the *Prabhāvatīpradyumnam* and the *Kaḷāpūrṇōdayam*. Like the other *utpādya* writers, he creates his own plot; but unlike them, he exhibits extraordinary originality and resourcefulness in handling his themes. Some of the characters of the *Prabhāvatīpradyumnam* are no doubt taken from the *Bhāgavatapurāṇa* or the *Harivamśa*; but the plot and the majority of characters owe their existence to Sūranna's creative genius. He shows great talent in infusing life into his characters, a quality which is rarely seen in the *prabandha* writers. Of all the Telugu writers Sūranna alone possesses the dramatic instinct, which imparts a special interest to his works. The *Kaḷāpūrṇōdayam* is somewhat different in character from the *Prabhāvatīpradyumnam*. The

poem is a perfect piece of art evolved from the highly creative brain of the author. The plot, the dramatic situations, and the characters fully pulsating with life are all created with consummate skill. The *Kaḷā-pūrṇōdayam* is a Telugu *Kādambarī* in verse, which the reader reluctantly lays down after reading it from cover to cover. Sūranna must be regarded as one of the greatest of the mediaeval poets, and there are very few who can bear comparison with him. His style is simple and vigorous; his descriptions are natural and appropriate; and his narrative runs smoothly and majestically like a stream swollen with winter floods.

(3) The *miśrabandha* or *miśra prabandha* is so called because its theme, though borrowed from a *purāṇa* or epic, is mixed up with incidents and situations introduced by the author. In other words, the author of a *miśrabandha* is free to modify the original story in whichever way he chooses. This class of *prabandha* appears to have acquired much popularity during the sixteenth century owing probably to the brilliant success that crowned the attempts of the early writers. According to one great poet of the century, the *prakyāta prabandha* is like a precious stone in its natural state, and an *utpādya* is but an artificial gem, whereas a *miśrabandha* is a genuine gem cut and polished. The view of this writer may be taken as an indication of the enormous popularity which this type of composition enjoyed during the sixteenth century.

Nandi Timmana, the author of the *Pārijātāpa-haraṇam*, appears to have been the earliest of the *miśra-bandha* poets. His poem, which he dedicated to Kṛṣṇa-rāya, takes its place among the best productions of the age. His language is sweet, his imagery polished, his sentiments fine, and his touch delicate. The greatest of *miśrabandha* poets was Peddana whose *Manucaritra* became the model which other writers attempted to emulate not only during his age, but in the succeeding centuries also. The traces of his influence appear in almost all the poems that had been written ever since. His style is sweet and majestic containing as it does a harmonious blending of the Sanskrit and the Telugu words. He is admired for his extraordinary skill, as one writer puts it, in 'weaving' words. By a few strokes of his pen, he can either conjure up a landscape of wonderful beauty, or infuse into his characters life, which raises them up to the human level. Kṛṣṇarāya, who seems to have been attracted by these qualities of his poetry, made him the poet-laureate and conferred upon him the title *Āndhrakavitāpitāmaha* or the creator of the Āndhra poesy. Kṛṣṇarāya himself was a poet of no mean order. He wrote a *prabandha* called the *Āmuktamālyada* which, in the opinion of modern critics, should be regarded as the most sublime poem in the whole range of the *prabandha* literature. The style of the poem is not attractive; it abounds in Sanskritisms, and is rugged and heavy. It repels the beginner, but offers him rare treasures, if he gets over his preliminary dislike. Although the work is generally ascribed to the Rāya, a bitter controversy still rages over its authorship. Some deny the authorship of Kṛṣṇarāya, and attribute it to Peddana, whereas several emphatically assert the contrary. The *Āmuktamālyada* should be regarded as a joint work of both the Rāya and Peddana. Even the most ardent of the pro-Rāya critics cannot deny that Peddana had a hand in the composition of the poem. The difference between the style of the *Manucaritra*, and that of the major portion of the *Āmuktamālyada* is a strong argument against the attribution of the whole work to Peddana.

Sankusāla Narasimha Kavi is also believed to have lived during the time of Kṛṣṇarāya. No evidence is brought forward to support this view. He wrote one of the few perfect *prabandhas* in Telugu called *Kavikarṇarasāyanam* in which it is said he describes forty-five topics. Although, in the opinion of some pandits, he occupies the first place among the *prabandha* poets his work must be regarded as dry and monotonous; and it creates a feeling of weariness in the mind of the reader. Judging it from its style and technique, it must be said to be a work of a later age when the *prabandha* became decadent. Tāḷḷapākam Peda-Tirumalārya composed a century of verse called the *Nīti-śatakam*, which throws some light on the social conditions of the period. His son, Tiruvengaḷanātha, the author of the *Aṣṭamahiṣīkalyāṇam*, was a contemporary of Acyutadēvarāya. Rāmarājabhūṣana flourished during the reign of Sadāśiva. He was a dependent of Rāmarāja, and of his brother, Tirumala, who later on usurped the throne of Vijayanagara. He wrote a *prabandha* called *Vasucaritra*, which is justly regarded as one of the greatest poems of the language. He lacks the creative genius of Peddana and Sūranna; but he surpasses both of them in the wonderful craftsmanship which he displays throughout his poem. Although he does not show much capacity in designing a plot, and the creation of characters, he successfully conceals this defect under the wonderful decorative art of which he is a master. Nevertheless, Rāmarājabhūṣana deserves a place among the greatest poets of the Telugu language. Rangapparāja, one of Rāmarāja's cousins, wrote the *Sambōpākhyāṇam*, a poem of considerable merit, though it has fallen out of taste at present on account of the many erotic descriptions in which the author revels.

The Religious Poetry:—The poems that have been written to glorify some deity, a place of pilgrimage, a saint, or a religious teacher fall under this head. They may be sub-divided into three classes for the convenience of treatment.

(*a*) *Poems written to glorify a deity*:—There are two poems of this class both written by Ellayārya *alias* Rādhamādhava who flourished at the court of Acyutadēvarāya. His *Tārakabrahmarājīya* which exists only in a fragmentary condition glorifies the Rāma incarnation of Viṣṇu. His *Viṣṇumāyāvilāsa* consists of a series of tales which extol the *māya* or illusion created by Viṣṇu to ensnare creatures in the interminable net of *samsāra*. The latter is a delightful poem of rare excellence written in a very elegant style. The descriptions once read linger long in memory and are not easily forgotten. Though the poem is unpublished at present, it is bound to take its place amongst the best productions of the century. *

(*b*) *Poems written to glorify a place of pilgrimage*:—The *Kāḷahastimahātmya* of Dhūrjaṭi (senior) is regarded as one of the classics of the Telugu language. The author's style is sweet and dignified; his characters are well-drawn; and his tale is narrated with considerable skill and charm. The greatest of the *mahātmya* writers was Tenāli Rāmakṛṣṇa, who produced two works of this class. His *Pāṇḍurangamahātmya* is a work of great literary excellence, and it is highly praised for the dignity of its style. In the art of telling stories, the skill of Rāmakṛṣṇa is unrivalled. His comparisons are apt, and homely, and his descriptions are characterised by their naturalness. In short,

* The poem has been recently published by the Telugu Department of the University of Madras.

he is one of those writers whose works always retain their popularity in spite of the changes of taste and fashion in the realm of letters. His *Ghaṭikācalamahātmya*, which was not published during his life-time, is less known; but, though not comparable to the *Pāṇḍurangamahātmya*, it should still be regarded as a great poem.

(*c*) *Poems written to glorify a saint or a religious teacher*:—Besides the two *mahātmyas* mentioned above Rāmakṛṣṇa wrote in his early days a poem called the *Udbhaṭārādhyacaritra*, describing the deeds of the Śaivite saint, Udbhaṭa. The work is available only in fragments, and it displays an early phase of the author's art which is still immature. The *Paramayōgivilāsa* of Tiruvengaḷanātha celebrates in *dvipada* metre the lives of the *Āḻwārs* or the Vaiṣṇava saints. The author is said to possess great command over *dvipada*; but it does not seem to be so pliable an instrument in his hands as it is in those of earlier writers such as Ranganātha and Gauranna. Another work of the same name was written by Timmarāja, a nephew of Aḷiya Rāmarāja. Although the style of the poem reaches the standard maintained by the *prabandha* writers, it appears to be void of any distinctive feature.

Many works of minor importance were produced during the Tuluva period; but they need not be taken into consideration here. What has been said above is enough to indicate the main lines on which the Telugu literature had developed during one of the greatest periods of its history.

Section 5: Art and Architecture:—The accession of Kṛṣṇadēvarāya to the throne of Vijayanagara marks the beginning of the most brilliant period in the history of the Vijayanagara art. It is said that "the time of its greatest prosperity was between the accession of Kṛṣṇadēva, 1508, and the death of Acyutarāya, 1542, and it is perhaps to their reigns that the finest monuments in the city should be ascribed." * The buildings that were erected during the period fall into two classes, *viz.* (1) temples and (2) palaces and public buildings. Though specimens of both classes of buildings still survive, no earnest attempt has yet been made to study them from an artistic point of view.

(1) *Temples* :—Soon after his accession in 1509, Kṛṣṇadēvarāya undertook to repair one of the *gōpuras* of the temple of Virūpākṣa at Hampi. At the same time, he also constructed a new *gōpura* at the eastern gate of the temple. During the course of his long war with the Gajapati, he built two new temples. One of them, the Kṛṣṇswāmi temple, was specially built to lodge the image of Bālakṛṣṇa, which Kṛṣnarāya had brought away from the fortress of Udayagiri when he captured it in 1513. The temple is large and handsome ; but it is devoid of ornamentation ; and there is nothing to relieve the monotony of its bare walls. The Hazāra Rāma temple which appears to have been built about the same time stood at the gate of the palace ; and it was intended to serve as a private chapel to the inmates of the imperial household. The Hazāra Rāma temple is said to be "one of the most perfect specimens of the Hindu temple architecture of the Vijayanagara period." "The temple is provided with a handsome porch in front, which leads into the central hall, the roof of which is mainly supported by four particularly beautiful and highly polished black stone pillars, richly carved and crowned with bracket capital

* Fergusson : *Hist. of India and Eastern Architecture* i. p. 401.

of the Indo-Cornithian appearance."* Its chief attraction however, lies in the beautiful sculptures which cover every inch of available space in the temple as well as on the walls of the enclosure. The construction of the imposing *gōpuram* at Cidambaram, and the thousand-pillared hall at Tiruvaṇṇāmalai must be ascribed to the same period. Kṛṣṇarāya seems to have erected a fine temple with many images in the new suburb of Nāgalāpūr about 1520. He must have undertaken to reconstruct the Viṭṭhalaswāmi temple during the last years of his reign,† which he was obliged to leave unfinished at the time of his death.

Some of the nobles appear to have been affected by Kṛṣṇarāya's love for fine temples. The Pemmasāni chiefs of Gaṇḍikōṭa built a shrine for the God Raghunātha in the fort; but the finest temples they built were at Tāḍpatri on the banks of the North Pennār

* Longhurst: *The Ruins of Hampi* pp. 69, 71.

† The construction of the Viṭṭhalaswāmi temple is usually attributed to Kṛṣṇadēvarāya; but he could not have built that temple, as it existed even during the time of Dēvarāya II. We learn from Haribhaṭṭa, who lived in the first quarter of the 16th century that Prōluganṭi Tippana, one of Dēvarāya's officers built a *bhōgamanṭapa* for Viṭṭhala at Hampi.

"ఆమంత్రీంద్రుడు ప్రౌఢరాయనృప దండాధీశ సంపత్కళా
సామగ్రి న్విలసిల్లి మల్లిసుమ భాస్వత్కీర్తి విస్ఫూర్తి న
ద్దామాసాధ్య మహోమహత్త్వమున సంధాయుక్తి దోశ్శక్తి వా
చామాధుర్యమునన్ బురావిభులతో జర్చించు వర్చస్వియై ॥

* * * * *

కదలని భక్తితో గట్టించె పంపావిరూపాక్షు దేవుని గోపురంబు
విఠ్ఠలపతికి గావించి యర్పణజేసె మహనీయతర భోగమంటపంబు
మాల్యవంతము రఘునాథమూర్తికి ఘనకిరీటం బుపాయన మొసంగె
దరిశెనంబిచ్చె మతంగ వీరన్నకుం గట్టాణిముత్యాల కంఠమాల."

Nārasimhapurāṇam.

It is evident that the shrine of Viṭṭhala as well as the temples of Virūpākṣa, Mālyavanta-Raghunātha, and Vīrabhadra were in existence during the time of Dēvarāya II.

These are regarded as the most splendid specimens of Vijayanagara art.

Acyuta continued the work of his brother by undertaking to complete the renovation of Viṭṭhala's shrine. He also built two new temples at the capital which deserve notice. The temple of Acyutarāyaswāmi which he built in 1539 A. D., was designed on the lines of Viṭṭhalaswāmi temple, although it must be considered far inferior to the latter from an artistic point of view. It contains a spacious verandah supported by finely carved granite pillars besides a few panels of exquisite workmanship. The Paṭṭābhirāma temple is the biggest shrine that was ever built at Vijayanagara. Though it is totally devoid of any kind of ornamentation, its huge proportions produce on the mind an impression of grandeur, which does not rapidly fade away. The large hall standing on lofty pillars facing the eastern *gōpura*, and the immense tank, with the granite *maṇḍapa* in its centre, are the most interesting features of this temple. The Paṭṭābhirāma temple is, perhaps, unsurpassed for its massive grandeur by any structure of its kind that still stands amidst the extensive ruins at Hampi.

The building activity of Acyuta was not confined only to his capital. He was a devout worshipper of God Venkaṭēśa of Tirupati, whose shrine he visited three or four times during his short reign of twelve years. Very early in his reign, he provided *Kapilatīrtham* on the Tirumalai with granite steps, and built *maṇḍapams* on its eastern and western sides to accommodate the Brahmans performing *sandhyāvandanam*. He also constructed the temple of Acyutarāyaperumāḷ, and around it an *agrahāra* of 120 houses.*

* *TDER.* p. 224.

Penugoṇḍa Virūpaṇṇa, one of his officers, built a beautiful temple at Lēpākṣi for his favourite deity Śiva. The temple is said to contain handsome sculptures and beautifully carved pillars.

(2) *Palaces and Public Buildings* :—Several palaces and public buildings were erected at Vijayanagara and other places during this period. Kṛṣṇarāya made fresh additions to the old palace in the city. At the close of the Kaḷinga war, he built the famous audience hall known as the *Bhuvana Vijaya* or 'the house of victory.' It was so called "as it was made when the King came back from the war against Orya."* The *Bhuvana Vijaya* was supported by pillars shaped like elephants, probably symbolising the eight mythical elephants bearing the burden of the earth on their backs. It was open in front, and people went up to it by staircases of stone ; around it there was a corridor paved with flag-stones. † About 1520, Kṛṣṇarāya added a new suburb to his capital, which he named Nāgalāpūr after his mother, Nāgalādēvī. Beside the royal palace, there were the mansions of the nobles and the merchants whom the Rāya induced to settle down in his new city. ‡ Probably some of the buildings that still stand amidst the ruins might owe their existence to the same monarch. If tradition can be trusted, the construction of the palaces at Candragiri and Penugoṇḍa should also be attributed to him. The palace at Candragiri gives us an idea of the external appearance of the royal residences of the time. The *Gagan Mahal*, as the Penugoṇḍa palace is called, where Kṛṣṇarāya is said to have usually resided during his visits to the place, is so sadly mutilated by the ravages of time and the vandalism

* *FE.* p. 263. † *ibid.* ‡ *ibid* p. 246.

of the people that no vestige of its former greatness can at present be detected ; but it retained something of its ancient grandeur during the eighteenth century. It consisted of two sections, the more ancient of which resembled closely the palace at Candragiri. The other was built in the style of the palaces of the Nāyaks of Tanjore and Madura. Judging its external appearance from an old wood-cut, * it must be regarded as a fine specimen of later Vijayanagara architecture. It must have been a grand building in the days of its glory. The chief point of interest is that it presents an early phase of the later secular architecture of the Vijayanagara period, which reached its zenith during the days of the Nāyaks.

No secular building appears to have been built by Acyuta ; however, the *Venkaṭavilāsa manṭapa* mentioned in the *Acyutarāyābhyudayam* might have been built by him. A few fine palaces were built during Sadāśiva's reign. The most noteworthy of them appears to be the *Ratnakūṭa*, which the musician Rāmayāmātya, who was also an engineer, built for Rāmarāja. The *Ratnakūṭa* stood in middle of an extensive garden containing fruit-bearing trees and artificial tanks. It was adorned with beautiful statues, and is said to have rivalled in magnificence, the *Vaijayanta*, the palace of the gods. † It is not unlikely that some of the buildings, such as the group of palaces in the Queen's Enclosure, and some of the gateways of the city were built at this time.

The Sculpture :—Abundant material is available for the study of the sculptor's art, though it remains almost unnoticed so far. Besides the Viṭṭhalaswāmi

* *The Oriental Annual* for 1840 ; see the frontispiece.

† *Sources* p. 190.

temple containing heaps of beautiful fragments of broken images and statues, there are other structures both at Vijayanagara and elsewhere that demand the attention of the artist and the historian. The Hazāra Rāma temple, the throne platform, and the temples at Tāḍpatri and Hampi must be regarded as the finest galleries of the Vijayanagara art that have come down to us. Some of the sculptures are "cut with exquisite sharpness and precision, in a fine close-grained horn-blende stone, and produce an effect richer, and on the whole perhaps in better taste than anything else in this style."* The hard granite obeyed the inspired mason, who by a few strokes of his chisel transformed its dull surface into forms and shapes that please the eye and gladden the heart. These sculptures are of two-fold interest: in the first place, they enable us to estimate the level of artistic excellence which the Vijayanagara sculptor had reached; and secondly, they give us a profound insight into the social and religious life of the people of Vijayanagara during the days of her greatest glory.

Painting:—Painting, as we have already noticed, flourished like the allied arts. It was customary to paint pictures representing stories from mythology on the walls of temples and palaces as well as the private dwelling-houses. Specimens of Vijayanagara painting are found in a few temples in a sadly mutilated condition. The ceiling of the temples at Tirupartikunṟam, Sōmpāḷem, Lēpākṣi and Hampi contain pictures representing the important scenes from the Jain mythology, the *Rāmāyaṇa* and the *Mahābhārata*. Unless these are copied and studied, it is not possible

* Fergusson: *The Indian and the Eastern Architecture* pp. 377-8.

to estimate the degree of skill which the Vijayanagara painter possessed, and the measure of success which he achieved in wielding his brush.

Music:—The South Indian music assumed more or less its present shape during the time of the Tuluvas, when it made considerable progress owing to the active interest which the Rāyas took in music and the musicians. Kṛṣṇadēvarāya learnt to play on the *vīṇa* from a famous musician called Kṛṣṇa, one of the ancestors of the Mādhwa *guru*, Rāghavēndra. * When he ascended the throne, he appointed as the music master of his zenana, Lakṣmīnārāyaṇa, the author of the *Sangītasūryōdaya*, who appears to have been a great authority in music at the time. Acyuta extended his patronage to Rāmayāmātya whom he appointed, probably as a mark of his appreciation of the musician's talents, as the governor of the province of Koṇḍavīḍu. Rāmarāja who was the *de facto* ruler of the empire during Sadāśiva's reign, not only permitted him to remain in that office, but placed his daughters under him to receive instruction in music. † It was during Sadāśiva's reign that Rāmayāmātya wrote his famous *Swaramēḷakaḷānidhi*, which had a large share in shaping the future course of development of the South Indian music.

The great popularity of music during the sixteenth century is evidenced by the contemporary literature, which is replete with references to music, musical instruments and contests. The musician was expected to possess an expert knowledge of the theory of music as well as of the *rāgas* and *tāḷas*. Like the scholar and the poet, he frequently wandered from place to place in search of patronage. He would challenge his fellow

* *Sources* p. 252.

† *ibid* p. 190.

musicians to a contest. If he won, he obtained rewards from a nobleman or the Rāya; and if he lost, he hastily retired from the place cursing his evil fate for his misfortune. Musical instruments of various kinds were in use; the most popular of them was, of course, the *vīṇa*, the ability to play on which was considered a special mark of culture. As the love of music permeated the whole society, musicians easily found patrons whose bounty enabled them to live in peace and comfort. An atmosphere favourable to the growth of the musical talent was thus created. It is only natural that it should thrive and bear fruit tenfold and hundred-fold.

APPENDIX A.

CATUIR OF NUNIZ.

According to Nuniz, Kṛṣṇarāya subdued the chief of Catuir, in the interval between his marriage with the daughter of the king of Orissa, and his campaign against the Ādil Shāh. Nuniz writes:—

"He (Kṛṣṇarāya) made ready a large army and prepared to attack Catuir, which is the land of a lord who had been in revolt for fifty years; this land is on the Charmáodel side. And he went against it, and laid siege to one of the principal cities, where the lord of the land was; and it is called......and is surrounded with water.

"Now at the time when Crisnarao attacked this city it was winter, for which cause the river that surrounded it was so swollen, and carried down so much water, that the king could do no harm to the place." *

This is all the data which Nuniz supplies for the identification of the place. The following points should be noted:—

(1) The lord of Catuir had been in revolt for fifty years.

(2) Catuir was on the Charamãodel side.

(3) Kṛṣṇadēvarāya laid siege not to the capital, but to one of the principal cities.

(4) The lord of the land was staying there.

(5) The place was 'surrounded' with water; and it was a river that surrounded it.

A few attempts have been made to identify the place, but so far without success. Unless the place

* *FE.* pp. 320-1.

which is to be identified with Catuir satisfies all the conditions of Nuniz, the identification may be taken as not established.

(1) The land of Catuir "had been in revolt for fifty years," when Kṛṣṇarāya attacked it. When did he attack it?

> "After Crisnarao had made peace, and had married the daughter of the King of Oria and had restored to him his wife and the lands beyond the river (Kṛṣṇā) as has been narrated above." *

The war with the king of Orissa came to an end in 1518-19 A. D. Therefore, the marriage of the Rāya with the daughter of the king of Orissa must have taken place in 1519. A. D. The attack upon Catuir must be placed in the same year.† The principality of Catuir appears to have been paying tribute to Vijayanagara about (1519—50) = 1469 A.D. The last emperor of Vijayanagara who could have received the tribute from the lord of the land was Mallikārjuna.

(2) The land of Catuir was on the Charamãodel side. There is no justification in looking for the place elsewhere. One should look for it along the coast of the Bay of Bengal. By 1519 A.D., all the Telugu country from Masulipatam downwards had already been conquered by the Rāya. The coastal region from Nellore to Madura was under the emperors of Vijayanagara ever since the Sāḷuva usurpation. Inscriptions make it clear that all this region was under the control of Sāḷuva Narasimha, Immaḍi Narasimha, Narasā Nāyaka and Vīra Narasimha. Probably, there was some disturbance during Vīra Narasimha's reign in the

* *ibid.*

† Sewell places the battle of Rāicūr on May 19, 1520. As the siege and capture of Catuir preceded Kṛṣṇarāya's attack upon Rāicūr, it is not unreasonable to suppose that the former had taken place a few months earlier.

Tuṇḍīra-maṇḍala; but it was suppressed by Kṛṣṇarāya as early as 1511 A. D. The Tuṇḍīra and the Cōḷa-maṇḍalas were so quiet during Kṛṣṇarāya's reign that he could not only embark on a long and arduous war with the Gajapati, but could pay frequent visits to their holy places. Catuir, which was in a state of rebellion for fifty years, could not have been in either of them. The Madura country was subdued by Narasā Nāyaka probably about 1501 A. D.* Inscriptions of Sāḷuva Narasingha Nāyaka, a subordinate of Vīra Narasimha and Kṛṣṇadēva reveal that their authority was recognised in the Madura country. Therefore, the land of Catuir, which was in a state of rebellion for fifty years preceding Kṛṣṇarāya's campaign, could not have been part of the Madura country. It appears that Catuir was somewhere to the south of Madura.

Catuir appears to be the same as Kāyattār, the capital of one of the branches of the Pāṇḍya royal family. It was known to several Portuguese writers. According to Pedro de Basto, "the Lord of Tuticorin, the capital of the town of that coast, was a knight whom they called King of Cayetarro, who was the lord of the other neighbouring towns besides Tuticorin."† Fr. Queyros alludes to the 'petty Kings of Caetarro.'‡ Cayetarro or Caetarro appears to be identical with Catuir, the chief of which, as seen already, was subjugated by Kṛṣṇarāya in 1519 A.D.

Was the principality of Kāyattār in a state of rebellion for fifty years before 1519 A.D.? No definite information is available on the subject. However, it is extremely probable that it had been so. Nuniz states

* *MER.* 36 of 1928–29.

† Queyros: *The Conquest of Ceylon* ii. p. 394 *n*. 1.

‡ *ibid* pp. 394-5.

that "the King of Coullao (Quilon) and Ceyllao and Paleacate and Peguu, and Tanaçary and many other countries paid tribute" to Dēvarāya II, whose reign came to an end in 1448-49 A.D.* That Dēvarāya's dominions extended as far south as Ceylon is proved by inscriptions and Abdur Razāk. The boundaries of Vijayanagara during the last years of Dēvarāya II, according to Razāk, "extended from the borders of Sarandip to those of Gulburga, and from Bengal to Malabar."† He also alludes to the invasion of Ceylon by 'the Daṇāik,' the minister of Dēvarāya II. ‡

It is evident that the kingdom of Quilon was tributary to Dēvarāya II; and the small principality of Kāyattār which was in its immediate neighbourhood could not have escaped the conqueror's arm. Mallikārjuna, the son and successor of Dēvarāya II, was a very weak monarch, and his authority in the south could not have survived the Orissan invasion under Kapilēśvara Gajapati, which took place in the middle of 1464 A.D.§ Quilon and other places in the extreme south must have asserted their independence about the time, which they enjoyed undisturbed almost until the time of Kṛṣṇadēvarāya.

(3) At the time of Kṛṣṇarāya's invasion, the lord of Kāyattār (Catuir) was not in his capital, but in one of his principal cities, which was surrounded by a river. What could have been the name of this city? It must have been Kāyal, the famous sea-port town in this part of the country. Kāyal stood in the delta of the Tāmraparṇī, surrounded by the branches into which the river splits itself, before falling into the sea. The difficulty of capturing the place in the height of winter

* *FE.* p. 302. † *ED.* iv. p. 105. ‡ *ibid* p. 116.

§ *MER.* 51, 92 of 1919.

floods must have been well-nigh insurmountable. This famous port belonged for several years to the king of Quilon; but it appears to have been conquered by the chief of Kāyattār subsequent to 1514 A.D. The following table* is bound to be instructive in this context.

1504. The king of Quilon was ruling from Quilon to Kāyal. He maintained a force of 60,000 archers. He defeated the king of Narasingha before that date.

1505. The king of Quilon maintained 20,000 horsemen; one of his cities was Kāyal.

1514. The kingdom of Quilon extended from Kāyamkulam to Kāyal.

1522. The kingdom of Quilon lay between Kāyamkulam and Travancore, and had two harbours, Quilon and Viliñjam.

This table makes it clear that between 1514 A.D. and 1522 A.D., there was a shrinkage in the north-eastern boundary of the kingdom of Quilon. Whereas in 1514 A.D., it extended as far as Kāyal, it was belimited by the kingdom of Travancore in 1522. Moreover, it had only two harbours, Quilon and Viliñjam. The omission of Kāyal as a port belonging to the kingdom of Quilon is significant. It indicates that the king of Quilon lost this port during the interval. Who could have taken it from him?

As the emperors of Vijayanagara were attempting to recover the whole of the south, as shown by Narasā Nāyaka's unsuccessful attempt about 1501 A.D.,† it may be argued that Kṛṣṇarāya, who was ruling at

* *JBHS*. ii. pp. 9-10.

† Albuquerque: *The Commentaries* i. p. 11.

Vijayanagara from 1509 to 1529 A.D., might have captured it. According to Nuniz, Caullim, which Sewell identifies with Kāyal,* was included in the province of Sāḷuva Nāyaka, at the time of the death of Kṛṣṇadēvarāya. Therefore, Caullim (Kāyal) appears to have been conquered by him on some occasion during his reign. An inscription at Pīrānmalai in the Ramnad district dated 1522-23 alludes to his conquest of Ceylon. † It may be pointed that he might have captured Kāyal about this time.

Although Kṛṣṇarāya's capture of Kāyal appears to be certain, nowhere have we an account of his campaign in the southern extremity of the peninsula. The *Rāyavācaka*, no doubt, refers to his pilgrimage to the holy shrines in the Ramnad and Tinnevelly districts; ‡ but it does not even remotely hint at a military campaign. However, as we have identified Catuir with the kingdom of Kāyattār, Nuniz may be said to have described Kṛṣṇarāya's military activities in the south in his account of the Catuir campaign. The topographic details which Nuniz gives about the place where the Rāya overcame the chief of Catuir (Kāyattār) apply exactly, as we have noticed, to Kāyal. Therefore, Kāyal appears to have been captured by the Rāya from the chief of Catuir. In that case, Kāyal must have changed hands twice between 1514 and 1522 A.D. It must have fallen first into the hands of the ruler of Kāyattār from whom Kṛṣṇarāya conquered it in 1519 A.D.

* *FE.* p. 384 *n.* 2.

† *MER.* 146 of 1903; 4 of 1894.

‡ *ASPP.* iii. pp. 208-10.

APPENDIX B.

THE ORIGIN OF THE NĀYAK KINGDOM OF MADURA.

It is said, in the *Tañjāvūru Āndhra Rājula Caritra*, that, during the last years of the emperor Kṛṣṇadēvarāya, Vīraśēkhara Cōḷa invaded the dominions of Candraśēkhara Pāṇḍya, and expelled him from his kingdom. Candraśēkhara complained to the Rāya against the unjust conduct of the Cōḷa king, and begged him to restore to him his territories. In response to this request, Kṛṣṇarāya commanded Nāgama Nāyaka, one of his officers, to punish Vīraśēkhara, and restore the Pāṇḍyan kingdom to its lawful owner. Nāgama proceeded to the south and defeated the Cōḷa king; but he did not care to restore the conquered territory to the Pāṇḍya in obedience to the commands of the Rāya. The Pāṇḍya king naturally complained to the Rāya against Nāgama. Kṛṣṇadēvarāya sent an order to Nāgama commanding him to hand over to the Pāṇḍya his dominions, and return to the capital with all possible haste; but Nāgama chose to disobey. The insubordination of Nāgama had so enraged the Rāya that he exclaimed in the open assembly, "Is there no one among my officers who has courage to chastise this rebel?" Viśwanātha, the only son of Nāgama, got up from his seat and begged that, if he were ordered to proceed against the rebel, he was ready to go. Further, he assured the Rāya that he would bring Nāgama dead or alive to the royal presence. The Rāya, thereupon, angrily enquired whether Viśwanātha was asking permission to go and join his father; but, on Viśwanātha making protestations of his loyalty, he was commanded by the Rāya to march upon Nāgama only with 6,000 *amaram* troops which he was entitled to maintain. No other help was given to him. Having obtained the royal command, Viśwanātha marched against his father, and he defeated him in a battle. Nāgama, who was taken prisoner, was carried away to Vijayanagara to be produced before the Rāya. Viśwanātha's extraordinary loyalty excited the admiration of the Rāya to such an extent that he not only forgave Nāgama but conferred the sovereignty of the Pāṇḍya and Cōḷa kingdoms on Viśwanātha with the title of 'the lord of the southern throne.' And Viśwanātha, having left the capital, repaired to Madura, where he soon after took charge of his new office. "Then Viśwanātha Nāyaka became the sole ruler of the Pāṇḍya and Cōḷa countries and governed them as a subordinate of the emperor at Vijayanagara." *

"The emperor Kṛṣṇadēvarāya died sometime after this and was succeeded by his younger brother Acyutarāya. His queen was Tirumalamma. Her younger sister, Mūrtyamma was married to Cevvappa Nāyaka. Acyutarāya appointed this Cevvappa as the sole viceroy over the Cōḷa country which was till then included in the viceroyalty of Madura along with the Pāṇḍya country." †

This account of the origin of the Madura Nāyak kingdom cannot be accepted as true for the following reasons :—

(1) According to the *Tañjāvūru Āndhra Rājula Caritra*, Viśwanātha "became the sole ruler of the Pāṇḍya and the Cōḷa countries" during the last years of Kṛṣṇadēvarāya's reign. He held this position for sometime even after Acyutarāya's accession.

* V. Prabhakara Sastri : *TARC.* (Vāviḷḷa Edition.)

† *ibid.*

This contradicts the evidence of contemporary writers. (i) Nuniz says: "After his (Kṛṣṇarāya's) death, Salvanay became minister of the kingdom, and governed it till the coming of King Achitarao."* "He is lord of Charamãodel and of Negapatao and Tamgor, and Bomgarin, and Dapatao, and Trueguel, and Caullim, and all these are cities; their territories all very large, and they border on Ceylon."† The names Charamãodel, Negapatao and Tamgor are easily identified. Bomgarin is Bhuvanagiri in the South Arcot district, in the neighbourhood of Cidambaram. Dapatao is Dēvīpaṭṇam in the Ramnad district. Caullim is said to be Kāyal in the Tinnevelly district. Trueguel is not yet identifiable. It is clear from this that the authority of Salvanay or Salvanayaque extended as far south as the Tinnevelly district. (ii) Rājanātha Ḍiṇḍima speaks of the Cōḷa country as the possession of one Sellappa who is identified with Salvanay or Salvanayaque mentioned above. (iii) Inscriptions of this Sāḷuva Nāyaka are found in the Cōḷa and the Pāṇḍya countries. Some of them are seen at Tirupattūr in the Ramnad district.

As Sāḷuva Nāyaka was the minister of Acyuta for a short time in 1530-31, his authority should have extended over the places mentioned above at that time; but the *Tañjāvūru Āndhra Rājula Caritra* would have us believe that at this very time Viśwanātha Nāyaka was ruling the Cōḷa and the Pāṇḍya countries as their sovereign. However, as the evidence of contemporary writers and the inscriptions is considered more trustworthy than that of the chronicles of later times, the latter may be set aside as unreliable.

* *FE*. p. 367.

† *FE*. p. 384.

(2) Nuniz gives a list of the principal *amaranāyakas* of Acyuta during the early years of his reign. The Nāyaka of Madura is conspicuous by his absence from the list. Sewell draws our attention to this omission: "Note that Madura is not mentioned in these lists."* If a great subordinate king like Viśwanātha Nāyaka was then ruling at Madura at the time, he could not have escaped the attention of Nuniz. The king of Madura is not mentioned by Nuniz, because Madura country was not, at this time, governed by a separate king, but was under the jurisdiction of Sāḷuva Nāyaka, one of the *amaranāyakas* of the Rāya.

(3) Some of the *Kaifiyats* preserved in the Mackenzie Mss. assert that Acyutadēvarāya crowned Viśwanātha Nāyaka king of Madura as a reward for meritorious services rendered to the state. †

(4) According to a palm leaf ms. called the *Pāṇḍyarājacaritra*, Viśwanātha Nāyaka obtained many titles from Acyutadēvarāya; and having become the master of the southern kingdom, he ruled over the Pāṇḍya *maṇḍala* with the city of Madura as his capital. ‡ This

* *FE*. p. 384 *n*. 2. † *LR*. 8 (*The Kaifiyat of Karṇāṭaka Koṭikam kings*) p. 319 ff.

‡ *The Pāṇḍyarājacaritra*.—Adyar Mss. Library.

అచ్యుతరాయ లేయవనీశమౌళికి సరుదులౌ పలువగ బిరుదు లిచ్చె
దక్షిణ సింహాస నాక్షిణ సామ్రాజ్య ధౌరేయుఁడయ్యె నే ధరణివిభుఁడు
ఘనముగా విజయదుర్గను మహాలక్ష్మి నే ధీరుఁడు తెచ్చి ప్రతిష్ఠఁజేసె
మధురాపురంబున మహనీయ పాండ్యభూమండలం బేలె నే మహిపమౌళి
అతఁడు నృపమాత్రుఁడా మహాహవజయాంకభూవరాహాదిబిరుద సంభూతకీర్తి
కార్తికీచంద్రధవళితగగనవాటి అలఘుఁడౌ విశ్వనాథనాయకకిరీటి ॥

V. Prabhakara Sastri, who was the first to notice this verse, drew attention to its importance in his short introduction to the *Satyabhāmāswāntanam*.

I am greatly obliged to Dr. C. Kunhan Rāja for securing me a loan of this ms. from the library of the Adyar Theosophical Society.

work does not tell us how he obtained the kingdom. It seems to suggest, in a vague manner, that he became the king of Madura after Acyuta.

Owing to these considerations, it is not possible to accept the view that the Nāyak Kingdom of Madura was founded during the time of Kṛṣṇadēvarāya.

It is suggested by some writers that Acyuta crowned Viśwanātha, king of Madura.* This suggestion has, as already noticed, the support of the *Kaifiyat of the Karṇāṭaka Koṭikam Kings* and other chronicles. Curiously enough, their evidence is contradicted by the *Maduraittala Varalāru.* According to this work, Viśwanātha was one of the governors that ruled at Madura before 1559 A.D.; his tenure of office was not continuous, as the period of his rule over Madura is divided into three periods, each period being separated by a fairly long interval.

"From the year Vijaya to the year Vibhava (Śubhakṛt (?)) A.D. 1533—42 for a period of nine years Viśwanāthanāyakaraiyan ruled the kingdom. Varada ruled in the year Śubhakṛt (A.D. 1542-43). Tumbiccināyakkar ruled from the year Śubhakṛt to the year Krōdhi (1543-44 A.D.) Kārtigai, for a period of a year. Viśwanāthanāyakaraiyan ruled from Krōdhi Mārgaḻi to the year Viśvāvasu (A.D. 1544-45) for a period of a year and seven months. One Viṭṭalarāja ruled from Prabhava (Parābhava ?) to the year Pingaḷa (1546—57 A.D.). The three kings Timmappanāyakkar, Cellappanāyakkar and Paṭṭukkōṭṭa Vīrappanāyakkar, ruled from Kāḷayukti to Raudri Kārthigai (1558-60). From Śaka 1246 to Śaka 1485 (A.D. 1324—1563) twenty-seven persons ruled in Madura."

"During the Śaka 1481 (1559 A.D.) current Raudri (A.D. 1560) Mārgaḻi, Viśwanāthanāyakkar, son of Kōṭṭiyam Nāgama Nāyakkar came under the orders of the Rāyar and died after a rule of twelve years extending from Raudri Mārgaḻi to Āngirasa Vaikāśi A. D. 1559—1572." †

* Heras: *The Āraviḍu Dynasty* p. 131.

† Satyanadhan: *The Nāyaks of Madura* App. F, p. 376.

According to this passage, Viśwanātha ruled at Madura, as a governor,—

(1) From A. D. 1533—A. D. 1542.

(2) From A. D. 1544—A. D. 1545.

(3) From A. D. 1559—A. D. 1572.

There is, therefore, an interval of two years between his first term and the second and another interval of fourteen years between his second and third terms. The dates that are given above do not seem to be very accurate. The earliest inscription of Viśwanātha in this region is dated in the year 1532 A.D.* He describes himself as the *ūḷiyam*, i.e., a menial servant of Acyutarāya. Acyutarāya himself made the grant to a temple of the village of Varagaṇaputtūr in the Tirupattūr tālūka of the Ramnad district in 1534-35 for the merit of Viśwanātha ; † and it is reasonable to suppose that Viśwanātha was holding some high office in that region; it is not unlikely that he held the office of the governor of the province of Madura. The exact period for which he held this office, it is difficult to ascertain at present. However, as Periya Rāmappa Nāyaka was Acyuta's *kāryakarta* in this region from 1538 A.D. to 1542, ‡ it may be said that Viśwanātha's term of office closed sometime before 1538 A.D. Viśwanātha does not make his appearance once again in any inscription of this region until 1547 A.D. In the light of available epigraphical evidence, it may be said that Viśwanātha might have held the governorship of Madura from 1532 to 1538 A.D. There is no justification whatever for the belief that Acyuta made Viśwanātha, the king of Madura with the title, 'the lord of the southern throne.'

* *MER.* 88 of 1928-9. † *ibid* 113 of 1908.

‡ *ibid* 121 of 1903 ; 65 of 1916 ; 30 of 1928-29.

APPENDIX B

During the first two years of Sadāśiva, Viśwanātha appears to have been holding some sort of office in the Cōḷa country. * Probably he accompanied Rāmarāja Viṭṭhala and Cina Timma to the south in A.D. 1544-45. According to Burgess and Natesa Sastri, he is mentioned in an inscription of Koṇḍagai dated A.D. 1546; he is said to have presided over an arbitration court, and an agent of the king called Timmappa-nāyakkar 'settled some disputes between the two sections of the inhabitants at Koṇḍagai.' † As a matter of fact, however, the said inscription does not at all seem to refer to Viśwanātha. It has been recently copied by the Government Epigraphist, and the name of Sāḷuva Nāyaka is found in it in the place of that of Viśwanātha. ‡ As he is said to be the agent of Rāmarāja Viṭṭhala in a record of Mēlaccevval (Tinnevelly Dt.) dated A.D. 1550, he could not have been the king of Madura. § He probably continued to hold this office until 1553 A.D. ¶ During this and the subsequent period, his authority was confined to the Ambā-samudram tālūka of the Tinnevelly district, as most of the inscriptions of himself and his son, Kṛṣṇappa Nāyaka are found in this region. ‖ He seems to have been promoted to a higher grade in A.D. 1558. According to a grant of Mannārkōvil (Ambāsamudram, Tinnevelly), Viśwanātha Nāyaka held the office of *kāryakarta* to Rāmarājadēva Mahārāja.** He is mentioned in a record of Āḻvārkurucci, dated A.D. 1560; but it gives no indication of his status. †† He was ruling the country around Tinnevelly until A.D. 1560, when he seems to have been transferred to the Tiruvaḍi

* *ibid* 99 of 1918.

† Satyanadhan : *NM*. App. E. p. 336.

‡ *MER*. 2 of 1923.

§ *ibid* 599 of 1916.

¶ *ibid* 721 of 1916.

‖ *ibid* 497 of 1916 ; 530 of 1916.

** *ibid* 385 of 1916.

†† *ibid* 119 of 1907.

rājya (South Arcot). Two grants of Viśwanātha dated 1560 A.D., are found at Aṇṇiyūr in the Viḷḷupuram tālūka of the South Arcot district.* One of these grants was made for the merit of Aḷiya Rāmarājayyan. No grant of Viśwanātha has so far been discovered bearing a date later than 1560 A.D., though in an epigrah of Kṛṣṇāpuram (Tinnevelly district) dated A.D. 1563, it is stated that Viśwanātha "had acquired the Tiruvaḍi *dēśa* "as *amaranāyakam* from Rāmarājar Ayyan." † Viśwanātha's son Kṛṣṇappa figures prominently in the inscriptions of subsequent years. Therefore, the year 1560 A.D., may be taken as the last year of the actual rule of Viśwanātha; it is just possible that he might have lived on for two or three years more. The *Maduraittala Varalāru* sums up the history of Madura up to A.D. 1563 by the statement that "from Śaka 1246 to Śaka 1485 twenty-seven persons ruled in Madura." ‡ Therefore, A.D. 1563 marks the end of one period and the commencement of another. According to the *Mṛtyuñjaya Ms.* Kṛṣṇappa Nāyaka was crowned on 25th January 1564 A.D. §

The foregoing study of the inscriptions shows that Viśwanātha was an ordinary *amaranāyaka* in the Ambāsamudram region of the Tinnevelly district until 1557 A.D. During this period, he was a humble subordinate of Rāmarāja Viṭṭhala. He was given an *amaram* in this district, because Rāmarāja wanted him to serve as a check against the rebellious propinquities of the Tiruvaḍi. This is why Rāmarājayyan granted him *amaranāyakam* over Tiruvaḍi *dēśa*. Viśwanātha had nothing to do with the government of Madura. Although he became the *kāryakarta* of Rāmarāja after this date, he was soon transferred

* *ibid* 622 of 1915; Sewell: *Ant.* i. p. 209. † *MER.* 17 of 1912.

‡ *The Nāyaks of Madura* App. E. p. 376. § *ibid* p. 68.

to a district in the Cōḷa country. Almost all the inscriptions of Kṛṣṇappa before 1564 A.D., come from the Tinnevelly district. Probably he was ruling his father's *amaram* on his behalf. There is absolutely nothing to indicate that either Viśwanātha or his son Kṛṣṇappa was anything but an ordinary *amaranāyaka* until A.D. 1564. The statement found in the chronicles that Kṛṣṇadēva or Acyuta crowned Viśwanātha as the king of Madura is not based upon facts. They are fabrications of later ages intended to throw a veil of legality over a treacherous and rebellious act. The truth appears to be that Kṛṣṇappa, taking advantage of the confusion caused by the disastrous battle of Tālikōṭa, seized the province of Madura, and declared himself to be its ruler. And the imperial government had neither strength nor time to prevent the usurpation of regal power by Kṛṣṇappa. Tirumala had probably to recognise the position which Kṛṣṇappa had claimed, in order to prevent the empire from falling to pieces. This seems to be the way in which the Nāyak Kingdom of Madura had originated.

APPENDIX C

VĪRA-NARASIMHA AND THE KŪCIPŪḌI MĒḶA.*

ఆయన (సంబెట గురవరాజు) చాలాదినములు జీవించి ప్రభుత్వము చేసినందున ఆయనను తాత గురవరాజు అని చెప్పు కొనేవారు... ఆ గురవరాజు ప్రభుత్వములో ప్రజలకు అతి దారుణ శిక్ష చేయిస్తూ వుండేవారు. ప్రజలవద్ద ద్రవ్య ఆకర్షణ చేశేయడల త్వరగా సొమ్ము యివ్వకపోతే స్త్రీలను తీసుక వచ్చి స్తనాలకు చిరుతలు పట్టించేవారు. ఆలాగంటి దినములలో వినుకొండ బెల్లంకొండ తట్టున కూచిపూండి అనే గ్రామం నుంచి బ్రాహ్మణులు భాగవతులనే వేషధారులు కీర్తన నిమిత్తమై యీ స్థళమునకు వచ్చివుండి సంబెట గురవరాజుయొక్క దారుణ ప్రభుత్వం చూచి యిక్కడ నుంచి లేచిపోయి విద్యానగరమునకు పోయి అక్కడ వీరనరసింహ రాయలు రాజ్యపరిపాలనం చేస్తూవుండగా భాగవతులు దర్శనం అయి కేళిక అడుగగా శెలవు యిచ్చినారు. కూచిపూడి మేళంవాండ్లు చాలా విద్యావంతులని ప్రశిద్ధిగా వినుకడి వున్నందున రాయలవారు స్త్రీలుసహా చూడవలెనని నగర్లవద్ద దివాణములో కీర్తనకు శెలవు యిచ్చినారు. అక్కడ కీర్తన వినికిచేశేటప్పుడు సంబెట గురవరాజు వేషంవేసికొని వొకడు, యిద్దరు బంట్రౌతుల వేషం వేసుకొని (యిద్దరు), వొకడు స్త్రీవేషం వేసుకొని, సంబెట గురవరాజువలెనే ఆ వేషగాడు కూర్చుండి, రాయల సమక్షమమందు ఆ స్త్రీయొక్క స్తనాలకు చిరుతలు పట్టించి సొమ్ము యివ్వమని తహశ్శీలు చేసినట్టు వినికిచేసినారు.

అప్పుడు రాయలవారు చూచి 'అదియేమ'ని అడుగగా ముఖస్తులయినవారు భాగవతుల ముఖతా ఆ వర్తమానము తెలిసి "శిద్ధవటం శీమలో సంబెట గురవరాజు అనే ఆయన ప్రజలవద్ద నుంచి ద్రవ్యాకర్షణ చేశేయెడల స్త్రీలను తీసుకపోయి యీ ప్రకారముగానే తహశ్శీలు చేస్తున్నారు; గనుక యేలినవారికి తేట పడేటందులకై యీప్రకారం వేషములు కట్టి వినికి చేశినార"ని

* *LR.* 56 (*The Kaifiyat of Mācupalle*) p. 66 ff.

APPENDIX C

విన్నపం శాయగా చాలాతీక్ష్ణంచేశి మరునాడు ఉదయమందు ఆ సంగతి తిరుగా జ్ఞాపకం శేయమని ముఖ్యస్తులయినవారికి ఆజ్ఞ యిచ్చినారు. ఆ రాత్రి కీర్తన సాంతనమయినవెనుక తెల్లవారిన పిమ్మట రాయలవారు కాలోచిత కృత్యములు తీర్చుకుని ఆస్థానమునకు వచ్చి పేరోలగముననుండి తమపద్ద కార్యభారకులు వచ్చి సంబెట గురవరాజుగారి వర్తమానం జ్ఞాపకం విజ్ఞాపన చేయగా విని ప్రధానులను సేనానాయకులను పిలిపించి మోహిముకు సైన్యము శిద్ధం చేయించవలసినదని శెలవు యివ్వగా ఆస్థాన పంజరములో చిలుక 'జయం జయం జయం' అని మూడుసార్లు పలికినది. ఆ పలుకులు మహారాజు విని 'యిదే మనకు శకునము' అని అప్పుడే పేషుఖానే బయట వేయించి కోట పశ్చిమద్వారము వెలుపట భానుజెండా వేయించి శిబ్బంది బట్టువాడాలుగ చేయించి సైన్యం యావత్తుకు ఖర్చు వెచ్చములకు యిప్పించి ఆ మోహిముకు రాయల కొమారుడు అనిపించుకొనివున్న యిసుమాలుఖానుడనే తురక సర్దారుడుగా మొకరర్రు చేసి అతనిని పిలుపించి సమక్షమందు వలసిన బుద్ధిమతులు శెలవుయిచ్చి తాంబూలం యివ్వగా ఆ సరదారుడు తాంబూలం అందుకొని సంబెట గురవరాజుతల తెస్తున్నానని ప్రతిజ్ఞపలికి సైన్యమును వెంటబెట్టుకవచ్చి గురవరాజుగారు వున్న కోటకు పశ్చిమం వైపున వున్న బండ్లకనమమీద లడాయిచేశి కనమపై వున్న చౌకీ విరగ బొడిచి కనమఘాటు అయివచ్చి కోటకు పశ్చిమభాగమందు దిగివుండి ఆదినంరాత్రి కోటకు పశ్చిమంవైపున వున్న గుండ్లకట్ట అనే సన్న కొండమీదను దమదమాలు యెత్తిమొహర్చాలు ఖాయంచేసి కోటమీద లడాయి షురువుచేశినంతట శక్తి వున్నంత మట్టుకు కోటలోనుంచిన్ని వేటువాడు జవాబుయిచ్చినారు. అంతట కోటలో నిభావుచెయ్యలేక కాలుమీద కోటయివ్వగా అప్పుడు గురవరాజును పట్టుకొని తలకోశి తీసుకొని పోయినారు. కోటలో స్త్రీలు బాలులు అందరు దేహత్యాగము చేశినారు.

INDEX

V—59

INDEX

INDEX

INDEX

INDEX

INDEX

G

INDEX

INDEX

INDEX

INDEX

INDEX

INDEX

INDEX

INDEX

INDEX

INDEX

INDEX

W

X

INDEX

CORRIGENDA

PAGE	LINE	FOR	READ
64	1	Durate	Duarte
79	22	intoleant	intolerant
125 Footnote	l.3	consisted 12	consisted of 12
178	6	Durate	Duarte
221	27	thrid	third
285	12	Arbas	Arabs
310	11 & 12	Desvara	Dēśāvara
374	8	olny	only
385	4	of court	of the court
400	17	who do not so	who do not do so
413 Footnote	l.3	दवस्य	देवस्य